mosaics FOCUSING ON ESSAYS

mosaics FOCUSING ON ESSAYS

Kim Flachmann

Wendy Wilson
Fanshawe College

Melissa Mackey
Fanshawe College

CANADIAN EDITION

PEARSON
Prentice
Hall

Toronto

Library and Archives Canada Cataloguing in Publication

Flachmann, Kim
Mosaics : focusing on essays / Kim Flachmann, Wendy Wilson, Melissa Mackey.—Canadian ed.

Includes index.
ISBN 0-13-127558-5

   1. Report writing. 2. English language—Rhetoric. I. Wilson, Wendy, 1946–
II. Mackey, Melissa, 1973– III. Title.

PE1408.F476 2005   808'.042   C2005-900530-0

ISBN 0-13-127558-5

Vice President, Editorial Director: Michael J. Young
Acquisitions Editor: Carolin Sweig
Marketing Manager: Cynthia Smith
Signing Representative: Beth Larsen
Developmental Editor: Jennifer Murray
Production Editor: Avivah Wargon
Copy Editor: Susan James
Proofreaders: Ann McInnis, Judith Turnbull
Production Coordinator: Janis Raisen
Manufacturing Coordinator: Susan Johnson
Page Layout: Janet Zanette
Photo Research: Sandy Cooke
Art Director: Mary Opper
Interior Design: Gail Ferreira Ng-A-Kien
Cover Image: Masterfile

1 2 3 4 5   10 09 08 07 06

Printed and bound in Canada

For Michael

—K.F.

To the memory of Mary Wilson, friend and mother-in-law.

—W.W.

To Jack and Betty Mackey, for inspiring me to go after my dreams.

—M.M.

Brief Contents

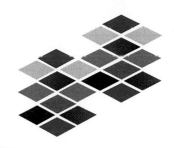

CONTENTS

CHAPTER **11** **Illustrating** **124**

CHAPTER **12** **Analyzing a Process** **141**

PREFACE

Experience tells us that students have the best chance of succeeding if they learn how to respond productively to the varying academic demands made on them throughout the curriculum. One extremely important part of this process is being able to analyze ideas and think critically about issues in many different subject areas. *Mosaics: Focusing on Essays* is the first in a series of three books that teach the basic skills essential to all good academic writing. This series illustrates how the companion skills of reading and writing are parts of a larger, interrelated process that moves back and forth through the tasks of prereading and reading, prewriting and writing, and revising and editing. In other words, the *Mosaics* series shows how these skills are integrated at every stage of the writing process.

THE *MOSAICS* SERIES

This Canadian edition of the *Mosaics* series consists of three books, each with a different emphasis: *Focusing on Essays, Focusing on Paragraphs in Context*, and *Focusing on Sentences in Context*. The first book highlights the composition of essays, the second book paragraph development, and the third sentence structure. Each book introduces the writing process as a unified whole and asks students to begin writing in the very first chapter. Each volume also moves from personal to more academic writing. The books differ in the length and level of their reading selections, the complexity of their writing assignments, the degree of difficulty of their revising and editing strategies, and the length and level of their student writing samples.

This entire three-book series is based on the following fundamental assumptions:

- Students develop confidence in their ability to read and write by reading and writing.
- Students learn best from discovery and experimentation rather than from instruction and abstract discussions.
- Students need to discover and develop their personal writing process.
- Students learn both individually and collaboratively.
- Students profit from studying both professional and student writing.
- Students benefit most from assignments that integrate thinking, reading, and writing.

- Students learn how to revise their writing by following clear guidelines.
- Students learn grammar and usage rules by editing their own writing.
- Students must be able to transfer their writing skills to their other courses.
- Students must think critically and analytically to succeed in school.

HOW THIS BOOK WORKS

Mosaics: Focusing on Essays teaches students how to write effective essays. For flexibility and easy reference, this book is divided into five parts:

Part I: The Writing Process
Part II: Writing Effective Essays
Part III: The Essay with Sources
Part IV: From Reading to Writing
Part V: The Handbook

Part I: The Writing Process   All eight chapters in Part I demonstrate the cyclical nature of the writing process. They begin with the logistics of getting ready to write and then move systematically through the interlocking stages of the process by following a student essay from prewriting to revising and editing. Part I ends with a quiz that students can take to identify their "Editing Quotient"—their strengths and weaknesses in grammar and mechanics.

Part II: Writing Effective Essays   Part II, the heart of the instruction in this text, teaches students how to write essays by introducing the rhetorical modes as patterns of development. It moves from personal writing to more academic types of writing: describing, narrating, illustrating, analyzing a process, comparing and contrasting, dividing and classifying, defining, analyzing causes and effects, and arguing. Within each chapter, students write their own essays, read professional essays, study the essays of other students, and finally revise and edit the essay they wrote earlier in the chapter. By following specific guidelines, students learn how to produce a successful essay using each rhetorical mode.

Part III: The Essay with Sources   The next section of this text helps students move from writing effective essays to writing essays with sources. It systematically illustrates the details of writing a source paper. Then it explains the source paper through student examples. Part III ends with a series of writing assignments and workshops designed to encourage students to write, revise, and edit an essay with sources and then reflect on their own writing process.

Part IV: From Reading to Writing   Part IV of this text is a collection of readings arranged by rhetorical mode. Multiple rhetorical strategies are at work in most of these essays, but each is classified according to its primary rhetorical purpose. As a result, you can refer your students to particular essays in this part that demonstrate a rhetorical mode you are studying in Part II. In this way, students can actually see the features of each rhetorical mode at work in different pieces of writing. Each professional essay is preceded by pre-reading activities that will help your students focus on the topic at hand. Each essay is followed by questions that move students from literal to analytical thinking as they consider the essay's content, purpose, audience, and paragraph structure.

Part V: The Handbook   Part V is a complete handbook, including exercises, that covers eight main categories: Sentences, Verbs, Pronouns, Modifiers, Punctuation, Mechanics, Effective Sentences, and Choosing the Right Word. These categories are coordinated with the Editing Checklist. Each chapter starts with five self-test questions so that students can check their strengths and weaknesses in a specific area. The chapters provide practice after each grammar concept, moving the students systematically from identifying grammar concepts to writing their own sentences. Each chapter ends with a practical editing workshop that asks students to use the skills they have just learned as they work with another student to edit their own writing.

APPENDICES

The appendices will help your students keep track of their progress in the various skills they are learning in this text. References to these appendices are interspersed throughout the book so that students will know when to use them as they study the concepts in each chapter.

Appendix 1: Revising and Editing Peer Evaluation Forms

Appendix 2: Editing Quotient Error Chart

Appendix 3: Error Log

Appendix 4: Spelling Log

Appendix 5: Presentation Techniques

Further appendices are available on the Companion Website for this book at **http://www.pearsoned.ca/flachmann**. Web Appendices 6 and 7 consist of Revising and Editing Peer Evaluation Forms for the following types of writing:

Web Appendix 6A: Describing

Web Appendix 6B: Narrating

Web Appendix 6C: Illustrating

Web Appendix 6D: Analyzing a Process

Web Appendix 6E: Comparing and Contrasting

Web Appendix 6F: Dividing and Classifying
Web Appendix 6G: Defining
Web Appendix 6H: Analyzing Causes and Effects
Web Appendix 6I: Arguing
Web Appendix 7A: Revising an Essay with Sources
Web Appendix 7B: Editing an Essay with Sources

Finally, Web Appendix 8, referred to frequently in the text, provides answers to the Test Yourself questions.

OVERALL GOAL

Ultimately, each book in the *Mosaics* series portrays writing as a way of thinking and processing information. One by one, these books encourage students to discover how the "mosaics" of their own writing process work together to form a coherent whole. By demonstrating the relationships among thinking, reading, and writing on progressively more difficult levels, these books promise to help prepare your students for success throughout the curriculum.

UNIQUE FEATURES

Several unique and exciting features separate this book from other basic writing texts:

- It moves students systematically from personal to academic writing.
- It uses both student writing and professional writing as models.
- It demonstrates all aspects of the writing process through student writing.
- It integrates reading and writing throughout the text.
- It teaches revising and editing through student writing.
- It features culturally diverse reading selections that are of high interest to students.
- It teaches rhetorical modes as patterns of thought.
- It helps students discover and develop their own writing process.
- It includes a complete handbook with exercises.
- It offers worksheets for students to chart their progress in reading and writing.

CANADIAN FEATURES

This text has been changed to reflect the needs of Canadian students. Fifteen high-interest readings by Canadian authors include essays by Mordecai Richler, Wayne Johnston, Patricia Pearson, and Lawrence Hill, among others. Examples throughout the text have been updated, and the grammar Handbook streamlined. At the same time, the integrity of the original text has been maintained. In the interests of keeping the book at a manageable size and providing electronic templates, some student material has been moved from the appendices to the Companion Website. As well, some of the self-assessment (Editing and Revising) charts from Part II are now on the website. These charts may still be seen in Chapters 7 and 8.

Supplements

To help both instructors and students get the most out of *Mosaics: Focusing on Essays*, we have provided both an Instructor's Manual and a Companion Website.

- The **Instructor's Resource Manual** (0-13-196951-X) provides over 350 pages of additional teaching strategies, collaborative activities, sample syllabi, chapter summaries, and two quizzes for each chapter. This supplement can be downloaded by instructors from a password-protected location on Pearson Education Canada's online catalogue. Simply search for the text, then click on "Instructor" under "Resources" in the left-hand menu. Contact your local sales representative for further information.
- The **Companion Website** (**www.pearsoned.ca/flachmann/mosaics**) offers students chapter objectives, quizzes, and internet activities, as well as further sample student essays.

ACKNOWLEDGMENTS

For the Canadian edition, we would like to thank our colleagues in the General Studies Division at Fanshawe College, Brian, Andrew, Haythem, Joe, Jennie, Kim, Rita, Diana, and Tony, for their help with Canadian trivia.

The following individuals graciously gave up their time to provide constructive criticisms of various drafts of the revisions. We are grateful to these people, and a few who wish to remain anonymous, for their many useful comments and suggestions.

Patricia Campbell, Red Deer College
Kathy Cocchio, Northern Alberta Institute of Technology
Calum Cunningham, Fanshawe College
Chandra Hodgson, Humber College
Kristine Kerins, Camosun College
Andrea Lovering, Georgian College
Helen Mendes, Kwantlen University College
Melanie Rubens, Seneca College

Wendy Wilson and Melissa Mackey

I want to express my gratitude to my students, from whom I have learned so much about the writing process, about teaching, and about life itself, and to Cheryl Smith's students, who tested various sections of the books and gave me good ideas for revising them over the past three years. Thanks finally to the students who contributed paragraphs and essays to this series: Josh Ellis, Jolene Christie, Mary Minor, Michael Tiede, and numerous others.

Finally, I owe a tremendous personal debt to the people who have lived with this project for the last few years; they are my closest companions and my best advisers: Michael, Christopher, and Laura Flachmann. To Michael I owe additional thanks for the valuable support and feedback he has given me through the entire process of creating and revising this series.

Kim Flachmann

A Great Way to Learn and Instruct Online

The Pearson Education Canada Companion Website is easy to navigate and is organized to correspond to the chapters in this textbook. Whether you are a student in the classroom or a distance learner you will discover helpful resources for in-depth study and research that empower you in your quest for greater knowledge and maximize your potential for success in the course.

[**www.pearsoned.ca/flachmann/mosaics**]

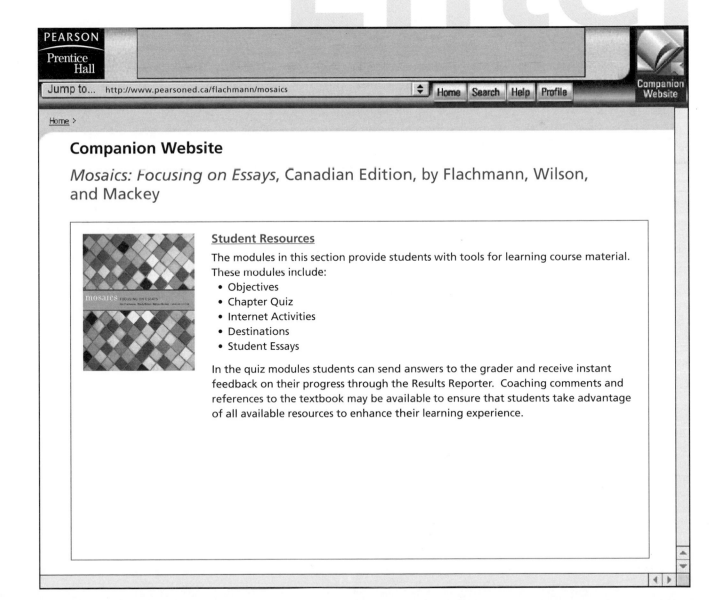

PEARSON
Prentice Hall

Jump to... http://www.pearsoned.ca/flachmann/mosaics   Home | Search | Help | Profile

Companion Website

Home >

Companion Website

Mosaics: Focusing on Essays, Canadian Edition, by Flachmann, Wilson, and Mackey

Student Resources

The modules in this section provide students with tools for learning course material. These modules include:

- Objectives
- Chapter Quiz
- Internet Activities
- Destinations
- Student Essays

In the quiz modules students can send answers to the grader and receive instant feedback on their progress through the Results Reporter. Coaching comments and references to the textbook may be available to ensure that students take advantage of all available resources to enhance their learning experience.

I

THE WRITING PROCESS

Writing, like life itself, is a voyage of discovery.

—HENRY MILLER

In Part I, you will be working with the entire writing process. The goal of this part is to help you develop self-confidence as a writer. It will give you the tools you need to construct your personal writing process. Then, as you move through these eight chapters, you will discover how to adjust the writing process to suit your own needs and preferences. As you become more aware of the choices you have to make, you will also develop a better understanding of your strengths and weaknesses as a writer. With practice, your personalized writing process will soon be a routine part of your academic life and will help you confirm your place in the community of writers.

1 WRITING IN COLLEGE

Words help us solve problems, discover new ideas, feel better, make people laugh, and understand the world around us. Writing is simply one way of using words. It lets us connect with our immediate environment. Eric Zorn, a reporter for the *Chicago Tribune*, tries to explain more precisely the power of writing in our everyday lives:

> We write to enlarge and preserve that which we know, that which we have felt. We write because organizing our jumbled impressions into sentences is sometimes the only way to figure out what we think. We write because words—inadequate as they always are—are the best and most lasting way to connect with ourselves and with others.

WHY LEARN HOW TO WRITE WELL?

The better you write, the more completely you can connect with your environment and the more control you have over your daily routine. Writing well lets you communicate exactly what you mean and actually helps you get what you want out of life. So writing well can give you power—in a variety of ways.

Writing as Discovery

Often you will not really know the points you want to make until you start writing. When you write, a very interesting process takes place: the physical act of writing helps your mind sort through lots of ideas and helps you decide exactly what you want to say. Sometimes new ideas will come out of something you have written. Or you might understand an idea better once you start writing about it.

The simple act of writing leads to understanding. Also, the more you write, the more ideas you generate. This is why your instructor might suggest that, when you are stuck on a topic or don't know what to say next, you should just keep on writing. Writing helps you discover and express the good ideas that are already in your mind.

Writing as Critical Thinking

Writing can also help you think critically. Critical thinking is the highest form of mental activity that human beings engage in, and it is a major source of success in college and in life.

Thinking critically involves grappling with the ideas, issues, and problems that surround you in your immediate environment and in the larger world. It means constantly questioning and analyzing different aspects of life. Since critical thinking is complex, it requires a great deal of concentration and practice. Once you have a sense of how your mind works at this level, you will be able to think critically whenever you want.

With some guidance, learning how to write according to different rhetorical modes or strategies (such as describing, narrating, or dividing and classifying) can give you the mental workout you need in order to think critically, in much the same way that physical exercise warms you up for various sports. As you move through the chapters in Part II, you will be asked to isolate each rhetorical mode—just as you isolate your abs, thighs, and biceps in a weight-lifting workout. Each rhetorical mode offers a slightly different way of seeing the world, processing information, and solving problems. So each rhetorical mode is really a different way of thinking and making sense of the world.

Writing as Necessity

Most important of all, writing is necessary for surviving both in college and on the job. You will have to write more in today's electronic age than any previous generation has. Some of your writing will be reports or projects that extend over a long period of time. Other writing tasks will have to be completed immediately, such as responses to e-mail messages. Whatever the terms, writing will be a significant part of your life throughout college and beyond.

The better your writing skills, the better grades you will make in college and the further you will get in a career. Everything you learn about writing in this text applies to writing in all your courses. These strategies will also be helpful on the job, especially when you have to write that difficult report or when you are asked to summarize your accomplishments so far. The same writing guidelines apply to all writing tasks.

THINKING OF YOURSELF AS A WRITER

Using words on paper or on the computer screen makes a person a writer. Whether you write a note on the refrigerator, e-mail a friend, write a paper for economics class, or draft a report for your boss, you are part of a community of writers. In fact, you *are* a writer.

Any piece of writing more formal than a note on the refrigerator, however, is usually the result of a sequence of activities that may seem on the surface to have nothing directly to do with the act of writing itself. This sequence of activities is called the **writing process,** and learning to use this process is what this book is all about.

Even though each writer is different, some general principles apply to everyone—students and professional writers alike. Before you actually begin to write, it is wise to get your surroundings ready. That involves setting aside a time and place for writing, as well as gathering supplies and establishing a routine.

1. ***Set aside a special time to write, and plan to do nothing else during that time.*** The bird's cage can wait to be cleaned until tomorrow, the furniture doesn't have to be dusted today, the garage can be hosed down some other time, and the dirt on your kitchen floor won't turn to concrete overnight. When you first get a writing assignment, a little procrastination can be good. Procrastinating lets your mind plan your approach to the writing task. The trick is to know when to quit procrastinating and get down to work.

2. ***Find a comfortable place with few distractions.*** Joyce Carol Oates, a famous contemporary writer, claims that writing is a very private act that requires lots of patience, time, and space. First, you need to set up a place to write that suits your particular needs as a writer. It should be a place where you are not distracted or interrupted. Some people work best in a straight-backed chair sitting at a table or desk, while others get their best ideas sitting cross-legged on the bed. The exact place doesn't matter, as long as you can write there.

   Even if you are fortunate enough to have a private study area, you may find that you still want to make some adjustments. You may decide to unplug your phone during your writing time. Or you may discover that an all-night R&B radio station helps you shut out all kinds of noises but doesn't distract you the way talk shows and rock stations do. One student may do her best writing after soaking in a hot tub; another might play jazz when he is getting down to work; and still another may have a pop on one side of his table and a chocolate bar on the other as he writes. Whatever your choices, you need to set up a comfortable working environment.

3. ***Gather your supplies before you begin to write.*** Don't risk losing your great ideas by not being able to find a pen and paper or a formatted disk. Some writers use a yellow tablet and a mechanical pencil to get started on a writing task; others go straight to their computers. One of the main advantages of working on a computer is that once you type your ideas into it, changing them or moving them around is easy. As a result, you are more likely to make revisions when you work on a computer, and you will therefore turn in a better paper. Whatever equipment you choose, make sure it is ready at the time you have set aside to write.

4. ***Establish a personal writing ritual.*** You are a member of the community of writers, and acknowledging your own writing habits and rituals is a major part of discovering your writing process. These rituals begin the minute you are given a writing assignment. What activities

help you get ready to write? Some people exercise, others catch up on e-mail, and still others clean their rooms before they write. Most people do these activities without even realizing why. But they are preparing their minds for writing. So in the course of confirming yourself as a writer, take a moment now to record some of your own preferences and rituals connected with your writing.

Practice 1   Explain the rituals you instinctively follow as you prepare to write. How do you prepare your mind for writing? Where do you write? At what time of day do you produce your best work? Do you like noise? Quiet? What other details describe your writing environment? What equipment do you use to write?

KEEPING A JOURNAL

The word **journal** refers to a daily log of your writing. It is a place where you can record ideas, snatches of conversation, dreams, descriptions of people, pictures of places, and thoughts about objects—whatever catches your attention.

If you use a notebook for your journal, choose one that you really like. You might even keep your journal on your computer. However, unless you have a hand-held computer, you won't have your electronic journal with you all the time. The choice is yours (unless your instructor has specific requirements). Just remember that a journal should be a notebook you enjoy writing in and carrying with you.

As you move from college to the professional world, you will find a personal journal a particularly valuable tool because—in the case of writing as in many other activities—the more you write, the more you will improve your writing. In addition, your journal can become an excellent bank of thoughts and topics for you. If used thoughtfully, it can become an incredible resource—a place to both generate and retrieve your ideas. Writing in your journal can help you discover your thoughts and feelings about specific issues as well as let you think through important choices you have to make. So writing can help you solve problems and work your way through various college projects.

A good way to establish the habit of journal writing is to use your journal for answering the questions that accompany the instruction in Parts II and III of this text, the readings in Part IV, and the writing exercises in the handbook (Part V). You can also use your journal to jot down ideas and plans for essays as they occur to you. In addition, you might want to complete your prewriting activities in your journal. Keeping track of a journal is much easier than finding notes on assorted scraps of paper.

Keeping a section of your journal private is also a good idea. Sometimes, when you think on paper or let your imagination run free, you don't want to share the results with anyone. Yet those notes can be very important in finding a subject to write about or in developing a topic.

The content of your journal entries depends to a great extent on your instructor's directions. But some basic advice applies to all entries, whether on paper or on a computer.

1. Date your entries, and note the time; you may find it useful to see when your best ideas occur.
2. Record anything that comes to your mind, and follow your thoughts wherever they take you (unless your instructor gives you different directions).
3. Glue or tape anything into your journal that stimulates your thinking or writing—cartoons, magazine ads, poems, pictures, advice columns; add URLs for useful Web sites.
4. Think of your journal as someone to talk to—a friend who will keep your cherished ideas safe and sound and won't talk back to or argue with you.

◆ *P r a c t i c e 2*   Begin your own journal.

1. Buy a notebook that you like, and write in it.
2. Make at least two journal entries on your computer.
3. Which type of journal do you prefer—notebook or disk? Write an entry explaining your preference.

WRITING WITH A COMPUTER

Many people—in school and at work—find that they write most efficiently directly on a computer. This strategy saves them time and energy and helps them meet deadlines. First of all, writing directly on a computer lets you change words and sentences as you go along. It also saves you time, since you don't have to write out a draft by hand and then input it later. When you complete a first draft on a computer, you can move your ideas around without having to rewrite the whole paper. Finally, you can correct grammar and spelling errors right on the final draft.

To compose on your computer, follow some simple rules so that you don't lose your work or make word processing more complicated than it really is. Here are five essential guidelines for writing on a computer:

1. Give your document a name before you start writing.
2. Save your work often (or set the computer to save at short intervals). This will help you avoid losing your writing in a power failure or other accident.
3. Save your work in two different places—on your hard drive and on a disk. Then if one becomes damaged, you always have the other.

4. Name and number each draft so that you can go back to earlier drafts if you want. For example, you might name and number an assignment this way: Description Essay D1, Description Essay D2, and so forth (D = draft).

5. Print out your work frequently so that you can refer to printed copies as well as electronic copies.

THE WRITING PROCESS

The writing process begins the minute you get a writing assignment. It involves all the activities you do, from choosing a topic to turning in a final draft, including trips to the library, phone calls, and late-night snacks. The main parts of the process are outlined here.

Prewriting

Prewriting refers to activities that help you explore a general subject, generate ideas about it, select a specific topic, establish a purpose, and learn as much as possible about your readers. Chapter 2 will teach you different strategies for accomplishing these goals before you actually begin to write a draft of your essay. Your mission at this stage is to stimulate your thinking processes before and during the act of writing. Whenever you generate new material, throughout the writing process, you are prewriting.

Writing

You can start writing after you have some ideas to work with. Writing includes developing some of your ideas further, organizing your thoughts with your purpose in mind, and writing a first draft. To begin writing, you should go back to your notes, journal entries, and other prewriting activities and then mould these ideas into a logical, coherent essay. As you write, you should concentrate on what you are saying and how your ideas fit together. Don't let grammar and spelling distract you from your task at this point. You can correct grammar and mechanical errors later.

Revising

Most people do not want to take the time to revise their writing. But revising always pays off, because it will make your writing stronger and better. Revising involves rethinking your content and organization so that your words say exactly what you mean. (Editing, the last step, focuses on grammar, punctuation, mechanics, and spelling.) Your main goal when revising is to make sure that the purpose of your essay is clear to your audience and that your main ideas are supported with enough details and examples. In addition, you should check that your paper is organized logically.

Editing

Editing is the final stage of the writing process. After you revise, read your writing slowly and carefully to find errors in grammar, punctuation, mechanics, and spelling. Such errors can distract your reader from the message you are trying to convey or can even cause communication to break down altogether. Editing gives you the chance to clean up your draft so that your writing will be clear, precise, and effective.

Once you start writing, these stages do not necessarily occur in any specific order. You may change a word (revise) in the very first sentence that you write, then think of another detail that you want to add to your opening sentence (prewrite), and next cross out and rewrite a misspelled word (edit)—all in the first two minutes of writing. Although you may never approach any two writing projects in the same way, the chapters in Part I will help you establish a framework for your personal writing process and start to feel comfortable as a writer working within that framework.

VISUALIZING THE WRITING PROCESS

Even though we talk about the stages of writing, writing is actually a cyclical process, which means that at any point you may loop in and out of other stages. As you work with the writing process in this textbook, the following graphic might help you understand how various stages of the process can overlap.

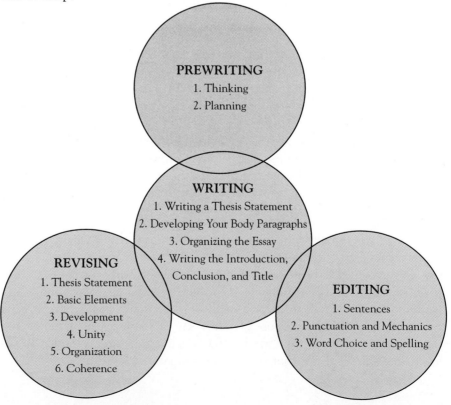

WRITING IN TANDEM WITH A STUDENT

In the rest of Part I, you will be writing in tandem with (along with) another student, Beth Olson, who has already completed the assignments you will be doing. In other words, this student writer will be demonstrating what you have to do for each essay. This approach will make the requirements for each writing task easy to follow, and you may find that you want to borrow Beth's ideas. If this happens, concentrate on discovering your own original ideas instead as you work through each assignment.

WRITING ASSIGNMENT

This first writing assignment is much like the writing tasks you will be asked to do throughout this book. You'll be working on this assignment yourself over the next seven chapters as you apply what you are learning about the writing process. At the same time, we will follow the work of student Beth Olson so you can see how she approaches and completes the same assignment. By the end of Chapter 8, you will have a feel for the entire writing process, which is essential to strengthening your writing and your identity as a writer.

Write Your Own Essay

We all learn about life in a variety of ways. These lessons help us become who we are. What have you learned over the years? How did you learn these lessons? What experiences have made you the person you are today? Drawing on a combination of your observations, your reading, and your personal experience, write an essay explaining how you learn best.

2

PREWRITING

Activities that take place before you actually start writing your paper fall into the general category of **prewriting.** This is a time when you should be generating as many new ideas on a topic as you can, using the right side of your brain over the left. This is the part of your brain that thinks up new ideas and sees relationships among old ideas. More specifically, prewriting consists of activities that help you do the following tasks:

- Explore a subject
- Generate ideas about the subject
- Settle on a specific topic
- Establish a purpose
- Analyze your audience

Let's begin by looking at some activities writers use to stimulate their minds as they approach a writing task. You will get a chance to try each one. Record your responses to the following exercises and questions in your journal or on a separate piece of paper, so that you can refer to them throughout the course.

THINKING

Thinking is always the place to start any writing project. Thinking means exploring your topic and letting your mind run freely over the ideas you generate. We'll look at six activities students often use to stimulate their best thoughts: reading, freewriting, brainstorming, clustering, questioning, and discussing. You will see how Beth Olson uses each strategy and then have a chance to try out the strategy yourself.

Reading

Sometimes a good way to start your writing process is to surf the Net or read an article on your topic. Taking notes on your reading will give you material to work with as you begin to write. In fact, you may find yourself wandering off into your own thoughts on the subject, which you should also get down in writing.

Beth's Reading Beth read the following paragraphs from an essay titled "Survive the Savage Sea" by Dougal Robertson. It stimulated her thoughts about learning in general because she believes that an important part of learning is taking risks. She jotted several notes to herself in the margins as she read.

My family would <u>never</u> have a Sunday like this.

That Sunday morning stands out clearly in my memory, however, as one of the nice days. I had put the kettle on the hot plate of the solid fuel cooker and while waiting for it to boil switched on the radio to listen to news, which contained a commentary on the Round the World yacht race. I had carried the mugs of tea upstairs on a tray, calling out to Anne, our sixteen-year-old daughter, to come through to our room where nine-year-old twins Neil and Sandy rocked with laughter as they lay in bed with their mother watching our son Douglas perform one of his special slapstick comedy acts. As Douglas rolled his eyes and cavorted around the bedroom in stiff-legged imitation of a disabled robot, Neil's face reddened as he laughed all the breath from his lungs, and even the more serious-minded Sandy chuckled in ecstasy as he watched his fifteen-year-old brother's antics.

I wish my dad were a sailor.

Sounds like a great learning experience!

Neil and Sandy had become silent while Anne and Douglas questioned and Lyn talked of our sailing adventures in Hong Kong before we had started farming, but suddenly Neil shouted, "Daddy's a sailor. Why can't we go round the world?" Lyn burst out laughing, and "What a lovely idea!" she exclaimed. "Let's buy a boat and go round the world." I realized that Neil, who thought Manchester was one of the four brown corners of the earth, had no conception of the meaning of his remark, and that his mother was entering into the spirit of the game, but suddenly, to me, it was no game. Why not? I looked at Anne and Douglas, both handsome children but the horizons of their minds stunted by the limitations of their environment. In two years they would both have reached school leaving age and neither had shown any leaning toward academic aptitude, and the twins, already backward compared with their contemporaries in town, were unlikely to blossom into sudden educational prodigies. In two years' time they would finish their primary schooling and then. . . . Why not indeed?

I can't believe they sold everything.   Two years later, after selling our entire holdings in stock and land, we had acquired enough money to embark on the initial stage of our planned circumnavigation of the world.   *I can't imagine spending so much time with my family.*

Later, Beth made this entry in her journal.

> The more I think about Robertson's essay, the more I think about how much I could learn from a trip like this. How great it would be to pick up and leave for a while! I could get some perspective on the world. I can't imagine not having any responsibilities except for those on a boat. My head might actually be clear. I would like to travel around the country for about a year or so, but in an RV or something. I've only been to Calgary and Edmonton, but I'd love to see the rest of the country. I can't imagine leaving my family or school, though. I think it would be a waste of time for me right now to just leave. I guess I can plan for that after I retire. That is, if I can get through school.

Your Reading   Read "I Just Wanna Be Average," an essay by Mike Rose (p. 308) on learning, and take notes in the margins as you read. Then, in your journal, write down any thoughts this essay stimulates.

Freewriting

The strategy of freewriting involves writing about anything that comes to your mind. You should write without stopping for five to ten minutes because the act of writing alone will make you think of other ideas. Don't worry about grammar, punctuation, mechanics, or spelling. If you get stuck, repeat an idea or start rhyming words. Just keep writing.

Beth's Freewriting   Beth had trouble freewriting, but she got going and then repeated some words to keep herself writing.

> My English teacher wants us to freewrite about whatever comes to our minds, but I can't think of anything to say. It's hard for me to just start writing. I still can't think of anything to say. And it's hard for me to just write. I don't even know what to write about. Everyone in here is writing furiously in their notebooks; I wonder what they're writing about. How many are writing about their girlfriends? their families? their dreams? I wonder what their dreams are. No one could

> ever guess that one of my dreams is to someday be my
> own boss in a company that will make enough money
> for my family to live comfortably. I suppose that's
> everyone's dream, really, but I don't think many people
> would think I had enough guts to go out on my own.
> But I will someday, and it's going to be a great life.

Focused freewriting is the same procedure, but focused on a specific topic—either one your instructor gives you or one you choose. Apply your guidelines for freewriting to a specific topic. Just write freely about a designated topic so that you find words for your thoughts and impressions.

Beth's Focused Freewriting   Beth produced the following focused freewriting in her journal. She is trying to get her mind ready to write her essay about learning.

> People can learn about life from just about
> everything they do. It seems that every action can
> result in some sort of lesson. It's like all those fairy
> tales that have morals at the end of the story. If we
> keep our eyes open, everything we do can have a
> moral at the end. We can learn about how to study
> when we join a study group. We can decide how to
> treat our boyfriends or girlfriends when we watch
> our friends. And we can even learn from what's on
> TV. I also like asking questions and talking to people
> about problems I'm having. I often get answers that
> way. Everywhere we look there's something to learn.

Your Freewriting   Try a focused freewriting assignment to prepare for the essay you are going to write by writing in your journal about some ways that you learn.

Brainstorming

Like freewriting, brainstorming is based on free association. When you are brainstorming, you let one thought naturally lead to another, generally in the form of a list. You can brainstorm by yourself, with a friend, or with a group. Regardless of the method, list whatever comes into your mind on a topic—ideas, thoughts, examples, facts. As with freewriting, don't worry about grammar, punctuation, mechanics, or spelling.

Beth's Brainstorming   Here is Beth's brainstorming on learning about life:

- everyone learns about life through everyday lessons
- from my parents
- from my brothers and sisters
- from friends
- by watching our friends make mistakes
- by listening to others
- by listening to the radio
- by making my own mistakes
- by asking questions
- by listening to music
- by taking risks
- by succeeding and failing
- by reading books or newspapers
- by studying or going to school
- by observing

Your Brainstorming   Brainstorm in your journal about how you think you learn.

Clustering

Clustering, like brainstorming, is based on free association, but it also shows how your thoughts are related. To cluster, take a sheet of blank paper, write a key word or phrase in the centre of the page, and draw a circle around it. Next, write down and circle any related ideas that come to mind. As you add ideas, draw lines to the thoughts they came from. After two or three minutes, you'll have a map of your ideas that can guide you toward a good essay.

Beth's Cluster   Here is Beth's cluster on learning about life:

Your Cluster   Write "Learning About Life" in the middle of a piece of paper, circle it, and create a cluster of your own associations with this concept.

Questioning

Journalists use the questions known as the "five *W*s and one *H*"—*Who? What? When? Where? Why?* and *How?*—to check that they've covered all the important information in a news story. Other writers use these questions to generate ideas on a writing topic. Ask yourself each question as it relates to a particular topic. Then answer the questions one by one.

Beth's Questions   Here is how Beth used questioning to generate ideas on her topic, learning about life:

Who?	everyone I know learns about life
What?	learning about life
When?	all day, every day
Where?	depends on what's being learned
Why?	to better themselves in life, for fun, for a variety of reasons
How?	by paying attention and taking action I guess we can even learn without realizing it.

Your Questions   In your journal, answer these six questions about learning in preparation for your essay: Who? What? When? Where? Why? How?

Discussing

Discussing involves talking your ideas out with friends, relatives, class-mates, tutors, or anyone who will listen. Often someone else will have a completely different perspective on your topic that will help you come up with even more ideas. Be sure to record your notes from these conversations so that you don't lose the ideas.

Beth's Discussion   Here are Beth's notes from a conversation she had with her running partner about how we learn about life.

> When I spoke with my friend Alison, I realized that we all learn about life from just about everything we do. I guess it really depends on how much we want to pay attention. Alison talked about the risks I took when I decided to leave my home town and study nursing at my current college. She also reminded me how much I learned from my cousin when she was involved in gangs. And we even reminisced about some of the bad choices I made and what they taught me. We talked about all the ways we learn in life, and realized we learn by watching what other people do, by taking risks throughout our

lives, and by actually making mistakes. We figured these were the best ways to learn about life—for us.

Your Discussion   Discuss learning about life with someone, and record notes from your conversation in your journal.

PLANNING

In this course, you'll be writing essays. Although essays may differ a great deal in design, organization, and content, they share certain identifying features that distinguish them from other types of writing. At the simplest level, how an essay looks on the page tells its audience "Here's an essay!" An essay usually has a title that names its broad subject. Many longer, more complex essays also have subtitles. When writers move from one topic to another, they indicate this shift by indenting a new paragraph. Most essays have a thesis that is either stated or implied in the introduction, several body paragraphs explaining or supporting that thesis, and a conclusion.

In content, essays are nonfiction, as opposed to short stories, poetry, or drama; that is, they deal with real-life subjects rather than made-up ones. Most essays concentrate on one specific subject and focus on a single purpose. For an essay to be successful, writers choose methods of development that both suit their purpose and appeal to the audience they hope to inform or persuade. A successful essay gets the reaction from the readers that its author hopes for—whether this response is to appreciate a special scene, identify with someone's grief, or leap into action.

You will learn in this book that writing an essay takes planning. If you make some decisions about your topic, audience, and purpose before you actually write, the job of writing will be much smoother and less stressful.

- *What is your subject (person, event, object, idea)?* An essay focuses on a single subject, along with related thoughts and details. So in approaching an essay assignment, deciding *what* you are going to write about is very important. Sometimes your topic is given to you, such as when your sociology instructor assigns a paper on rural depopulation. But other times, you choose your own subject. In such cases, choose a subject that interests you. You will have more to say, and you will enjoy writing much more if you know something about your topic.

- *What is your purpose?* Your purpose is your reason for writing an essay. Your purpose could be to explore your feelings about a topic (*to do personal writing*), to tell a friend about something funny that happened to you (*to entertain*), to explain something or share information (*to inform*), or to convince others to agree with your position on a controversial issue (*to persuade*). Whatever your purpose, deciding on it in advance makes writing the rest of your essay easier.

- *Who is your audience?* Your audience consists of the people your message is intended to reach. The more you know about your audience, the more likely you are to accomplish your purpose. The audience for your writing in college is usually your instructor, who represents what is called a "general audience"—people with an average amount of knowledge on most subjects. A general audience is a good group to aim for in all your writing, unless you are given other directions.

Practice 1   Identify the subject, purpose, and audience of each of the following paragraphs.

1. Schools have been dealing with the issue of bilingual education for many years. The big debate is whether or not students should be allowed to study in their native language while learning English. Many people believe that students should be forced to learn in English, even if they don't know the language. Other people believe that this method of teaching will cause students not to learn, but they know bilingual education programs aren't teaching the students either. Obviously, a compromise must be reached in order to help the students.

   Subject: _____

   Purpose: _____

   Audience: _____

2. The world of computers has reached a point where people can conduct all their business transactions from the comfort of their own homes. Internet companies have made it possible for people to shop and do all of their business online. While most people using these services enjoy the convenience of being able to have a business meeting in their bathrobes, the idea of never having to leave the house worries other computer users. People will be able to do everything from home and won't have to interact with other people face to face. Eventually, the art of human interaction will be lost.

   Subject: _____

   Purpose: _____

   Audience: _____

Beth's Plans   Beth made the following decisions before beginning to write on learning about life:

Subject: learning about life

Purpose: informative—to really talk about the different ways of learning

Audience: general—anyone from the general population

Your Plans   Identify the subject, purpose, and audience of the essay you will write on learning about life.

Subject: _____

Purpose: _____

Audience: _____

CHAPTER 3

WRITING A THESIS STATEMENT

By now, you have a subject (learning about life), and you have used several prewriting techniques with this subject, which means you have generated a number of thoughts that you can use in your essay. You have also decided on a purpose and an audience. In this chapter, you will learn how to write a thesis statement, which you will develop into an essay in the next three chapters. Again, you will be writing alongside Beth Olson as she works through her writing process.

Writing assignments in college usually have broad subjects. To compose a good essay, you need to narrow a broad subject to an idea that you can discuss in a limited number of pages. Your thesis statement is what puts limits on your essay. A **thesis statement** is the controlling idea of an essay. It is the main point that all other sentences relate to. Like a high-powered telescope, your thesis statement zooms in on the specific topic that you will discuss in the body of your essay. The decisions you made in Chapter 2 about subject, purpose, and audience lead you to your thesis statement.

A thesis statement is usually found in the first paragraph of an essay. It works best as the last sentence of the opening paragraph. Ending the introduction with the thesis statement lets the writer use the beginning of the paragraph to capture the reader's interest or give background information.

A thesis statement has two parts: a topic and an opinion you hold on that topic.

Subject	Limited Subject	+	Opinion	=	Thesis Statement
Sports	Playing a team sport		has lots of benefits		Playing a team sport teaches a person self-discipline, cooperation, and leadership.

Subject	Limited Subject	+	Opinion	=	Thesis Statement
Anger	Road rage		is very dangerous		Road rage is dangerous because it puts the driver, the victim, and the surrounding cars at risk.

◆ **P r a c t i c e   1**   Limit the following subjects that aren't already limited. Then add an opinion to all subjects, and make them into thesis statements.

	Subject	Limited Subject	+	Opinion	=	Thesis Statement
1.	Friendship	_____		_____		_____
2.	Work	Managers		_____		_____
3.	Winning	_____		_____		_____
4.	Love	Dating		_____		_____
5.	Winter	_____		_____		_____

When you write a thesis statement, keep the following guidelines in mind:

1. ***Your subject should not be too broad or too narrow.*** A subject or topic that is too broad would need a book to develop it. One that is too narrow leaves you nothing to say. A manageable subject is one that you can write about in roughly three body paragraphs. You may find it necessary to limit your subject several times before you arrive at one that will work.

Subject:	Television
Too broad:	Prime-time TV
Still too broad:	New TV shows of the 2004 season
Good:	*The Bachelor*
Too narrow:	My favourite competitor

2. ***State your opinion clearly.*** When you give your opinion on the topic, choose your words carefully. Be direct and take a stand. Opinions such as "is interesting," "are not good," "is a problem," or "can teach us a lot" are vague and boring. In fact, if you are specific enough about the opinion you hold, you will be very close to a thesis statement.

Vague Opinion:	*The Bachelor* is fun to watch.
Specific Opinion:	*The Bachelor* teaches us about choosing a mate.

3. ***Do not simply announce your topic.*** Make an interesting statement about your topic.

> **Announcement:**   My paper is going to be about *The Bachelor.*
>
>   *The Bachelor* is the topic of this essay.
>
> **Statement:**   *The Bachelor* is a TV show that teaches us how to choose a mate.

4. ***Try your thesis statement (TS) as a question.*** This does not mean that you should actually express your thesis statement as a question in your essay. Rather, you should try thinking of your thesis statement as a question that you will answer in the rest of your essay. You might want to write out your "TS Question" and keep it in front of you as you draft your paper. It will help you keep your focus.

> **Thesis Statement:**   The television program *The Bachelor* teaches us how to choose a mate.
>
> **TS Question:**   How does *The Bachelor* teach us about choosing a mate?

◆ P r a c t i c e   2   Which of the following are good thesis statements? Mark B for too broad, N for too narrow, MO for missing opinion, and C for complete. Test each thesis statement by turning it into a question.

_____ 1. Schools have good education programs.

_____ 2. In Canada today, we face the problem of keeping our air clean.

_____ 3. Vehicles powered by natural gas will cut down on the pollution expelled by automobiles.

_____ 4. When using a computer, the user should know many things.

_____ 5. Human cloning is being studied to determine the scientific and moral consequences of the process.

_____ 6. Children in Canada are becoming desensitized to violence because of TV.

_____ 7. Many people do not eat meat because they cannot stand the thought of eating something that was once alive.

_____ 8. A lot of people avoid math because they have difficulty with analytical problem solving.

_____ 9. Our campus drama department will be performing *Noises Off* this spring.

_____ 10. Since the early 1980s, people have been on various health-craze diets and exercise programs.

◆ *P r a c t i c e   3*   Complete the following thesis statements.

1. Marriage today _____.

2. _____ is my favourite class because _____.

3. Sleeping _____.

4. TV award shows _____.

5. _____ is a role model for students today.

Beth's Thesis Statement   Beth writes a thesis statement by stating her opinion about her subject.

Limited Subject   **Opinion**

I know that I learn   from many things in life.

Your Thesis Statement   Write a thesis statement here that can serve as the controlling idea for your essay.

Limited Subject   **Opinion**

_____   _____

Thesis Statement

_____

CHAPTER 4

DEVELOPING BODY PARAGRAPHS

Now that you have written a thesis statement that comes at the end of your introduction, you are ready to write the body paragraphs of your essay. The body paragraphs explain and support the thesis statement.

SUPPORT FOR YOUR THESIS STATEMENT

What ideas will support the statement you make in your thesis? This is the question you need to answer at this point. The supporting ideas are what make up the body of your essay. Each body paragraph covers one major idea of your thesis. The body paragraphs consist of a topic sentence and concrete details that support that topic sentence.

Practice 1A For each of the following lists, cross out any ideas that do not support the thesis statement.

1. Thesis: Children are desensitized to violence by television, video games, and comic books.

   Children don't react to the violent acts they see on TV.

   Children do not care when the heroes beat up the villains in comic books.

   Many video games cost too much.

   Children often want to be just like the sports figures they watch on TV.

   Most children learn very early in life to shoot figures in video games.

2. Thesis: Political campaigns often bring out the worst in candidates.

   Most people are either Liberal or Conservative.

   Candidates try to find secrets from their opponents' pasts.

   Candidates use the media to try to ruin other candidates' reputations.

   Federal elections occur every few years.

   Some candidates even resort to name-calling and twisting their opponents' words.

3. Thesis: Starting your own business takes a lot of planning and work.

    Prospective business owners must create a business plan in order to borrow money from a bank.

    Owning your own business is rewarding.

    People should research current trends in the market when deciding what type of business they plan to open.

    Sometimes business owners can get their families to work for free.

    People should calculate how much money they will spend and how much money they will make so they can project possible earnings.

4. Thesis: To maintain a long-distance relationship, both people must be willing to sacrifice.

    Couples often separate when they go to different universities.

    Both parties must be sensitive to the other's needs—even at a distance.

    People have to communicate often with each other, even if it's hard to find the time.

    Both people must put extra effort into the relationship to make it work.

    My parents had a long-distance relationship.

◆ *P r a c t i c e   1 B*   For each of the following thesis statements, list three supporting ideas.

1. People should always look for three qualities when searching for a job.

    _____

    _____

    _____

2. Moving away from home for the first time can be hard.

    _____

    _____

    _____

3. Animals can help people live longer.

_____

_____

_____

4. Vacations can sometimes be more strenuous than restful.

_____

_____

_____

Essays can be different lengths and often have a varying number of ideas that support their thesis statements. The thesis statement generally determines the length of an essay and the amount of support needed to make a point. Some statements require very little proof and might need only one body paragraph; others require much more support and might need four or more body paragraphs for a complete explanation. An essay that falls somewhere in the middle has an introduction, three body paragraphs, and a conclusion.

Beth's Supporting Ideas   Beth decided on three supporting ideas for her essay, which calls for three body paragraphs.

Thesis Statement: I know that I learn from many things in life.
Supporting Idea 1:   Taking risks
Supporting Idea 2:   Watching others
Supporting Idea 3:   Making mistakes

Your Supporting Ideas   Now list the support you might use for your thesis statement.

Your Thesis Statement: _____

Supporting Idea 1: _____

Supporting Idea 2: _____

Supporting Idea 3: _____

OUTLINING

At this stage of the writing process, many people benefit from putting their main ideas in the form of a rough, or working, outline. A rough outline can help you plan your essay and let you see how your ideas relate to one another. Then you can easily identify ideas that don't support your thesis and spot places where you need more information. A rough outline can evolve and become more detailed as your paper develops.

Beth's Rough Outline   Here is a rough outline of Beth's ideas so far:

Thesis Statement: I know that I learn from many things in life.

    A. I learn from taking risks.

    B. I learn from watching others.

    C. I learn from making mistakes.

Your Rough Outline   Now put your ideas so far into outline form.

Thesis Statement: _____

    A. _____

    B. _____

    C. _____

TOPIC SENTENCES

Writing is made up of several steps that lead you to your first draft. So far, you have been given a subject (learning about life) and have worked through a number of prewriting techniques. You also have generated ideas that you can use in your essay and have decided on a purpose and audience. Now you will learn how to write topic sentences for your body paragraphs. Then you will add some specific, concrete details from your prewriting activities and choose a method of organization for each paragraph. At that point, you will be ready to write your essay. This portion of the chapter will help you start your first draft, which you will then revise and edit in Chapters 7 and 8. Again, you will be writing alongside Beth as she works through the writing process with you.

First, you need to state each of your supporting ideas in the form of a topic sentence that will be developed into a body paragraph. The decisions you made in Chapter 2 about subject, purpose, and audience will lead you to your topic sentences. Look back at your prewriting notes and think about which topics will best support your thesis statement. These will be the topics of your body paragraphs. The body paragraphs will each include a topic sentence.

The **topic sentence** of a paragraph is its controlling idea. A typical paragraph consists of a topic sentence and details that expand on that topic sentence. A topic sentence performs two important tasks in its paragraph: (1) It supports the essay's thesis statement, and (2) it tells what the paragraph will be about. It functions best as the first sentence in its paragraph. Beginning a paragraph with the topic sentence gives direction to the paragraph and provides a kind of road map for the reader.

Like a thesis statement, a topic sentence has two parts—a topic and a statement about that topic. The topic should be limited enough that it can be developed in a paragraph. It should also be focused, not vague or scattered.

Topic	Limited Topic	Statement
Reading	Frequent reading	improves thinking skills.
Lotteries	Winning the lottery	will change a person's life forever.
Children	Having children	is a huge responsibility.
Hate	Hate crimes	are one of life's worst horrors.

◆ **P r a c t i c e   2 A**   Limit the following topics. Then develop them into statements that could be topic sentences.

Topic	Limited Topic	Statement
1. Mondays	_____	_____
2. Hobbies	_____	_____
3. Theme parks	_____	_____
4. Writing	_____	_____
5. Summer	_____	_____

◆ **P r a c t i c e   2 B**   Complete the following topic sentences. Make sure they are general enough to be developed into a paragraph, but not too broad.

1. Work-related injuries _____.

2. _____ is my favourite television show.

3. Sex education _____.

4. Stray dogs and cats _____.

5. _____ must be looked at on my college campus.

◆ *P r a c t i c e   2 C*   Write topic sentences for the following paragraphs.

1. _____

She watches the old ones like *Perry Mason* and can't get enough of the newer ones like *CSI*. But my mom really prefers the not-old and not-new mystery shows like *Matlock* and *Murder, She Wrote*. My mom will watch any of these shows for hours. My dad has a joke that she's watching all these TV shows so she can learn how to get rid of him and get away with it. I think she's just gathering information to write a book similar to these shows she loves to watch.

2. _____

First, you must follow the directions to install it onto your computer. Then you must read the directions to learn what you should do first with the program. It's best to read all the directions first, but most of the time people just go straight to the program and try to navigate their way through it. Once you get a handle on how to work the program, it's best just to play around and use the book only when you have questions. Mastering computer programs can be hard, but once you've done it, you can be sure you'll never forget how to use them.

3. _____

Because she wanted to save money for other parts of her wedding, the consultant was the first expense she cut. Everything went fine until the day of the wedding. My sister didn't get the flowers she ordered, but the ones that were delivered were OK. The cake arrived four hours late, and the reception hall wouldn't let us attach anything to the walls. And just before my sister walked into the church, she discovered that the train on her wedding dress was completely inside out. Luckily, no one but my sister and our family knew of the mishaps, but a consultant would have been worth every penny on the actual day of the wedding.

◆ *P r a c t i c e   3 A*   Supply three topic sentences for each thesis statement.

1. Many people enjoy resting on Sundays.

_____

_____

_____

2. Teachers should encourage all students to learn.

_____

_____

_____

3. Computers enable people to function more efficiently at work, at home, and at play.

_____

_____

_____

4. Planning is the key to a successful vacation.

_____

_____

_____

5. Being able to think critically, act quickly, and communicate clearly is essential in the business world.

_____

_____

_____

◆ *P r a c t i c e   3 B*   Fill in the following rough outlines.

1. Subject: Student life

Limited Subject: _____

Thesis Statement: _____

Topic Sentence: _____

Topic Sentence: _____

Topic Sentence: _____

2. Subject: Animal rights

    Limited Subject: _____

    Thesis Statement: _____

    Topic Sentence: _____

    Topic Sentence: _____

    Topic Sentence: _____

3. Subject: Intercollegiate sports

    Limited Subject: _____

    Thesis Statement: _____

    Topic Sentence: _____

    Topic Sentence: _____

    Topic Sentence: _____

4. Subject: Summer jobs

    Limited Subject: _____

    Thesis Statement: _____

    Topic Sentence: _____

    Topic Sentence: _____

    Topic Sentence: _____

5. Subject: The Internet

    Limited Subject: _____

    Thesis Statement: _____

    Topic Sentence: _____

    Topic Sentence: _____

    Topic Sentence: _____

Beth's Topic Sentences   Beth writes three topic sentences that she thinks will support her thesis statement.

> Thesis Statement: I know that I learn from many things in life.
>
>   Topic Sentence: I have discovered that I learn a lot by taking risks.
>
>   Topic Sentence: I also benefit from watching other people.
>
>   Topic Sentence: I believe that I learn from making mistakes.

Your Topic Sentences   Develop each of the ideas you listed on page 26 into a topic sentence that is directly related to your thesis statement. List your thesis first.

Thesis Statement: _____

   Topic Sentence: _____

   Topic Sentence: _____

   Topic Sentence: _____

SPECIFIC DETAILS

Now you are ready to generate the specific details that will make up the bulk of your body paragraphs. Later in this text, you will learn about different methods of developing your ideas, such as describing, comparing and contrasting, and analyzing causes and effects. For now, we are simply going to practise generating concrete supporting details and examples that are directly related to a specific topic. Concrete words refer to anything you can see, hear, touch, smell, or taste, such as *trees, boats, water, friends, fire alarm,* and *bread.* They make writing come alive because they help the reader picture what the writer is talking about.

◆ *Practice   4A*   Put a check by the details and examples listed that support each topic sentence.

1. Many people are addicted to soap operas.

       _____ viewers get caught up in the story

       _____ people care about the characters

       _____ soap operas are often springboards for actors wanting more work

_____ people are anxious to see what happens next

_____ mindless but entertaining TV

_____ viewers often strongly identify with the characters

_____ CBS has had the number one soap opera for years

2. My parents have reversed the stereotypical roles in their marriage.

    _____ my dad decorates the house

    _____ my mom and dad both work

    _____ my sister wants to be just like our mom

    _____ my mom mows and takes care of the lawn

    _____ my dad cleans the inside of the house

    _____ I hope to marry someone like my mom

3. Students change their majors often throughout their academic careers.

    _____ general education courses make students learn about a variety of subjects

    _____ in college, students discover new interests in subjects they have never been exposed to before

    _____ professors bring new subjects to life for many students

    _____ math is difficult for many students

    _____ other students often influence a student's decision about a major

    _____ the reality of the job market creates changes in majors

    _____ academic performance sometimes makes students look for alternative interests

◆ *P r a c t i c e   4 B*   For each of the following topic sentences, list five details or examples to develop them.

1. Everywhere I go, I seem to see someone that I know.

   _____

   _____

   _____

   _____

   _____

2. When I was in high school, I enjoyed many extracurricular activities.

   _____

   _____

   _____

   _____

   _____

3. People are beginning to use their personal computers for many different types of business transactions.

   _____

   _____

   _____

   _____

   _____

Beth's Development   To come up with concrete details and examples that would support her topic sentence, Beth uses the brainstorming and focused freewriting techniques she learned in Chapter 2. This is what she wrote:

I have discovered that I learn a lot by taking risks.

- buying a used car
- quitting my new job
- leaving Aaron to come to this school
- driving way too fast
- trying new foods
- changing majors
- procrastinating in school

I also benefit from watching other people.

- moving in with roommates I don't know
- watching my friends make mistakes with their boyfriends
- looking at my parents make rules
- seeing my cousin ruin her life
- watching my brother mess up
- observing people around me get involved with drugs
- learning about other people's mistakes from my friends

I believe that I learn from making mistakes.

- cheating on the test
- believing the rumour about my best friend
- lying to my parents
- not believing my sister
- waiting too long to write a paper
- watching TV instead of studying

Here is Beth's new freewriting:

I know I learn a lot by taking risks, watching other people, and making mistakes. I'm sure I learn in other ways too, but these are the ways that seem to give me the most information about life in general.

Taking risks really helps everyone learn in life, but I think this is especially true for me. I mean, right now I'm sitting here in this class thinking about Aaron and how we want to get married some day. But I left my home town and Aaron to come here for the nursing program. So far everything is great, but I knew it was a risk coming here. But how could I learn if I didn't?

I also learn by watching other people. My parents are great role models, but it's hard to really learn from them because they are so much older. I mean, they *tell* me not to join a gang, but they're my parents. I learned more about gangs from my cousin than from my parents. Watching my cousin go through her experiences was way better than just listening to my parents. I definitely learn by watching others.

And I definitely learn by making mistakes. And boy do I have tons of those. Most of my mistakes are pretty small, but I still learn from them. I think I learned the most from Mr. Turner, though, when he caught me cheating on his test. He talked to me, and that really helped. In fact, I think it's because of him that I started paying attention in class and decided to pursue nursing at this school.

I will always learn about life from these sources. I guess I will always learn about life as long as I keep my eyes open, but these ways seem the most important to me right now.

Your Development   Choose at least one of the prewriting strategies that you learned in Chapter 2, and use it to generate more specific details and examples for each of your topic sentences.

ORGANIZING YOUR ESSAY

CHAPTER 5

You are moving along quite well in the writing process. You have determined your subject, purpose, and audience, and you have written your thesis statement. You have also written topic sentences for your body paragraphs and thought of details, examples, and facts to develop those topic sentences. You are now ready to organize your ideas. What should come first? What next?

To organize the ideas in your essay, you need to consider the purpose of your essay and the way each body paragraph serves that purpose. Then you should arrange your body paragraphs in a logical manner to achieve that purpose. If your essay's main purpose is informative—to describe the layout of a building, for example—you would probably arrange the details spatially. That is, you might begin with the entrance and move to the other parts of the building as if you were strolling through it. If, however, you want to persuade a reader to buy one type of car over another, you might arrange the essay so that it moves from one extreme to another—for example, from the least important feature of the car to the most important. Once you decide on the order of your paragraphs, you need to organize the details in each paragraph.

Most paragraphs and essays are organized in one of the following five ways:

1. From general to particular
2. From particular to general
3. Chronologically (by time)
4. Spatially (by physical order)
5. From one extreme to another

Let's look at these methods of organization one by one.

GENERAL TO PARTICULAR

The most common method of organizing an essay or paragraph is from general to particular. This method begins with a general topic and becomes more specific as it progresses. A paragraph organized from general to particular might look like this:

Topic Sentence
    Detail
    Detail
    Detail
    Detail

Here is an example of a paragraph organized from general to particular:

    When I began attending college, I was very nervous because I was afraid I would not do very well in my classes. My first year, I took general education classes that reviewed a lot of the material I learned in high school. There was a lot of studying involved in these classes, but I was able to pass all of them. Soon I decided that my major would be business, so I began taking classes that dealt with business. All of the business classes were harder than the classes I had taken in general education. Just when I thought I would not pass a class, I would do well on a test, which would raise my confidence level again. I worked very hard in every class I took and was able to pass every one. Tomorrow I am graduating with my bachelor's degree in business.

This paragraph moves from the general idea of going to college to the specific notion of taking classes, graduating, and receiving a degree. Notice that it includes such transitions as *when*, *but*, *soon*, and *which*. They show the relationships among the writer's thoughts.

The skeleton of a general-to-particular essay looks like this, although the number of paragraphs and details will vary:

Introduction
    Topic sentence stating the most general point
        Detail
        Detail
        Detail
    Topic sentence stating a more specific supporting point
        Detail
        Detail
        Detail
    Topic sentence stating the most specific supporting point
        Detail
        Detail
        Detail
Conclusion

An example of an essay organized from general to particular is "A Family Dilemma: To Scout or Not to Scout" on page 354. The essay begins by introducing the nephew of the author and the U.S. Supreme Court's ruling that the Boy Scouts can legally fire gay men from their organization. The author then explains how these two general topics are affecting his present life, moving to topics that become more and more specific as the essay progresses. You might want to read this selection to see how this method of organization works in a full essay.

 Practice 1   Write a topic sentence for the following group of sentences. Then organize the sentences into a paragraph using general-to-particular order. Add words, phrases, or sentences as necessary to smooth out the paragraph.

Topic Sentence: _____

During these events, not only do you get to watch the athletes play their games, but you get to see former athletes announcing the action play-by-play.

Anytime you turn on the TV, there are at least a dozen sporting events happening at one time.

You can see anything from basketball to golf to racing to fishing.

Let's face it—the likelihood of seeing a sports figure on TV is great.

And just when you think you've seen enough of the players, you are bombarded by commercials that have athletes selling various products.

PARTICULAR TO GENERAL

When you reverse the first method of organization, you arrange your material from particular to general. In this case, more specific ideas start the essay or paragraph and lead up to a general statement. This type of organization is particularly effective if you suspect that your reader might not agree with the final point you are going to make. With this method, you can lead your reader to your opinion slowly and carefully.

A paragraph organized from particular to general looks like this:

Detail

Detail

Detail

Detail

Topic Sentence

Here is a paragraph of particular-to-general organization.

> The water is so crystal-clear that I can see every pebble settled on the bottom. A small sandy beach reaches the water's edge and makes a perfect spot to spend the afternoon. Across the water I can see the mountainside covered in the greenest trees imaginable. A log cabin also sits amongst the trees halfway up the mountain, so peaceful and secluded. The puffy white clouds make the sky appear to be a brighter blue, and the birds seem to enjoy floating on the soft breeze. I could sit all day next to the lake in the valley and just stare at my surroundings.

This paragraph starts with specific details about the area around the lake and ends with a topic sentence. Such transitions as *and, across the water*, and *also* move readers through the paragraph.

This is how a particular-to-general essay looks, though the number of details will vary:

Introduction
    Topic sentence stating the most specific point
      Detail
      Detail
      Detail
    Topic sentence stating a less specific point
      Detail
      Detail
      Detail
    Topic sentence stating the most general point
      Detail
      Detail
      Detail
Conclusion

The essay titled "Healing Myself with the Power of Work" on page 349 is a good example of organization from particular to general. It moves from examples out of the writer's life to his thesis at the end—that work is his therapy. If you read this selection, you will see first-hand how this method of organization works in a complete essay.

◆ **P r a c t i c e   2 A**   Turn to the essay "What Are Friends For?" on page 342, and find two paragraphs that demonstrate particular-to-general organization.

◆ *P r a c t i c e   2 B*   Write a topic sentence for the following group of sentences. Then organize the sentences into a paragraph using particular-to-general order. Add words, phrases, or sentences as necessary to smooth out the paragraph.

Topic Sentence: _____

My mom hopes I'll order something more grown-up, but I never will.

My family knew I loved pizza and always let me order one once a week.

I have always loved pepperoni, even on sandwiches and in soups.

I used to love pizza night when I lived at home.

I believe that pizza is the best food ever created.

Now when I go home, we just go to an Italian restaurant where I can order pizza.

CHRONOLOGICAL ORDER

When you organize ideas chronologically, you are organizing them according to the passage of time—in other words, in the order in which they occurred. Most of the time, when you tell a story or explain how to do something, you use chronological order: First this happened, and then that. Or first you do this, next you do that, and so on.

A paragraph organized chronologically looks like this:

Topic Sentence
  First
  Then
  Next
  Finally

Here is an example of a paragraph organized chronologically:

Preparing to go snowboarding for the first time can be a lot of fun. First of all, you must get into full gear when you arrive at the mountain. Then you ride a ski lift to the top of the mountain. Once at the top, it is time to buckle your boots into the bindings on the board. The bindings must be tight, but not so tight that they are uncomfortable. Next, you are ready to begin your descent. On the way down the mountain, pay attention to how the board moves when pressure is applied to the toes and heels of your feet. Finally, you need to learn which way to lean in order to turn right and left so you can fly down the mountain. Once you have mastered the basics, you will have fun perfecting your new hobby.

This paragraph is chronological because it explains snowboarding according to a time sequence and uses transitions such as *first of all*, *then*, *next*, and *finally*.

Here is what an essay organized chronologically looks like:

Introduction
    What happened first
      Detail
      Detail
      Detail
    What happened next
      Detail
      Detail
      Detail
    What happened after that
      Detail
      Detail
      Detail
Conclusion

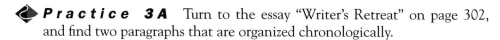 **Practice 3A** Turn to the essay "Writer's Retreat" on page 302, and find two paragraphs that are organized chronologically.

Practice 3B Write a topic sentence for the following group of sentences. Then organize the sentences into a paragraph using chronological order. Add words, phrases, or sentences as necessary to smooth out the paragraph.

Topic Sentence: _____

Spread the jam on top of the peanut butter.
Unscrew the lid from a jar of peanut butter and from a jar of jam.
Using the knife again, remove a small amount of jam from the jar.
Place two slices of bread on a plate.
Using the knife, remove a small amount of peanut butter from the jar.
Place the second slice of bread on top of the slice with the peanut butter and jam on it.
First, remove a knife from the drawer.
Spread the peanut butter on one slice of bread with the knife.

SPATIAL ORDER

Another method of arranging details is by their relationship to each other in space. You might describe the layout of your campus from its front entrance to its back exit or the arrangement of a beautiful garden from one end to the other. Explaining a home page from top to bottom and describing a screened-in porch from inside to outside are also examples of spatial order. Beginning at one point and moving detail by detail around a specific area is the simplest way of organizing by space.

A paragraph organized spatially might look like this:

Topic Sentence
   Here
   There
   Next
   Across
   Beyond

Here is an example of a paragraph organized spatially:

It was the first football game of the season and her first football game ever as a cheerleader. Standing in front of the huge crowd made the butterflies in her stomach begin to flutter again. In the front row sat a group of her friends cheering her on. Two rows behind them sat her psychology professor. Next to her professor sat a few of her new sorority sisters. As the cheerleader looked across the aisle, she noticed a group of rowdy students screaming and cheering for their team. Beyond the crowd, the tall announcer's booth where all of the press people and the athletic director sat seemed to glare down at her. Any minute the music would begin to blare from that very booth, and she would begin her first half-time dance routine.

This paragraph is arranged spatially because it moves physically around the football stadium, using such words as *in front of*, *behind*, *next to*, and *beyond* as transitions.

Here is what an essay organized spatially looks like:

Introduction
   Here
      Detail
      Detail
      Detail

> There
>   Detail
>   Detail
>   Detail
> Next
>   Detail
>   Detail
>   Detail
> Across
>   Detail
>   Detail
>   Detail
> Beyond
>   Detail
>   Detail
>   Detail
> Conclusion

◆ ***Practice 4***   Write a topic sentence for the following group of sentences. Then write a paragraph putting the sentences in spatial order. Add words, phrases, or sentences as necessary to smooth out the paragraph.

Topic Sentence: _____

The hotel's check-in desk is located on the left side of the lobby.

Two little boys are sitting quietly on the couches next to the check-in desk, waiting for their parents to finish checking in.

In the centre of the lobby are four massive couches arranged in a conversational setting.

Directly across from the check-in desk is the activities counter where people can plan their days.

Inside the front door, the guests' attention is immediately drawn to the ceiling.

Painted to look like a sky, the ceiling gives guests the feeling that they have never left the outdoors.

Framing the front door are two huge dolphins, each perched in the centre of a water fountain.

ONE EXTREME TO ANOTHER

Sometimes the best way to organize a paragraph is from one extreme to another: from most expensive to least expensive, from most humorous to least humorous, from most frustrating to least frustrating, and so on. (Of course, you can also move from least to most.) Use whatever extremes make sense for your topic. You might explain how to choose a pet by elaborating on the most important qualities of an animal and then considering the least important. For example, an apartment dweller's most important consideration might be the size of the pet and its need for exercise. Least important might be watchdog qualities. To accomplish another purpose, you might reverse this order and begin with the least important quality; this method is good in persuasive writing because you end with your most important idea.

This method of organization has one distinct advantage over the other four approaches: It is the most flexible. When no other method of organization works, you can always arrange details from one extreme to another.

Here is an outline of a paragraph organized from one extreme to another:

Topic Sentence
  Most
  Next most
  Somewhat
  Least

Here is an example of a paragraph that moves from one extreme to another:

> Ever since I was old enough to join Little League teams, I have played a variety of sports. I would have to say that my favourite sport has always been football. Absolutely nothing can top the feeling of running for a touchdown and passing the defensive safety. My next favourite sport would have to be baseball. I used to love to pitch to catchers when we would work together as though we were one athlete. My next favourite sport is basketball. As a teenager, I played guard in basketball, but eventually I got bored with the position. My least favourite sport is soccer. No matter how much I trained and ran before soccer season, I always got exhausted during the games—all we did was run up and down the field. Now that I'm in college, I'm grateful for the intramural teams that let me keep playing the sports that I love.

This paragraph moves from most to least preferred sports and is marked by such words as *favourite*, *next favourite*, and *least favourite*.

Here is what an essay organized according to extremes looks like:

Introduction
  Most
    Detail
    Detail
    Detail
  Next most
    Detail
    Detail
    Detail
  Somewhat
    Detail
    Detail
    Detail
  Least
    Detail
    Detail
    Detail
Conclusion

"What Are Friends For?" on page 342 is a good example of this method of organization. It begins with a discussion of "relative friends" and moves to an explanation of "new friends." The author organizes her essay from least meaningful to most meaningful friends. Reading through it will help you understand this strategy.

Practice 5   List the best method of development for paragraphs on the following topics.

1. How to make homemade salsa.

2. I think I am going to rearrange my dorm room to create more space.

3. What I will have for dinner tonight.

4. Today, people question the ethics of capital punishment.

5. I lift weights for an hour and run five miles every day.

Practice 6   Write a topic sentence that introduces the following details in a paragraph. Then arrange the details in logical order, and write a paragraph.

Topic Sentence: _____

> exercising three times a week
> the advantages of aerobic exercise
> exercising with a friend
> the difficulty of starting an exercise routine

Beth's Organization   Beth decided to organize her essay from one extreme to another—from the most important ways of learning for her to the least important. She first wants to introduce the idea of taking risks, which she believes is very important. Next she will discuss watching others and finally write about learning from mistakes because she thinks she learns a lot from her own mistakes. She thinks this order might work, so she lists as many concrete details as she can under each main idea.

Here is Beth's working outline at this point:

Thesis Statement: I know that I learn from many things in life.

  Taking Risks (*most important*):   taking risks and learning from them

    Specific Details: finding a good nursing program
                      leaving my boyfriend back home
                      going to college

  Watching Others (*less important*):   learning from watching others

    Specific Details: watching my cousin in gangs
                      living in fear
                      not in a gang because of her

  Making Mistakes (*least important*):   making mistakes and learning
                                  from those mistakes

    Specific Details: cheating on test
                      talking with Mr. Turner
                      learning to pay more attention in school
                        for a better future

Concluding Thoughts: people can learn from everything they do
  Specific Details: taking risks
                      watching others
                      making mistakes

Does the method of organization that Beth has chosen suit her topic? Would any other method of organization work as well?

Your Organization   What method of organization will work best for your ideas about learning? Why do you think this method will work best?

WRITING THE INTRODUCTION, CONCLUSION, AND TITLE

By now, you have written your thesis statement and topic sentences for your body paragraphs. You've thought of supporting details, facts, examples, and the most effective way of organizing your thoughts. At the end of this chapter, you will write a complete first draft of your essay. First, though, let's look at three important parts of your essay: the introduction, the conclusion, and the title.

You might have written some of these parts already. Some people write their introduction with their thesis; others write the introduction last. Some have an idea of how they want to conclude from the time they begin their papers; others write the conclusion last. Some struggle with a title; others write their titles as they generate their drafts. The order in which you write these three parts of an essay depends on your own personal writing process. All that matters is that your papers have a title, an introduction, several body paragraphs, and a conclusion that work together.

INTRODUCTION

The introduction to your essay—your first paragraph—should both introduce your subject and stimulate your audience's interest. The introduction of an essay captures the readers' interest, supplies necessary background information, and presents your thesis statement. This paragraph essentially tells readers what the essay is going to cover without going into detail or discussing specifics.

Writers generally use the introduction to lead up to their thesis statement. As a result, the sentences at the beginning of the introductory paragraph need to grab your readers' attention. Some effective ways of capturing your audience's interest and giving necessary background information are to (1) furnish a vivid description, (2) tell a brief story, (3) state a revealing fact, statistic, or definition, (4) make an interesting comparison, (5) present a dramatic example, and (6) use an exciting quotation.

Also be sure that your introduction gives your readers any information that they may need to have in order to follow your train of thought. One way to check that your readers have enough background information is to apply the five Ws and one H: *Who, What, When, Where, Why,* and *How.* Any of this information that is important to your readers' understanding of your thesis statement should go in the introduction. You might also ask a friend to read your first draft and tell you if any background information is missing.

Beth's Introduction and Thesis   Beth wrote a first draft of her introduction just to get started. She knew she would have to work on it later, but at least she was able to get some of her ideas down on paper.

> Everyone learns in different ways. Some people learn by watching, some by reading, and others by themselves. The way people learn is a part of who they are. Knowing how we learn can help us understand ourselves better. I know that I learn from many things in life.

Your Introduction   Use the guidelines suggested here to capture your readers' interest and, if necessary, give them background information. Write two different introductions for your essay. End each with your thesis statement.

CONCLUSION

The concluding paragraph is the final paragraph of an essay. It completes your essay, giving readers a sense of closure. That is, readers feel that all the loose ends are wrapped up and the point of the essay is clear. As with introductions, there are many good techniques for writing a conclusion. You might (1) summarize the main ideas, (2) highlight the most important issue, (3) ask a question that gets readers to think about something in particular, (4) predict the future, (5) offer a solution to a problem, or (6) call readers to action. In some cases, you might want to use several of these strategies.

You should avoid two common problems in writing a conclusion. First, do not begin your conclusion with the words "in conclusion," "in summary," or "as you can see." Your conclusion should *show*—not *tell*—that you are at the end of your essay. Second, do not introduce a new idea. The main ideas of your essay should be in your body paragraphs. The conclusion is where you *finish* your essay, leaving your readers with a sense of closure or completeness.

Beth's Conclusion   Here is a rough outline of what Beth wants to include in her conclusion. These are the notes that she came up with at this point.

People can learn about life from just about anything.

- made me the person I am
- watching other people
- taking some risks myself
- making mistakes

Your Conclusion   Sketch an outline or write a draft of a possible conclusion for your essay.

TITLE

A title is a phrase, usually no more than a few words. A title gives a hint about the subject, purpose, or focus of what is to follow. For example, the main title chosen for this book, *Mosaics,* reflects a particular view of the writing process—as many bright pieces logically connected to complete a picture. In other words, that title expresses in capsule form this textbook's purpose, which is to guide writers through the process of fitting the separate pieces of their ideas into a single meaningful whole to make an essay. The title of this chapter, however, is a straightforward naming of its contents: "Writing the Introduction, Conclusion, and Title."

Besides suggesting an essay's purpose, a good title catches an audience's attention or "hooks" readers so that they want to read more. Look at some of the essay titles in the readings in Part IV. For example, "What Are Friends For?" is a title that will naturally draw in most readers. And "I Just Wanna Be Average" is intriguing because the title is not a typical goal for most people. Do not underline or use quotation marks around your essay titles. Do not put a period at the end of your titles, and be sure to capitalize them correctly. The first word and last word in a title are always capitalized. Capitalize all other words except articles (*a, an, the*), short prepositions (such as *in, by, on,* or *from;* see page 383 for a more complete list of prepositions), and coordinating conjunctions (such as *and, but,* and *or*).

Beth's Title   Beth has several possible titles for her essay. She doesn't really know which one to use.

Learning About Life

The Way We Learn

Everyone Can Learn

Your Title   Write three titles for your essay: (1) one that gives a hint of your subject, (2) one that gives a hint of your purpose, and (3) one that gives a hint of your focus. Make each title as catchy as you can.

Beth's First Draft   In Chapters 1 through 5, and again in this chapter, you have watched Beth thinking about, planning, developing, and organizing her essay. It is time now to get a complete first draft down on paper. Here is Beth's first draft, including a few grammar errors that we will deal with later on in this unit.

The Way We Learn

Everyone learns in different ways. Some people learn by watching, some by reading, and others by themselves. The way people learn is a part of who they are. Knowing how we learn can help us understand ourselves better. I know that I learn from many things in life.

1

I have discovered that I learn a lot by taking risks. Coming to this school was a risk. I have a boyfriend back home, we want to get married some day. We are hoping for a spring wedding with all of our friends and family. I left my boyfriend to come here. Coming here was a risk to our relationship. But if I am ever going to make it, I have to be willing to take risks.

2

I also benefit from watching other people. When my cousin became heavily involved with gangs, I watched my cousin live in constant fear. By watching my cousin, I made a conscious decision to be nothing like my cousin. By watching and understanding my cousin's life. I learned to live mine better.

3

I believe that I learn from making mistakes. When I was in high school, I didn't study for a major science test. So I cheated. My sister cheated once. I was so scared to do it. The teacher caught me. The teacher took the time to talk to me about the mistake I was making. This mistake made me re-evaluate my education. I could have laughed off the cheating experience. I decided to slow down and learn from the experience.

4

People can learn about life from almost anything they do. They just have to be willing to do so. When I take risks, I think about what I will learn. I definitely try to learn as much as I can from watching others. When I make mistakes, I figure out why I made each mistake and how to avoid it a second time.

5

Your First Draft   Now write a complete first draft of your essay on how you learn.

CHAPTER 7

REVISING

No matter how hard you wish, writing does not end with your first draft. The fun of revising and editing still lies ahead of you. **Revising** means "seeing again," and that is exactly what you should try to do when you revise to improve your writing—see it again from as many different angles as possible.

More specifically, revising your writing means changing it so that it says exactly what you mean in the most effective way. Revision involves both *content* (what you are trying to say) and *form* (how you deliver your message). Having a friend or tutor read your paper before you revise it is a good idea so that you can see whether or not you are communicating clearly.

Revising content means working with your words until they express your ideas as accurately and completely as possible. Revising form consists of working with the organization of your writing. When you revise, you should look closely at the six basic categories listed in the following checklist.

REVISING CHECKLIST ✔

THESIS STATEMENT
- ✔ Does the thesis statement contain the essay's controlling idea and an opinion about that idea?
- ✔ Does the thesis appear as the last sentence of the introduction?

BASIC ELEMENTS
- ✔ Does the title draw in the reader?
- ✔ Does the introduction capture the reader's attention and build up to the thesis statement effectively?
- ✔ Does each body paragraph deal with a single topic?
- ✔ Does the conclusion bring the essay to a close in an interesting way?

DEVELOPMENT
- ✔ Do the body paragraphs adequately support the thesis statement?
- ✔ Does each body paragraph have a focused topic sentence?

✔ Does each body paragraph contain *specific* details that support the topic sentence?

✔ Does each body paragraph include *enough* details to explain the topic sentence fully?

UNITY

✔ Do the essay's topic sentences relate directly to the thesis statement?

✔ Do the details in each body paragraph support its topic sentence?

ORGANIZATION

✔ Is the essay organized logically?

✔ Is each body paragraph organized logically?

COHERENCE

✔ Are transitions used effectively so that paragraphs move smoothly and logically from one to the next?

✔ Do the sentences move smoothly and logically from one to the next?

Let's look at these revision strategies one by one.

Thesis Statement

✔ Does the thesis statement contain the essay's controlling idea and an opinion about that idea?

✔ Does the thesis appear as the last sentence of the introduction?

As you learned in Chapter 3, every successful essay has a thesis statement that states the essay's controlling idea. This sentence gives direction to the rest of the essay. It consists of a limited subject and the writer's position on that subject. Although a thesis statement can appear anywhere in an essay, it is usually the last sentence of the introduction.

Here are two examples:

Limited Subject	+	Opinion	=	Thesis Statement
1. Children today		grow up too fast		Children today grow up too fast.
2. Children today		grow up too fast		Children today grow up too fast because of television, advertising, and working parents.

As in the second example, the thesis statement should introduce all the topics in its essay. The first example includes the limited subject and the writer's position on that subject, but it also needs to introduce its topics.

◆ *P r a c t i c e   **1A***   Review the guidelines for developing a thesis statement in Chapter 3. Then write a thesis statement for each group of topic sentences listed here.

1. Thesis Statement: _____

> Everyone needs a friend who likes to do the same things.
>
> Everyone needs someone to share good news with.
>
> Equally important, everyone needs a good listener during bad times.

2. Thesis Statement: _____

> Watching a movie on the big screen of a theatre makes the story and characters bigger and more interesting than life.
>
> The sound system in a movie theatre makes me feel that I'm right there in the action.
>
> The concession stand has all sorts of candy and goodies, and I don't have to clean up my own mess afterward.

3. Thesis Statement: _____

> Being behind slow drivers can cause people to experience road rage.
>
> Likewise, tailgating can cause people to get angry.
>
> People who weave in and out of traffic at extreme speeds make many drivers furious.

◆ *P r a c t i c e   **1B***   Write thesis statements for the following introductions.

1. _____

No matter how much I tell myself I am going to get up in the morning and go, I cannot seem to do it. Every night before I go to bed, I lay out my sweats and shoes and set my alarm. In the morning when the alarm rings, I push the snooze button and promise myself that I will get up in five minutes. This routine goes on for the next hour until I have to get up in order to make it to work on time. Once again, I have failed to get up and go to the gym, and I have deprived myself of one more hour of sleep.

2. _____

The most important detail is to determine the number of rooms in the house. A family must consider the needs of the people living in the house and their plans for the near future. Of course, don't forget the backyard. Does the family need a fenced yard for animals or an area for the kids to play? And the family must pay attention to how well the house has been kept up. All of these items are very important details when looking for a new home.

3. _____

Every morning, at precisely 8:00, the couple eat breakfast at the corner café. Afterward, they go to the market for fresh fruit or vegetables and run errands. If they have no shopping to do, the couple go home and do housework or yard work. Every afternoon at 1:00, they sit down to lunch and watch a little television. In the late afternoon, they go for a walk around the lake for a bit of exercise before preparing their dinner. After dinner, they watch the news and play a hand of cards. Soon the sun dips behind the mountain, and the couple retire for the night.

Beth's Revision   When Beth looks back at her thesis statement, she realizes it does not completely introduce what she talks about in her essay. Her thesis tells readers only that she learns about life from different things, not that she has three important ways that she learns about life.

Thesis Statement: I know that I learn from many things in life.

She decides to expand her thesis statement so that it more accurately introduces the topics that will follow in her essay:

Revised Thesis Statement: I know that I learn ~~from many things in life~~ best from taking risks, watching others, and making mistakes.

She feels that this thesis statement introduces the notion of learning and the different ways that she has learned.

Your Revision   With these guidelines in mind, revise your thesis statement.

Your Revised Thesis Statement: _____

_____

Basic Elements

✔ Does the title draw in the reader?

✔ Does the introduction capture the reader's attention and build up to the thesis statement effectively?

✔ Does each body paragraph deal with a single topic?

✔ Does the conclusion bring the essay to a close in an interesting way?

These revision items ask you to check that all the basic elements of the essay are present and are doing the jobs they are supposed to do. If all the essay's parts are in place, you can spend more time polishing what you have to say.

Now that you have written a complete draft of your essay, this is the time to review these basic elements. What changes do you want to make in your title? In your introduction? In your conclusion? Is your thesis statement at the end of your introduction? Do you need to split any body paragraphs?

◆ *Practice 2A* Write an alternative title for the essay "The Truth About Stories" (page 333).

◆ *Practice 2B* Write an alternative introduction for "Don't Be Cruel" (page 318).

◆ *Practice 2C* Write an additional body paragraph for "Wild Weather" (page 313).

◆ *Practice 2D* Write an alternative conclusion for "Writer's Retreat" (page 302).

Beth's Revision Beth sets out to answer each of these questions one by one. Here are her responses.

✔ Does the title draw in the reader?

No. It's kind of boring.

✔ Does the introduction capture the reader's attention and build up to the thesis statement effectively?

Not really—it's too short; I could use one of the ideas introduced in Chapter 6 to make it more interesting.

✔ Does each body paragraph deal with a single topic?

Yes. So I don't have to break any of them into two or more paragraphs.

✔ Does the conclusion bring the essay to a close in an interesting way?

Sort of. I guess I should look at it again and try to apply some of the material in Chapter 6 to my conclusion.

You saw Beth's first draft at the end of Chapter 6. Here is the second draft of her introduction, conclusion, and title with her changes highlighted.

Introduction

Everyone learns in different ways. Some people learn by watching, **while others learn by doing.** Some **learn** by reading, **while others learn by listening** ~~and others by themselves.~~ **Some learn best when they work independently, while others do better in groups.** The way people learn is a **major** part of who they are. Knowing how we learn can help us understand ourselves better. I know that I learn best from taking risks, watching others, and making mistakes.

Conclusion

People can learn about life from almost anything they do. They just have to be willing to do so. When I take risks, I think about what I will learn. I definitely try to learn as much as I can from watching others, **which I believe, in the case of my cousin, has already saved my life.** When I make mistakes, I figure out why I made each mistake and how to avoid it a second time. **These three ways of learning are all part of who I am today. I know I'm not finished learning yet. In fact, I don't know if I ever will be.**

Title

~~The Way We Learn~~

The Learning Curve

Your Revision   Apply these questions one by one to your essay.

☐ Does the title draw in the reader?

☐ Does the introduction capture the reader's attention and build up to the thesis statement effectively?

☐ Does each body paragraph deal with a single topic?

☐ Does the conclusion bring the essay to a close in an interesting way?

Development

> ✔ Do the body paragraphs adequately support the thesis statement?
>
> ✔ Does each body paragraph have a focused topic sentence?
>
> ✔ Does each body paragraph contain specific details that support the topic sentence?
>
> ✔ Does each body paragraph include enough details to explain the topic sentence fully?

When you develop an essay, you build the body paragraphs. Body paragraphs provide supporting evidence for the thesis statement. They are made up of a clearly focused topic sentence and details that support the topic sentence. Supporting details should be as specific as possible, and you need to provide enough details to support the point you are making in each paragraph.

Specific Details

An important part of developing a good essay is being able to recognize ideas that are more general (for example, *entertainment* and *exercise*) and more specific (the opening scene in *The Green Mile*). Two other essential terms to know in choosing details are *abstract* and *concrete*. As you learned in Chapter 3, concrete words refer to items you can see, hear, touch, smell, or taste—as opposed to abstract words, which refer to ideas and concepts, such as *entertainment, frustration,* and *peacefulness.* Look at the following examples, and notice how each line becomes more detailed.

entertainment (general, abstract)
    movies
        suspense films
            Stephen King films
                The Green Mile
                    opening scene in *The Green Mile* (specific, concrete)

exercise (general, abstract)
    sports
        team sports
            football
                university football
                    varsity football championship
                        Vanier Cup
                            2003 Vanier Cup at the SkyDome in Toronto (specific, concrete)

Don't confuse levels of detail with examples. Compare the previous ladder with this one:

sports
> team sports
>> football
>>> varsity football
>>>> McMaster Marauders
>>>> St. Mary's Huskies
>>>> Laval Rouge et Or
>>>> Western Mustangs

In this ladder, the four varsity teams are at the same level of detail. One is not more specific than another. So these last four items are just a list of examples.

As a rule, your thesis statement should be the most general statement in your essay. Your topic sentences are more specific than your thesis, and the details in your body paragraphs are the most specific items in the essay. So an outline of these elements looks like this:

Thesis statement (general)
> Topic sentence
>> Detail (specific and concrete)
>> Detail (specific and concrete)
>> Detail (specific and concrete)

Making your essay more specific involves adding as well as rewriting words, phrases, and whole sentences. Here is one of Beth's body paragraphs with more specific details in bold type in her revision.

First Draft

I have discovered that I learn a lot by taking risks. Coming to this school was a risk. I have a boyfriend back home, we want to get married some day. We are hoping for a spring wedding with all of our friends and family. I left my boyfriend to come here. Coming here was a risk to our relationship. But if I am ever going to make it, I have to be willing to take risks.

Revised with Specific Details

I have discovered that I learn a lot by taking risks.
If I didn't take risks, I think I'd never mature. Coming to
this school was a risk. I have a boyfriend back home, we
want to get married some day. We are hoping for
a spring wedding with all of our friends and family.
I left my boyfriend to come here. Coming here was a
risk to our relationship. **Taking this risk taught me to
be responsible and trust my boyfriend back home.** But
if I am ever going to ~~make it~~ **reach my potential,** I have
to be willing to take risks.

◆ *P r a c t i c e   3A*   Underline the most specific word or phrase in each
group.

1. books, library, shelves, page 42, stairs

2. computer, technology, software, power button, online help

3. backyard, swimming pool, Coppertone lotion, pool party

4. drinks, thirst, pop, Dr. Pepper, root beer in a frosty mug

5. pink candles on a birthday cake, dessert, dinner, sweets, chocolate candy

◆ *P r a c t i c e   3B*   Fill in each blank with a new level of concrete detail
as indicated by the indentions.

1. _____

   The lottery

      _____

      _____

2. _____

   brother

      _____

      _____

3. boat

   _____

   _____

   _____

4. _____

   _____

   _____

   blue shirt with stripes

5. _____

   _____

   Thursday's newspaper

   _____

Enough Details

Not only should your details be specific and concrete, but you should furnish enough details to support your topic sentence. No matter how good one detail is, it is not enough to develop a topic sentence. Without enough details, facts, or reasons, a paragraph can be too short and weak to support a thesis statement. So Beth needs to add more details to her paragraph.

Here is Beth's body paragraph on learning with more details.

Revised with More Details

I have discovered that I learn a lot by taking risks. If I didn't take risks, I think I'd never mature. Coming to this school was a risk. I have a boyfriend back home, we want to get married some day. We are hoping for a spring wedding with all of our friends and family. **But I knew that this school's nursing program was better than the one in my home town.** I left my boyfriend to come here. Coming here was a risk to our relationship. **Not coming here would have been a risk to my career.** Taking this risk taught me to be responsible and trust my boyfriend back home. **I know that I will take many risks like this throughout my life and that not all of them will work out.** But if I am ever going to reach my potential, I have to be willing to take risks.

◆ *P r a c t i c e **4A***   List three details that could support each of the following topic sentences.

1. My favourite pastime is swimming.

    _____

    _____

    _____

2. Eating a balanced diet is an important part of feeling good.

    _____

    _____

    _____

3. A simple gift is often the best.

    _____

    _____

    _____

4. Working for people you like is easy.

    _____

    _____

    _____

5. Spending time outdoors can change a person's mood.

    _____

    _____

    _____

◆ *P r a c t i c e **4B***   Develop the following topic sentences with enough specific details.

1. Before taking a test, take a moment to relax.
2. Always discuss major decisions with someone you trust.
3. When interviewing for a job, dress appropriately.

4. My roommate is a real neat freak.

5. When reading a book, think about what you are reading.

Beth's Revision   Beth's essay needs *more* details and *more specific* details to help it communicate its message. She accomplishes this by adding more details about learning throughout her essay. The details she added to her first draft are highlighted below.

The Learning Curve

Everyone learns in different ways. Some people learn by watching, while others learn by doing. Some learn by reading, while others learn by listening. Some learn best when they work independently, while others do better in groups. The way people learn is a major part of who they are. Knowing how we learn can help us understand ourselves better. I know that I learn best from taking risks, watching others, and making mistakes.   1

I have discovered that I learn a lot by taking risks. If I didn't take risks, I think I'd never mature. Coming to this school was a risk. I have a boyfriend back home, we want to get married some day. We are hoping for a spring wedding with all of our friends and family. But I knew that this school's nursing program was better than the one in my home town. I left my boyfriend to come here. Coming here was a risk to our relationship. Not coming here would have been a risk to my career. Taking this risk taught me to be responsible and trust my boyfriend back home. I know that I will take many risks like this throughout my life and that not all of them will work out. But if I am ever going to reach my potential, I have to be willing to take risks.   2

I also benefit from watching other people. When my cousin became heavily involved with gangs **and drugs,** I watched my cousin live in constant fear. **She was worried that she would end up in jail, overdose on drugs, or become a "plaything" for other gang members. She worked hard to overcome that lifestyle. She talked a lot to me about those experiences.** By watching my cousin **go through these horrible experiences,** I made a conscious decision ~~to be nothing like my cousin~~ never to make the bad choices that my cousin made. **I had plenty of opportunities to do so. Turning away from that life was difficult, but I did it.** By watching and understanding my cousin's life. I learned to live mine better.   3

4   I believe that I learn from making mistakes. When I was in high school, I didn't study for a major science test. **I knew the test was important, but I decided to go to a party with my friends. I really needed the grade, S**so I cheated. My sister cheated once. I was so scared to do it. **I cut my notes into small strips of paper that I put in my desk, but T**the teacher caught me. **Thank goodness the teacher was a nice person.** The teacher took the time to talk to me about the mistake I was making**, not only cheating for a grade, but cheating myself out of the knowledge that I could have.** This mistake made me re-evaluate my education. **This mistake led me into nursing by making me re-evaluate what subjects I really enjoyed.** I could have laughed off the cheating experience **and the teacher.** I decided to slow down and learn from the experience.

5   People can learn about life from almost anything they do. They just have to be willing to do so. When I take risks, I think about what I will learn. I definitely try to learn as much as I can from watching others, which I believe, in the case of my cousin, has already saved my life. When I make mistakes, I figure out why I made each mistake and how to avoid it a second time. These three ways of learning are all part of who I am today. I know I'm not finished learning yet. In fact, I don't know if I ever will be.

Your Revision   Add more relevant details to your essay, making your explanations and descriptions as specific as possible. Also make sure all of your body paragraphs have focused topic sentences that support your thesis statement.

Unity

> ✔ Do the essay's topic sentences relate directly to the thesis statement?
> ✔ Do the details in each body paragraph support its topic sentence?

An essay is unified when its topic sentences are all related to the thesis statement and when each body paragraph discusses only one idea. Irrelevant paragraphs in essays are those that don't support their essay's thesis statement. They should be deleted or revised to fit into the essay's plan.

A paragraph's main idea is introduced in its topic sentence. All other sentences in a paragraph should expand on this idea and relate to it in some way. Information that is not about the topic sentence is irrelevant and does not belong in the paragraph.

◆ *Practice* **5A**   Cross out the topic sentences that don't support each thesis statement.

1. Thesis: Holidays are fun times in my family.

    My favourite holiday is Thanksgiving.
    July 1st always scares my dogs.
    Chanukah is a time of great celebration in my house.
    My boyfriend doesn't understand my family.

2. Thesis: I love working with children.

    Children's games still make me laugh.
    I hate foods that are good for me.
    I want a job that pays well.
    I have always liked babysitting.
    I have applied to work at the Children's Centre on our campus.

3. Thesis: Exercise is essential for good health.

    Exercise keeps our hearts in good shape.
    Exercise is fun.
    Exercise is difficult when you are on a tight schedule.
    Exercise is necessary for weight control.
    Exercise is good for us emotionally.

4. Thesis: I have learned over the years how to control my anger.

    One way is to count to ten before I do anything.
    I get angry easily.
    Another solution is to take a deep breath before I act.
    The solution I use most often is to take a walk.

5. Thesis: I really like to cook, but I never have the time.

    I am most creative at breakfast.
    The dish I like to make the most is frittata.
    My class schedule keeps me busy right through dinner.
    My philosophy class is my toughest class.
    I don't like spicy foods.

◆ *P r a c t i c e   5 B*   Cross out the three irrelevant sentences in the following paragraph.

I have a very bad habit of waiting until the night before an exam to begin studying, so it is very important for me to have a well-planned and productive cramming session. One time in high school, I failed a test. I begin by putting on comfortable clothes so that when I start to squirm and twist to try and get comfortable, I am able to move around. Next, I get a big glass of milk and several cookies to snack on. Peanut-butter cookies have always been my favourite. Once I have my snack, I spread out all my books and study materials on the living room floor. I have a hardwood floor. Finally, I am ready to begin studying for the next few hours.

◆ *P r a c t i c e   5 C*   Cross out the three irrelevant sentences in the following paragraph.

Most people wonder what it would be like to win the lottery and be able to spend money as they please. The odds are that even the people who buy a lottery ticket every day will never win the lottery. Winning the lottery would change most people's lives dramatically. Many people say that they would begin by paying off all their debts. There are people in the world who buy so many items on credit that they are constantly trying to get out of debt. Other people say that they would buy a new house or a new car to spoil themselves a little bit. Some people simply say that they would invest the money and use it when they retire so that they can live comfortably. Many elderly people are unable to continue the lifestyles they are accustomed to after retirement.

Beth's Revision   When Beth reads her paper for unity, she sees that three sentences are off topic. So she deletes them.

In Paragraph 2:   ~~We are hoping for a spring wedding with all of our friends and family.~~

In Paragraph 3:   ~~My sister cheated once. I was so scared to do it.~~

Your Revision   Read your essay carefully, and cross out any irrelevant sentences or paragraphs.

Organization

✔ Is the essay organized logically?
✔ Is each body paragraph organized logically?

In Chapter 3, you learned five ways to organize your paragraphs and essays:

1. From general to particular
2. From particular to general
3. Chronologically (by time)
4. Spatially (by physical arrangement)
5. From one extreme to another

The organization that you choose for your essay depends chiefly on your topic and overall purpose. What are you trying to accomplish? In what order should you present your evidence? Is point A the most important? Maybe it should be in the last body paragraph so you can build up to it.

After you put your paragraphs in order, you are ready to look at the organization of each individual paragraph. It's very likely that your essay will be organized one way (say, from least important to most important) and each of your body paragraphs will have its own method of organization. As you revise, you should check to see that your essay is organized as effectively as possible for what you are trying to accomplish and that your body paragraphs are each arranged logically as well.

Practice 6 A   Reorganize the following topics so that they are in a logical order. Then label your method of organization.

1. east at the mall to the stop light

   west at the grocery store to the flower shop

   north at the flower shop until you get to Anita's

   south at the stop light until you hit the grocery store

   Method of Organization: _____

2. sitcoms

   dramas

   documentaries

   musicals

   awards shows

   Method of Organization: _____

3. community servants

   police badges

   police officers

   police office staff

   police uniforms

   Method of Organization: _____

◆ *P r a c t i c e   6 B*   Reorganize the following sentences so that they are in a logical order. Then identify your method of organization.

Next, I decide what I will have for dinner and begin to cook.

Then I change into comfortable clothes.

Before I completely wind down, I lay out my clothes for the next day and set my alarm clock.

This is always a good time to look at the mail or return phone calls.

While I am cooking, I listen to music or turn on the evening news.

First, I begin to relax by taking a shower.

When I return home in the evenings, I always follow the same routine.

After I eat, I do the dishes and sit down in the living room.

Finally I watch television or read a book until I fall asleep.

Method of Organization: _____

◆ *P r a c t i c e   6 C*   Reorganize the following sentences so that they are in a logical order. Then identify your method of organization.

Sweatshirts belong next to long-sleeved shirts, so they come next.

When I walk in the closet door, all of my T-shirts are hanging directly to my left in the closet.

My shoes follow the same pattern on the floor as the clothes on hangers.

Next to the T-shirts are my long-sleeved shirts.

Starting the summer clothes are the tank-tops, followed by summer dresses.

Everything in my closet must be in order, or I will never be able to find anything.

All of my sweaters can be found stacked neatly on the shelf just above my long-sleeved sweatshirts.

Jackets, of course, go along with sweatshirts, so they are hanging next to the sweatshirts.

I have winter shoes immediately as I walk in the door, with sandals for summer toward the back of the closet.

After the jackets come the summer clothes.

Method of Organization: _____

Beth's Revision   In Chapter 3, Beth decided that the best way to organize her essay was from one extreme to another (from most to least important). But now she needs to make sure that this is the most effective order for her ideas and that every paragraph is in the right place.

This is the order of the main ideas in her first draft:

Most important:	Taking risks
Next most important:	Watching others
Least important:	Making mistakes

After thinking about this order, Beth realizes that she learns more from making mistakes than from watching others. So she decides to reverse these two topics. She also remembers that she has to revise her thesis statement and her conclusion to reflect this new order.

Revised Thesis Statement:	I know that I learn best from taking risks, making mistakes, and watching others.
Revised Conclusion:	People can learn about life from almost anything they do. They just have to be willing to do so. When I take risks, I think about what I will learn. **When I make mistakes, I figure out why I made each mistake and how to avoid it a second time. I definitely try to learn as much as I can from watching others, which I believe, in the case of my cousin, has already saved my life.** These three ways of learning are all a part of who I am today. I know I'm not finished learning yet. In fact, I don't know if I ever will be.

Also in Chapter 3, Beth organized her three body paragraphs from general to particular. At this point, she checks to see if this is the most effective order for these ideas. She thinks that this order is a good choice for her body paragraphs.

Your Revision   Double-check the method of organization you chose in Chapter 3 for your essay. Do you still think this is the most effective order for what you are trying to say? Then check each body paragraph to see that the details are arranged logically.

Coherence

> ✔ Are transitions used effectively so that paragraphs move smoothly and logically from one to the next?
>
> ✔ Do the sentences move smoothly and logically from one to the next?

A well-written paragraph is coherent—that is, its parts cohere or stick together. It is smooth, not choppy, and readers move logically from one thought to the next, seeing a clear relationship among the ideas. Here are four different strategies that writers use to help their readers follow their train of thought from one paragraph to the next and within paragraphs: *transitions, repeated words, synonyms,* and *pronouns.*

Transitions

Transitional words and phrases provide bridges or links between paragraphs and ideas. They show your readers how your paragraphs or thoughts are related or when you are moving to a new point. Good use of transitions makes your writing smooth rather than choppy.

Choppy: I could have laughed off the cheating experience and the teacher. I decided to slow down and learn from the experience.

Smooth: I could have laughed off the cheating experience and the teacher. **However,** I decided to slow down and learn from the experience.

Transitions have very specific meanings, so you should take care to make logical choices that help you communicate your exact thoughts.

Confusing: I could have laughed off the cheating experience and the teacher. **In addition,** I decided to slow down and learn from the experience.

Here is a list of some common transitional words and phrases that will make your writing more coherent. They are classified by meaning.

Some Common Transitions

Addition:	*again, and, and then, also, besides, finally, first, further, furthermore, in addition, last, likewise, moreover, next, nor, second, third, too*
Comparison:	*in like manner, likewise, similarly*
Contrast:	*after all, and yet, at the same time, but, however, in contrast, nevertheless, on the contrary, on the other hand, otherwise, still, yet*

Emphasis:	*actually, after all, essentially, in any event, indeed, in fact, of course, to tell the truth*
Example:	*for example, for instance, in this case*
Place:	*adjacent to, beyond, here, near, nearby, next to, opposite, there*
Purpose:	*for this purpose, to this end, with this objective*
Result:	*accordingly, as a result, consequently, hence, so, then, therefore, thus*
Summary:	*as I have said, in brief, in other words, in short, in sum, on the whole, that is, to conclude, to sum up, to summarize*
Time:	*after a few days, afterward, at length, (at) other times, immediately, in the meantime, later, meanwhile, now, sometimes, soon, subsequently, still, then*

See pages 410–411 in the Handbook (Part V) for more information on transitions.

Sometimes longer phrases provide transitions between paragraphs or main ideas. See if you can find the long transition that Beth adds to the beginning of one of the paragraphs that she moved (pages 75–76). This phrase helps her readers shift gears to a new topic and makes her essay easier to follow.

◆ *P r a c t i c e   7 A*   Fill in the blanks in the following paragraph with logical transitions.

Today, an unlimited amount of information is available through the Internet. _____, some of this information may not be suitable for younger audiences. Many concerned parents asked for a way to block Internet sites that they did not want their children to view. _____, a system was developed by which a parent uses a password to choose which Internet sites the household computer will and won't access. _____, children who do not know the password cannot access the blocked Internet sites. _____ , parents have control over the technology in their homes and feel their children are safe when they use the Internet.

◆ *Practice   7B*   Rewrite the following paragraph, adding at least three transitions to make it more coherent.

> In high school, I thought I had everything figured out. I never considered what I would do after graduation. I never made any plans. When I graduated, I was completely lost. I went to see a guidance counsellor at the local college. I decided to go to college. I am in college and have made many plans for the future.

Repeated Words

Repeating key words is another way of binding the ideas of an essay together and guiding readers through the details. A key word is usually a main idea in an essay. You should also know that too much repetition becomes boring.

Effective Repetition: Coming here was a **risk** to our relationship. Not coming here would have been a **risk** to my career.

◆ *Practice   8A*   Underline four effective repeated words in the following paragraph.

> All my life, I have gone to my grandmother's house near a lake out in farm country during the summer. This year, I'm taking my best friend from college with me. What I like most about summers at the lake is that the weather is so warm that I can swim all day long. I swim near the bridge and see the small fish darting around the columns. Sometimes I even swim over to the docks where all of the people are loading and unloading their boats. I used to try to swim faster and faster to beat my own record. Now I just go to relax, forget about school, and think about the future.

◆ *Practice   8B*   Underline at least five effective repeated words in the following paragraph.

> For many people, reading the daily newspaper is their main source of information about the world. The front page usually gives the national news or an international political event that affects Canada. Major world events, such as an earthquake, always make front-page news. On the second page of the first section is the op-ed (opposite editorial) page, where editors and readers give their opinions on current news. The editorial and op-ed pages are among the few places in the newspaper where the writing is not objective, along with book and movie reviews and columns such as *Dear Abby*. Most newspapers have separate sections for sports, business, entertainment, classified ads, and comics. All in all, a half hour spent with the newspaper over morning coffee keeps a person up-to-date on world affairs and local people, places, and events.

Synonyms

Synonyms are another way to link your ideas and help you avoid ineffective repetition. Synonyms are words that have identical or similar meanings—*movie/film, feeling/emotion, fantastic/unbelievable*. They add variety and interest to your writing. A thesaurus, or book of synonyms, can help you choose synonyms for specific words. Be aware, however, that all the words in a thesaurus listing are not interchangeable. *Retreat,* for example, is listed as a synonym for *escape,* but the two words suggest two very different ways of leaving a place. In the following example from Beth's essay, Beth uses *incidents* in place of one of her references to *experiences.*

Boring Repetition:	She talked a lot to me about those **experiences.** By watching my cousin go through these horrible **experiences,** I made a conscious decision never to make the bad choices that my cousin made.
Synonym:	She talked a lot to me about those **experiences.** By watching my cousin go through these horrible ~~**experiences**~~ **incidents,** I made a conscious decision never to make the bad choices that my cousin made.

◆ *P r a c t i c e 9 A* Underline four different synonyms for *friend* in the following paragraph.

My younger brother and his friends were always starting clubs when I was young. The clubhouse and the club name were very important. The pals usually decided on a name first. I think my favourite name that they had was "The Three Amigos," even though it was not very original. Every once in a while, an acquaintance of the boys would be allowed to join the club, and the name would have to be changed. Since the boys always thought that they were such sophisticated companions, they had a sign on the door that read "Associates Only—No Girls Allowed." The boys are all grown now, but I still smile every time I think about all of the meetings of "The Three Amigos" that I sat outside and listened to.

◆ *P r a c t i c e 9 B* Replace two uses of the word *actor* with two different synonyms in the following paragraph.

Being an actor seems like a glamorous career choice, but becoming famous is not easy. Many actors start out waiting on tables in restaurants, hoping to be discovered by agents dining there. Other actors go from bit part to bit part in movies and never really earn enough for a living. In the unlikely event that an actor makes it big, he or she suddenly loses all privacy. Still, there are advantages to fame, and most actors adjust quite well to the lifestyle.

Pronouns

Finally, you can link your sentences with *pronouns*. Pronouns not only help you avoid needless repetition, they also keep your writing moving along at a fairly brisk pace. Personal pronouns (*I, you, he, she, it, we, they*) and indefinite pronouns (*any, some, other, one*) are the ones most commonly used as replacements.

Beth can use a pronoun to get rid of her repetition of the words *my cousin*.

> **Repetition:**   When my cousin became heavily involved with gangs and drugs, I watched my cousin live in constant fear.
>
> **Revision:**   When my cousin became heavily involved with gangs and drugs, I watched ~~my cousin~~ **her** live in constant fear.

For more information on pronouns, see pages 381–382 in the Handbook (Part V).

◆ **P r a c t i c e   1 0 A**   Underline ten personal and indefinite pronouns in the following paragraph.

The people down the street have a very large family, which means that there is always something going on in their house. Sometimes when I am at their house, I cannot keep up with everything that is happening. For example, when Sandy answers the phone, she yells that it's for Ryan. Of course, Ryan has to know who it is, and the yelling continues back and forth until Ryan decides to finally pick up the phone. Sometimes when the family members are really busy, they all make dinner individually. Everyone is in the kitchen at one time trying to find something to eat while trying not to step on one another. I'm not sure I could live at the Mitchells' house, but I definitely like visiting.

◆ **P r a c t i c e   1 0 B**   Add five pronouns where appropriate in the following paragraph.

A few days ago, Brian, Carol, Katie, and I went out to dinner. Brian, Carol, Katie, and I went to a new Italian restaurant on Queen Street. As soon as Brian, Carol, Katie, and I walked in the door, Brian, Carol, Katie, and I could smell the garlic, basil, and oregano in the rich tomato sauces of pizza, lasagna, and, of course, spaghetti and meatballs. Brian, Carol, Katie, and I couldn't stand it, so

Brian, Carol, Katie, and I ordered immediately. The food tasted even better than it smelled. Before the dinner was over, Brian, Carol, Katie, and I set a date to return.

Beth's Revision   When Beth checks her essay for coherence, she thinks her writing could be smoother if she used some of these techniques. So she makes the following revisions that help bind her sentences together and show the specific relationships between her ideas.

Here is Beth's essay with transitions, repeated words, synonyms, and pronouns highlighted.

The Learning Curve

Everyone learns in different ways. Some people learn by watching, while others learn by doing. Some learn by reading, and others learn by listening. Some learn best when they work independently, but others do better in groups. **In fact,** t~~T~~he way people learn is a major part of who they are. **So** knowing how we learn can help us understand ourselves better. I know that I learn best from taking risks, making mistakes, and watching others.

First, I have discovered that I learn a lot by taking risks. If I didn't take risks, I think I'd never mature. Coming to this school was a risk. I have a boyfriend back home, we want to get married some day. But I knew that this school's nursing program was better than the one in my home town~~,~~ **so** I left my boyfriend to come here. Coming here was a risk to our relationship. **However,** n~~N~~ot coming here would have been a risk to my career. Taking this risk taught me to be responsible and trust my boyfriend back home. I know that I will take many risks like this throughout my life and that not all of them will work out. But if I am ever going to reach my potential, I have to be willing to take risks.

Also, I believe that I learn from making mistakes. **For example, w**~~W~~hen I was in high school, I didn't study for a major science test. I knew the test was important, but I decided to go to a party with my friends. I really needed the grade, so I cheated. I cut my notes into small strips of paper that I put in my desk, but the teacher caught me. Thank goodness ~~the teacher~~ **he** was a nice person. ~~The teacher~~ **He** took the time to talk to me about the mistake I was making, not only **cheating** for a grade, but **cheating** myself out of the knowledge that I could have. This mistake made me re-evaluate my education. ~~This mistake~~ It led me into nursing by making me ~~re-evaluate~~ realize what subjects I really enjoyed. I could have laughed off the cheating experience and the teacher. However, I decided to slow down and learn from the experience.

In addition to learning from my own actions, I also benefit from watching other people. **For instance,** ~~w~~When my cousin became heavily involved with gangs and drugs, I watched her live in constant fear. She was worried that she would end up in jail, overdose on drugs, or become a "plaything" for other gang members. She worked hard to overcome that lifestyle. She talked a lot to me about those experiences. By watching my cousin go through these horrible incidents, I made a conscious decision never to make the bad choices that ~~my cousin~~ she made. I had plenty of opportunities to do so. Turning away from that life was difficult, but I did it. By watching and understanding my cousin's life. I learned to live mine better.

Essentially, p~~P~~eople can learn about life from almost anything they do. They just have to be willing to do so. **Now, w**~~W~~hen I take risks, I think about what I will learn. When I make mistakes, I figure out why I made each mistake and how to avoid it a second time. **Also,** I definitely try to learn as much as I can from watching others, which I believe, in the case of my cousin, has already saved my life. These three ways of learning are all part of who I am today. I know I'm not finished learning yet. In fact, I don't know if I ever will be.

Transitions   In addition to *however*, Beth added 12 more transitions to her essay. What are they?

_____

_____

Repeated Words   When Beth checked her essay for repeated key words, she saw that she referred directly to *cheating* twice in the same sentence. She decided this was an effective repetition and chose to keep it in her essay.

Effective Repetition: He took the time to talk to me about the mistake I was making, not only **cheating** for a grade, but **cheating** myself out of the knowledge that I could have.

Synonyms   When Beth looked at her essay again, she found another opportunity to use a synonym to link her ideas more clearly. Besides the addition of *incidents* for *experiences*, what other synonym does Beth use in her revision?

_____ for _____

Pronouns   Finally, in addition to substituting *her* for *my cousin*, Beth found four more places to use pronouns to bind key parts of her essay together. Where are these places in her essay?

_____ for _____

_____ for _____

_____ for _____

_____ for _____

Your Revision   Now it's time to make your essay more coherent.

Transitions   Check the transitions in your essay. Do you use enough transitions so that your essay moves smoothly and logically from one paragraph to the next and from one sentence to the next? Do you use your transitions logically?

Repeated Words   Look at your essay to see when you might want to repeat a key word. Then revise your essay accordingly.

Synonyms   Now look for places in your essay where you might add synonyms to link your sentences. Use a thesaurus (in book or electronic form) if you need help.

Pronouns   Now check your essay for opportunities to use pronouns. Add appropriate pronouns.

Beth's Revised Essay   After revising her thesis statement, her development of ideas, and the unity, organization, and coherence of her writing, Beth produced the following revised essay. All of her revisions are highlighted.

~~**The Way We Learn**~~

The Learning Curve

  Everyone learns in different ways. Some people learn   1
by watching, **while others learn by doing.** Some **learn** by
reading, ~~**while**~~ and others learn by listening ~~**and others
by themselves.**~~ Some learn best when they work
independently, ~~**while**~~ but others do better in groups. In

fact, t~~T~~he way people learn is a **major** part of who they are. Knowing how we learn can help us understand ourselves better. I know that I learn ~~from many things in life~~ best from taking risks, making mistakes, and watching others.

2   **First,** I have discovered that I learn a lot by taking risks. **If I didn't take risks, I think I'd never mature.** Coming to this school was a risk. I have a boyfriend back home, we want to get married some day. ~~We are hoping for a spring wedding with all of our friends and family.~~ But I knew that this school's nursing program was better than the one in my home town~~.~~ so I left my boyfriend to come here. Coming here was a risk to our relationship. **However, n~~N~~ot coming here would have been a risk to my career. Taking this risk taught me to be responsible and trust my boyfriend back home. I know that I will take many risks like this throughout my life and that not all of them will work out.** But if I am ever going to ~~make it~~ **reach my potential,** I have to be willing to take risks.

3   **Also,** I believe that I learn from making mistakes. **For example, w~~W~~**hen I was in high school, I didn't study for a major science test. **I knew the test was important, but I decided to go to a party with my friends. I really needed the grade, S~~s~~**o I cheated. ~~My sister cheated once. I was so scared to do it.~~ I cut my notes into small strips of paper that I put in my desk, but ~~T~~the teacher caught me. **Thank goodness** ~~the teacher~~ he was a nice person. ~~The teacher~~ **He** took the time to talk to me about the mistake I was making, **not only cheating for a grade, but cheating myself out of the knowledge that I could have.** This mistake made me re-evaluate my education. ~~This mistake~~ **It** led me into nursing by making me ~~re-evaluate~~ **realize what subjects I really enjoyed.** I could have laughed off the cheating experience **and the teacher. However,** I decided to slow down and learn from the experience.

4   **In addition to learning from my own actions,** I also benefit from watching other people. **For instance, w~~W~~**hen my cousin became heavily involved with gangs and drugs, I watched ~~my cousin~~ **her** live in constant fear. ~~My cousin~~ **She** was worried that she would end up in jail, overdose on drugs, or become a "plaything" for other gang members. **She worked hard to overcome that lifestyle. She talked a lot to me about those experiences.**

By watching my cousin **go through these horrible** ~~experiences~~ **incidents,** I made a conscious decision ~~to be nothing like my cousin~~ **never to make the bad choices** that ~~my cousin~~ **she** made. **I had plenty of opportunities to do so. Turning away from this life was difficult, but I did it.** By watching and understanding my cousin's life. I learned to live mine better.

     Essentially, p~~P~~eople can learn about life from almost   5 anything they do. They just have to be willing to do so. **Now, w**~~W~~hen I take risks, I think about what I will learn. **When I make mistakes, I figure out why I made each mistake and how to avoid it a second time. Also, I definitely try to learn as much as I can from watching others, which I believe, in the case of my cousin, has already saved my life. These three ways of learning are all part of who I am today. I know I'm not finished learning yet. In fact, I don't know if I ever will be.**

Your Revised Essay   Now that you have applied all the revision strategies to your own writing, rewrite your revised essay.

8

EDITING

After you have revised your writing, you are ready to edit it. Editing involves finding and correcting errors in grammar, punctuation, mechanics, and spelling. Correct writing is as important to communicating as well-chosen words. Nothing distracts readers from what you are saying more than editing errors.

As the checklist here shows, we have divided the editing strategies into three categories: sentences, punctuation and mechanics, and word choice and spelling. This checklist doesn't cover all the grammar and usage problems you may find in your writing; rather, it focuses on the main errors college students make.

EDITING CHECKLIST

SENTENCES
✔ Does each sentence have a main subject and verb?
✔ Do all subjects and verbs agree?
✔ Do all pronouns agree with their nouns?
✔ Are modifiers as close as possible to the words they modify?

PUNCTUATION AND MECHANICS
✔ Are sentences punctuated correctly?
✔ Are words capitalized properly?

WORD CHOICE AND SPELLING
✔ Are words used correctly?
✔ Are words spelled correctly?

YOUR EQ (EDITING QUOTIENT)

A good way to approach editing is by finding your EQ (Editing Quotient). Knowing your EQ will help you look for specific errors in your writing and make your editing more efficient.

◆ *P r a c t i c e   1* **EQ Test** In each of the following paragraphs, underline the errors you find, and label them a, b, c, and so on. Then list them on the lines below the paragraph. The number of lines corresponds to the number of errors in each paragraph.

The possible errors are listed here:

apostrophe	end punctuation	pronoun agreement
capitalization	fragment	spelling
comma	fused sentence	subject–verb agreement
comma splice	modifier error	verb form
confused word	pronoun	

1. Many people seem to have a telephone permanently attached to one ear people have several phone lines going into their homes. And cell phones hanging off of their belts. People are talking on their cell phones in restaurants, in cars, and even in public washrooms. When they go home, they go online to check e-mail. While the second line is ringing off the hook. Why would someone want to be available every second of the day? This rushed society will eventually have to slow down, people can't live at this pace for long.

(a.) _____

(b.) _____

(c.) _____

(d.) _____

2. Recently, a major computer software company was accused of being a monopoly. That is, it seemed to be trying to control the whole software industry. The company, reality software, sells many different types of software at reasonable prices. Which results in the company selling more products than its competitors. Reality Software also signed contracts with Computer Manufacturers that allow the manufacturers to install Reality programs on computers before they are sold. The courts, which guard against monopolies, say this is unfair to consumers, buyers should be able to choose their software. It is also unfair to other software companies. Because they are not given a fair chance to sell their products.

(a.) _____

(b.) _____

(c.) _____

(d.) _____

(e.) _____

3. Public speaking is a valuable tool no matter what career path a person take. At some point in every career, if a person is going to advance, they will have to speak to a group. In fact, the higher up the career ladder a person climb, the more public speaking will be required. It is good preparation, therefore, to take a public speaking course in college, a public speaking course not only teaches the skills involved in making a presentation but also builds a person's confidence.

(a.) _____

(b.) _____

(c.) _____

(d.) _____

4. If I had my way, I would require every college student to take a course in geography. It is embarassing how little the average Canadian knows about his own country, to say nothing of other countries. For instance, do you know the capital of new brunswick? Could you name all the Great Lakes? On which continent is greece? If you can answer these questions you are one of very few people. People think geography is boring but it isn't. Its fascinating to learn about the world we live in.

(a.) _____

(b.) _____

(c.) _____

(d.) _____

(e.) _____

(f.) _____

(g.) _____

5. I believe that fast-food restaurants should change there names to "fast food sometimes, but at least faster than a sit-down restaurant." When I go through the drive-up window at a fast-food restaraunt, it is because I am in a hurry and want to get something to eat quickly, however, sometimes it would be quicker for me to go home and cook a three-course meal. I do not understand what could take so long. I pull up to the intercom, order my food, procede to the window, and wait. If fast food always lived up to its name I would be able to get food fast.

(a.) _____

(b.) _____

    ⓒ _____

    ⓓ _____

    ⓔ _____

6. Doing the family laundry used to be a chore for me but now I am a pro. First, I sort the clothes according to colours or whites. Before I learned this basic rule, my poor brother had to wear pink underwear from time to time. Next, I put the clothes in the washing machine, and add detergent. If I'm doing whites I also add bleach. I close the lid, turn the dial to hot wash and cold rinse, and push the "start" button. I allow the washing machine to do it's work while I read a magazine. When it's time to put the clothes in the dryer, I pay attention to the drying instructions on the tags. Once I neglected this step, and my favourite pants shrinked. When the dryer has done its work, I remove the clothes immediately so they do not become rinkled.

    ⓐ _____

    ⓑ _____

    ⓒ _____

    ⓓ _____

    ⓔ _____

    ⓕ _____

7. It's fun to watch a person with their animals. For instance, the lady down the street takes her dog for a walk every morning. The dog is a tiny rat terrier, it is really cute. The lady puts a little leash on the dog. To keep him from running away. Even though the dogs legs are short, he can run real fast. The dog seems so happy during his walks. He jumps and yips. The lady and her dog are a good pair they enjoy walking with each other and keeping each other company.

    ⓐ _____

    ⓑ _____

    ⓒ _____

    ⓓ _____

    ⓔ _____

    ⓕ _____

◆ *P r a c t i c e   2*   EQ Answers Score your answers in Practice 1 using the following answer key.

1. [a]<u>Many people seem to have a telephone permanently attached to their ear people have several phone lines going into their homes.</u> [b]<u>And cell phones hanging off of their belts.</u> People are talking on their cell phones in restaurants, in cars, and even in public bathrooms. When they go home, they go online to check e-mail. [c]<u>While the second line is ringing off the hook.</u> Why would someone want to be available every second of the day? [d]<u>This rushed society will eventually have to slow down, people can't live at this pace for long.</u>

   (a.) *fused sentence or end punctuation*

   (b.) *fragment*

   (c.) *fragment*

   (d.) *comma splice or end punctuation*

2. Recently, a major computer software company was accused of being a monopoly. That is, it seemed to be trying to control the whole software industry. The company, [a]<u>reality software</u>, sells many different types of software at reasonable prices. [b]<u>Which results in the company selling more products than its competitors.</u> Reality Software also signed contracts with [c]<u>Computer Manufacturers</u> that allow the manufacturers to install Reality programs on computers before they are sold. [d]<u>The courts, which guard against monopolies, say this is unfair to consumers, buyers should be able to choose their software.</u> It is also unfair to other software companies. [e]<u>Because they are not given a fair chance to sell their products.</u>

   (a.) *capitalization*

   (b.) *fragment*

   (c.) *capitalization*

   (d.) *comma splice or end punctuation*

   (e.) *fragment*

3. Public speaking is a valuable tool no matter what career path a [a]<u>person take.</u> At some point in every career, if a person is going to advance, [b]<u>they</u> will have to speak to a group. In fact, the higher up the career ladder a [c]<u>person climb</u>, the more public speaking will be required. [d]<u>It is good preparation, therefore, to take a public speaking course in college, a public speaking course not only teaches the skills involved in making a presentation but also builds a person's confidence.</u>

   (a.) *subject–verb agreement*

   (b.) *pronoun agreement*

(c.) subject–verb agreement _____

(d.) comma splice or end punctuation _____

4. If I had my way, I would require every college student to take a course in geography. It is ⓐembarassing how little the average Canadian knows aboutⓑhis own country, to say nothing of other countries. For instance, do you know the capital ofⓒnew brunswick? Can you name all the Great Lakes? On which continent is ⓓgreece? If you can answer these questionsⓔyou are one of very few people. People think geography is boringⓕbut it isn't. ⓖIts fascinating to learn about the world we live in.

(a.) spelling _____

(b.) pronoun _____

(c.) capitalization _____

(d.) capitalization _____

(e.) comma _____

(f.) comma _____

(g.) confused word or apostrophe _____

5. I believe that fast-food restaurants should changeⓐthere names to "fast food sometimes, but at least faster than a sit-down restaurant."ⓑWhen I go through the drive-up window at a fast-foodⓒrestaraunt, it is because I am in a hurry and want to get something to eat quickly, however, sometimes it would be quicker for me to go home and cook a three-course meal. I do not understand what could take so long. I pull up to the intercom, order my food, ⓓprocede to the window, and wait. If fast food always lived up to its nameⓔI would be able to get food fast.

(a.) confused word _____

(b.) comma splice or end punctuation _____

(c.) spelling _____

(d.) spelling _____

(e.) comma _____

6. Doing the family laundry used to be a chore for meⓐbut now I am a pro. First, I sort the clothes according to colours or whites. Before I learned this basic rule, my poor brother had to wear pink underwear from time to time. Next, I put the clothes in the washing machine,

(b)and add detergent. If I'm doing whites (c)I also add bleach. I close the lid, turn the dial to hot wash and cold rinse, and push the "start" button. I allow the washing machine to do (d)it's work while I read a magazine. When it's time to put the clothes in the dryer, I pay attention to the drying instructions on the tags. Once I neglected this step, and my favourite pants (e)shrinked. When the dryer has done its work, I remove the clothes immediately so they do not be-come(f)rinkled.

(a.)   *comma* _____

(b.)   *comma* _____

(c.)   *comma* _____

(d.)   *confused word or apostrophe* _____

(e.)   *verb form* _____

(f.)   *spelling* _____

7. It's fun to watch a person with (a)their animals. For instance, the lady down the street takes her dog for a walk every morning. (b)The dog is a tiny rat terrier, it is really cute. The lady puts a little leash on the dog. (c)To keep him from running away. Even though the (d)dogs legs are short, he can run (e)real fast. The dog seems so happy during his walks. He jumps and yips. (f)The lady and her dog are a good pair they enjoy walking with each other and keeping each other company.

(a.)   *pronoun agreement* _____

(b.)   *comma splice or end punctuation* _____

(c.)   *fragment* _____

(d.)   *apostrophe* _____

(e.)   *modifier error* _____

(f.)   *fused sentence or end punctuation* _____

HOW TO EDIT

Editing is a two-part job: First, you must find the errors. Then you must know how to correct them.

Finding Your Errors

A major part of editing is proofreading. Proofreading is reading to catch grammar, punctuation, mechanics, and spelling errors. If you do not proofread carefully, you will not catch your errors and make the final changes that will improve your writing.

There are some specific techniques for finding errors. One good method is to read your essay backward, sentence by sentence, starting with the last sentence. Taking sentences out of context lets you concentrate on individual sentences and not get caught up in reading for meaning.

Many students like to keep error logs like the one for grammar, punctuation, and mechanics in Appendix 3 and the one for spelling in Appendix 4. By the second or third paper you write, the logs will show you the types of errors you make most often. Then you can proofread your paper for one type of error at a time. For example, if you often write run-on sentences, you should read your paper once just to catch run-ons. Then read it again to find a second type of error, and so on. The error logs can help you reduce the number of errors in your writing. By recording the correction for each error you find, you will eventually learn the corrections.

You can also use the grammar-check or spell-check features on your computer. The grammar check will point out possible grammar errors and suggest ways to reword sentences, but it is not foolproof. You need to decide if you want to accept or reject the grammar suggestions the computer makes. The spell-check is also not completely reliable because it misses errors, so you should use it cautiously.

Asking a tutor or a friend to read your writing is also a good idea. A fresh pair of eyes may see errors you have missed. When others read your writing, they might want to use the editing symbols on the inside back cover to highlight your errors for you. You can then use the page references on the chart to guide you to the part of this textbook that explains how to correct those errors.

Correcting Your Errors

Whenever you find errors, you need to correct them. To guide you through this phase of the writing process, Part V of this text provides a complete handbook of grammar and usage. You may also want to refer to the list on the inside back cover if your instructor uses editing symbols when reading your essays.

As you proofread, record your errors in the Error Log in Appendix 3 and the Spelling Log in Appendix 4. If you do this regularly as you write, these logs will eventually help you control the most common errors in your writing.

Finally, use the Editing Checklist at the beginning of this chapter. Apply each question in the checklist to your essay. If you are not sure whether you have made an error or not, look up the problem in Part V. Work with your writing until you can answer yes to every question on the checklist.

◆ *P r a c t i c e   3*   **Using the Handbook**   Using the Handbook in Part V, list the page references for the 15 different types of errors you worked with in Practice 1. This will help you learn to use the Handbook as a reference guide.

apostrophe   page ＿＿＿＿＿

capitalization   page ＿＿＿＿＿

comma   page ＿＿＿＿＿

comma splice   page ＿＿＿＿＿

confused word   page ＿＿＿＿＿

end punctuation   page ＿＿＿＿＿

fragment   page ＿＿＿＿＿

fused sentence   page ＿＿＿＿＿

modifier error   page ＿＿＿＿＿

pronoun   page ＿＿＿＿＿

pronoun agreement   page ＿＿＿＿＿

spelling   page ＿＿＿＿＿

subject–verb agreement   page ＿＿＿＿＿

verb form   page ＿＿＿＿＿

◆ *P r a c t i c e   4*   **Using the Error Log and Spelling Log**   Turn to Appendixes 3 and 4, and start an Error Log and a Spelling Log of your own with the errors you didn't identify in Practice 1. For each error, write out the mistake and the rule from the Handbook. Then make the correction. See Appendix 3 for an example.

◆ *P r a c t i c e   5*   **Using the Editing Checklist**   Using the Editing Checklist at the beginning of this chapter, edit two of the paragraphs from Practice 1. Rewrite the entire paragraphs, and correct all errors.

Beth's Editing   When Beth proofreads her paper for grammar, punctuation, mechanics, and spelling, she finds two errors that she looks up in Part V and corrects. The first error is a comma splice:

> **Comma Splice:**   I have a boyfriend back home, we want to get married some day.

Beth realizes that this sentence has too many subjects and verbs without any linking words or end punctuation between them. She looks up "comma splice" on page 406 of Part V and corrects the error by putting a coordinating conjunction (*and*) between the two clauses.

Correction: I have a boyfriend back home, **and** we want to get married some day.

Beth also finds a sentence that doesn't sound complete—it's not a sentence but a fragment:

Fragment: By watching and understanding my cousin's life.

When she looks up the problem in Part V (page 394), she learns that a fragment is easily corrected by connecting it to another sentence.

Correction: By watching and understanding my cousin's life., I learned to live mine better.

Beth's Edited Draft   Both of these errors are corrected here in Beth's edited draft.

The Learning Curve

Everyone learns in different ways. Some people learn by watching, while others learn by doing. Some learn by reading, and others learn by listening. Some learn best when they work independently, but others do better in groups. In fact, the way people learn is a major part of who they are. Knowing how we learn can help us understand ourselves better. I know that I learn best from taking risks, making mistakes, and watching others.

First, I have discovered that I learn a lot by taking risks. If I didn't take risks, I think I'd never mature. Coming to this school was a risk. **I have a boyfriend back home, and we want to get married some day.** But I knew that this school's nursing program was better than the one in my home town, so I left my boyfriend to come here. Coming here was a risk to our relationship. However, not coming here would have been a risk to my career. Taking this risk taught me to be responsible and trust my boyfriend back home. I know that I will take many risks like this throughout my life and that not all of them will work out. But if I am ever going to reach my potential, I have to be willing to take risks.

Also, I believe that I learn from making mistakes. For example, when I was in high school, I didn't study for a major science test. I knew the test was important, but I decided to go to a party with my friends. I really needed the grade, so I cheated. I cut my notes into small

1

2

3

strips of paper that I put in my desk, but the teacher caught me. Thank goodness he was a nice person. He took the time to talk to me about the mistake I was making, not only cheating for a grade, but cheating myself out of the knowledge that I could have. This mistake made me re-evaluate my education. It led me into nursing by making me realize what subjects I really enjoyed. I could have laughed off the cheating experience and the teacher. However, I decided to slow down and learn from the experience.

4   In addition to learning from my own actions, I also benefit from watching other people. For instance, when my cousin became heavily involved with gangs and drugs, I watched her live in constant fear. She was worried that she would end up in jail, overdose on drugs, or become a "plaything" for other gang members. She worked hard to overcome that lifestyle. She talked a lot to me about those experiences. By watching my cousin go through these horrible incidents, I made a conscious decision never to make the bad choices that she made. I had plenty of opportunities to do so. Turning away from that life was difficult, but I did it. **By watching and understanding my cousin's life, I learned to live mine better.**

5   Essentially, people can learn about life from almost anything they do. They just have to be willing to do so. Now, when I take risks, I think about what I will learn. When I make mistakes, I figure out why I made each mistake and how to avoid it a second time. Also, I definitely try to learn as much as I can from watching others, which I believe, in the case of my cousin, has already saved my life. These three ways of learning are all a part of what I am today. I know I'm not finished learning yet. In fact, I don't know if I ever will be.

Your Editing   Proofread your paragraph carefully to find errors, using at least two of the methods described in this chapter. Record your grammar, punctuation, and mechanics errors in the Error Log (Appendix 3) and your spelling errors in the Spelling Log (Appendix 4).

Your Edited Draft   Now write out a corrected draft of your essay.

REVIEW OF THE WRITING PROCESS

Clues for Review

♦ **The writing process** is a series of tasks that involve prewriting, writing, revising, and editing. At any time, one activity may loop in and out of another.

♦ **Prewriting** consists of thinking about and planning your essay.
Thinking: Reading, freewriting, brainstorming, clustering, questioning, discussing
Planning: Deciding on a subject, purpose, and audience

♦ **Writing** includes writing a thesis statement, developing your ideas, organizing your essay, and writing a first draft.
Writing a thesis statement: Stating a limited subject and an opinion about that subject
Developing: Explaining your ideas and adding specific details, examples, facts, and reasons
Organizing: Arranging ideas from general to particular, particular to general, chronologically, spatially, or from one extreme to another
Drafting: Writing a first draft, then revising to write a second draft, a third draft, and so on, until you have written your final draft

♦ **Revising** means "seeing again" and improving all aspects of an essay's organization and development.
Thesis statement
Basic elements
Development
Unity
Organization
Coherence

♦ **Editing** involves proofreading and correcting your grammar, punctuation, mechanics, and spelling errors.

◆ *Review Practice 1*   Write a thesis statement for three of the following topics. Then develop one thesis statement into a first draft of an essay.

1. My best adventure
2. In the middle of the night
3. My future career
4. The best car
5. Parents should never

◆ *Review Practice 2*   Revise the essay you wrote for Review Practice 1, using the checklist on pages 52–53.

◆ *Review Practice 3*   Edit the essay you revised for Review Practice 2, using the checklist on page 80.

II

WRITING EFFECTIVE ESSAYS

Writing is not hard. Just get a paper and pencil,
sit down and write it as it occurs to you. The writing
is easy—it's the occurring that's hard.

—STEPHEN LEACOCK

In Part I of *Mosaics,* you learned about the different stages of the writing process—prewriting, writing, revising, and editing—and the form of an essay. You know that essays typically have an introduction with a thesis statement, several body paragraphs, and a conclusion. Part II of *Mosaics* focuses on ways to develop and organize an essay's body paragraphs. You will learn strategies for thinking on paper that will help you discover your best thoughts on a particular topic. Then you will find out your options for organizing those ideas.

The nine basic writing strategies—also called rhetorical modes—are introduced in this part. Each chapter begins with an explanation of a strategy and then gives specific guidelines for using that strategy with examples from a model essay. Then the chapter helps you apply the chapter guidelines to two writing samples: (1) a real student essay and (2) your own essay. Students can usually see patterns in other students' writing more easily than they can in their own. As a result, you are asked to look at another student's writing first. In both cases, however, with the help of detailed instruction on a writing strategy, on revising, and on editing, you can see systematically how to improve your writing.

DESCRIBING

CHAPTER 9

When you show, you get out of the readers' way and
let them come right at the experience itself.

—DONALD MURRAY

Description is an essential part of your life every day. Your friends might
want to know what kind of car you just bought; your parents may ask what
your new friend is like; your supervisor might need a description of the
project you just finished. You constantly need to describe people, places,
objects, and activities for different audiences if you want to communicate
clearly and effectively.

In addition, you frequently use description when writing. Actually, description is a major part of our writing in our personal lives, at school, and
at work:

You describe your new leather jacket in an e-mail message to a
friend.

You describe the damage to your car in an insurance report.

A student describes a cell and its parts on a biology exam.

A nurse describes the appearance of a wound in a patient report.

A landscape contractor describes a design for a rock garden.

Description creates a picture in words to help a reader visualize something a writer has seen, heard, or done. It helps the reader understand or share
a sensory experience through "showing" rather than "telling." Description is
one of our primary forms of self-expression.

At times, description is used as an end in itself. That is, you write a description for the sole purpose of telling what something looks, sounds, feels,
tastes, or smells like. For instance, you might use pure description to tell a
friend about your new apartment. More often, though, description is used to
help accomplish another purpose—to explain a problem, to analyze the
causes and effects of an event, or to persuade your readers to change their
thinking or take some specific action.

WRITING A DESCRIPTION ESSAY

In his fictionalized account of the life of Newfoundland premier Joey Smallwood, Wayne Johnston describes the real-life seal hunt tragedy of March, 1914. He imagines Smallwood on the *S.S. Newfoundland* as the men discover the fourth watch, which has been missing on the ice for three days. First-hand accounts of natural disasters are common these days. In what ways has nature played a role in your life? What is this role? Is it a positive or a negative one?

WAYNE JOHNSTON

from *The Colony of Unrequited Dreams*

On the third day, when we looked through the porthole at mid-morning, we saw something other than the single shade of white we had become accustomed to—the many subtle shades of white that comprised the ice-field.

It was several hours more before the master watch came down and told me to go to my sleeping quarters.

I did as he said. I heard the boiler being fired up and felt the ship begin to move through the ice pack, which had loosened because the wind had changed.

About three o'clock in the afternoon, they found what they were looking for. Far off on the ice, I saw a couple of dozen men trudging about in a circle. The shout no sooner went up that the men of the *Newfoundland* were found than the ship's whistle shrieked in celebration. I looked out through the porthole, but that side of the ship was at too oblique an angle to the rescue site. As the ship ploughed on through the ice, however, the stem slowly drifted starboard and I was able to see round the curvature of the hull. The men were not a hundred feet away, still tramping in a circle as if even the ship's whistle had not roused them, each man with his hand on the shoulder of the man in front. They were so coated in snow I could not tell what they were wearing or make out their faces, which were rimed with frost. Most of them were limping badly; outside the circle was a man walking an even slower circle of his own and at the same time holding beneath the armpits another man whose feet made a feeble step now and then but otherwise dragged behind him on the ice.

As we drew closer to them, some of them at last noticed the ship and stopped walking. Some dropped to their knees or toppled over onto their backs, others stared as if they doubted that what they saw was real. The crew poured over the side and led the sealers or carried them on stretchers to the ship.

We moved on. I had counted twenty-three men. That left eighty unaccounted for. I stayed at the porthole. The ship came hard about, and for half an hour we crashed on through the ice, then stopped again.

My heart rose when I saw what looked to be the balance of the crew standing on a mile-wide ice pan in the near distance. From on deck, there were shouts of "Hurray" and footsteps thumped on the ceiling overhead as once again the ship's whistle sounded.

Gradually we drew up close to the ice pan. Mooring lines with grapnels on the end were cast onto the ice, and the pan was slowly pulled towards the ship until it thumped against it.

For several minutes after the ship stopped, no one disembarked. I saw what I had not been able to through my binoculars: that these were not survivors but a strange statuary of the dead. I was not repulsed by what I saw. I could not take my eyes away.

Two men knelt side by side, one man with his arm around the other, whose head was resting on his shoulder in a pose of tenderness between two men that I had never seen in life.

Three men stood huddled in a circle, arms about each other's shoulders, heads together like schoolboys conferring on a football field.

A man stood hugging himself, his hands on his arms, shoulders hunched, in the manner of someone who has momentarily stepped out of his house into the cold in shirtsleeves to bid a guest goodbye.

One man knelt, sitting back on his heels, while another stood behind him, his hands on his shoulders, as if they were posing for a photograph.

Two sealers stood in a fierce embrace, the taller man with both arms wrapped round the other, holding him against his chest, while the arms of the shorter man hung rigid at his sides.

Four men lay on their stomachs side by side, all facing the same way as if they had lain down for some purpose or agreed together that they would.

Only a few men knelt or lay alone, perhaps those who had lasted longer than the others.

One man sat by himself, his elbows resting on his drawn-up knees, his bare hands frozen to his face.

The storm had started out as freezing rain. A man who must have been among the first to fall lay encased within a mould of silver thaw.

I later learned that some who, in their delirium, thought they saw a light ran off in pursuit of it and were never found.

Joined in some manner of embrace were men who before this journey to the ice had never met, men who had outlasted those they knew best and for warmth or fellowship in death embraced some stranger.

They were all there, the boys too young and the men too old, who to get a berth had lied about their ages or agreed to half a share; boys younger than me and men older than my father.

Perhaps, too tired to walk but still standing, they had been buried in snow that had blown away when the storm let up, by which time they were rooted in the ice that lay like pedestals about their feet.

Some men lay in the lee of a low shelter they had managed to erect, a wall of ice and snow that was barely three feet high.

I recognized a few of them, but only because of some distinctive article of clothing, like the orange watch cap of the man who every morning made the tea. He lay on his side, his knees drawn up almost to his chest, his head resting on his hands, which were clasped in a prayer-like pillow, palm to palm.

They had been transformed by their passion on the ice. Each had assumed in death some posture emblematic of his life. Or else they were refined to men that no one knew, as if in each face and posture was inscrutably depicted the essence of the person they had been.

Everywhere lay evidence of futile acts of courage and self-sacrifice. A man stripped down to his undershirt and coveralls lay prone beside a boy bulked out in two sets of clothes.

In various places the snow was scorched where small fires had been lit. From each a smudge of soot trailed out, a stain left from the smoke that had been flattened by the wind.

I did not want to see them moved or see the scene disturbed. I closed the porthole and sat down on my bunk.

I heard above the wind and the droning of the ropes the sound of ice being hacked and chopped. I heard the coal crank of the hatch at the far end of the ship lurch into motion. The chopping and shouting and winching of the crank went on for hours. When it stopped, I considered opening the porthole but could not bring myself to do it.

I looked around the sleeping quarters at all the empty bunks. Not all the men had been lost. Not every bunk represented a man who would not be going home. It was impossible to tell which ones did. Three-quarters of them did, but I didn't know which ones. Except for the bunk of the man who made the tea.

Something deep within me, which I hadn't known was there, gave way. My body grieved but not my mind. I felt as though someone who was sitting right beside me was crying, and though I wanted to console him, I could not.

I felt the ship reach open water. The grinding of the ice against the hull ceased suddenly, the keel rocked from side to side until it balanced and we moved smoothly on. I got up and pounded on the door to be let out. As if, in all the commotion, I had been forgotten, I heard the sound of footsteps running. The hatch slid open and I saw the sky.

PREPARING TO WRITE YOUR OWN DESCRIPTION

What are some memorable experiences you have had with nature (for example, a snowstorm, a sunny day, a drought, a tornado, a thunderstorm)? Why do you remember these experiences? Do any of them form a single impression when you think about them? Use one or more of the prewriting techniques that you learned in Chapter 2 to generate your thoughts about these memories.

How to Write a Description Essay

Describing is a very natural process that is based on good observing. But some people describe things more vividly than others. When they describe an experience, you feel as though you were there too. We can all improve our skill at describing by following a few simple guidelines:

1. *Decide on a dominant impression—the feeling or mood you want to communicate.* How do you want your readers to feel after reading your description? Good about the characters in the scene? Angry at the situation? Satisfied with the outcome? Choosing a dominant impression gives your description focus and unity. You can't possibly write down everything you observe about a person, place, incident, or object. The result would be a long, confusing—and probably boring—list. But if you first decide on a dominant impression for your description, you can then choose the details that will best convey that impression.

    The dominant impression Johnston conveys is his feeling of awe, both at the sight of the men frozen in the ice and the forces of nature that did this to them, and at the nobility depicted in the various human tableaux. This dominant impression gives his writing focus and helps him choose the details that will best communicate this feeling.

2. *Decide how much of your description should be objective (factual) and how much should be subjective (personal reactions).* An objective description is like a dictionary definition—accurate and without emotion. Scientific and technical writing are objective. If, for example, you are describing a piece of equipment used in a chemistry experiment or the packaging needed to ship a computer, you would be objective. Subjective description, in contrast, tries to produce a specific emotional response in the reader. It focuses on feelings rather than facts and tries to activate as many senses as possible. An advertisement describing a Caribbean cruise might be very subjective, as might a restaurant or movie review. Most descriptive writing has a combination of objective and subjective elements. The degree to which you emphasize one over the other depends on your purpose and your audience.

    Johnston's essay demonstrates a good balance of objective and subjective writing. He presents the facts of what he sees through the porthole, vividly describing the image of the group of men walking in the unending circle, or the orange watch cap of the man who made the tea. Then he becomes more subjective, noting that some men seemed to be praying or huddled together in fellowship. At times he also becomes analytical, commenting that the men were frozen in a position that depicted their essence. This combination of objective and subjective elements makes the writing realistic and powerful at the same time. Note also how Johnston uses similes to create images familiar to the reader: "heads together like schoolboys conferring on a football field."

3. ***Draw on your five senses to write a good description.*** Although observing is at the heart of good description, limiting yourself to what you see is a mistake. Good description relies on all five senses: seeing, hearing, touching, smelling, and tasting. If you use all your senses to relay your description, your readers will be able to see, hear, touch, smell, and taste what you are describing as if they were there with you, participating in the same experience.

   Look again at Johnston's description. He draws primarily on sight throughout the essay, moving from a distant image seen through binoculars to a close-up view through the porthole of his cabin. When sight becomes too overpowering, the narrator closes the porthole and relies on sound—the droning of the ropes, the sound of the ice being hacked. As he *feels* the ship move, he *hears* the sound of running feet, and then the hatch opens and once more he sees outside, this time the open sky. The sensory details make the writing more vivid, but are also used in a literary way to create a changing sense of distance between the reader and the subject matter.

4. ***When you describe, try to show rather than tell your readers what you want them to know.*** Your ultimate goal in writing a description essay is to give your readers an experience as close to yours as possible. Therefore, do not simply tell your readers what you saw or experienced; show them. Use your writing skills to re-create the event so that your readers can see, hear, feel, smell, taste, and understand as if they were there. For example, you can tell someone you bought a "terrific new car." But if you say you bought a "beautiful, new blue Mustang with a grey interior, custom wheels, and an awesome stereo," you're *showing* your readers why you are so excited about your purchase.

   If Johnston had simply stated his dominant impression (that the young Joey Smallwood was awed by the sight of the sealers frozen on the ice pans) with no examples or details to support his statement, he would only be *telling* his readers how the narrator felt. Instead, he shows them. His sensory details demonstrate his main point.

5. ***Organize your description so that your readers can easily follow it.*** Most descriptions are organized from general to particular (from main idea to details), from particular to general (from details to main idea), or spatially (from top to bottom or left to right). Because the organization of your essay often depends on your point of view, you should choose a specific perspective from which to write your description. If your description jumps around your house, referring to a picture on the wall in your bedroom, then to the refrigerator in the kitchen, and next to the quilt on your bed, your readers are likely to become confused and disoriented. They will not be able to follow you. If, however, you move from room to room in a logical way, your audience will be able to stay with you. In fact, your vision will become their vision.

Johnston organizes his description so that the narrator becomes a stand-in for the reader, looking through the porthole in the same way that the reader is looking into the pages of the book. The narrator becomes a guide for the reader, telling us exactly what to think, but also what to feel. The seal hunt has been the subject of much controversy throughout the world, and this description gives a sympathetic look at a group of men who are not often seen this way. They become real and honest and noble, even as "statuary" frozen on the ice pans of Newfoundland.

WRITING YOUR OWN DESCRIPTION ESSAY

What direct encounters have you had with nature? What are some of the details of these encounters? Was your general impression good or bad? Write an essay describing one of these encounters. Describe your experience through the senses, following the guidelines for writing a description essay. Remember to show rather than tell your readers about your memory. Begin by reviewing your prewriting notes. Then choose your dominant impression, and put it into a thesis statement.

WORKING WITH A STUDENT ESSAY

In an essay about a fond memory, a student named Abby Reed reminisces about her grandfather. As you read this draft, ask yourself what dominant impression Abby is trying to communicate to her readers.

Grandma's House

My grandma lives in the country, near a large, blue lake and a small, green forest. I look forward to visiting her house. I think of my grandpa when I'm there. 1

Whenever I walk into my grandma's house, I always go directly to my grandpa's favourite room—the den. I am immediately reminded of my grandpa in this room. My grandma has a soft, brown sofa and a brown leather loveseat in this small, dark room, but all I see is the old, worn chair that was my grandpa's. The chair was re-covered in an itchy tweed fabric. I used to pretend to be asleep in his chair so my grandpa would gently lift me from the coarse fabric and place me on his lap. I would lie there even though I wasn't sleeping and enjoy the warmth of his body. I remember the times I sat on his sturdy lap in that chair while he read <u>One Fish, Two Fish, Red Fish, Blue Fish</u> or <u>The Cat in the Hat</u> in his deep voice. 2

Now when I sit in his chair, I look on the mantel and see an old Air Force picture of my grandpa and three of his Air Force buddies. They are 3 all dressed in informal flight clothes and are standing in front of a World War II airplane. Next to this picture is a single portrait of my grandpa when he was 70. This picture represents the way I still see him in my mind. His grey hair is thin, his face has light brown sun spots on it that show his years of working outdoors. His gentle, light blue eyes sparkle in a way that usually meant he was up to something mischievous. But most of all. I love looking at his smile. The right side of his mouth always turned slightly downward, but it is a smile that I would give anything to see in person just one more time.

4   I also love to play with the pipe stand that sits on the table next to my grandpa's chair. I like the worn feeling of the pipe. It once was rough with ridges but is now smooth from use. When I quietly pick up his pipe and smell the sweet tobacco that was once housed in its shell, I think of all the times I knew my grandpa were near me because of this same aroma.

5   I have wonderful memories of my grandpa. When I go to my grandma's house, I can sit in my grandpa's old chair in my grandpa's favourite room and reminisce about all the times I felt safe when my grandpa was near. I will always treasure this one tiny room, with its smells from the past and its picture of my grandpa smiling.

Discovering How the Essay Works

1. This essay creates a certain mood. What is the dominant impression that Abby creates?

     _____

2. Is this description primarily subjective or objective? Explain your answer.

     _____

     _____

3. In this particular essay, the student writer describes her subjects mainly through the sense of sight, with a few references to hearing, touching, and smelling. Find at least one example of each of these senses in this essay.

     Seeing: _____

     Hearing: _____

     Touching: _____

     Smelling: _____

4. Abby works hard in this essay to *show* rather than *tell* us what she sees in the house. List three details that go beyond telling to *show* us what she observes.

_____

_____

_____

5. How does Abby organize her essay? List the topics of each of her body paragraphs, and then identify her method of organization.

_____

_____

_____

Method of Organization:_____

Revising and Editing the Student Essay

This essay is Abby's first draft, which now needs to be revised and edited. First, apply the Revising Checklist from Chapter 7 (pages 52–53) to the content of Abby's draft. When you are satisfied that her ideas are fully developed and well organized, use the Editing Checklist in Chapter 8 (page 80) to correct her grammar and punctuation errors. Answer the questions below. Then write your suggested changes directly on Abby's draft.

Revision Questions

Thesis Statement

1. Put brackets around the last sentence in Abby's introduction. Does it contain her dominant impression?

_____

2. Rewrite Abby's thesis statement if necessary so that it states her dominant impression as clearly as possible.

_____

_____

Basic Elements

1. Give Abby's essay an alternate title.

   _____

2. Rewrite Abby's introduction so that it captures the reader's attention and builds up to the thesis statement at the end of the paragraph.

   _____

   _____

   _____

   _____

3. Does each of Abby's body paragraphs deal with only one topic?

   _____

4. Rewrite Abby's conclusion, using at least one suggestion from Part I.

   _____

   _____

   _____

   _____

Development

1. Write out Abby's thesis statement (revised, if necessary), and list her three topic sentences below it.

   Thesis statement: _____

   _____

   Topic 1: _____

   _____

   Topic 2: _____

   _____

Topic 3: _____

_____

2. Do Abby's topics adequately support her thesis statement?

_____

3. Does each body paragraph have a focused topic sentence?

_____

4. Does the essay draw on all five senses?

_____

5. Add at least one detail to Abby's essay that refers to a new sense. Label the detail you are adding.

Sense: _____   Detail: _____

6. In what way does Abby's essay *show* rather than *tell* her readers about her memories of her grandfather?

_____

_____

Unity

1. Read each of Abby's topic sentences with her thesis statement (revised, if necessary) in mind. Do they go together?

_____

2. Revise them if necessary so they are directly related.

3. Drop or rewrite any of the sentences in her body paragraphs that are not directly related to their topic sentences.

Organization

1. Read Abby's essay again to see if all the paragraphs are arranged logically.

2. Move any paragraphs that are out of order.

3. Look closely at Abby's body paragraphs to see if all her sentences are arranged logically within paragraphs.

4. Move any sentences that are out of order.

For a list of transitions, see pages 70–71.

Coherence

1. Circle five transitions Abby uses.

2. Explain how two of these make Abby's essay easier to read.

_____

_____

Now rewrite Abby's essay with your revisions.

Editing Questions

Sentences

Subjects and Verbs

For help with subjects and verbs, see Chapter 32.

1. Underline the subjects once and verbs twice in paragraphs 3 and 4 of your revision of Abby's essay. Remember that sentences can have more than one subject–verb set.

2. Does each sentence have at least one subject and verb that can stand alone?

_____

For help with fragments, see Chapter 33.

For help with run-ons, see Chapter 34.

3. Did you find and correct Abby's fragment? If not, find and correct it now.

4. Did you find and correct Abby's run-on sentence? If not, find and correct it now.

Subject–Verb Agreement

For help with subject–verb agreement, see Chapter 36.

1. Read aloud the subjects and verbs you underlined in your revision of Abby's essay.

2. Did you find and correct the subject and verb that do not agree?

_____

Pronoun Agreement

For help with pronoun agreement, see Chapter 39.

1. Find any pronouns in your revision of Abby's essay that do not agree with their nouns.

2. Correct any pronouns that do not agree with their nouns.

Modifiers

For help with modifier errors, see Chapter 42.

1. Find any modifiers in your revision of Abby's essay that are not as close as possible to the words they modify.

2. Rewrite sentences if necessary so that modifiers are as close as possible to the words they modify.

Punctuation and Mechanics
Punctuation

1. Read your revision of Abby's essay for any errors in punctuation.
2. Find the fragment and the run-on sentence you revised, and make sure they are punctuated correctly.

For help with punctuation, see Chapters 43–46.

Mechanics

1. Read your revision of Abby's essay for any errors in capitalization.
2. Be sure to check Abby's capitalization in the fragment and run-on sentence you revised.

For help with capitalization, see Chapter 47.

Word Choice and Spelling
Word Choice

1. Find any words used incorrectly in your revision of Abby's essay.
2. Correct any errors you find.

For help with confused words, see Chapter 53.

Spelling

1. Use spell-check and a dictionary to check the spelling in your revision of Abby's essay.
2. Correct any misspelled words.

For help with spelling, see Chapter 54.

Now rewrite Abby's essay again with your editing corrections.

 ## WORKING WITH YOUR OWN ESSAY

Returning to the description you wrote earlier in this chapter, revise and edit your own writing. Use the same techniques you used for Abby's essay.

PRACTISING DESCRIPTION

Reading Suggestions

In Chapter 23, you will find two essays that demonstrate good descriptive writing: "Underground Toronto" by Allen Abel describes people and places associated with the Toronto subway system, "Dryden's Backyard" by Ken Dryden describes a backyard hockey rink. You might want to read these selections before writing another description essay. As you read, notice how the writers pull you into each experience through sensory details.

Writing Workshop

Guidelines for Writing a Description Essay

1. Decide on a dominant impression—the feeling or mood you want to communicate.

2. Decide how much of your description should be objective (factual) and how much should be subjective (personal reactions).

3. Draw on your five senses to write a good description.

4. When you describe, try to *show* rather than *tell* your readers what you want them to know.

5. Organize your description so that your readers can easily follow it.

1. Place yourself in the scene above, and describe it in as much detail as possible. Imagine that you can see, hear, touch, smell, and taste everything in this picture. What are your sensations? How do you feel? Before you begin to write, decide on the dominant impression you want to convey. Then choose your details carefully.

2. Describe for your classmates a class environment that is ideal for you. What kind of classroom atmosphere makes you thrive? What should the people in your class understand about you as a student? What kind of instructor brings out the best in you? Why?

3. A national travel magazine is asking for honest descriptions (positive or negative) of places people have visited. They are offering $100 to the writers of the essays chosen for publication. You may decide to write about a place with a marvellous beach or about an absolutely awful hotel. In either case, remember to begin with the dominant impression you want to create.

4. Create your own description assignment (with the help of your instructor), and write a response to it.

Revising Workshop

Small Group Activity (5–10 minutes per writer)   Working in groups of three or four, each person should read his or her description essay to the other members of the group. Those listening should record their reactions on a copy of the Peer Evaluation Form in Appendix 1A. After your group goes through this process, give your evaluation forms to the appropriate writers so that each writer has two or three peer comment sheets for revising.

Paired Activity (5 minutes per writer)   Using the completed Peer Evaluation Forms, work in pairs to decide what you should revise in your essay. If time allows, rewrite some of your sentences, and have your partner look at them.

Individual Activity   Rewrite your paper, using the revising feedback you received from other students.

Editing Workshop

Paired Activity (5–10 minutes per writer)   Swap papers with a classmate, and use the editing portion of your Peer Evaluation Form (Appendix 1B) to identify as many grammar, punctuation, mechanics, and spelling errors as you can. If time allows, correct some of your errors, and have your partner look at them. Record your grammar, punctuation, and mechanics errors in the Error Log (Appendix 3) and your spelling errors in the Spelling Log (Appendix 4).

Individual Activity   Rewrite your paper again, using the editing feedback you received from other students.

CHAPTER 10

NARRATING

There are things to confess that enrich the world, and things that need not be said.

—JONI MITCHELL

Because we are constantly telling other people about various events in our lives, we all know how to use narration. Think of how many times a day you tell someone about an event that happened to you: your accident on the way to school; the conversation you had at the bus stop yesterday; your strange experience at the restaurant last night. Narrating is an essential part of all of our lives. In fact, stories can teach us how to live our lives.

Narration also plays an important role in our writing. Think about how many times we tell a story when we write—in our personal lives, in classes, and at work:

You tell a friend in an e-mail about how you met the person you're now dating.

On a history exam, a student summarizes the chain of events that led to Newfoundland joining Confederation.

A student summarizes a short story in an English class.

An emergency medical technician gives an account of her 911 calls for the day.

A supervisor writes a report explaining an employee's accident on the job.

Narration, or storytelling, is an interesting way of getting someone's attention by sharing thoughts or experiences. Like description, narration is sometimes used as an end in itself (for example, when you tell a friend a joke or the plot of a movie). But very often it's used in conjunction with explaining or persuading. You might start a term paper analyzing drug abuse, for example, with a brief story of one addict's life. Basically, people use storytelling to help focus their readers' or listeners' attention.

WRITING A NARRATION ESSAY

Jane Maher, who teaches in New York City, wrote the following auto-biographical essay to help her come to terms with the loss of her father. Can you think of an event that taught you something important about life? What was the event? What did you learn?

GIRL

by Jane Maher

I don't remember exactly when I began to be offended when my father   1
called me, or other girls or women, "girl." I guess he always did it; at least I don't remember him ever not doing it. He'd often use it as a term of affection: "How's my girl today?" But just as often, he'd use it carelessly or callously, the way some men use the expression "sweetie." "Listen, girl," my father would say, "I make the rules around here."

Women, girls, were perceived by my father as less than men: less im-   2
portant, less intelligent, less capable, less in need of education or direction. In fact, for a long period of my life, I was so indoctrinated by my father's views, and by society's confirmation of those views, that I agreed with him.

But as I grew older, the term "girl" began to hurt me and make me   3
angry. As my father became aware of my strong and growing aversion to the word, he'd use it even more often. "What's the matter," he'd ask. "You don't like it anymore when your old man calls you girl? You're my daughter; I'll call you whatever I want." Or he'd ask my mother, pretending I wasn't in the room, "What kind of daughter did you raise that she wants to become a man? Is she ashamed to be a girl?" The word took on stronger and stronger connotations for me as I began to realize how permanently, and adversely, my father's attitudes had affected my life. I had been sent to an all-girls commercial high school. "Listen, girl," my father declared, "as long as you know typing and stenography, you'll never starve." College was not mentioned very much in our house. I was one of three daughters. If one of us had a date, my father would tell my mother to remind us "what can happen to a girl if she's not careful." When I got married, I heard my father joking with my uncle: "One down, two to go." We were objects to be dispensed with, burdens of no conceivable use to him.

This does not mean that he did not love us or care for us; for my entire   4
childhood, he worked two jobs so that he could afford to send us away to the country every summer. But it was the terms upon which he loved and cared for us which were so distressing to me. Nor did I always get angry when he used the term. When my first daughter was born, he arrived at the hospital carrying a silver dollar he had saved in his collection for many years as a gift for her. "Now I've got four of you girls instead of three," he

said, knowing that I knew at this special time he was only teasing and did not intend to hurt me.

5   I saw less and less of my father after I moved to Connecticut in 1980. He and my mother kept their house in Brooklyn but spent most of the winter months in Florida. Sometimes when I called on the phone, I could tell how happy he was to hear my voice. "Hey, girl, is that husband of yours taking as good care of you as I did?" But other times, over Thanksgiving dinner or while opening Christmas presents, he'd use the term as he had when I was young. "Girl, get me a little more coffee will you?" Or when I enrolled my daughter in an expensive private school: "Why spend money you don't have to, girl? She's just going to get married the way you did." I'd keep my countenance at those times; I had grown wise to my father—I wouldn't give him the satisfaction of showing my anger. That's not to say he didn't keep trying: "So now you like it when your old man calls you girl, huh? You're finally getting wise to the fact that men aren't so bad to have around when you need something."

6   And I suspected that secretly he was proud of me. Soon after I got married, I returned to college, part-time, in the evening, and graduated magna cum laude. By then, both of my daughters were in school, so I earned my master's degree from Columbia University, again part-time. It was my father who picked up my daughters from the school bus stop on the day I took my comprehensive exam. When I began to teach part time at a local community college, my father asked my mother, again pretending I wasn't in the room, "if there was a girl around here who thought her father was going to start calling her Professor."

7   My father had always had a heart condition, exacerbated by twenty-two years as a New York City fireman, two packs of cigarettes a day, and my mother's delicious Italian cooking. When he suddenly became seriously ill, my mother got him home from Florida and into a hospital in Brooklyn in less than 24 hours. But it still wasn't soon enough. My father died before they could perform a triple bypass, and before I got to say goodbye to him.

8   I had left Connecticut at nine in the morning, intending to wait out the surgery with my mother and to be with my father when he awoke. Instead, when I arrived at the hospital, one of my sisters and my mother were in a small, curtained-off section of the intensive care unit being told by a busy, preoccupied young resident that my father had experienced very little discomfort before he died. It sounded too pat, too familiar, too convenient to me. I was overcome with the fear that my father had been alone that entire morning, that no one in that overcrowded municipal hospital had even known that he was dead until they arrived to prepare him for surgery.

9   They left us alone to say goodbye to him, but I was so concerned over my mother's anguish that I didn't take the time I should have to kiss him or even to touch his forehead. A nurse came in and suggested, gently, that it was time to leave. She was right, of course; another moment and my mother would have collapsed.

I thanked the nurse and asked her, nonchalantly, if she knew exactly   10
when my father had died, secretly convinced that she didn't have an answer, that he had been alone all morning. "I didn't see him this morning,"
she replied, "but I'll get the nurse who did."

A young, pretty nurse appeared several minutes later. "My shift is over,"   11
she said, "but I was waiting around to see the family."

"Was he in pain?" my mother asked.   12

"No, not at all. He even teased me a bit. I remember his exact words. "Go   13
take care of the patients who need you, girl," he said. "I'm perfectly fine."

I wasn't exactly fine, but I have never felt more comforted in my life than   14
when I heard that word.

 PREPARING TO WRITE YOUR OWN NARRATION ESSAY

We have all learned important lessons from various events in our
lives. Over time, we find that some lessons are more worthwhile than
others. What events in your life have taught you important lessons?
Use one or more of the prewriting techniques you learned in Chapter 2 to gather your thoughts on these events. What lessons did you
learn?

How to Write a Narration Essay

Narrating involves telling a story about an experience—one of yours or
someone else's. When you write a narrative essay, you focus on a particular
event and make a specific point about it. You should provide enough detail
so that readers can understand as completely as possible what your experience was like. Here are some guidelines to help you make your narrative
interesting.

1. ***Make sure your essay has a point.*** The most important feature of a
   narrative essay is that it makes a point. Simply recording your story step
   by step is a boring exercise for both writer and reader. Writing an
   account of your walk to class in the morning might not be particularly
   interesting. But the walk becomes interesting when something important or significant happens on the way. An event is significant if it
   helps both writer and reader understand something about themselves,
   about other people, or about the world we live in. If you can complete
   one of the following sentences, you will produce a focused narrative:

   This essay shows that . . .

   This essay teaches us that . . .

In Jane Maher's essay, the narrator focuses on the pain she felt, growing up, when her father referred to her as a "girl." She thought the term was degrading until she understood, after he died, that it was really a term of endearment. Maher is able to communicate the process of growing up through her experience with this one word. Her essay teaches us that the relationship between words and emotions is complex.

2. ***Use the five Ws and one H to construct your story.*** The five Ws and one H are the six questions—*Who? What? When? Where? Why?* and *How?*—that journalists use to make sure they cover all the basic information when they write a news story. These questions can help you come up with details and ideas for a well-developed narrative essay. You should make sure that your essay answers all of these questions in detail.

   When you look at Maher's narrative again, you can see that she covered the answers to all these questions:

   Who was involved? Maher, her father, her mother, and the nurses
   What was the central problem? Maher was offended by her father's use of the word "girl."
   When did this story take place? As Maher was growing up
   Where were they? At home and in a hospital
   Why was Maher offended? Because she thought the word "girl" was degrading to her as a person and to other females
   How did the author learn from this event? She finally understood that her father's use of "girl" wasn't as offensive as she thought it was.

   Since Maher covers all these basic details, the reader can appreciate her full story and understand its significance.

3. ***Develop your narrative with vivid details.*** Your readers will be able to imagine the events in your narrative essay if you provide them with specific details. In fact, the more specific your details, the more vivid your essay will become. These details should develop the ideas you generated with the six journalistic questions. At the same time, you should omit any irrelevant details that don't support your thesis statement.

   Look again at Maher's essay. In this narrative, the author provides many vivid details about the narrator: She is a girl whose father thinks girls are less important than boys; he calls her "girl"; this term starts to bother the narrator as she is growing up; she gets married and moves to Connecticut; she has two daughters; she gets her master's degree at Columbia University and starts teaching at a local community college; and her father dies of a heart attack. The amount of detail in Maher's essay helps us participate in her narrative.

4. ***Build excitement in your narrative with careful pacing.*** To be most effective, narration should prolong the exciting parts of a story and

shorten the routine facts that simply move the reader from one episode to another. If you were robbed on your way to work, for example, a good narrative describing the incident would concentrate on the traumatic event itself rather than on such boring details as what you had for breakfast or what clothes you were wearing. One writer might say, "I fell and hurt myself this morning." A better writer would draw out the exciting parts: "As I was running to my English class this morning, I slipped on a patch of black ice and landed flat on my back beside a group of smokers huddled by the entrance." The details themselves tell the story.

Maher reveals the details in her story through some of her father's quotations that bothered her: "Listen, girl, I make the rules around here"; "Listen, girl, as long as you know typing and stenography, you'll never starve." She feels frustrated and belittled by her father, even as an adult: "Hey, girl, is that husband of yours taking as good care of you as I did?" Finally, she works through the hurtfulness when her father dies. At this point, Maher draws out the search for the nurse who could tell her if her father died alone. The pacing of her story holds our interest throughout the essay.

5. *Organize your narration so that your readers can easily follow it.* Most narrative essays follow a series of actions through time, so they are organized chronologically, or according to a time sequence. Once you choose the details you will use, you should arrange them so that your story has a clear beginning, middle, and end. If you add clear, logical transitions, such as "then," "next," "at this point," and "suddenly," you will guide your readers smoothly through your essay from one event to the next.

Jane Maher organizes her narrative chronologically. It moves through time from her childhood to going to high school to getting married and having a baby as her father raises her, retires, and grows old. In other words, the two main characters—Maher and her father—move through normal life events. Because it follows a logical time sequence and does not jump around, Maher's narrative is easy to follow. She guides her readers through her essay with such transitions as "in fact," "as I grew older," "when," "sometimes," and "soon."

✎ Writing Your Own Narrative Essay

Choose one of the events from your prewriting notes that taught you an important lesson in life, and write a narrative essay explaining this incident and the lesson you learned. Follow the guidelines in this chapter to develop your essay.

WORKING WITH A STUDENT ESSAY

In an essay about a dramatic incident, student writer Tommy Poulos tells a story that taught him an important lesson in life. Here is his first draft. As you read this paragraph, try to figure out what Tommy's main point is.

"My Brother"

1   My family and I lead a fairly quiet life. My parents go to work, and my brother and I go to school. We never make headlines with sports events or science fairs. We essentially live a normal, average life out of the spotlight. It was quite a shock, then, when a lot of attention was focused on our family.

2   My brother, Wayne, was driving on a highway that is nicknamed "The Death Loop." It got its name because it's a two-lane highway that loops around the city, and many people have died because of drivers who take too many chances and cause head-on collisions. One afternoon, Wayne saw a woman's car wrecked into a guardrail with her passenger side of the car completely smashed in. The driver's side was mangled, and my brother could tell the woman inside was in trouble. Wayne didn't think twice about running up to help them. She was badly injured, but my brother knew not to move her!

3   The woman had not been wearing her seat belt. Her car was too old to have an airbag. She had obviously hit her head because she had blood gushing from a gaping wound in her forehead. She was conscious, so my brother sat with her, trying to keep her calm and awake. He kept asking her questions like if she had any children? Two other cars stopped, and my brother remembers telling one man to call 911. Wayne stayed with the woman until the paramedics arrived.

4   Wayne left the scene after giving a statement to the police. Later, he heard from the local newspapers and news stations that his heroic actions had saved the woman. In these stories, the woman's husband said he believed his wife was still alive because she had a guardian angel keeping her awake. Even the paramedics said Wayne probably kept her alive. By keeping her awake. In public, Wayne acts very humble, but in private, he is loving the attention.

5   Now my brother is the local hero. Our house used to be quiet, but since Wayne's act of heroism, it's become Grand Central Station. Everyone wants to talk to Wayne. I'm happy for him. But most of all, I'm glad Wayne realizes the importance of seat belts. He used to be macho and say seat belts were too uncomfortable to wear. Now he won't leave the driveway until everyone has buckled their seat belts. Perhaps the woman will save Wayne's life as well.

Discovering How the Essay Works

1. All the details in Tommy's essay lead to one main point. What is that point?

   _____

2. Tommy covers all the journalistic questions in his essay. Record at least one detail he uses for each question:

   Who? _____

   What? _____

   When? _____

   Where? _____

   Why? _____

   How? _____

3. In your opinion, which two details of Tommy's are the most vivid? What makes them so vivid?

   _____

   _____

4. How does Tommy pace his essay to build excitement?

   _____

   _____

   _____

   _____

5. How does Tommy organize his essay? List the topic of each of his body paragraphs; then identify his method of organization.

   Paragraph 2: _____

   Paragraph 3: _____

   Paragraph 4: _____

   Method of Organization:_____

Revising and Editing the Student Essay

This essay is Tommy's first draft, which now needs to be revised and edited. First, apply the Revising Checklist in Chapter 7 (pages 52–53) to the content of Tommy's draft. When you are satisfied that his ideas are fully developed and well organized, use the Editing Checklist on page 80 in Chapter 8 to correct his grammar and mechanics errors. Answer the questions below. Then write your suggested changes directly on Tommy's draft.

Revision Questions

Thesis Statement

1. Put brackets around the last sentence in Tommy's introduction. Does it contain his main point? Does it express his opinion about that point?

   _____

2. Rewrite Tommy's thesis statement if necessary so that it states his main point and an opinion about that main point.

   _____

   _____

   _____

Basic Elements

1. Give Tommy's essay an alternate title. Also drop the quotation marks, since original titles should not be in quotation marks.

   _____

2. Rewrite Tommy's introduction so that it captures the reader's attention and builds up to the thesis statement at the end of the paragraph.

   _____

   _____

   _____

3. Does each of Tommy's body paragraphs deal with just one topic?

   _____

4. Rewrite Tommy's conclusion, using at least one suggestion from Part I.

_____

_____

_____

Development

1. Write out Tommy's thesis statement (revised, if necessary), and list his three topic sentences below it.

   Thesis statement: _____

   _____

   Topic 1: _____

   Topic 2: _____

   Topic 3: _____

2. Do Tommy's topics adequately support his thesis statement?

   _____

3. Does each body paragraph have a focused topic sentence?

   _____

4. Add more specific information to two of Tommy's supporting details.
5. Add two new details to Tommy's essay that support his main idea.

Unity

1. Read each of Tommy's topic sentences with his thesis statement (revised, if necessary) in mind. Do they go together?

   _____

2. Revise them if necessary so they are directly related.
3. Drop or rewrite any of the sentences in his body paragraphs that are not directly related to their topic sentences.

Organization

1. Read Tommy's essay again to see if all the paragraphs are arranged chronologically.
2. Move any paragraphs that are out of order.
3. Look closely at Tommy's body paragraphs to see if all his sentences are arranged logically within paragraphs.
4. Move any sentences that are out of order.

Coherence

1. Circle five words or phrases Tommy repeats.
2. Explain how two of these make Tommy's essay easier to read.

_____

_____

Now rewrite Tommy's essay with your revisions.

Editing Questions

Sentences

Subjects and Verbs

For help with subjects and verbs, see Chapter 32.

1. Underline the subjects once and verbs twice in paragraph 4 of your revision of Tommy's essay. Remember that sentences can have more than one subject–verb set.
2. Does each sentence have at least one subject and verb that can stand alone?

_____

For help with fragments, see Chapter 33.

3. Did you find and correct Tommy's fragment? If not, find and correct it now.

Subject–Verb Agreement

For help with subject–verb agreement, see Chapter 36.

1. Read aloud the subjects and verbs you underlined in your revision of Tommy's essay.
2. Correct any subjects and verbs that do not agree with each other.

Pronoun Agreement

For help with pronoun agreement, see Chapter 39.

1. Find any pronouns in your revision of Tommy's essay that do not agree with their nouns.
2. Did you find and correct the two pronouns that do not agree with their nouns? If not, find and correct them now.

Modifiers

1. Find any modifiers in your revision of Tommy's essay that are not as close as possible to the words they modify.
2. Rewrite sentences if necessary so that modifiers are as close as possible to the words they modify.

For help with modifier errors, see Chapter 42.

Punctuation and Mechanics

Punctuation

1. Read your revision of Tommy's essay for any errors in punctuation.
2. Find the fragment you revised, and make sure it is punctuated correctly.
3. Did you find and correct Tommy's two other punctuation errors?

For help with punctuation, see Chapters 43–46.

Mechanics

1. Read your revision of Tommy's essay for any errors in capitalization.
2. Be sure to check Tommy's capitalization in the fragment you revised.

For help with capitalization, see Chapter 47.

Word Choice and Spelling

Word Choice

1. Find any words used incorrectly in your revision of Tommy's essay.
2. Correct any errors you find.

For help with confused words, see Chapter 53.

Spelling

1. Use spell-check and a dictionary to check the spelling in your revision of Tommy's essay.
2. Correct any misspelled words.

For help with spelling, see Chapter 54.

Now rewrite Tommy's essay again, including your editing corrections.

WORKING WITH YOUR OWN ESSAY

Returning to the narrative you wrote earlier in this chapter, revise and edit your own writing. Use the Checklists for Revising and Editing the student essay in Chapters 7 and 8.

PRACTISING NARRATION

Reading Suggestions

In Chapter 24, you will find two essays that illustrate good narrative writing: "The Worth of Women's Work," in which Nina Lee Colwill tells the story of her grandmother and what she learned from her, and "Writer's Retreat" by Stan Higgins, which talks about his life as a writer in prison. You might want to read these selections before writing another narration essay. As you read, notice how the writers cover the journalistic questions and use vivid descriptive details to pull you into their narratives, making the main point of the essays all the more meaningful.

Writing Workshop

Guidelines for Writing a Narration Essay

1. Make sure your essay has a point.
2. Use the five *W*s and one *H* to construct your story.
3. Develop your narrative with vivid details.
4. Build excitement in your narrative with careful pacing.
5. Organize your narrative so that your readers can easily follow it.

---

1. Place yourself in the scene pictured below, and write a narrative about what is happening. How did you get here? Why are you here? Where are you going from here? Be sure to decide on a main point before you begin to write.

2. Your old high school has asked you, as a graduate, to submit an essay to the newsletter recalling a job or volunteer experience that you enjoyed. The editors want to inform current high school students about options for volunteer and paid work. Your purpose is to tell your story in enough interesting detail so that you convince the current high school students that the job you had is worth looking into.

3. Your college class is putting together a collection of essays that explain how classmates decided to go to their college. What happened first? When did you decide? What helped you decide? What activities or

people influenced your decision the most? Tell your story in vivid detail.

4. Create your own narration assignment (with the help of your instructor), and write a response to it.

Revising Workshop

Small Group Activity (5–10 minutes per writer)   Working in groups of three or four, each person should read his or her narration essay to the other members of the group. Those listening should record their reactions on a copy of the Peer Evaluation Form in Appendix 1A. After your group goes through this process, give your evaluation forms to the appropriate writers so that each writer has two peer comment sheets for revising.

Paired Activity (5 minutes per writer)   Using the completed Peer Evaluation Forms, work in pairs to decide what you should revise in your essay. If time allows, rewrite some of your sentences, and have your partner look at them.

Individual Activity   Rewrite your paper, using the revising feedback you received from other students.

Editing Workshop

Paired Activity (5–10 minutes per writer)   Swap papers with a classmate, and use the editing portion of your Peer Evaluation Form (Appendix 1B) to identify as many grammar, punctuation, mechanics, and spelling errors as you can. If time allows, correct some of your errors, and have your partner look at them. Record your grammar, punctuation, and mechanics errors in the Error Log (Appendix 3) and your spelling errors in the Spelling Log (Appendix 4).

Individual Activity   Rewrite your paper again, using the editing feedback you received from other students.

CHAPTER 11

ILLUSTRATING

When I began to write, I found it was the best way to make sense out of my life.

—JOHN CHEEVER

Giving examples to make a point is a natural part of communication. For example, if you are trying to demonstrate how much time you waste, you can cite the fact that you talk on the phone for about two hours every day. Or to tell your friends how much fun you are having, you might say, "Residence is great because no one tells me what to do or when to go to bed. I am completely on my own." The message is in the examples you choose.

We also use examples every day to make various points in our writing. Think about the following situations that take place in our personal lives, at school, and at work.

In a letter to your parents, you tell them how hard you are studying by giving them examples of your weekend study schedule.

A student gives examples of gestures, facial expressions, and posture in a paper on nonverbal communication for a psychology course.

A student answers a sociology exam question by giving examples to show how children are integrated into society.

A human resources director of a large company writes a memo on sexual harassment in the workplace, including examples of inappropriate behaviour.

The owner of a catering business writes a brochure listing examples of dinners available in different price ranges.

An example is an **illustration** of the point you want to make. Well-chosen examples, then, are the building blocks of an illustration essay. You draw examples from your experience, your observations, and your reading. They help you show rather than tell what you mean, usually by supplying concrete details (what you see, hear, touch, smell, or taste) to support abstract ideas (such as hope, understanding, and love), by providing specifics ("I like chocolate") to explain generalizations ("I like sweets"), and by giving definite references ("Turn left at the second stoplight") to clarify vague statements ("Turn left in a few blocks").

Not only do examples help you make your point, but they also add interest to your writing. Would you like to read an essay stating that being a server in a restaurant is a lot harder than it looks? Or would you be more interested in reading an essay describing what it is like having to serve too many tables, carrying heavy trays, taking the wrong order to a table, and dealing with rude customers? The first statement *tells*, but vivid examples *show* your readers the point you want to make.

WRITING AN ILLUSTRATION ESSAY

In his essay "The Question," taken from his book *Black Berry, Sweet Juice: On Being Black and White in Canada*, Lawrence Hill writes about the insensitivity of Canadians who assume that if your skin is a different colour from theirs, you must be from somewhere else. Have you ever visited a foreign country where you stood out (or blended in) because of your appearance? Have you been part of a group that blended two or more cultures? What did you learn?

THE QUESTION
by Lawrence Hill

Canadians have a favourite pastime, and they don't even realize it. 1 They like to ask—they absolutely have to ask—where you are from if you don't look convincingly white. They want to know it, need to know it, simply must have that information. They just can't relax until they have pinpointed, to their satisfaction, your geographic and racial coordinates. They can go almost out of their minds with curiosity, as when driven by the need for food, water, or sex, but once they've finally managed to find out precisely where you were born, who your parents were, and what your racial make-up is, then, man, do they feel better. They can breathe easy and get back to the business of living.

I don't have the math background of, say, an actuary, but I can manage 2 the following calculation. I am forty-four years old. Since about age ten, I have been asked "So what are you, anyway?" and all its variations. ("Where are you from?" "Yes, but where are you really from?" "Yes, but where were your parents born?") That's thirty-four years I've been fielding The Question.

Let's assume I have been asked The Question once a day over these 3 past thirty-four years. $34 \times 365 = 12{,}410$. But that would be an underestimation because it fails to factor in the two years I lived in Quebec. During those two years, I was most certainly asked The Question five times per day. (*"D'où viens-tu?" "Quelles sont tes souches?" "Tes parents sont de quel pays?"*) An extra four times per day for two years in Quebec City would add on another 2,920 questions. $12{,}410 + 2{,}920 = 15{,}330$.

4   That, ladies and gentlemen, is the absolute minimum number of times Canadians have asked me either "Where are you from?' or *"D'où viens-tu?"* or any of the multitudinous variations.

5   Minelle Mahtani, whose doctoral thesis at the University of London examined identity among mixed-race Canadian women, tells a story of how she was walking alone one day in Toronto's St. Lawrence Market area, when someone tapped on her shoulder. Minelle turned around to find a woman who seemed motivated by a particular urgency—she had obviously been watching Minelle and just had to know where she was from.

6   "Ah," you may say, "but it's just curiosity. What's wrong with people being curious?"

7   I am a patient man. So patient that my children can confidently remove a chocolate chip cookie right from the edge of my fingers, or raid my dish of French vanilla ice cream and leave nothing but the cloudy bowl, and still know that I won't lose my cool. But even this patience was exhausted some time around the 5,000 mark of the 15,330 questions I have faced.

8   What is wrong with The Question? Nothing at all—when it is asked at the right time, when it results from a genuine interest in you as a person, and when the person asking the question actually accepts the answer.

9   Let's dissect the interrogation process. Imagine me at a party, sipping mineral water. A stranger walks up.

10   STRANGER: "Do you mind my asking where you are from?" [This is code for "What is your race?"]

11   ME: "Canada." [This is code for "Screw off."]

12   STRANGER: "Yes, but you know, where are you really from?" [This is code for "You know what I mean, so why are you trying to make me come out and say it?"]

13   ME: "I come from the foreign and distant metropolis of Newmarket. That's Newmarket, Ontario. My place of birth." [Code for "I'm not letting you off the hook, buster."]

14   STRANGER: "But your place of origin? Your parents? What are your parents?" [Code for "I want to know your race, but this is making me very uncomfortable because somehow I feel that I'm not supposed to ask that question."]

15   This exchange is like the opening of a chess game. The first few moves are pretty standard: White moves Pawn to King Four, Black responds with Pawn to King Four, White answers with Knight to King Bishop Three, and Black answers with Knight to King Bishop Three. From this point on, the possibilities multiply.

16   I can give a teaser, such as "My parents came up from the States," which frustrates the questioner, who really wants to know my parents' racial background.

17   I can give it all up and explain that I have a black father and a white mother.

18   I can invent an answer, such as "My father is a White Russian and my mother is an Ethiopian Jew."

Or I can turn the question around, as in "Why are you asking me this?"   19

And that is the nub of the issue. Why am I always asked that question?   20
Why do people need to know the answer so desperately?

Have you ever noticed that black people rarely put other people of any   21
race through the wringer like this? That's because many of them have been
asked The Question more times than they care to count. They're sophisticated enough—by virtue of their own experiences—to understand that
many people resent this line of interrogation.

Is it truly innocent? Can The Question be chalked up to basic curiosity?   22
I don't think so. Children are the most innocent and curious of all human
beings, yet they never hammer me with these questions. As a rule, adults
aren't all that curious about other people. With me, they are generally interested in just one thing: my ancestry.

Do you suppose that—15,330 times in thirty-four years—strangers will   23
ask an indisputably white Canadian with a traditional Anglo-Canadian
accent where he is from, where he was born, or where his parents were
born? Absolutely not. Strangers will assume that he is a true Canadian,
and leave that part of his identity unmolested. The offence-causing kernel
at the centre of this line of interrogation is its implication: "You are not white,
you don't look like me, so you're clearly not Canadian." It also suggests
"Since you're clearly not Canadian, and I am, I am within my rights to ask
you just exactly where you're from."

We grow up learning that certain questions are off limits in polite con-   24
versation. Any properly socialized Canadian knows, by the teenage years
at the latest, that it would be considered grossly impolite to walk up to
strangers and ask how much money they make, how they vote, whether
they believe in God, or whether they sleep with men, women, or both.
These questions are deemed intrusive. But to my way of thinking, they are
eminently preferable to "Where are you from?" After all, what is wrong
with asking what people do or think? But to ask what they *are*, and to presume to know at least part of the answer—that they are not white and
therefore are not Canadian—is very different.

Digging into someone's identity—especially a stranger's identity—is   25
tricky business. Hell, people can spend top dollar on psychotherapists to
figure out their own identities and still fall short of satisfaction. When I wake
up in the morning, stumble to the mirror, and brush my teeth, I'm certainly
not saying to myself, "Hello, black man, how are you today?" Nor am I saying, "Hello, white and black mix-up, what are you doing today?"

Obviously, the blackness and the whiteness within me are reflected   26
back at me by society. But I don't care to have my identity boiled down to
race. My identity may, at any given time, comprise a hundred elements.

I suppose the reason many of us mixed-race people find The Question   27
offensive is not just that it makes assumptions, which are often false, about
our identity, but because it attempts to hang our identity on one factor: our
race.

28   Not everybody I interviewed had the same take on this issue. Interestingly, two of the strongest opposing views came from young men, both in their twenties, university-educated, and living in southern Ontario.

29   Stefan Dubowski, of Hamilton, told me The Question doesn't bother him. When he is asked about his background, he just says he is part Ukrainian, part Barbadian. "Then we get into a discussion of what they thought I was. I've had Armenian, Egyptian, Pakistani, East Indian . . . It's just a question of curiosity. I've been asked so many times. If I got mad about it every single time, I'd just be this really angry person. I certainly don't feel any anger about it when people ask me about it, but my back does go up when I read it on an application form or on a government census."

30   Tyson Brown, who was raised in Burlington and now lives in Toronto, said he takes The Question as an opportunity to educate people about issues of mixed race and blackness. "I say, 'I'm mixed, African Canadian and white Canadian.' " Tyson emerged from a largely white high school to embrace his black identity completely as a young man. He read black literature, listened to black music, wore funky black clothes, dated black women, and chose to immerse himself completely in the black student community at York University. Later, he lived with his girlfriend for a year in Barbados, and there the constant references to his race grated on him. "They called me 'red man' the whole time I was there," he complained.

31   However, my brother, Dan, described The Question as a painful experience, especially during childhood. "I was definitely asked that question a lot. And a lot of times, when I said part black, or half black, people would then decide to argue with me and tell me that no, I wasn't, 'cause I didn't look black enough. I can remember it happening a lot when I was a boy, at summer camp. When I went up to camp for the first time, I was sitting on the bus with this kid who was probably a year or two older than I was. And this kid was saying, 'You're not. You can't be.' So there I was arguing with him about this."

32   Like Dan, most of the people I interviewed—and virtually all of the women—expressed impatience with constant questions about their racial background.

33   Karyn Hood, of Toronto, said, "People think I'm everything under the flipping sun, and it drives me insane. I get North African, Moroccan, Italian, Sicilian, Greek, Spanish, Jewish . . . Whenever I meet someone, I know it's going to be 'What are you? What background are you?' I usually try to put it to bed with one answer: 'My father is West Indian, my mother's Irish Canadian.' It's annoying. But life's a puzzle, and they want to know how you fit into their world." Karyn resents being perceived as "exotic," cultivates friendships in the black community, and prefers to date black men. "You can't live in two worlds. You have to make a choice. Saying you're white isn't really an option. So this makes it clear to people. If there's any doubt, that's the choice I'm making."

Natalie Wall, of Toronto, concurred. "I've been asked what I am so many   34
times. It is the rudest question in the world. It's the basest form of labelling
I've ever seen. People on the street are always guessing. 'You're Spanish,
right? Indian? What the hell are you?' I tell them I'm Canadian. 'But where
are you from?' 'Canada.' 'What about your parents?' 'My mom is from Nova
Scotia, my dad is from Trinidad.' 'So what are you?' 'Black.' I get a surprised
look. 'You *are*?' "

Jazz Miller, of Toronto, is so sick of The Question that when people ask   35
her what she is, she has taken to answering "aardvark." "It is designed to
embarrass the person asking the question. There's always a little bit of nervous laughter."

Aaron Cavon, who has a white father and a black mother, was a grad-   36
uate student at Dalhousie University when I interviewed him. He said people always look astonished when he says that The Question irritates him
and he won't answer it. He described the attitude of the questioner as un-
consciously aggressive, a stance that suggests the person being questioned is inferior. Underneath The Question, Aaron argued, is this unarticu-
lated belief: "It's not necessary for me to explain my origins, but it's
necessary for you to tell me who you are." He told me, "The assumption behind The Question is, 'I'm just white. You are the person who answers the
question because you are the one who is unknown.' "

Sara, one of my anonymous interviewees, fumed as she recalled the   37
numerous times she had dealt with The Question.

"Sometimes I'm very rude. I don't give much information. I might just   38
say, 'I'm from here.' Some days, if I don't feel like it, I just say, 'Africa.' And
they're happy, not realizing that Africa's a continent and that there are fifty-
two countries in it. It's just what they want to hear. They want to place you
somewhere because it makes them feel comfortable, helps them compart-
mentalize you.

"Where the hell are they from? No one's from here unless they're First   39
Nations peoples. But they're trying to make you feel strange. It's a displace-
ment. They're just trying to let you know that you don't belong . . . They are
not coming from a position of intelligence, asking those questions. White
privilege doesn't operate from a level of consciousness. It operates from a
position of privilege. Because they're privileged, they don't have to think
about stuff. They really don't. Does it mean that they're not well inten-
tioned? These can be people you love dearly, you know? But that's the way
the world is. They're operating from a position of belligerent white privilege, and they don't have to look at stuff and think about stuff. So they ask
these reckless questions."

PREPARING TO WRITE YOUR OWN ILLUSTRATION ESSAY

When did you last try something new in your life? Was it difficult? Did you plan this new experience, or did it just happen? Do you like new experiences, or do you prefer keeping your life routine? Use one or more of the prewriting strategies you learned in Chapter 2 to recall several times you tried something new, planned or not. Then think about the positive and negative aspects of trying new experiences. What value do they have in your life? What are the disadvantages of trying new experiences?

How to Write an Illustration Essay

In the art world, a good illustrator is someone who makes an image or an idea come alive with the perfect drawing. The same principle applies in writing: Someone who uses illustrations, or examples, effectively makes an essay or other piece of writing come alive. Moreover, in college, most essay exam questions are based on illustration—finding the best examples to support your main point. Here are some guidelines to help you use examples effectively:

1. *State your main point and your opinion about that point in the last sentence of your introduction.* Write a thesis statement that clearly and plainly states the main idea of your essay, and place it at the end of your introduction. This is the controlling idea of your essay and should consist of a limited subject and your opinion about that subject. You will explain this main point through the examples you furnish in the following body paragraphs.

   In the sample essay, Hill starts his essay with his main point in the second sentence of the introduction: "They [Canadians] have to ask where you are from if you don't look convincingly white." The essay that follows is a series of examples that illustrate that question and how those who are asked it react to it. He then closes the essay with Sara's opinion on the matter: "They're operating from a position of belligerent white privilege . . . so they ask these reckless questions." This movement of a thesis from general to specific is the inductive method of writing an essay. The more common method for students, which places the specific opinion first, is called the deductive method.

2. *Choose examples that are relevant to your point.* In an illustration essay, examples serve as the writer's explanation. Well-chosen examples are an essay's building blocks. They help you prove your point and must directly support the point you are trying to make. Examples that are not relevant are distracting, causing readers to lose their train of

thought. Your readers will appreciate the point you are making not because you tell them what to think but because you show them with relevant examples what you are trying to say. Keep in mind, too, that the more specific your examples are, the more likely your readers are to agree with your point.

Finding relevant examples is a fairly easy task. The best examples often come from your own experience and observation. You can also draw examples from your reading—books, newspapers, magazines. In addition, as technology advances, more and more information is available online, making the Internet a good place to find examples for an illustration essay.

In Hill's essay, all his examples focus on examples of The Question. Since his point is that Canadians of mixed race are always asked that question, he interviews several people and relates their experiences in addition to his own. Although not everyone he talks to finds The Question offensive, most of them do. He combines their speculations about the reasons people must have for asking The Question with his own. These focused examples make the essay coherent and unified.

3. ***Choose examples that your readers can identify with.*** To do this, you need to know as much as possible about your audience. Once you know who your readers are, you can tailor your examples to them. In this way, your readers are most likely to follow your line of reasoning. Suppose, for instance, that you want your parents to finance an off-campus apartment for you. You are not likely to make your point by citing examples of European universities that do not provide any student housing because this is not an example that Canadian parents can identify with. You need to furnish examples that address your specific situation.

Hill's essay is a chapter in his book, *Black Berry, Sweet Juice: On Being Black and White in Canada.* He has two audiences: Canadians who ask The Question, and Canadians who are asked The Question. It is the first group he hopes will understand his point. His numerous examples make it clear that The Question is asked frequently. However, he also needs to convince his readers that it is offensive. For this reason he inserts a comment by an imagined reader: " 'Ah,' you may say, 'but it's just curiosity. What's wrong with people being curious?' " As an answer, he can then give examples to show that it is indeed offensive to those who are asked.

4. ***Use enough examples to make your point.*** Nobody has a set formula for determining the perfect number of examples, because that depends on the point you are trying to make. Sometimes several short examples will make your point best. Or perhaps three or four fairly detailed examples each in its own body paragraph—work best. At other times the most effective way to develop an essay is with a single extended

example. Usually, however, three or four examples are sufficient. If you are in doubt whether to add another example or more vivid details, you should probably do so. Most students err on the side of using too few examples or not adding enough detail to their examples.

In addition to his own experiences, Hill gives nine examples throughout his essay. The first example, Minelle Mahtani's story, sets up the opposing idea that it may just be curiosity. He then leads with two examples of people who are not offended, and follows with six examples of people who *are* offended. The variety of examples keeps the essay interesting and the reader engaged.

5. ***Organize your examples to make your point in the clearest, strongest way.*** When you have gathered enough relevant examples, you are ready to organize them into an essay. Most illustration essays are organized from general to particular (from a general statement—the thesis—to specific examples that support the general statement) or chronologically (according to a time sequence).

The examples themselves must also be organized within their paragraphs in some logical way—chronologically, spatially, or by extremes. Which example should come first? Second? Last? The simple act of arranging examples can help you—and your reader—make sense of an experience or idea. Use basic logic to guide you to different patterns.

Hill opens his essay with what Canadians will recognize as a rant. The rant is, however, presented in a semi-humorous way. Humour is also evident in the math, and in the totalling up of how many times the author may have been asked The Question. The first few examples give the reader a chance to express some polite Canadian doubts, and then Hill overwhelms the reader with the negative examples. Leading with the reader's question and the opposing views is a good persuasive technique, as it deals with any doubts the reader might have up front.

 WRITING YOUR OWN ILLUSTRATION ESSAY

Based on the prewriting that you did earlier, write an essay about three new experiences you have had. Which were planned? Which were unplanned? Did they affect you in positive ways? In negative ways? Or were the outcomes mixed? What did you learn from these experiences? Draft a thesis statement. Then write a first draft of your essay, including an introduction and a conclusion. Use examples in your body paragraphs to support your thesis statement.

WORKING WITH A STUDENT ESSAY

In the following essay, student writer Taleah Trainor uses examples to explain her relationship with Murphy's Law. As you read this draft of her essay, try to find Taleah's main point.

Murphy's Law

Murphy's Law: If something can go wrong, it will. I have always been familiar with the concept of this law, but never from actual experience. It was not until the summer before my first year in college that different events taught me about Murphy's Law.   1

The first event was when my father informed me that on our family trip to Winnipeg we would be using my car. Since I had made previous plans I was not bubbling with enthusiasm. I had 14 "fun-filled" days in Winnipeg. And to top it all off, on the way home, my car decided to have a breakdown between two northern Ontario towns. Northern Ontario has a really long stretch of highway that driver's hate. People feel like they're on it forever. Luckily, my father had CAA, our delay was short.   2

This particular instance had familiarized me with Murphy's Law, and for the remainder of the summer, I began to notice it every time I turned around. At first it was little things like catching the flu just hours before a date. After a while, it turned into bigger hussles, like getting flat tires on the way to job interviews. I prayed my luck would take a turn for the better rather then the worse.   3

Murphy showed up again on August 29, when I left my home town to travel to my new school. Having to entrust my 397-mile journey to an old CAA map, I pictured getting sidetracked onto an out-of-the-way farm road leading me to an uncharted town. But I did not get lost until arriving at the infamous "traffic circle" in my new home town. Realizing my highway map was of know use in town, I frantically looked around and happened to catch a glimpse of the "I ♥ Ti-Cats" bumper sticker plastered on the car in front of me. I said to myself, "Now how many cars could have that sticker?" I convinced myself that I was in luck and that the car in front of me was headed toward campus. I decided to follow it. After arriving in a gruesome alley, which accurately resembled the pictures I had seen of a Third World country, I came to the conclusion the car was not headed toward campus but probably to the local chicken fights. Pulling in to the nearest Petro-Can station, directions were given to me. Three service stations later, their I was, at my new dorm on campus. Once again, I knew that Murphy's Law had decided to play with me.   4

I realized Murphy's Law was becoming a permanent part of my life. If something in my life could possibly go wrong, Murphy would be there to make sure of it. I had finally come to the conclusion that Murphy, and I would be friends for life—unless, of course, something went wrong.   5

Discovering How the Essay Works

1. What main idea do you think Taleah is trying to communicate in this essay?

    _____

    Does her thesis communicate this main idea?

    _____

2. How does each of Taleah's examples relate to her main point? List three examples she furnishes, and explain how they are related to her thesis statement. ·

    _____

    _____

3. Knowing that this essay was written for her college writing class, do you think Taleah's audience could identify with these examples? Explain your answer.

    _____

    _____

4. Does Taleah include enough examples to make her point? Explain your answer.

    _____

    _____

5. How are the examples in Taleah's essay arranged? List some of her examples in the order they appear; then identify her method of organization.

    _____   _____

    _____   _____

    _____   _____

    Method of Organization:_____

Revising and Editing the Student Essay

This essay is Taleah's first draft, which now needs to be revised and edited. First, apply the Revising Checklist in Chapter 7 to the content of Taleah's draft. When you are satisfied that her ideas are fully developed and well organized, use the Editing Checklist in Chapter 8 to correct her grammar and mechanics errors. Answer the questions below. Then write your suggested changes directly on Taleah's draft.

Revision Questions

Thesis Statement

1. Put brackets around the last sentence in Taleah's introduction. Does it introduce her main point? Does it include her opinion about that point?

   _____

2. Rewrite Taleah's thesis statement if necessary so that it states her main point and her opinion about that point.

   _____

   _____

Basic Elements

1. Give Taleah's essay an alternate title.

   _____

2. Rewrite Taleah's introduction so that it captures the readers' attention and builds up to the thesis statement at the end of the paragraph.

   _____

   _____

   _____

3. Does each of Taleah's body paragraphs deal with only one topic?

   _____

4. Rewrite Taleah's conclusion, using at least one suggestion from Part I.

_____

_____

_____

Development

1. Write out Taleah's thesis statement (revised, if necessary), and list her three topic sentences below it.

   Thesis statement: _____

   _____

   Topic 1: _____

   _____

   Topic 2: _____

   _____

   Topic 3: _____

   _____

2. Do Taleah's topics adequately support her thesis statement?

   _____

3. Does each body paragraph have a focused topic sentence?

   _____

4. Are Taleah's examples specific?

   _____

   Add another, more specific, detail to one of the examples in her essay.

5. Does she offer enough examples to make her point?

   _____

   Add at least one new example to strengthen Taleah's essay.

Unity

1. Read each of Taleah's topic sentences, keeping her thesis statement (revised, if necessary) in mind. Do they go together?

   _____

2. Revise them if necessary so they are directly related.

3. Drop or rewrite the two sentences in paragraph 2 that are not directly related to their topic sentence.

Organization

1. Read Taleah's essay again to see if all the paragraphs are arranged logically.

2. Move any paragraphs that are out of order.

3. Look closely at Taleah's body paragraphs to see if all her sentences are arranged logically within paragraphs.

4. Move any sentences that are out of order.

Coherence

1. Circle five transitions, repetitions, synonyms, or pronouns Taleah uses.

2. Explain how two of these make Taleah's essay easier to read.

   _____

   _____

For a list of transitions, see pages 70–71.

For a list of pronouns, see pages 381–382.

Now rewrite Taleah's essay with your revisions.

Editing Questions

Sentences

Subjects and Verbs

1. Underline the subjects once and verbs twice in paragraph 2 of your revision of Taleah's essay. Remember that sentences can have more than one subject–verb set.

2. Does each one of Taleah's sentences have at least one subject and verb that can stand alone?

   _____

3. Did you find and correct Taleah's run-on sentence? If not, find and correct it now.

For help with subjects and verbs, see Chapter 32.

For help with run-ons, see Chapter 34.

Subject–Verb Agreement

For help with subject–verb agreement, see Chapter 36.

1. Read aloud the subjects and verbs you underlined in your revision of Taleah's essay.

2. Correct any subjects and verbs that do not agree.

Pronoun Agreement

For help with pronoun agreement, see Chapter 39.

1. Find any pronouns in your revision of Taleah's essay that do not agree with their nouns.

2. Correct any pronouns that do not agree with their nouns.

Modifiers

For help with modifier errors, see Chapter 42.

1. Find any modifiers in your revision of Taleah's essay that are not as close as possible to the words they modify.

2. Did you find and correct her dangling modifier? If not, find and correct it now.

Punctuation and Mechanics

Punctuation

For help with punctuation, see Chapters 43–46.

1. Read over your revision of Taleah's essay to find any errors in punctuation.

2. Find the run-on sentence you revised, and make sure it is punctuated correctly.

3. Did you find and correct Taleah's two comma errors?

Mechanics

For help with capitalization, see Chapter 47.

1. Read your revision of Taleah's essay for any errors in capitalization.

2. Be sure to check Taleah's capitalization in the run-on sentence you revised.

Word Choice and Spelling

Word Choice

For help with confused words, see Chapter 53.

1. Find any words used incorrectly in your revision of Taleah's essay.

2. Did you find and correct the three confused words in Taleah's essay? If not, find and correct them now.

Spelling

For help with spelling, see Chapter 54.

1. Use spell-check and a dictionary to check the spelling in your revision of Taleah's essay.

2. Correct any misspelled words.

Now rewrite Taleah's essay again with your editing corrections.

WORKING WITH YOUR OWN ESSAY

Returning to the illustration you wrote earlier in this chapter, revise and edit your own writing. The checklists in Chapters 7 and 8 will help you apply what you have learned to your essay.

PRACTISING ILLUSTRATION

Reading Suggestions

In Chapter 25, you will find two essays that use examples to make their point: "I Just Wanna Be Average" by Mike Rose gives examples from his life to show the importance to him of being average, and "Wild Weather" by Chris Wood uses examples to talk about global "wettening." You might want to read these selections before writing another illustration essay. As you read, notice how the writers use examples to support and advance their ideas.

Writing Workshop

Guidelines for Writing an Illustration Essay

1. State your main point in the last sentence of your introduction.
2. Choose examples that are relevant to your point.
3. Choose examples that your readers can identify with.
4. Use enough examples to make your point.
5. Organize your examples so as to make your point in the clearest, strongest way.

1. Identify some common themes in the news photo on page 139. Then come up with a thesis statement that explains one of the themes. Write an essay to support your thesis statement that is developed with relevant examples from the picture and from your own experience.

2. Share with your classmates your opinion on salary caps for professional athletes or funding for non-professional Olympic athletes. Use examples in your body paragraphs to support your main point.

3. Why do you think Canadians are interested in exercise and weight loss? What actions illustrate your attitude? Use examples or illustrations to explain your observations on the current interest in health and weight.

4. Create your own illustration assignment (with the help of your instructor), and write a response to it.

Revising Workshop

Small Group Activity (5–10 minutes per writer)   Working in groups of three or four, each person should read his or her illustration essay to the other members of the group. Those listening should record their reactions on a copy of the Peer Evaluation Form in Appendix 1A. After your group goes through this process, give your evaluation forms to the appropriate writers so that each writer has two or three peer comment sheets to use in revising.

Paired Activity (5 minutes per writer)   Using the completed Peer Evaluation Forms, work in pairs to decide what you should revise in your essay. If time allows, rewrite some of your sentences, and have your partner look at them.

Individual Activity   Rewrite your paper, using the revising feedback you received from other students.

Editing Workshop

Paired Activity (5–10 minutes per writer)   Swap papers with a classmate, and use the editing portion of your Peer Evaluation Form (Appendix 1B) to identify as many grammar, punctuation, mechanics, and spelling errors as you can. If time allows, correct some of your errors, and have your partner look at them. Record your grammar, punctuation, and mechanics errors in the Error Log (Appendix 3) and your spelling errors in the Spelling Log (Appendix 4).

Individual Activity   Rewrite your paper again, using the editing feedback you received from other students.

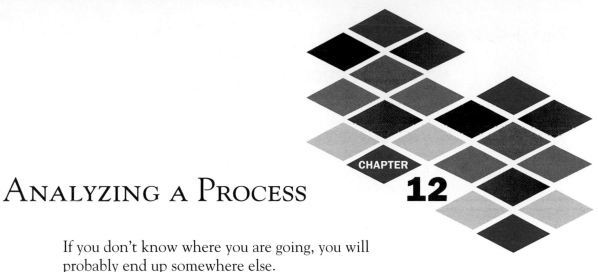

ANALYZING A PROCESS

CHAPTER 12

If you don't know where you are going, you will probably end up somewhere else.

—LAURENCE PETER

Process analysis satisfies our natural desire for basic information—how to be more assertive, how to invest in the stock market, how to eat more healthfully, or how to help your child do a better job in school.

Process analysis writing, more than other types of writing, helps you understand the world around you and improve yourself—in your personal life, in school, and in the workplace. Consider the following situations:

People who are coming to visit you from out of town e-mail you for directions to your house.

A student needs to write a paper on how to improve employee morale for a course in business management.

A student needs to explain how to be a good listener for the midterm exam in speech communication.

The owner of an apartment building posts a notice in the laundry room explaining how to operate the new washers and dryers.

The manager of a shoe store has to write a memo reminding employees about the correct procedure for taking returns.

Process analysis is a form of explaining. Process analysis essays fall into one of two main types—giving directions or giving information. The first type, giving directions, tells *how to do something*, such as how to write a research paper or change the oil in your car. The second type, giving information, analyzes *how something works*, such as satellite TV or a bread machine, or *how something happened*, such as how the Soviet Union broke into separate nations. In each case, the explanation starts at the beginning and moves step by step, usually in chronological order, to the end result. Process analysis can be about something mental (how to solve a math problem) or something physical (how to pitch a tent).

WRITING A PROCESS ANALYSIS ESSAY

In "Dare to Change Your Job and Your Life in 7 Steps," Carole Kanchier explains how to take the right risks in order to change jobs and improve your life. In other words, the essay demonstrates the first type of process analysis: how to do something. Kanchier tells you what to do first, then second, and so on until reaching the desired outcome—success in a job you like. Have you ever held a job that you intensely disliked? Were you able to quit? Why or why not? Do you know what career you want to follow? What steps are you taking to prepare for it?

DARE TO CHANGE YOUR JOB AND YOUR LIFE IN 7 STEPS

by Carole Kanchier

1   Small, dark-haired, attractive, and warm, Melissa belies her 44 years. In a sharp gray suit and becoming blouse, she projects a professional yet approachable image. She is now director of training and development for a large retail outlet—and loves it.

2   "I feel good about myself," she says, "and at the end of the day, I have lots of energy left over." Melissa feels content because she believes she is doing something worthwhile. Her new position gives her life meaning and purpose. But getting there wasn't easy.

3   First a flight attendant, then a high school English teacher, then a manager in a retail store, Melissa stumbled about from what was for her one dead-end job to another. How did she finally find a meaningful, fulfilling, well-paid career? And how did she do what so many of us fail to do—dare to change?

4   A career change can take months or even years of soul-searching—10 months in Melissa's case. You need to know the steps, how to master the troublesome feelings that accompany change, where the possible dangers lie, and how to maximize your gains while minimizing your losses. While creating a life worth living isn't easy, Melissa and millions of others have shown that anything is possible.

5   In interviews and surveys with more than 30,000 people over the past 25 years, I have identified seven steps that are key to a successful career and life shift.

1. Become AWARE of Negative Feelings

6   Your body and mind may be sending you messages about your job satisfaction. The messages may be physical—lingering colds, flu or headaches—or verbal—"23 minutes till lunch!" or "One more day till Friday!"

7   Perhaps you've been working for several years in your job, and it appears to be going well. You've had steady promotions, praise from superiors,

and admiration from colleagues. Then one day you get a queasy feeling that something is lacking. But what? You run the film of your life in reverse but you can't figure it out. These feelings may persist for months or even years, depending on your ability to tolerate them, but, sooner or later, you have to admit you have a problem.

2. DEFINE the Problem

A good written definition of your problem can help to put you on the road toward change.   8

First, ask yourself, "What's making me feel this way? What is it about my situation that is unpleasant? Does this job help me reach my goals?" If not, why?   9

Next, describe any barriers that may be blocking you from making a move—perhaps fear of change; fear of losing a secure income, pension or other benefits; fear that the change will interfere with your relationships; or fear that you'll lose power or status.   10

Fear is the result of conditioning, and because it is learned, it can be unlearned. Reprogram your old attitudes and beliefs with new ones by learning and practicing specific ways to overcome the fears blocking your path toward change. Think of FEAR as an acronym for "False Expectations Appear Real." Don't spend time worrying about what might happen. Focus on the now.   11

3. Listen to AMBIVALENCE

Milton, a rehabilitation counselor, was approached by a prospective partner to start an executive recruitment agency. For weeks before making the move, he went straight to bed immediately after dinner and pulled the sheets up over his head. He tried to make light of this behavior, but he had undertaken many risks before and had never felt this way about them.   12

His underlying fears were prophetic. He later discovered that the hardsell, aggressive style required for executive recruiting was not for him. The difference in basic values between Milton and his partner proved such a handicap that, within five months, the two parted ways.   13

The decision to change can provoke mixed feelings. A certain amount of ambivalence is natural. Inner emotional preparation—weighing losses as well as gains, fears as well as hopes—is a necessary prerequisite for successful risk taking.   14

But if the prospect of undertaking a change is so great that your stomach is churning, you can't sleep, you have constant headaches, or you feel you're developing an ulcer, your body, in its wisdom, is telling you to forgo the risk.   15

4. PREPARE for Risk

The key to avoiding potential potholes is to set tentative career goals before you explore new roads. Goals force you to focus on what you really   16 want. Years from now, as you review your life, what would you regret not having done?

17   Fantasize about the ultimate goal, your shining star. If you could do anything in the world, what would it be? Write all of your ideas or fantasies in a notebook. Include everything you want to do, be, and have. The sky is the limit. Once you know what you want, you'll be more willing to take the risks necessary to achieve it.

18   Choosing a satisfying career and lifestyle also requires a basic understanding of yourself. A variety of exercises can help. To identify your strengths, for example, list some of the successes you've had—say, substituting for your son's soccer coach. Next to each success, identify what gave you the positive feelings. Did you contribute to the team's first win of the season?

19   Also list the skills and abilities you used to bring about that success. Were you well organized and adept at working with parents? Finally, decide how your interests, needs, accomplishments, and other personal strengths add up. What pattern do they form?

20   Self-exploration is just part of the process. You also need to take a careful look at your current situation, as well as the available alternatives. Some popular reference tools, available at your local library, can help. Check out the *Occupational Handbook*, the *Dictionary of Occupational Titles*, and the *Encyclopedia of Careers and Work Issues*. The Internet also offers excellent sites for exploring general occupational fields, job descriptions, and educational opportunities.

5. NARROW Your Options

21   Successful career management hinges on finding a position that's compatible with your personal qualities and goals. Do you have the necessary intelligence and skills to do the work? Can you afford the training required for the job? Might your shortcomings—health, vision, size, or strength, for example—pose a problem?

22   To help narrow your options, draw a series of vertical and horizontal lines so that your paper is divided into squares. Across the top of the page, list the most important elements of your ideal job: income, responsibility, public image, creativity, challenge, and so on (one in each square). Down the left side of the page, list each occupational option you're considering.

23   Next, for each alternative, place a −1 in the appropriate box if that job option doesn't satisfy the criterion listed at the top of the page. If the criterion is met, but not as much as you'd like, record a 0. If the criterion is well met, record a +1. Add the points for each job option and place them in a column labeled "total" at the far right. The job with the highest score meets the greatest number of criteria that you have deemed important.

6. Take ACTION

Once you've determined your occupational goal, take steps to realize it. 24
You'll need a well-planned campaign to market yourself for the job, establish your own business, or return to school.

Stay focused on your goals, and believe you will achieve them. View 25
failures along the way as learning experiences—detours that might offer
an unexpected dividend.

7. EVALUATE the Decision

When you have worked hard at making a decision, take the time not 26
just to enjoy the outcome, but to evaluate it. Ask yourself:

- Do I feel good about the move?
- What other gains did I derive from the move? What did I lose?
- What factors contributed to the success of my move?
- If I could do it all over again, what would I do differently?
- Who was most helpful in the process? Who let me down?

Evaluation is a continuous process. Assess your needs, goals, and job 27
satisfaction periodically to determine if your developing personality fits
your position and lifestyle. Don't wait for a crisis to clear your vision.

There really is no substitute for risk as a way to grow. Knowing you have 28
honestly faced the painful struggle and accepted the trade-offs, and yet
proceeded in spite of them, is extremely gratifying.

Melissa learned that the tremendous investment of energy a successful 29
job search demands is exactly what enables people to look back and say,
"Win, lose, or draw, I gave it my everything." Being able to say with satisfaction that you risked all for a dream may be the biggest prize of all.

To remain fulfilled, however, you'll need to risk again and again until 30
you've created a life in which you feel comfortable being yourself, without
apology or pretense—a life in which you can continue to have choices.

 PREPARING TO WRITE YOUR OWN PROCESS ANALYSIS

Think of some advice that you would like to give to a friend or classmate—for example, how to survive your first year of college, how to
find the partner of your dreams, how to buy a used car, or how to find
good day care for your child. Use one or more of the prewriting
strategies you learned in Chapter 2 to generate ideas about advice
you have for others.

How to Write a Process Analysis Essay

Both types of process analysis call for careful step-by-step thinking, but especially the first—how to do something. If you leave out even one detail, you may confuse your reader or even endanger someone's life. If, for example, you forget to tell a patient who is coming to a doctor's office for some tests that she shouldn't eat after midnight and she has breakfast, the test results will not be accurate, and a serious medical condition might go unnoticed.

Good process analysis of the second type—how something works or how something happened—can help your reader see a product or an event in a totally new light. Someone looking at a product that is already assembled or at a completed event has no way of knowing how it got to the final stage without an explanation. Good process analysis gives the reader a new way of seeing something. The following guidelines will help you write clear and complete process analysis essays.

1. *State in the thesis statement what the reader should be able to do or understand by the end of the essay.* Stating the end result at the beginning, in the thesis statement, gives your reader a road map for what follows. The thesis statement in a process essay should also state the number of steps or stages in the process. For example, someone giving directions might start by saying, "It's easy to get to the library from here with just four turns." Even if a process involves many separate steps, you should divide the list into a few manageable groups: "Most experts agree that there are four stages in overcoming an addiction." Stating the end result and the number of steps or stages in the thesis statement helps the reader follow your explanation. These statements set up the tasks.

   Carole Kanchier's thesis statement, which appears in paragraph 5, at the end of her introduction, tells her readers exactly what they will be able to do by the end of her article: make "a successful career and life shift." She also tells them how many steps are involved—seven. In this way, she provides a very clear road map for reading her essay.

2. *Know your audience.* In a process analysis essay, more than in others, the success of your essay depends on how well you know your audience. Knowing your audience helps you decide how much detail to include, how many examples to add, and which terms to define. Also keep in mind that your readers won't be able to ask you questions, so if they can't follow your explanation, they will become confused and frustrated. Whoever your audience is, explaining clearly is essential.

   Kanchier's essay was first published in *Psychology Today,* which is read mostly by educated adults. The author's audience seems to be working adults of any age who are unhappy in their jobs. Kanchier addresses them in a very businesslike way; she doesn't talk down. Knowing that being unhappy in a job is very discouraging, she strives for an upbeat "you can do it" tone.

3. ***Explain the process clearly in the body of your essay.*** By the end of a how-to essay, the reader should be able to perform the activity. By the end of a how-something-works essay, the reader should understand what is going on behind the scenes, and by the end of a how-something-happened essay, the reader should understand more about a specific event.

   In writing the body paragraphs of a process essay, pay special attention to transitions. Use transitions such as *first, next, then, after that,* and *finally* to guide your reader through the process from beginning to end.

   Since Kanchier's process has seven parts, she numbers each step. This is a good idea if a process is complicated. If you are writing about a process with only three or four steps, you can use transitions to indicate to your readers where you are in the process.

4. ***Organize your material logically.*** Most process analysis essays are organized chronologically or according to a time sequence. The explanation starts at one point and progresses through time to the final point. If a process is complicated, figure out the most logical organization for the process you are explaining. For instance, playing the guitar involves pressing the strings with the fingers of one hand and strumming with the other hand. You might therefore explain each part of the process separately and then explain how the hands work together to make music.

   Kanchier's essay is organized chronologically. She moves from recognizing the problem to taking action and then to evaluating the action. To help readers follow along smoothly, she numbers the steps and uses transitions such as *first, next,* and *then.*

5. ***End your essay by considering the process as a whole.*** Don't just stop after you have explained the last step of a process. Instead, in the conclusion, look at the process as a whole. There are many ways to do this. You might state why knowing about this process is important: Knowing how to perform CPR (cardiopulmonary resuscitation) can save a life; knowing how your car runs might save you money in repair bills. Or you might review your introduction, summarize the steps of the process, call for action, or end with a fitting quotation. Whatever your method, leave your reader feeling that your essay has reached a natural close.

   Kanchier concludes by returning to her introduction. She brings back Melissa, the person from the opening example, to emphasize the rewards of taking risks. She ends her essay by saying that a satisfying life requires taking risks over and over again.

WRITING YOUR OWN PROCESS ANALYSIS ESSAY

Look at the prewriting you did earlier on the topic of giving advice to a friend or classmate. If your directions involve many steps, divide them into three groups. Come up with a thesis statement that states the end result of the process and tells how many steps or stages are involved. Then write the first draft of your essay by following the guidelines for writing a process analysis essay. Make sure you have an introduction and a conclusion.

WORKING WITH A STUDENT ESSAY

A student writer named Emily Bliss wrote the following essay about procrastination. See if you can follow her steps as you read her first draft.

You Too Can Procrastinate

1   My name is Emily, and I am a procrastinator. But I have discovered over the years that procrastination is not all bad. Especially when I have to write. At my college, the English instructors requires rough drafts. I have somehow mastered the art of procrastinating but still meeting deadlines with my papers. So I have perfected a successful plan for procrastinating that I now want to share with the world.

2   You will know the dreaded day you have to write has arrived when you wake up with a start. This day is different from the rest. You actually have to do something about your paper today. But whatever you do, resist the temptation to sit down and write early in the day by following two more steps. First (step 1), to avoid sitting down to write, you can clean, take a bike ride, do the laundry, rearrange the furniture, dust the light bulbs, and so on. But don't write. Then (step 2), when you finally think you are ready to start writing, call a friend. Talk about anything but your paper for about 15 or 20 minutes. This final delay is what creates the tension that a real procrastinator needs to do his or her best work.

3   Whether you want to or not, you will naturally think about the assignment from the moment you get it. If you have two weeks or two months, you will spend most quiet moments haunted by your paper topic. No matter what you do, your paper topic will be bouncing around in your head giving you headaches, making you worry, wanting attention. But that's OK. Don't give in and write. Ignore it until the day before it is due.

4   At this point, your third step is to prepare your immediate environment for work. You need to get ready for serious business. Sharpen your pencils, and lay them in a row. Get out the white paper if you can't think on yellow, or get out the yellow paper if you can't think on white. Go to the kitchen for snacks. Whether or not you actually drink or eat these item's is irrelevant—as long as they are by your side. You can't be distracted if

you don't have them next to you. My stomach growls really loudly when I'm hungry. Some sort of bread usually takes away the hunger pangs. Step 4 is to sit back in your chair and stare at the computer while you think long and hard about your paper. Fifth, brainstorm, list, or cluster your ideas on the coloured paper of your choice. Sixth, put all your procrastination strategies aside. Its finally time to write.

If you follow these six simple steps, you too can become a master procrastinator. You can perform your very own procrastinating ritual and still get your first draft in on time. If you go through the same ritual every time you write. You can perfect it and get your own system for writing essays down to a science. The trick is just to make sure you start writing before you has to join Procrastinators Anonymous.   5

Discovering How the Essay Works

1. What should the reader be able to do by the end of this essay?

     _____

2. Who do you think Emily's audience is? Does she meet their needs?

     _____

     _____

3. Do you understand how to procrastinate and still meet your deadlines? If so, list the six steps of this process.

     Step 1: _____

     Step 2: _____

     Step 3: _____

     Step 4: _____

     Step 5: _____

     Step 6: _____

     If you do not understand, what else do you need to know?

     _____

4. Are the details in the essay organized logically? Is this order effective for what the author is trying to say? Why or why not?

     _____

     _____

     _____

5. Does the essay conclude by considering the process as a whole? Explain your answer.

_____

_____

_____

Revising and Editing the Student Essay

This essay is Emily's first draft, which now needs to be revised and edited. First, apply the Revising Checklist in Chapter 7 (pages 52–53) the content of Emily's draft. When you are satisfied that her ideas are fully developed and well organized, use the Editing Checklist in Chapter 8 (page 80) to correct her grammar and mechanics errors. Answer the questions below. Then write your suggested changes directly on Emily's draft.

Revision Questions

Thesis Statement

1. Put brackets around the last sentence in Emily's introduction. Does it state her purpose?

_____

2. Rewrite Emily's thesis statement if necessary so that it introduces her process and states her purpose.

_____

_____

Basic Elements

1. Give Emily's essay an alternate title.

_____

2. Rewrite Emily's introduction so that it captures the reader's attention and builds up to the thesis statement at the end of the introduction.

_____

_____

_____

3. Does each of Emily's body paragraphs deal with only one topic?

    _____

4. Rewrite Emily's conclusion, using at least one suggestion from Part I.

    _____

    _____

    _____

Development

1. Write out Emily's thesis statement (revised, if necessary), and list her three topic sentences below it.

    Thesis statement: _____

    _____

      Topic 1: _____

      _____

      Topic 2: _____

      _____

      Topic 3: _____

      _____

2. Do Emily's topics adequately support her thesis statement?

    _____

3. Do Emily's details in the essay explain the process step by step?

    _____

4. Where do you need more information?

    _____

5. Add at least two new details to make the steps clearer.

Unity

1. Read each of Emily's topic sentences with her thesis statement (revised, if necessary) in mind. Do they go together?

   _____

2. Revise them if necessary so they are directly related.

3. Drop or rewrite the two sentences in paragraph 4 that are not directly related to their topic sentence.

Organization

1. Read Emily's essay again to see if all the paragraphs are arranged logically. Look at your list of steps in response to question 3 after Emily's essay (page 149).

2. Reverse the two paragraphs that are out of order.

3. Look closely at Emily's body paragraphs to see if all her sentences are arranged logically within paragraphs.

4. Move any sentences that are out of order.

Coherence

For a list of transitions, see pages 70–71.

1. Circle five transitions Emily uses.

2. Explain how two of these make Emily's essay easier to read.

   _____

   _____

   _____

Now rewrite Emily's essay with your revisions.

Editing Questions

Sentences

Subjects and Verbs

For help with subjects and verbs, see Chapter 32.

1. Underline the subjects once and verbs twice in paragraphs 1 and 5 of your revision of Emily's essay. Remember that sentences can have more than one subject–verb set.

2. Does each sentence have at least one subject and verb that can stand alone?

   _____

For help with fragments, see Chapter 33.

3. Did you find and correct Emily's two fragments? If not, find and correct them now.

Subject–Verb Agreement

1. Read aloud the subjects and verbs you underlined in your revision of Emily's essay.

2. Did you find and correct the two subjects and verbs that do not agree? If not, find and correct them now.

For help with subject–verb agreement, see Chapter 36.

Pronoun Agreement

1. Find any pronouns in your revision of Emily's essay that do not agree with their nouns.

2. Correct any pronouns that do not agree with their nouns.

For help with pronoun agreement, see Chapter 39.

Modifiers

1. Find any modifiers in your revision of Emily's essay that are not as close as possible to the words they modify.

2. Rewrite sentences if necessary so that modifiers are as close as possible to the words they modify.

For help with modifier errors, see Chapter 42.

Punctuation and Mechanics

Punctuation

1. Read your revision of Emily's essay for any errors in punctuation.

2. Find the two fragments you revised, and make sure they are punctuated correctly.

3. Did you find and correct Emily's two apostrophe errors? If not, find and correct them now.

For help with punctuation, see Chapters 43–46.

Mechanics

1. Read your revision of Emily's essay for any errors in capitalization.

2. Be sure to check Emily's capitalization in the fragments you revised.

For help with capitalization, see Chapter 47.

Word Choice and Spelling

Word Choice

1. Find any words used incorrectly in your revision of Emily's essay.

2. Correct any errors you find.

For help with confused words, see Chapter 53.

Spelling

1. Use spell-check or a dictionary to check the spelling in your revision of Emily's essay.

2. Correct any misspelled words.

For help with spelling, see Chapter 54.

Now rewrite Emily's essay again with your editing corrections.

WORKING WITH YOUR OWN ESSAY

Returning to the process analysis you wrote earlier in this chapter, revise and edit your own writing. The checklists in Chapters 7 and 8 will help you apply what you have learned to your essay.

PRACTISING PROCESS ANALYSIS

Reading Suggestions

In Chapter 26, you will find two essays that illustrate good process analysis writing: "Don't Be Cruel" by Dr. Roger Flax explains how to criticize people without humiliating them, and "Why We Have a Moon" by David Levy explains the role of the moon in relation to the earth. You might want to read these selections before writing another process analysis essay. As you read, notice how the writers explain every step of the process carefully and completely.

Writing Workshop

Guidelines for Writing a Process Analysis Essay

1. State in the thesis statement what the reader should be able to do or understand by the end of the essay.
2. Know your audience.
3. Explain the process clearly in the body of your essay.
4. Organize your material logically.
5. End your essay by considering the process as a whole.

1. Place yourself in a scene similar to the one opposite, and write a process analysis essay explaining something that you find as interesting as this person finds this activity. Be sure to cover all steps or stages of the process you are discussing.

2. Choose an appliance or a piece of equipment that you understand well, and write a process analysis essay explaining how it works. Don't identify the item in your essay. Then see if the class members can guess what device you are talking about.

3. Research the history of your college or university, and write an essay explaining its background to prospective students. Be sure to give a focus to your study and decide on a purpose before you begin writing.

4. Write your own process analysis assignment (with the help of your instructor), and write a response to it.

Revising Workshop

Small Group Activity (5–10 minutes per writer) In groups of three or four, each person should read his or her process analysis essay to the other members of the group. Those listening should record their reactions on a copy of the Peer Evaluation Form (Appendix 1A). After your group goes through this process, give your evaluation forms to the appropriate writers so that each writer has two or three peer comment sheets for revising.

Paired Activity (5 minutes per writer) Using the completed Peer Evaluation Forms, work in pairs to decide what you should revise in your essay. If time allows, rewrite some of your sentences, and have your partner look at them.

Individual Activity Rewrite your paper, using the revising feedback you received from other students.

Editing Workshop

Paired Activity (5–10 minutes per writer) Swap papers with a classmate, and use the editing portion of your Peer Evaluation Form (Appendix 1B) to identify as many grammar, punctuation, mechanics, and spelling errors as you can. If time allows, correct some of your errors, and have your partner look at them. Record your grammar, punctuation, and mechanics errors in the Error Log (Appendix 3) and your spelling errors in the Spelling Log (Appendix 4).

Individual Activity Rewrite your paper again, using the editing feedback you received from other students.

13

COMPARING AND CONTRASTING

The difference between the right word and the almost-right word is really a large matter—'tis the difference between the lightning-bug and the lightning.

—MARK TWAIN

Comparison and contrast are at the heart of our democratic society. Our competitive natures lead us to compare our lives to those of others so we can try to better ourselves. Even if we simply attempt to improve on our "personal best," comparison and contrast keep us striving for more. In school, we learn about different writers, different cultures, different musical instruments, and different political platforms by comparing them to one another. And every day we make decisions based on comparisons of one kind or another—which clothes to wear, which person to date, which apartment to rent, which job to take. Comparisons help us establish a frame of reference and figure out where we fit into the larger world around us.

On another level, comparison and contrast are also part of our writing. They play an important role in our personal lives, in our college courses, and in the workplace, as in the following situations:

Someone looking for a new car does comparison shopping on the Internet.

A student doing a report in a nursing course compares and contrasts traditional and alternative approaches to medical care.

A student compares and contrasts two cultures for an exam in anthropology.

An insurance agent prepares a report for a client that compares and contrasts several different insurance policies.

A travel agent compares and contrasts two vacation packages for a client.

Comparison and contrast help us understand one subject by putting it next to another. When we *compare,* we look for similarities, and when we *contrast,* we look for differences. Nearly always, however, comparison and contrast are part of the same process. For this reason, we often use the word *compare* to refer to both techniques.

WRITING A COMPARISON/CONTRAST ESSAY

In the essay "D'oh! An Analysis of the Medical Care Provided to the Family of Homer J. Simpson," Robert Patterson and Charles Weijer compare and contrast two doctors from the television show *The Simpsons* to make a tongue-in-cheek case for the likely direction of medical care in Canada. What problems do you see as a consumer of medical care in Canada? Do the authors make a good case, even though they are using amusing examples?

D'OH! AN ANALYSIS OF THE MEDICAL CARE PROVIDED TO THE FAMILY OF HOMER J. SIMPSON
by Robert Patterson and Charles Weijer

These are hard times for physicians. Governments blame doctors for 1
spiralling health care costs as they slash spending. Ethicists decry medical paternalism. Our patients—sorry, our clients—demand to be treated like consumers. And political correctness has changed the way we speak. It's enough to give your average doctor an identity crisis. Who are we? Who should we aspire to be?

Working on the premise that life imitates art, we searched for and found 2
a role model for physicians to follow in these difficult times. We found him in a long-running cartoon series, *The Simpsons*, and spent many hard hours in front of the television, collecting and collating data for analysis. We hope readers will give our conclusions the attention they deserve.

In the quiet town of Springfield,[1] noted for its substandard nuclear 3
power plant and eccentric citizenry, Drs. Julius Hibbert and Nick Riviera frequently come in contact with Springfield's everyman, Homer J. Simpson, and his family. Homer, who works at the power plant, is known for his love of donuts and Duff's beer.

Like the forces of good and evil battling for the soul of medicine itself, 4
these two physicians are polar opposites. Julius Hibbert is an experienced family physician with a pleasant, easygoing manner, while Nick Riviera is an ill-trained upstart who is more interested in money than medicine. Knowing that appearances can be deceiving (and first impressions rarely correct), we explored this question: Which of these two physicians should Canada's future physicians emulate?

We briefly entertained Hibbert as a potential role model. He is a trusted 5
family physician who provides care not only to Homer but also to his spouse Marge and their three children: Bart, Lisa and Maggie. He delivered all of the children and has weathered many a Simpson medical crisis, from Bart's broken leg to Lisa's primary depression.

6   Generally the quality of care he provides is solid, although there was an incident when he accidentally left the keys to his Porsche inside a patient. We decided to ignore this incident, since such a mishap can befall any physician.

7   Hibbert has diagnostic acumen of Oslerian proportions. He uses this regularly to identify a variety of baffling conditions, from Marge's alopecia areata to Homer's unique form of hydrocephalus.

8   "Don't worry, it's quite beneficial," he told Homer about the latter condition. "Your brain is cushioned by a layer of fluid one-eighth of an inch thicker than normal. It's almost as if you're wearing a football helmet inside your own head. Why, I could wallop you all day with this surgical 2-by-4, without ever knocking you down."[2]

9   Another positive trait is Hibbert's sense of humour, which he uses to put patients and their families at ease. When Homer was critically injured and rushed to hospital after opening a can of beer that spent some time in a paint mixer thanks to Bart, Hibbert's levity helped relieve an otherwise tense situation.

10   "Mrs. Simpson, I'm afraid your husband is dead," he said.

11   "Oh my god!" Marge responded.

12   "April Fools!"

13   Deeper analysis, however, reveals that Hibbert is no Semmelweiss. He treats the health care system like his personal cash cow by taking time to talk to his patients and distributing lollipops to children. No wonder the U.S. system is so expensive. Worse yet, he stocks his office with patient education materials that either contain value judgements or are poorly written.

14   When Homer first courted his bride-to-be, Hibbert gave a pamphlet entitled *So You've Ruined Your Life* to a pregnant but unmarried Marge. Fair enough. But later on, when Homer was poisoned after eating an incorrectly prepared blowfish at a Japanese restaurant, Hibbert handed him another brochure, *So You're Going to Die*. By giving away the conclusion in the title, Hibbert ruined the surprise ending. What fun is that?

15   Another gross violation of ethics occurred when Bart stuck various objects to his skin with Krazy Glue. In a scene reminiscent of the Spanish Inquisition, Dr. Hibbert showed him the instruments of surgery, thereby frightening the poor youngster so badly that he began to sweat, causing the objects to fall off.

16   Obviously, informed consent and truth-telling mean little or nothing to this medical Machiavelli. Any ethicist worth her salt would flail him for such an act of unbridled paternalism. Perhaps worst of all, Hibbert shows about as much sensitivity to politically correct language as Howard Stern, as demonstrated by this conversation with Lisa.

17   "Yes, I remember Bart's birth well," he said. "You don't forget a thing like Siamese twins!" "I believe they prefer to be called 'conjoined twins,' " Lisa replied.

18   "And hillbillies prefer to be called 'sons of the soil,' " Hibbert responded, "but it ain't gonna happen."

19   No, the true medical hero for whom we search is Julius Hibbert's foil, the enterprising Dr. Nick Riviera, an international medical graduate who at-

tended the Club Med School. He practises with an enthusiasm that is matched only by his showmanship. Unfortunately, this has led to 160 complaints from Springfield's narrow-minded Malpractice Committee, but artists like Riviera are rarely understood in their time. Dr. Nick, as he is known, may be a tad weak on anatomy. "What the hell is that?" he asked after making the incision for Homer's coronary artery bypass. However, he does possess all the requisite traits for the doctor of tomorrow: he is resource conscious and he gives the customer what she wants.

Ever resourceful, Dr. Nick finds innovative new uses for underutilized medical materials, such as cadavers. By placing several of them in his vehicle, he can drive in the car-pool lane and get to work more quickly. This commendable behaviour is also environmentally conscious.   20

And he's no shill for the medical establishment. Knowing that physicians' fees are the real cause of the health care funding crisis, Dr. Nick produced a TV ad in which he offered to do any surgical procedure for just $129.95 (Can$193.95 at time of writing). Cost-effective and consumer conscious, Riviera would never let quality of care interfere with discount-rate fees.   21

His greatest asset, though, is his willingness—no, his mission—to satisfy every whim and fancy of his patients.   22

He is acutely aware that many patients actually want to be sick and, like Albert Schweitzer, he compassionately helps them. When Bart was run over by a car but appeared unhurt, his parents considered a lawsuit against the driver. Dr. Nick was very eager to assist them. "Your son is a very sick boy," he said. "Just look at these X-rays! You see that dark spot there? Whiplash. And this smudge here that looks like my fingerprint? That's trauma."   23

In another touching moment, Homer discovered that he would qualify for disabled benefits and be able to work at home if he weighed more than 300 pounds, and immediately sought a way to increase his weight. Dr. Nick was there in his time of need.   24

"You'll want to focus on the neglected food groups, such as the whipped group, the congealed group and the choc-o-tastic," he advised. "Be creative. Instead of making sandwiches with bread, use Pop-Tarts. Instead of chewing gum, chew bacon."   25

Being so burdened with his patients' wishes, Riviera often sacrifices his personal needs. Every now and then, however, he manages to think of his own well-being. "The coroner—I'm so sick of that guy," he told Homer as he prepared to perform cardiac surgery on him. "Now if something should go wrong, let's not get the law involved. One hand washes the other."   26

In these turbulent times, we need a hero to guide us into the next millennium. As a profession, we must shed the dark past embodied by Dr. Hibbert—a wasteful, paternalistic and politically incorrect physician. Instead, the physician of the future must cut corners to cut costs, accede to the patient's every whim and always strive to avoid the coroner. All hail Dr. Nick Riviera, the very model of a 21st-century healer.   27

"See you at the operating place!"   28

References

1. It is unclear where Springfield is located. According to *Webster's Ninth New Collegiate Dictionary*, it could be in Illinois, Massachusetts, Ohio, Missouri or Oregon.

2. All quotations taken from our TV screens were checked against those from Richmond, R. (ed). *The Simpsons: A complete guide to our favorite family.* New York: HarperCollins Publishers; 1997.

 PREPARING TO WRITE YOUR OWN COMPARISON/CONTRAST ESSAY

Think of several ways you escape or relieve stress. What do you like about these methods of relaxation? Use one or more of the prewriting strategies you learned in Chapter 2 to generate ideas about these forms of relaxation. Why do they work for you?

How to Write a Comparison/Contrast Essay

To write a comparison/contrast essay, you should consider two items that have something in common, such as cats and dogs (both are family pets) or cars and motorcycles (both are means of transportation). A discussion of cats and motorcycles, for example, would not be very interesting or useful because the two do not have common features. This is the basic rule underlying the following guidelines for writing a good comparison/contrast essay.

1. *Decide what point you want to make with your comparison, and state it in your thesis statement.* A comparison/contrast essay is usually written for one of two purposes: to examine the subjects separately or to show the superiority of one over the other. This purpose should be made clear in your thesis statement.

   In the sample essay, Patterson and Weijer outline the problems facing doctors today and look for a role model for the future in a cartoon: " . . . we searched for and found a role model for physicians to follow in these difficult times." The essay compares two doctors from the television show *The Simpsons* and finds that Dr. Nick Riviera is the superior role model. Of course, because the essay is ironic, the ideal role model is someone who is able to "cut corners to cut costs, accede to the patient's every whim and always strive to avoid the coroner." The authors use their sense of humour to make a point about government expectations of doctors in Canada today.

2. *Choose items to compare and contrast that will make your point most effectively.* Usually, the subjects you plan to compare and contrast have

many similarities and differences. Your task, then, is to look over the ideas you generated in prewriting and choose the best points for making your comparison clearly and strongly.

In their essay, the authors compare their subjects—Dr. Hibbert and Dr. Riviera—on two main points:

- Positive traits
- Faults

3. ***Use as many specific details and examples as possible to expand your comparison.*** The most common way of developing a comparison/contrast essay is to use description and example. Generate as many details and examples as you can for each of your subjects. Try to think of both obvious and not-so-obvious points of comparison.

In "D'oh! An Analysis of the Medical Care Provided to the Family of Homer J. Simpson," Robert Patterson and Charles Weijer rely heavily on examples from the television show. The topics covered are summarized in the final paragraph. Instead of being wasteful, paternalistic and politically incorrect, as they have been accused of being, doctors should cut corners, accede to patients' whims, and strive to avoid litigation. The examples are outrageous: Dr. Riviera makes practical use of cadavers by loading them into his car so he can drive in the car-pool lane and get to work sooner, for example. These specific examples draw the readers into the essay.

4. ***Develop your comparison in a balanced way.*** Having selected the points on which you will compare your two subjects, you are ready to develop the comparison in your body paragraphs. You should make sure that your treatment of each subject is balanced. That means, first, you should cover the same topics for each subject. In other words, you should give equal coverage to both subjects, no matter what your conclusion is. In addition, you should spend the same amount of time on each point. If you describe one of your subjects in detail, you should describe the other in detail as well. In like manner, you should provide a similar number of examples for both subjects. In this way, your readers will feel that you have been fair to both subjects and that you are not presenting a biased discussion that favours one subject over the other.

Patterson and Weijer spend approximately the same amount of time on each subject. They begin by discussing Dr. Hibbert's positive traits (undercutting each one), and then discuss his problems. Dr. Hibbert is greedy, unethical, and politically incorrect. The authors then turn to Dr. Riviera, beginning with his problems and concluding with his positive traits. He satisfies his customers, he is compassionate, and he sacrifices his own personal needs. By reversing the order of the points, the authors appear to indicate that Dr. Riviera is the superior role model.

5. *Organize your essay subject by subject or point by point—or combine the two approaches.* When you are ready to write, you have three choices for organizing a comparison-and-contrast essay: (1) subject by subject (AAA, BBB), (2) point by point (AB, AB, AB), or (3) a combination of the two.

In the subject arrangement, you say everything you have to say about the first subject, A, before you move on to talk about the second subject, B. In a point-by-point arrangement, both subjects are compared on point 1; then both are compared on point 2; and so on through all the points.

To choose which method of organization will be most effective, just use your common sense. If the subjects themselves are the most interesting part of your essay, use the subject pattern. But if you want single characteristics to stand out, use the point-by-point pattern.

Patterson and Weijer's essay is organized subject by subject. Here is what the organization pattern looks like:

Subject 1: Dr. Hibbert
A.   Positive traits
   a.   trustworthy
   b.   reliable
   c.   good diagnostician
B.   Problems
   a.   greedy
   b.   unethical
   c.   politically incorrect

Subject 2: Dr. Riviera
A.   Problems
   a.   opened himself to litigation
   b.   doesn't understand anatomy
B.   Positive traits
   a.   resourceful
   b.   satisfies customers' needs
   c.   avoids litigation

 WRITING YOUR OWN COMPARISON/CONTRAST ESSAY

Write an essay comparing and contrasting two methods of escape, based on the ideas you generated in your prewriting activities. How are they alike? How are they different? Decide what point you want to make before you start writing. Then spend some time choosing and organizing your topics and deciding on your method of organization (subject by subject, point by point, or a combination of the two). Form a clear thesis statement, and follow the guidelines for writing a comparison/contrast essay.

WORKING WITH A STUDENT ESSAY

Let's look at a student's management of a comparison/contrast essay. This next essay, called "The Truth About Cats and Dogs," was written by a student named Maria Castillo. See if you can identify her main point as you read this draft of her essay.

The Truth About Cats and Dogs

The majority of people in the world will say that dogs are man's best friends and that cats were put on this earth to aggravate dogs. Some people are closet cat lovers, meaning he or she is afraid to tell family and friends that they actually like cats. Others will proudly state, "I hate cats, except for yours." People who resist cats do so because they believe they are; aloof, self-centred, and dull. People prefer dogs because they are friendly, protective, and playful. However, cats exhibit these same qualities and deserve the same respect as dogs.   1

Dogs have always been considered to be friendly, but cats can also fit this description. Dogs stay by their owners' sides and live to make their masters happy. They are the first to greet their family at the front door, they want nothing more than to be praised by their owners. Yet cats are much the same way. They, too, will be at the front door when their family gets home and are always excited to see them. They usually sit near their owners just to be by their sides. And despite what some people believe, a cat does come when they're called. Birds do not sit with their owners unless they are trained. Cats are very friendly to their owners.   2

As much as dogs love to play, so do cats. Most dogs love to play with chew toys, searching for the hidden-squeaker treasure. They often parade around with their "kill" until their masters notice their triumph. Some owners will awaken to find that their dogs have strewn all their toys all over the house. Dogs love the toys they know are theirs. However, so do cats. Cats will make a toy out of anything that will slide across a tile floor, whether it's a hair clip, a milk jug ring, a toy mouse, or a spool of thread. They can amuse themselves for hours. If the toy-of-the-day gets trapped under the refrigerator, cats will whine and wait for their owner to get the toy. Cats just love to play.   3

Even though dogs are great defenders, cats have been known to protect the family as well. Dogs bark or growl whenever they want to alert their owners to possible danger. They stand at the door and wait for their owners to check for danger. If they see their owner being attacked, they will attack the enemy. Most people think cats would just stand by and watch, but this simply isn't true. Cats also alert their owners of danger by growling or standing to stiff attention. They, too, stand near the door waiting for their owner to react. Cats have been   4 known to bite people who harm their loved ones. Cats can be excellent watch animals.

5   Dogs and cats are a lot alike. People say cats are very different from dogs, but this is not the case. The truth is, most people love to hate cats. It's now an old established pastime. But it's time for all cat lovers to unite and prove that it can be a cat-eat-cat world too.

Discovering How the Essay Works

1. What is Maria's main point in this essay?

    _____

2. What exactly is Maria comparing or contrasting in this essay? List her points under the subjects below.

    Dogs   Cats

    _____   _____

    _____   _____

    _____   _____

    _____   _____

3. Does Maria use as many specific details and examples as possible? List three of her specific references.

    _____

    _____

4. Does Maria develop her comparison in a balanced way? Explain your answer.

    _____

    _____

5. How does Maria organize her essay: subject by subject, point by point, or a combination of the two?

    _____

Revising and Editing the Student Essay

This essay is Maria's first draft, which now needs to be revised and edited. First, apply the Revising Checklist in Chapter 7 (pages 52–53) to the content of Maria's draft. When you are satisfied that her ideas are fully developed and well organized, use the Editing Checklist in Chapter 8 (page 80) to correct her grammatical and mechanical errors. Answer the questions below. Then write your suggested changes directly on Maria's draft.

Revision Questions

Thesis Statement

1. Put brackets around the last sentence in Maria's introduction. Does it contain her main point?

   _____

2. Rewrite Maria's thesis statement if necessary so that it states her main point and introduces her topics.

   _____

   _____

   _____

Basic Elements

1. Give Maria's essay an alternate title.

   _____

2. Rewrite Maria's introduction so that it captures readers' attention and builds up to the thesis statement at the end of the paragraph.

   _____

   _____

   _____

3. Does each of Maria's body paragraphs deal with only one topic?

   _____

4. Rewrite Maria's conclusion, using at least one suggestion from Part I.

_____

_____

_____

Development

1. Write out Maria's thesis statement (revised, if necessary), and list her three topic sentences below it.

   Thesis statement: _____

   _____

   _____

   Topic 1: _____

   _____

   Topic 2: _____

   _____

   Topic 3: _____

   _____

2. Do Maria's topic sentences adequately support her thesis statement?

   _____

3. Does each body paragraph have a focused topic sentence?

   _____

4. Do Maria's details adequately characterize both cats and dogs?

   _____

5. Where do you need more information?

   _____

6. Make two of Maria's details more specific.
7. Add at least two new details to make her comparison clearer.

Unity

1. Read each of Maria's topic sentences with her thesis statement (revised, if necessary) in mind. Do they go together?

_____

2. Revise them if necessary so they are directly related.
3. Drop or rewrite the sentence in paragraph 2 that is not directly related to its topic sentence.

Organization

1. Read Maria's essay again to see if all the paragraphs are arranged logically.
2. Reverse the two paragraphs that are out of order.
3. Look closely at Maria's body paragraphs to see if all her sentences are arranged logically within paragraphs.
4. Move any sentences that are out of order.

Coherence

1. Add two transitions to Maria's essay.
2. Circle five synonyms that Maria uses.
3. Explain how two of these make Maria's essay easier to read.

For the list of transitions, see pages 70–71.

_____

_____

_____

Now rewrite Maria's essay with your revisions.

Editing Questions

Sentences

Subjects and Verbs

1. Underline Maria's subjects once and verbs twice in paragraph 2 of your revision of Maria's essay. Remember that sentences can have more than one subject–verb set.
2. Does each of Maria's sentences have at least one subject and verb that can stand alone?

For help with subjects and verbs, see Chapter 32.

_____

For help with run-ons, see Chapter 34.

3. Did you find and correct Maria's run-on sentence? If not, find and correct it now.

Subject–Verb Agreement

For help with subject–verb agreement, see Chapter 36.

1. Read aloud the subjects and verbs you underlined in your revision of Maria's essay.
2. Correct any subjects and verbs that do not agree.

Pronoun Agreement

For help with pronoun agreement, see Chapter 39.

1. Find any pronouns in your revision of Maria's essay that do not agree with their nouns.
2. Did you find and correct the two pronouns that do not agree with their nouns?

Modifiers

For help with modifier errors, see Chapter 42.

1. Find any modifiers in your revision of Maria's essay that are not as close as possible to the words they modify.
2. Rewrite sentences if necessary so modifiers are as close as possible to the words they modify.

Punctuation and Mechanics
Punctuation

For help with punctuation, see Chapters 43–46.

1. Read your revision of Maria's essay for any errors in punctuation.
2. Find the run-on sentence you revised, and make sure it is punctuated correctly.
3. Did you find and correct Maria's semicolon error? If not, find and correct it now.

Mechanics

For help with capitalization, see Chapter 47.

1. Read your revision of Maria's essay for any errors in capitalization.
2. Be sure to check Maria's capitalization in the run-on sentence you revised.

Word Choice and Spelling
Word Choice

For help with confused words, see Chapter 53.

1. Find any words used incorrectly in your revision of Maria's essay.
2. Correct any errors you find.

Spelling

For help with spelling, see Chapter 54.

1. Use spell-check and a dictionary to check the spelling in your revision of Maria's essay.
2. Correct any misspelled words.

Now rewrite Maria's essay again with your editing corrections.

WORKING WITH YOUR OWN ESSAY

Returning to the comparison/contrast you wrote earlier in this chapter, revise and edit your own writing. The checklists in Chapters 7 and 8 will help you apply what you have learned to your essay.

PRACTISING COMPARISON/CONTRAST

Reading Suggestions

In Chapter 27, you will find two essays that illustrate good comparison/contrast writing: "That Is Not the Image We Have of Canada," by Tom Hayden, and "The Truth About Stories," by Thomas King. You might want to read these selections before writing another comparison/contrast essay. As you read, notice how the writers make their points through well-thought-out, detailed comparisons and contrasts.

Writing Workshop

Guidelines for Writing a Comparison/Contrast Essay

1. Decide what point you want to make with your comparison, and state it in your thesis statement.
2. Choose items to compare and contrast that will make your point most effectively.
3. Use as many specific details and examples as possible to expand your comparison.
4. Develop your comparison in a balanced way.
5. Organize your essay subject by subject or point by point—or combine the two approaches.

1. Compare and contrast the two buildings on the previous page. What details in both buildings are different? What are the same? What is the overall message you get from these two buildings? Look at both the obvious and the not-so-obvious.

2. Choose a job being advertised in your local newspaper's classified section, and write a cover letter to the employer comparing yourself to your probable competition. What are your best qualifications compared to others who might be applying for this job? What are your weaknesses in comparison to them? Why would you be the best candidate for the job?

3. Discuss the similarities and differences between two cities that you know well. How are they the same? How are they different? What do you think accounts for these similarities and differences? When you write your essay, consider whether a subject-by-subject or a point-by-point organization would be more effective.

4. Create your own comparison/contrast assignment (with the help of your instructor), and write a response to it.

Revising Workshop

Small Group Activity (5–10 minutes per writer)   Working in groups of three or four, each person should read his or her comparison/contrast essay to the other members of the group. Those listening should record their reactions on a copy of the Peer Evaluation Form (Appendix 1A). After your group goes through this process, give your evaluation forms to the appropriate writers so that each writer has two or three peer comment sheets for revising.

Paired Activity (5 minutes per writer)   Using the completed Peer Evaluation Forms, work in pairs to decide what you should revise in your essay. If time allows, rewrite some of your sentences, and have your partner look over them.

Individual Activity   Rewrite your paper, using the revising feedback you received from other students.

Editing Workshop

Paired Activity (5–10 minutes per writer)   Swap papers with a classmate, and use the editing portion of your Peer Evaluation Form (Appendix 1B) to identify as many grammar, punctuation, mechanics, and spelling errors as you can. If time allows, correct some of your errors, and have your partner look at them. Record your grammar, punctuation, and mechanics errors in the Error Log (Appendix 3) and your spelling errors in the Spelling Log (Appendix 4).

Individual Activity   Rewrite your paper again, using the editing feedback you received from other students.

Dividing and Classifying

There is an art of reading, as well as an art of thinking
and an art of writing.

—Isaac D'Israeli

Division and classification ensure that we have a certain amount of order
in our lives. In fact, we constantly use these two processes to navigate
through our days. Thanks to classification, you know where to find the milk
in the grocery store and the chapter on the fur trade in your history
textbook. Also, when you choose a major and a career, you use division and
classification to make your choice. Division and classification are such a
natural part of everyday life that we often don't even know we are using
them.

In addition, we regularly use division and classification when we write.
Actually, division and classification are a vital part of our written communication every day—in our personal lives, in school, and at work:

You divide your expenses into categories to create a budget.

A student explains three types of bacteria on a biology exam.

A student writes a report on types of hazardous materials for a
science course.

A personal banker prepares a flyer about the types of savings
accounts that are available.

The manager of a music store suggests to head office a new system
for arranging CDs.

Like comparison and contrast, division and classification are really two
parts of the same process. **Division** is sorting—dividing something into its
basic parts, such as a home into rooms. Division moves from a single, large
category (home) to many smaller subcategories (kitchen, bathroom, living
room, bedroom, and so forth). **Classification,** grouping items together,
moves in the opposite direction, from many subgroups to a single, large category. For example, several pieces of furniture in a home can be classified as
living room furniture or bedroom furniture. Division and classification help
us organize information so that we can make sense of our complex world.

Dividing large categories into smaller ones (division) and grouping many items into larger categories (classification) both help us put a lot of information into useful groups.

WRITING A DIVISION/CLASSIFICATION ESSAY

Here is a sample division/classification essay by Fran Lebowitz called "The Sound of Music: Enough Already." It classifies the types of music Lebowitz dislikes the most. What are some of your dislikes? Are these also your biggest pet peeves? Why do you dislike these things or behaviours?

THE SOUND OF MUSIC: ENOUGH ALREADY
by Fran Lebowitz

1   First off, I want to say that as far as I am concerned, in instances where I have not personally and deliberately sought it out, the only difference between music and Muzak is the spelling. Pablo Casals practicing across the hall with the door open—being trapped in an elevator, the ceiling of which is broadcasting "Parsley, Sage, Rosemary, and Thyme"—it's all the same to me. Harsh words? Perhaps. But then again these are not gentle times we live in. And they are being made no more gentle by this incessant melody that was once real life.

2   There was a time when music knew its place. No longer. Possibly this is not music's fault. It may be that music fell in with a bad crowd and lost its sense of common decency. I am willing to consider this. I am willing even to try and help. I would like to do my bit to set music straight in order that it might shape up and leave the mainstream of society. The first thing that music must understand is that there are two kinds of music—good music and bad music. Good music is music that I want to hear. Bad music is music that I don't want to hear.

3   So that music might more clearly see the error of its ways, I offer the following. If you are music and you recognize yourself on this list, you are bad music.

1. Music in Other People's Clock Radios

4   There are times when I find myself spending the night in the home of another. Frequently the other is in a more reasonable line of work than I and must arise at a specific hour. Ofttimes the other, unbeknownst to me, manipulates an appliance in such a way that I am awakened by Stevie

Wonder. On such occasions I announce that, if I wished to be awakened by Stevie Wonder, I would sleep with Stevie Wonder. I do not, however, wish to be awakened by Stevie Wonder and that is why God invented alarm clocks. Sometimes the other realizes that I am right. Sometimes the other does not. And that is why God invented many others.

2. Music Residing in the Hold Buttons of Other People's Business Telephones

I do not under any circumstances enjoy hold buttons. But I am a woman of reason. I can accept reality. I can face the facts. What I cannot face is the music. Just as there are two kinds of music—good and bad—so there are two kinds of hold buttons—good and bad. Good hold buttons are hold buttons that hold one silently. Bad hold buttons are hold buttons that hold one musically. When I hold, I want to hold silently. That is the way it was meant to be, for that is what God was talking about when he said, "Forever hold your peace." He would have added, "and quiet," but he thought you were smarter.

3. Music in the Streets

The past few years have seen a steady increase in the number of people playing music in the streets. The past few years have also seen a steady increase in the number of malignant diseases. Are these two facts related? One wonders. But even if they are not—and, as I have pointed out, one cannot be sure—music in the streets has definitely taken its toll. For it is at the very least disorienting. When one is walking down Fifth Avenue, one does not expect to hear a string quartet playing a Strauss waltz. What one expects to hear while walking down Fifth Avenue is traffic. When one does indeed hear a string quartet playing a Strauss waltz while one is walking down Fifth Avenue, one is apt to become confused and imagine that one is not walking down Fifth Avenue at all but rather that one has somehow wound up in Old Vienna. Should one imagine that one is in Old Vienna, one is likely to become upset when one realizes that in Old Vienna there is no sale at Charles Jourdan. And that is why when I walk down Fifth Avenue I want to hear traffic.

4. Music In the Movies

I'm not talking about musicals. Musicals are movies that warn you by saying, "Lots of music here. Take it or leave it." I'm talking about regular movies that extend no such courtesy but allow unsuspecting people to come to see them and then assault them with a barrage of unasked-for tunes. There are two major offenders in this category: black movies and movies set in the fifties. Both types of movies are afflicted with the same misconception. They don't know that movies are supposed to be movies. They think that movies are supposed to be records with pictures. They have failed to understand that if God had wanted records to have pictures, he would not have invented television.

5. Music in Public Places Such as Restaurants, Supermarkets, Hotel Lobbies, Airports, Etc.

8   When I am in any of the above-mentioned places, I am not there to hear music. I am there for whatever reason is appropriate to the respective place. I am no more interested in hearing "Mack the Knife" while waiting for the shuttle to Boston than someone sitting ringside at the Sands Hotel is interested in being forced to choose between sixteen varieties of cottage cheese. If God had meant for everything to happen at once, he would not have invented desk calendars.

Epilogue

9   Some people talk to themselves. Some people sing to themselves. Is one group better than the other? Did not God create all people equal? Yes, God created all people equal. Only to some he gave the ability to make up their own words.

   PREPARING TO WRITE YOUR OWN DIVISION/CLASSIFICATION ESSAY

Everyone has pet peeves. What are yours? How did you develop these pet peeves? Do your pet peeves form any particular patterns? Use one or more of the prewriting strategies that you learned in Chapter 2 to explore this topic.

How to Write a Division/Classification Essay

To write a division/classification essay, keep in mind that the same items can be divided and classified in many different ways. Your friends probably don't all organize their closets the way you do, and no two kitchens are organized exactly alike. Similarly, in writing you can divide and classify a topic in different ways. Whatever your method of dividing or classifying, use the following guidelines to help you write an effective division/classification essay.

1. *Decide on your purpose for writing, and make it part of your thesis statement.* Dividing and classifying in themselves are not particularly interesting. But they are very useful techniques if you are trying to make a specific point. That point, or purpose, should be in your thesis statement. Look at these two examples:

    A. There are three types of dangerous drivers on the road today.
    B. Being aware of three types of dangerous drivers on the road today could save your life.

Both thesis statements name a category—dangerous drivers—but only thesis statement B gives the reader a good reason to keep reading: Knowing the three types could save your life.

In our sample essay, Lebowitz uses division and classification to make fun of the types of music she dislikes. She divides all music into good music and bad music. Then she breaks bad music into five categories. She captures the humour of her essay in her thesis at the end of paragraph 3: "If you are music and you recognize yourself on this list, you are bad music."

2. ***Divide your topic into categories that don't overlap.*** Since most subjects can be classified in different ways, your next task in writing a division/classification essay is to decide on what basis you will divide your subject into categories. First, gather information to come up with a list of all the possible topics. Second, decide on what basis you will put these topics into categories. Next, make sure that some of your topics don't fall into more than one category. Your categories should be separate enough that your topics fall into only one category. Also, don't add a category at the last minute to accommodate a topic. Keep adjusting your categories until they work with your thesis.

   In the sample essay, the author uses a combination of division and classification to make her point. First, she divides all music into good and bad. Then she classifies bad music into five categories: (1) music in other people's clock radios, (2) music in the hold buttons of other people's business telephones, (3) music in the streets, (4) music in the movies, and (5) music in public places such as restaurants, supermarkets, hotel lobbies, and airports. She might have tried to classify bad music in other ways, such as public and private; indoor, outdoor, and a combination of the two; or personal, business-related, and involving other people. But none of these options would be effective. The first two groupings are too general to supply the detailed information that Lebowitz's categories give us. The third set of categories would force the author to classify many topics, like music in the movies and music in public places, in two categories, which would be confusing. Lebowitz's more specific categories are all about the same size and are very effective in sending her humorous message.

3. ***Clearly explain each category.*** With division, you are trying to show what differences break the items into separate groups or types. With classification, you let the similarities in the items help you set up categories that make sense. In either case, you need to explain each category fully and provide enough details to help your readers see your subject in a new way. To do this, use vivid description and carefully chosen examples. Comparison and contrast (Chapter 13) is also a useful technique because when you classify items, you are looking at how they are alike (comparison) and how they are different (contrast).

Lebowitz uses comparison and contrast to place her ideas into categories. Then she describes each category and provides detailed examples, such as Stevie Wonder, a Strauss waltz, and "Mack the Knife," to fill out her descriptions. As a result, she explains each of her categories fully and clearly.

4. *Organize your categories logically.* Your method of organization should make sense and be easy for readers to follow. Most often, this means organizing from one extreme to another. For example, you might organize your types from most obvious to least obvious. Or you might move from least important to most important, from least humorous to most humorous, from largest to smallest—or the other way around. In every case, though, try to end with the category that is most memorable.

Fran Lebowitz's essay is arranged from one extreme to another—from personal to public. The categories move from clock radios to business phones to music in the streets to music in movies to music in public places. Each category gets farther from the personal realm, which helps Lebowitz prove that bad music is everywhere.

5. *Use transitions to move your readers through your essay.* Transitions will help your readers move from one category to another and follow your train of thought. They will also keep your essay from sounding choppy or boring.

Since Lebowitz gives her categories headings, she doesn't need to use transitions to move from one category to another. But she does use transitions within her paragraphs. Here are some effective transitions from Lebowitz's essay: "first off" (paragraph 1), "there was a time when" (paragraph 2), "frequently" (paragraph 4), "on such occasions" (paragraph 4), "but" (paragraph 5), and "when" (paragraphs 6 and 8). These words and phrases serve as traffic signals that guide Lebowitz's readers through her essay.

 WRITING YOUR OWN DIVISION/CLASSIFICATION ESSAY

Write an essay explaining your various pet peeves. How did these pet peeves start? Why do you have them? Begin by reviewing your prewriting notes. Next, divide your subject into distinct categories, and write a clear thesis statement. Then develop your essay with specific examples that explain each category.

 ## WORKING WITH A STUDENT ESSAY

Sergio Mendola, a student writer, uses division and classification in an essay about neighbours. Called "Won't You Be My Neighbour?" it divides and classifies neighbours into specific categories to prove a point. See if you can identify his main point as you read this draft of his essay.

Won't You Be My Neighbour?

Neighbourhoods can be strange places. Every one is different, but they are all made up of the same ingredient—neighbours. In today's world, though, most people don't know there neighbours. It's not like the '50s. When people knew what their neighbours were doing. But in every neighbourhood today, you can find at least one Mystery Neighbour, one Perfect Cleaver Family, and one Good Neighbour Family.   1

The first type of neighbour everyone has is the Perfect Cleaver Family. This family has the perfect parents and the perfect children. They are the June and Ward Cleavers of today. They have 2.5 perfect children. Although these children get in their share of minor trouble, the children never repeat the same mistake after the parents express their disappointment. And then, to avoid future disappointments, the children always keep their parents' values in mind before making decisions. Eddie Haskell left a lot to be desired. I don't know what his values are. The Cleaver-type children later become heart surgeons or police chiefs in order to help the world around them. These neighbours are the role models for everyone else.   2

Then there is the Mystery Neighbour. The Mystery Neighbour remains aloof, and the only way the other neighbours know someone lives at the Mystery House is because the newspaper disappears sometime during the day and the lawn somehow gets mowed every week. Every once in a while, a car will sit in the driveway, but no one knows for sure if the car belongs to the people who own the house. Neighbourhood children make up stories about the Mystery Neighbour, which are based on nothing and compete with the best urban legends. The Mystery Neighbour is usually a workaholic or a traveling salesperson, but this doesn't stop the neighbours from wondering.   3

The best type of neighbour in any neighbourhood is the Good Neighbour Family. Made up of very reliable people. This family is always reaching out to other neighbours. Whenever something goes wrong, someone from the Good Neighbour Family is the first person at the doorstep to lend a helping hand. These neighbours will water the plants and feed the animals for people on vacation who always want to help others. They create the kinds of friendships that continue even when one family moves away. Sometimes the parents might try to "fix up" their boy and girl children so that the families relationship can be legally cemented for life. The Good Neighbour Family is one that everyone hopes to encounter at least once in a lifetime.   4

This mixture of neighbours makes up a very good neighbourhood. It creates a neighbourhood that functions smoothly and thoughtfully. And   5 even though people don't no their neighbours like they used to 50 years ago, they will probably find at least three different types of neighbours if they look hard enough: the Perfect Cleaver Family, the Mystery Neighbour, and the Good Neighbour Family. It would be sad to be missing any one of them.

Discovering How the Essay Works

1. This essay doesn't simply classify neighbours for their own sake. It has a broader message. What is Sergio's general purpose in this essay?

   _____

   _____

2. Does Sergio divide his subject into categories that don't overlap?

   _____

   _____

3. Does Sergio clearly explain each of his categories? Explain your answer.

   _____

   _____

4. How does Sergio organize his categories? Is this the most logical order for this purpose? Explain your answer.

   _____

   _____

5. What transitions does Sergio use to move his essay along smoothly?

   _____

   _____

   _____

Revising and Editing the Student Essay

This essay is Sergio's first draft, which now needs to be revised and edited. First, apply the Revising Checklist in Chapter 7 (pages 52–53) to the content of Sergio's draft. When you are satisfied that his ideas are fully developed and well organized, use the Editing Checklist in Chapter 8 (page 80) to correct his grammar and mechanics errors. Answer the questions below. Then write your suggested changes directly on Sergio's draft.

Revision Questions

Thesis Statement

1. Put brackets around the last sentence in Sergio's introduction. Does it introduce his purpose?

   _____

2. Rewrite Sergio's thesis statement if necessary so that it states his purpose and introduces his topics.

   _____

Basic Elements

1. Give Sergio's essay an alternate title.

   _____

2. Rewrite Sergio's introduction so that it captures the readers' attention and builds up to the thesis statement at the end of the paragraph.

   _____

   _____

   _____

3. Does each of Sergio's body paragraphs deal with only one topic?

   _____

4. Rewrite Sergio's conclusion using at least one suggestion from Part I.

   _____

   _____

   _____

Development

1. Write out Sergio's thesis statement (revised, if necessary), and list his three topic sentences below it.

   Thesis statement: _____

   _____

   _____

      Topic 1: _____

   _____

      Topic 2: _____

   _____

      Topic 3: _____

   _____

2. Do Sergio's topics adequately support his thesis statement?

   _____

3. Does each body paragraph have a focused topic sentence?

   _____

4. Do Sergio's details adequately explain his categories?

   _____

5. Where do you need more information?

   _____

6. Make two of Sergio's details more specific.
7. Add two new details to make his essay clearer.

Unity

1. Read each of Sergio's topic sentences with his thesis statement (revised, if necessary) in mind. Do they go together?

   _____

2. Revise them if necessary so they are directly related.

3. Drop or rewrite the two sentences in paragraph 2 that are not directly related to their topic sentences.

Organization

1. Read Sergio's essay again to see if all the paragraphs are arranged logically.

2. Reverse the two paragraphs that are out of order.

3. Look closely at Sergio's body paragraphs to see if all his sentences are arranged logically within paragraphs.

4. Move any sentences that are out of order.

Coherence

1. Add two transitions to Sergio's essay.

2. Circle five transitions, repetitions, synonyms, or pronouns Sergio uses.

3. Explain how two of these make Sergio's essay easier to read.

For a list of transitions, see pages 70–71.

For a list of pronouns, see pages 381–382.

_____

_____

Now rewrite Sergio's essay with your revisions.

Editing Questions

Sentences

Subjects and Verbs

1. Underline the subjects once and verbs twice in paragraphs 1 and 4 of your revision of Sergio's essay. Remember that sentences can have more than one subject–verb set.

For help with subjects and verbs, see Chapter 32.

2. Does each sentence have at least one subject and verb that can stand alone?

_____

3. Did you find and correct Sergio's two fragments? If not, find and correct them now.

For help with fragments, see Chapter 33.

Subject–Verb Agreement

1. Read aloud the subjects and verbs you underlined in your revision of Sergio's essay.

For help with subject–verb agreement, see Chapter 36.

2. Correct any subjects and verbs that do not agree.

Pronoun Agreement

1. Find any pronouns in your revision of Sergio's essay that do not agree with their nouns.

For help with pronoun agreement, see Chapter 39.

2. Correct any pronouns that do not agree with their nouns.

Modifiers

For help with modifier errors, see Chapter 42.

1. Find any modifiers in your revision of Sergio's essay that are not as close as possible to the words they modify.
2. Did you find and correct Sergio's modifier error? If not, find and correct it now.

Punctuation and Mechanics

Punctuation

For help with punctuation, see Chapters 43–46.

1. Read your revision of Sergio's essay for any errors in punctuation.
2. Find the two fragments you revised, and make sure they are punctuated correctly.
3. Did you find and correct the missing apostrophe in Sergio's essay?

Mechanics

For help with capitalization, see Chapter 47.

1. Read your revision of Sergio's essay for any errors in capitalization.
2. Be sure to check Sergio's capitalization in the fragments you revised.

Word Choice and Spelling

Word Choice

For help with confused words, see Chapter 53.

1. Find any words used incorrectly in your revision of Sergio's essay.
2. Did you find and correct his three confused words? If not, find and correct them now.

Spelling

For help with spelling, see Chapter 54.

1. Use spell-check and a dictionary to check the spelling in your revision of Sergio's essay.
2. Correct any misspelled words.

Now rewrite Sergio's essay again with your editing corrections.

WORKING WITH YOUR OWN ESSAY

Returning to the division/classification essay you wrote earlier in this chapter, revise and edit your own writing. The checklists in Chapters 7 and 8 will help you apply what you have learned to your essay.

PRACTISING DIVISION AND CLASSIFICATION

Reading Suggestions

In Chapter 28, you will find two essays that illustrate good division and classification writing: "Bad Boys" by Mordecai Richler categorizes dating losers, while "What Are Friends For?" by Marion Winik discusses different types of friends. You might want to read these selections before writing another division and classification essay. As you read, notice how the authors' categories support the points they are making.

Writing Workshop

Guidelines for Writing a Division/Classification Essay

1. Decide on your purpose for writing, and make it part of your thesis statement.
2. Divide your topic into categories that don't overlap.
3. Clearly explain each category.
4. Organize your categories logically.
5. Use transitions to move your readers through your essay.

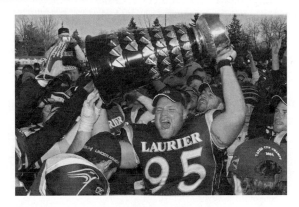

1. Looking at the picture above, think of the types of activities students do in their spare time. Classify these activities into a few categories, and explain their advantages and disadvantages.

2. What are some rituals that you follow in your own life? Do these rituals serve a purpose in your life? Use division and classification to explain three rituals that you follow.

3. We all dream about trips we'd like to take. Sometimes we get to take one of these trips. Others have to remain dreams. What are your ideal trips? Discuss the types of trips you would like to take. What categories do they fall into? Why do you dream about these types of travel?

4. Create your own division/classification assignment (with the help of your instructor), and write a response to it.

Revising Workshop

Small Group Activity (5–10 minutes per writer)   Working in groups of three or four, each person should read his or her division/classification essay to the other members of the group. Those listening should record their reactions on a copy of the Peer Evaluation Form (Appendix 1A). After your group goes through this process, give your evaluation forms to the appropriate writers so that each writer has two or three peer comment sheets for revising.

Paired Activity (5 minutes per writer)   Using the completed Peer Evaluation Forms, work in pairs to decide what you should revise in your essay. If time allows, rewrite some of your sentences, and have your partner look at them.

Individual Activity   Rewrite your paper, using the revising feedback you received from other students.

Editing Workshop

Paired Activity (5–10 minutes per writer)   Exchange papers with a classmate, and use the editing portion of your Peer Evaluation Form (Appendix 1B) to identify as many grammar, punctuation, mechanics, and spelling errors as you can. If time allows, correct some of your errors, and have your partner look at them. Record your grammar, punctuation, and mechanics errors in the Error Log (Appendix 3) and your spelling errors in the Spelling Log (Appendix 4).

Individual Activity   Rewrite your paper again, using the editing feedback you received from other students.

DEFINING

> Writers, most of all, need to define their tasks . . . their themes, their objectives.
>
> —HENRY SEIDAL CANBY

All communication depends on our understanding of a common set of definitions. If we did not work from a set of shared definitions, we would not be able to carry on coherent conversations, write clear letters, or understand any form of media.

It's no surprise, then, that we regularly use definitions in writing as well—in our personal lives, in school, and in the workplace:

You e-mail a friend to tell him or her about the equipment at the fitness centre you just joined.

A student has to define melody, harmony, and rhythm on a music appreciation quiz.

A student begins a report for a criminal justice course with a definition of criminal law.

A financial planner prepares a summary sheet defining the basic financial terms a client should know.

The manager of a sporting goods shop writes a classified ad for an opening on the staff.

Definition is the process of explaining what a word, an object, or an idea is. A good definition focuses on what is special about a word or an idea and what sets it apart from similar words or concepts. Definitions help us understand basic concrete terms (*cell phone, large fries, midterm exams*), discuss events in our lives (*baseball game, graduation, dentist appointment*), and grasp complex ideas (*friendship, courage, success*). Definitions are the building blocks that help us make certain both writer and reader (or speaker and listener) are working from the same basic understanding of terms and ideas.

Definitions vary greatly. They can be as short as one word (a "hog" is a motorcycle) or as long as an essay or even a book. Words or ideas that require such extended definitions are usually abstract, complex, and controversial. Think, for example, how difficult it might be to define an abstract idea like *equality* compared to concrete words such as *dog* or *cat*.

WRITING A DEFINITION ESSAY

In the following essay, Patricia Pearson defines the term "bullying," comparing her own memories of bullies with her daughter's stories, and with the definitions currently used by experts. Have you ever been the subject of bullying? Have you ever watched someone else being bullied and stood by? How do you feel about bullying? What type of kids are bullies, in your experience?

WHEN KIDS ARE CRUEL
by Patricia Pearson

I read my seven-year-old daughter a storybook the other day. It had been designed to address the question of bullying. Not a rip-roaring great story like *Walter the Farting Dog*, but, rather, one of those socially instructive tales that abound in children's literature, such as *Heather Has Two Mommies*, or *Everyone Poops*. Given the current near-obsession on childhood obesity, I reckon it's only a matter of time before we see *Emma's Roomy Pants*. Likewise, perhaps you've noticed that "bullying" has become a pervasive catchword of late. There've been newspaper headlines, school pamphlets, public seminars, government studies, all centred on what to do about bullying at school.

It is unclear, actually, whether incidents of bullying have increased since I attended elementary school in the 1970s. But certainly the concept has gained more urgency, and initiatives to combat bullying are flying out from every level of government, from municipal school boards putting on plays to the National Film Board producing a classroom short called *No More Bullies*.

In Clara's storybook, a little boy finds himself being tormented by a *taniwha*, a Maori monster with sharp teeth and wild eyes that's rampaging around the schoolyard. His grandfather urges him to befriend the *taniwha*. He shares his lunch; he invites the *taniwha* to play ball. Ultimately, they forge a happy friendship. The book's illustrations gradually shift, so that the *taniwha* looks less and less like a monster and more like an ordinary boy. "You see?" I said to Clara. "Bullies are really just insecure children trying to get attention. Instead of being scared of them, try to befriend them and see what happens."

My daughter chewed on her lip, looking decidedly unsure, and possibly wondering if I had a screw loose. Clara knows that there is an adult label for kids who bug you: "bully." And like other children, she is eager to put her knowledge of adult labels to use. But, in the highly complicated universe of her elementary school, it is difficult to picture what adults actually mean by bully. From Clara's point of view, all children pick on each other, in one way or another. That is her experience. I ought to know this, because whenever I listen to conversations between little girls in her class, I can't decide whether to laugh or cry, they're so outrageously cutting.

Some morning, one of them might come up to me and say: "Who's prettier, Zoe or me?" Unlike adults, who suppress their feelings and make nice, and would therefore say, "Oh, I think you both look lovely," young children insult one another with brutal frankness. "You're prettier, by far—Zoe's hair looks stupid," a kid might respond.

Under the circumstances, it is hard for children to pick out the "bullies" among all the garden-variety offenders who hurt their feelings—and whose feelings they hurt right back—on a daily basis. On reflection, Clara helpfully identified as "a bully" a boy who actually suffers from ADHD. He is hyperactive and impulsive, and will often throw chalk. In effect, he harasses her. Is that what adults mean by bullying? I asked the principal of Clara's school. She said she would dearly like to see more information out there for parents on "what bullying is not." In her view, bullying involves a powerful child picking on a weaker or less secure victim. She distinguishes this from peer aggression, which is also perceived to have increased in Canadian schools, although—again—there is little concrete data.

I seem to recall throwing a rock at someone when I was in elementary school. I also remember that bullying essentially involved the so-called cool kids picking on the nerd, or the fat girl, and this dynamic apparently persists. A study published last December in the journal *Pediatrics* reported that bullies were not like the *taniwha* in Clara's book. "Despite increased conduct problems," wrote author Jaana Juvonen of UCLA's psychology department, "bullies were psychologically strongest, and enjoyed high social standing among their classmates."

In other words, bullies are popular. They are not socially isolated or lonely. It is their victims—some of whom, the UCLA study points out, are aggressive or provocative themselves—who are more likely to have been demonized or rendered "monstrous," like the *taniwha*. That complicates our picture of the playground jungle.

PREPARING TO WRITE YOUR OWN DEFINITION ESSAY

What do you think of when you hear the word *harassment?* What associations do you make with this word? What examples does it bring to mind? Use one or more of the prewriting strategies you learned in Chapter 2 to generate ideas for writing an extended definition of *harassment.*

How to Write a Definition Essay

Clear definitions give writer and reader a mutual starting point on the road to successful communication. Sometimes a short summary and an example are all the definition that's needed. But in the case of abstract and complex words or ideas, a writer may use several approaches to a definition. Use the following guidelines to help you write an extended definition essay.

1. ***Choose your word or idea carefully, and give a working definition of it in your thesis statement.*** First, you need to choose a word or idea that can be defined and explained from several angles, or you will end up with a short, lifeless essay. At the same time, you need to give your readers a working definition right at the start. Put that brief, basic definition in your thesis statement so that readers have a mental hook on which to hang the definitions and explanations in the rest of your essay. Also include the purpose of your essay in your thesis statement.

   Pearson does not give an initial definition of "bully," partly because it is a word that is all too familiar to most people. However, she notes that bullying has "become a pervasive catchword." The best definitions of bullying come in the last two paragraphs, which works best in this case because the essay follows the author's own investigation into bullying.

2. ***Decide how you want to define your term: by synonym, by negation, or by category.*** These are the three common ways to develop a definition.

   When you define by using a *synonym*, you furnish readers with a similar word or a short explanation with synonyms. Pearson compares a bully to a character she finds in a child's book, a "taniwha," which she describes as "a Maori monster with sharp teeth and wild eyes that's rampaging around the schoolyard." This description is meant to evoke the emotion that bullies arouse in children, rather than their actual appearance. As the appearance of the taniwha changes, Pearson offers her daughter a definition: "Bullies are really just insecure children trying to get attention. Instead of being scared of them, try to befriend them and see what happens."

   When you define a word by *negation*, you say what the term is not. That is, you define a term by contrasting it with something else. Pearson combines the use of negation with the use of expert opinion, quoting an expert who distinguishes bullying from peer aggression. She returns to definition by negation when she notes later in the essay that bullies are not like the taniwha in Clara's book. The principal of Pearson's daughter's school also tells Pearson that she would like to have more information out there for parents on "what bullying is not."

   Defining a term by *category* is a more formal type of definition, as in a dictionary. Defining by category has two parts: the class or general category that the word belongs to and the way the word is different from other words in that group. For example, *heart* might be defined as "the organ that pumps blood through the body." The general category is *organ*, and it is different from other organs (brain, lungs, stomach, liver, and so on) because it pumps blood. Pearson does not use this type of definition directly. However, she does imply that bullying is part of a wider range of schoolyard aggression and problems. She also talks about "garden-variety offenders" as a larger group that includes bullies. She does not give information on this larger group, however, other than saying that they are people who "hurt feelings." This larger group could also be seen as existing in the "playground jungle" mentioned in the last paragraph.

3. ***Develop your definition with examples.*** Nearly every definition can be improved by adding examples. Well-chosen examples show your definition in action. Definitions can be *objective*—strictly factual, as in a dictionary definition—or *subjective*—combined with personal opinions. A definition essay is usually more subjective than objective because you are providing your personal opinions about a word or concept. You are explaining to your readers your own meaning, which is what makes your essay interesting. If your readers wanted an objective definition, they could go to a dictionary.

   Pearson uses examples throughout her essay to both expand and limit her definition. Clara's descriptions of the boy with ADHD who throws things and of the casual cruelty of children when asked who is prettier are examples of what bullying is not. Pearson combines the use of negation with the use of examples. She uses more general examples to explain her own idea of bullies: "the so-called cool kids picking on the nerd, or the fat girl . . ."

4. ***Use other rhetorical strategies, such as description, comparison, or process analysis, to support your definition.*** When you write a definition essay, you want to look at your word or idea from many different angles. The other techniques you have learned for developing body paragraphs can help you expand your definition even further. Perhaps a description, a short narrative, or a comparison will make your definition come alive.

   In addition to examples, Pearson uses comparison and contrast and narration to expand her definition. She uses comparison by looking at her own past experiences with bullying and comparing them to her daughter's experience. She also compares what adults will say when asked questions related to appearance with what children will say. She narrates short stories about her own experience of being a bully—"I seem to recall throwing a rock at someone."

5. ***Organize your essay in a logical way.*** Because a definition essay can be developed through several strategies and techniques, there is no set pattern of organization. So you need to figure out the most logical way to explain your word or idea. You might move from particular to general or

from general to particular. Or you might arrange your ideas from one extreme to the other, such as from most important to least important, least dramatic to most dramatic, or most familiar to least familiar. In some cases, you might organize your definition chronologically or spatially. Or you might organize part of your essay one way and the rest another way. What's important is that you move in some logical way from one point to another so that your readers can follow your train of thought.

Pearson organizes her essay by moving from specific examples to specific definitions, using what is called an inductive pattern. As noted above, this pattern follows her actual investigation of the word bullying. She questions people, from her own daughter to her daughter's principal to experts, until she finds a definition she can accept. The essay makes logical sense because it allows the reader to follow the same path of investigation as the writer.

 WRITING YOUR OWN DEFINITION ESSAY

Bullying is one type of harassment. Write an essay defining "harassment." Begin by reviewing your prewriting notes. Then decide how you are going to approach your subject. Next, write your essay, starting with a clear thesis statement.

 # WORKING WITH A STUDENT ESSAY

In the following essay, titled "True Friends," a student named Francine Feinstein defines friendship. See if you can identify her main point as you read this draft of her essay.

True Friends

1   Many people throw the term "friend" around loosely. They think they have friends at work, friends at school, and friends from the Internet. But is all these people really friends? The word "friend" seems to be used today to refer to anyone from long-term to short-term relationships. However, a true friend is someone who will always be there in times of need, who will always be the best company, and who will always listen and give advice.

2   Without any questions asked, a good friend will always be there in times of need. No matter how bad a problem is, a true friend will be the person who sits up nights and take days off work just to sit with a friend. If someone is in trouble with a difficult paper a friend will help brainstorm to figure out the problem. If someone is sick, a friend will be the first one at the door with chicken soup and will baby-sit the kids until the sick person feel better. I hate the feeling of being sick. If someone is stranded across town with a broken-down car, a friend will drop every-

thing to make a rescue and drive the person wherever he or she needs to go. Not everyone has a friend like this a true friend will always be the first one there, no matter what.

Most of all, a true friend is also someone who will listen and give reliable advice. Some people will listen to problems and then give the advice that they think will work best for them, but that advice isn't necessarily best for their friend. Other people will listen but then interject personal stories that relate to the problem but don't solve it. But a true friend listens to a problem and gives suggestions to help a friend figure out the best solution for himself or herself. In other words, a true friend knows how to <u>listen</u> and help a person solve problems.   3

In addition, a friend is someone who is always great company, because friends have so much in common with each other. Imagine working out together, grabbing a sandwich, and then spending the evening just talking— about life, about good times, about bad times, about classes at school. Right now my classes are really hard. At the end of the day, friends might rent their favourite DVD and make some fresh popcorn. Sometimes they even seem to be on the same biological clock, getting tired and waking up at the same time. Friends can always be themselves around each other.   4

The word "friend" may be misused in the English language, but at least we can agree on what true friends are. True friends are hard to find. But once you find them, they will always be there, listen to you and be the best people to spend time with. No wonder true friends are so rare!   5

Discovering How the Essay Works

1. What is this essay defining?

    _____

2. Does this author define mainly by synonym, by negation, or by category in her essay? Explain your answer.

    _____

    _____

3. List three specific examples that Francine uses to develop her definition.

    _____

    _____

    Are her examples more objective or subjective?

    _____

4. What other techniques does Francine use to develop her definition?

_____

_____

5. How does Francine organize the examples in her essay?

_____

Explain your answer.

_____

_____

_____

Revising and Editing the Student Essay

This essay is Francine's first draft, which now needs to be revised and edited. First, apply the Revising Checklist in Chapter 7 (pages 52–53) to the content of Francine's draft. When you are satisfied that her ideas are fully developed and well organized, use the Editing Checklist in Chapter 8 (page 80) to correct her grammar and mechanics errors. Answer the questions below. Then write your suggested changes directly on Francine's draft.

Revision Questions

Thesis Statement

1. Put brackets around the last sentence in Francine's introduction. Does it state her purpose?

_____

2. Rewrite Francine's thesis statement if necessary so that it states her purpose and introduces her topics.

_____

Basic Elements

1. Give Francine's essay an alternate title.

_____

2. Rewrite Francine's introduction so that it captures the reader's attention and builds up to the thesis statement at the end of the paragraph.

_____

_____

_____

3. Does each body paragraph deal with only one topic?

_____

4. Rewrite Francine's conclusion, using at least one suggestion from Part I.

_____

_____

_____

Development

1. Write out Francine's thesis statement (revised, if necessary), and list her three topic sentences below it.

Thesis statement: _____

_____

_____

Topic 1: _____

_____

Topic 2: _____

_____

Topic 3: _____

_____

2. Do Francine's topic sentences adequately support her thesis statement?

    _____

3. Does each body paragraph have a focused topic sentence?

    _____

4. Do the examples in the essay help define "friend"?

    _____

5. Where do you need more information?

    _____

6. Make two of Francine's details more specific.
7. Add at least two new details to make her essay clearer.

Unity

1. Read each of Francine's topic sentences with her thesis statement in mind. Do they go together?

    _____

2. Revise them if necessary so they are directly related.
3. Drop or rewrite the sentences in paragraph 2 and in paragraph 4 that are not directly related to their topic sentence.

Organization

1. Read Francine's essay again to see if all the paragraphs are arranged logically.
2. Reverse the two paragraphs that are out of order.
3. Look closely at Francine's body paragraphs to see if all her sentences are arranged logically within paragraphs.
4. Move any sentences that are out of order.

Coherence

For a list of transitions, see pages 70–71.

1. Add two transitions to Francine's essay.
2. Circle five transitions Francine uses.
3. Explain how two of these make Francine's essay easier to read.

    _____

Now rewrite Francine's essay with your revisions.

Editing Questions

Sentences

Subjects and Verbs

1. Underline the subjects once and verbs twice in paragraphs 1 and 2 of your revision of Francine's essay. Remember that sentences can have more than one subject–verb set.

2. Does each sentence have at least one subject and verb that can stand alone?

For help with subjects and verbs, see Chapter 32.

3. Did you find and correct Francine's run-on sentence? If not, find and correct it now.

For help with run-ons, see Chapter 34.

Subject–Verb Agreement

1. Read aloud the subjects and verbs you underlined in your revision of Francine's essay.

2. Did you find and correct the three subjects and verbs that did not agree?

For help with subject-verb agreement, see Chapter 36.

Pronoun Agreement

1. Find any pronouns in your revision of Francine's essay that do not agree with their nouns.

2. Correct any pronouns that do not agree with their nouns.

For help with pronoun agreement, see Chapter 39.

Modifiers

1. Find any modifiers in your revision of Francine's essay that are not as close as possible to the words they modify.

2. Rewrite sentences if necessary so that modifiers are as close as possible to the words they modify.

For help with modifier errors, see Chapter 42.

Punctuation and Mechanics

Punctuation

1. Read your revision of Francine's essay for any errors in punctuation.

2. Find the run-on sentence you revised, and make sure it is punctuated correctly.

For help with punctuation, see Chapters 43–46.

3. Did you find and correct the two comma errors in Francine's essay?

Mechanics

For help with capitalization, see Chapter 47.

1. Read your revision of Francine's essay for any errors in capitalization.
2. Be sure to check Francine's capitalization in the run-on sentence you revised.

Word Choice and Spelling

Word Choice

For help with confused words, see Chapter 53.

1. Find any words used incorrectly in your revision of Francine's essay.
2. Correct any errors you find.

Spelling

For help with spelling, see Chapter 54.

1. Use spell-check and a dictionary to check the spelling in your revision of Francine's essay.
2. Correct any misspelled words.

Now rewrite Francine's essay again with your editing corrections.

WORKING WITH YOUR OWN ESSAY

Returning to the definition essay you wrote earlier in this chapter, revise and edit your own writing using the checklists in Chapters 7 and 8.

PRACTISING DEFINITION

Reading Suggestions

In Chapter 29, you will find two good definition essays: "Ways to Ai" by Wang Ping defines love from the point of view of her Chinese heritage, and "Healing Myself with the Power of Work" by Michael Norlen reveals through definition how work helps the author overcome depression. You might want to read these selections before writing another definition essay. As you read, notice how the writers make their points through well-chosen examples and details.

Writing Workshop

Guidelines for Writing a Definition Essay

1. Choose your word or idea carefully, and give a working definition of it in your thesis statement.
2. Decide how you want to define your term: by synonym, by negation, or by category.
3. Develop your definition with examples.
4. Use other rhetorical strategies, such as description, comparison, or process analysis, to support your definition.
5. Organize your essay in a logical way.

1. What does education mean to you? Define "education" as portrayed in this picture.
2. The concept of "family" has undergone a number of changes over the past few years. How would you define this term in our current society?
3. Define one of the following abstract terms: *fear, love, inferiority, wonder, pride, self-control, discipline, anger, freedom, violence, assertiveness, courtesy, kindness*.
4. Create your own definition assignment (with the help of your instructor), and write a response to it.

Revising Workshop

Small Group Activity (5–10 minutes per writer)   Working in groups of three or four, each person should read his or her definition essay to the other members of the group. The listeners should record their reactions on a copy of the Peer Evaluation Form (Appendix 1A). After your group goes through this process, give your evaluation forms to the appropriate writers so that each writer has two or three peer comment sheets for revising.

Paired Activity (5 minutes per writer)   Using the completed Peer Evaluation Forms, work in pairs to decide what you should revise in your essay. If time allows, rewrite some of your sentences and have your partner look at them.

Individual Activity   Rewrite your paper, using the revising feedback you received from other students.

Editing Workshop

Paired Activity (5–10 minutes per writer)   Swap papers with a classmate, and use the editing portion of your Peer Evaluation Form (Appendix 1B) to identify as many grammar, punctuation, mechanics, and spelling errors as you can. If time allows, correct some of your errors, and have your partner look at them. Record your grammar, punctuation, and mechanics errors in the Error Log (Appendix 3) and your spelling errors in the Spelling Log (Appendix 4).

Individual Activity   Rewrite your paper again, using the editing feedback you received from other students.

Analyzing Causes and Effects

The act of writing is one of the most powerful
problem-solving tools humans have at their disposal.

—TOBY FULWILER

We are born with a natural curiosity. Wanting to know why things happen is one of our earliest, most basic instincts: Daddy, why is the sky blue?
Closely related to this desire to understand *why* is our interest in *what* will
happen as a result of some particular action: If I stay outside much longer,
will I get a bad sunburn? But thinking about causes and effects is not only
part of human nature; it is also an advanced mental process and the basis for
most decisions we make. When faced with a decision, we naturally consider
it from different perspectives. If we choose option A, what will happen?
What if we choose B—or C? In other words, we look at the possible results—
the effects—of the choices and then make up our minds.

Analyzing causes and effects is also an essential part of our writing lives.
We use cause-and-effect writing in our personal lives, in school, and in the
marketplace:

A volunteer for a mayor's campaign designs a poster telling how a
vote for this candidate will benefit the city.

A student discusses the causes of schizophrenia in a paper for a
psychology course.

A student explains the effects of repatriating the Constitution on a
history exam.

A sales representative writes a report to her manager explaining
why she didn't meet her sales projections.

The owner of a florist shop writes a letter of complaint to one of the
suppliers about the negative effect of late deliveries on sales.

Analyzing causes and effects requires the ability to look for connections
between two or more items or events and to analyze the reasons for those
connections. As the name implies, this writing strategy is composed of two
parts: cause and effect. To understand **causes,** we look in the past for reasons

why something happened. To discover **effects,** we look to the future for possible results of an action. In other words, we break a situation into parts so we can look at the relationships between these parts and then reach conclusions that are logical and useful.

WRITING A CAUSE/EFFECT ESSAY

In "Why Do Schools Flunk Biology?" Lynnell Hancock makes the point that education in the United States is stuck in the nineteenth century. She deals with both the causes and the effects of students' ability to learn. What do you think of our educational system on the high school level? How does the Canadian system compare to the U.S. system described here?

WHY DO SCHOOLS FLUNK BIOLOGY?
by Lynnell Hancock

1   Biology is a staple at most American high schools. Yet when it comes to the biology of the students themselves—how their brains develop and retain knowledge—school officials would rather not pay attention to the lessons. Can first graders handle French? What time should school start? Should music be cut? Biologists have some important evidence to offer. Not only are they ignored, but their findings are often turned upside down.

2   Force of habit rules the hallways and classrooms. Neither brain science nor education research has been able to free the majority of America's schools from their 19th-century roots. If more administrators were tuned in to brain research, scientists argue, not only would schedules change, but subjects such as foreign language and geometry would be offered to much younger children. Music and gym would be daily requirements. Lectures, worksheets, and rote memorization would be replaced by hands-on materials, drama, and project work. And teachers would pay greater attention to children's emotional connections to subjects. "We do more education research than anyone else in the world," says Frank Vellutino, a professor of educational psychology at State University of New York at Albany, "and we ignore more as well."

3   Plato once said that music "is a more potent instrument than any other for education." Now scientists know why. Music, they believe, trains the brain for higher forms of thinking. Researchers at the University of California, Irvine, studied the power of music by observing two groups of preschoolers. One group took piano lessons and sang daily in chorus. The other did not. After eight months the musical 3-year-olds were expert puzzlemasters, scoring 80 percent higher than their playmates did in spatial intelligence—the ability to visualize the world accurately.

This skill later translates into complex math and engineering skills. 4 "Early music training can enhance a child's ability to reason," says Irvine physicist Gordon Shaw. Yet music education is often the first "frill" to be cut when school budgets shrink. Schools on average have only one music teacher for every 500 children, according to the National Commission on Music Education.

Then there's gym—another expendable hour by most school standards. 5 Only 36 percent of school children today are required to participate in daily physical education. Yet researchers now know that exercise is good not only for the heart. It also juices up the brain, feeding it nutrients in the form of glucose and increasing nerve connections—all of which make it easier for kids of all ages to learn. Neuroscientist William Greenough confirmed this by watching rats at his University of Illinois at Urbana-Champaign lab. One group did nothing. A second exercised on an automatic treadmill. A third was set loose in a Barnum & Bailey obstacle course requiring the rats to perform acrobatic feats. These "supersmart" rats grew "an enormous amount of gray matter" compared with their sedentary partners, says Greenough. Of course, children don't ordinarily run such gantlets; still, Greenough believes, the results are significant. Numerous studies, he says, show that children who exercise regularly do better in school.

The implication for schools goes beyond simple exercise. Children also 6 need to be more physically active in the classroom, not sitting quietly in their seats memorizing subtraction tables. Knowledge is retained longer if children connect not only aurally but emotionally and physically to the material, says University of Oregon education professor Robert Sylwester in *A Celebration of Neurons*.

Good teachers know that lecturing on the American Revolution is far 7 less effective than acting out a battle. Angles and dimensions are better understood if children chuck their work sheets and build a complex model to scale. The smell of the glue enters memory through one sensory system, the touch of the wood blocks another, the sight of the finished model still another. The brain then creates a multidimensional mental model of the experience—one easier to retrieve. "Explaining a smell," says Sylwester, "is not as good as actually smelling it."

Scientists argue that children are capable of far more at younger ages 8 than schools generally realize. People obviously continue learning their whole lives, but the optimum "windows of opportunity for learning" last until about the age of 10 or 12, says Harry Chugani of Wayne State University's Children's Hospital of Michigan. Chugani determined this by measuring the brain's consumption of its chief energy source, glucose. (The more glucose it uses, the more active the brain.) Children's brains, he observes, gobble up glucose at twice the adult rate from the age of 4 to puberty. So young brains are as primed as they'll ever be to process new information. Complex subjects such as trigonometry or foreign language shouldn't wait for puberty to be introduced. In fact, Chugani says, it's far easier for an elementary-school child to hear and process a second language—and even speak it without an accent. Yet most U.S. districts wait until junior high to introduce Spanish or French—after the "windows" are closed.

9   Reform could begin at the beginning. Many sleep researchers now believe that most teens' biological clocks are set later than those of their fellow humans. But high school starts at 7:30 a.m., usually to accommodate bus schedules. The result can be wasted class time for whole groups of kids. Making matters worse, many kids have trouble readjusting their natural sleep rhythm. Dr. Richard Allen of Johns Hopkins University found that teens went to sleep at the same time whether they had to be at school by 7:30 a.m. or 9:30 a.m. The later-to-rise teens not only get more sleep, he says; they also get better grades. The obvious solution would be to start school later when kids hit puberty. But at school, there's what's obvious, and then there's tradition.

10   Why is this body of research rarely used in most American classrooms? Not many administrators or school-board members know it exists, says Linda Darling-Hammond, professor of education at Columbia University's Teachers College. In most states, neither teachers nor administrators are required to know much about how children learn in order to be certified. What's worse, she says, decisions to cut music or gym are often made by noneducators, whose concerns are more often monetary than educational. "Our school system was invented in the late 1800s, and little has changed," she says. "Can you imagine if the medical profession ran this way?"

PREPARING TO WRITE YOUR OWN CAUSE/EFFECT ESSAY

What can be improved in our educational system on the high school level? What do you want to change? What would be the possible results of these changes? What do you want to keep the same? Use one or more of the prewriting techniques that you learned in Chapter 2 to generate ideas on this subject.

How to Write a Cause/Effect Essay

When you write a cause/effect essay, your purpose is to give your readers some insight into the causes and effects of an event or a situation. Cause/effect writing is based on your ability to analyze. Good cause/effect essays follow a few simple guidelines.

1. ***Write a thesis statement that tells what you are analyzing.*** Cause/effect thinking requires that you look for connections between two or more situations. That is, you want to discover what caused an incident or what its results might be. Then you can focus on the causes (what

made something else happen) or the effects (the results), or some combination of the two.

In her essay, Hancock puts her thesis statement at the end of her first paragraph: "Not only are they [biologists] ignored, but their findings are often turned upside down." She goes on to say that if school administrators paid attention to research (the cause), we would see many changes (the effects), which she names. The rest of the essay examines each effect in detail.

2. **Choose facts, details, and reasons to support your thesis statement.** Cause/effect essays are usually written to prove a specific point. As a result, your body paragraphs should consist mainly of facts, details, and reasons—not opinions. Your reader should be able to check what you are saying, and any opinions that you include should be based on clear evidence.

Since Hancock sets out to prove that American education ignores research, she must name specific research studies that help her prove her point. She breaks her subject into five areas: music, gym, teaching methods, curriculum (subjects studied), and school hours. She then cites evidence in each area. For example, in the area of music, she describes research at the University of California, Irvine; for gym, she discusses rat studies from the University of Illinois; for curriculum, she describes research done at Wayne State University's Children's Hospital.

Hancock also quotes many experts, such as Frank Vellutino, a professor of educational psychology at State University of New York at Albany (paragraph 2), and gives statistics from the National Commission on Music Education (paragraph 4). A reader could check every one of Hancock's research studies, quotations, statistics, and observations (such as when most high schools begin classes in the morning). By providing facts and reasons rather than opinions in her body paragraphs, Hancock proves her point—that American education is not paying attention to current research about learning.

3. **Do not mistake coincidence for cause or effect.** If you get up every morning at 5:30, just before the sun rises, you cannot conclude that the sun rises *because* you get up. The relationship between these two events is coincidence. Confusing coincidence with cause and effect is faulty reasoning—reasoning that is not logical. To avoid this kind of faulty reasoning, you can look more deeply into the issues connected with your subject. The more you search for real causes and effects, the less likely it is that you will be thrown off by coincidence.

Hancock does not seem to mistake coincidence for cause or effect in any part of her essay. If, however, she had said that ignoring research on how teens learn has resulted in fewer students studying foreign languages today compared to 40 years ago, her reasoning would be faulty. She has no evidence to prove that the research about how students learn and the decline in students taking foreign languages in high school are related. It's only a coincidence that the research has been ignored and that fewer students study foreign languages today.

4. *Search for the real causes and effects connected with your subject.*
Just as you wouldn't stop reading halfway through a good murder mystery, you shouldn't stop too early in your analysis of causes and effects. Keep digging. The first reasons or results that you uncover are often not the real reasons or results. Suppose that a character in a mystery dies by slipping in the shower. You should try to find out what caused the fall. A good detective who keeps digging might find that someone administered a drug overdose, which caused her to fall in the shower. In other words, you are looking for the most basic cause or effect.

Hancock shows us through the large amount of evidence she presents that she has searched hard to discover the real causes and effects of education's lagging behind the times. She names two causes—administrators ignore research and noneducators make decisions about education—and gives the effects of ignoring research in five areas of education.

5. *Organize your essay so that your readers can easily follow your analysis.* Though it may be difficult to think through the causes and effects of a situation, organizing this type of essay is usually straightforward. Your thesis statement tells what you are going to analyze. Then your body paragraphs discuss the main causes or main effects in the order they occurred, from one extreme to another, from general to particular, or from particular to general. You might, for example, use chronological order to show how one effect led to another and then to a third. Or you might move from the most important cause or effect to the least important. Your goal in a cause/effect essay is to get your readers to agree with you and see a certain issue or situation the way you do. To accomplish this purpose, your readers need to be able to follow what you are saying.

Hancock discusses five effects of ignoring research on how students learn, moving from particular to general. First, she deals with the two subjects that school boards cut most often for budget reasons: music and gym. From these specific classes she moves to more general concerns—teaching methods and curriculum. Finally, she discusses high school hours, the most general topic of all. In other words, she organizes her essay from specific to general, moving from specific classes to the general logistics of the school day.

 WRITING YOUR OWN CAUSE/EFFECT ESSAY

Write an essay analyzing one of the changes you think is needed in our high school educational system. What caused the current problem as you see it? Why is this change necessary? What will be the results of this change? Review your prewriting notes first. Then draft a thesis statement and write your analysis, following the guidelines for writing a cause/effect essay.

WORKING WITH A STUDENT ESSAY

Jefferson Wright, the student writer of the following essay, titled "The Budget Crisis," explores the problems of budget cuts at his local college. Can you find the points in this draft of his essay when he deals with causes? When does he focus on effects?

The Budget Crisis

The local community college has a budget crisis. Now, when a staff person quits their job or retires, no one is hired to replace that person. This wouldn't be of great concern to most students, except now the lack of money is starting to affect the campus grounds. The college no longer has the money to replace some of the maintenance and facilities crew, which means the campus grounds, classrooms, and offices are no longer well maintained.

1

A campus that used to be beautiful has turned into a wasteland because of the neglect in keeping up its grounds. The small maintenance crew simply cannot handle the workload necessary to maintain the campus. The flower beds in front of the buildings have not been weeded, so now it has more weeds than flowers. Garbage that is thrown around the campus has not been picked up. Around every doorway are cigarette butts ground into the concrete. People shouldn't smoke anyway. It's not a great habit. There are old newspapers and candy wrappers caught on grass that has not been mowed in over two weeks, making the grounds look like the aftermath of a concert. Cans are overflowing with garbage and have colonies of flies circling them. The outside of the campus just looks unkempt and uncared for.

2

However, the campus grounds are not all that is ugly. The classroom buildings are also neglected. Everything inside is as messy as outside. The floors that used to shine are now covered with a sticky gray film. There are spills on the floors by all the soft drink machines. The bulletin boards are never cleaned off, so people just put new flyers over three or four layers of old flyers. On warm days, a strange smell overwhelms the classrooms, which the students have named "the biohazard." Washrooms are in desperate need of attention. And would probably fail any government check. The campus is really disgusting.

3

But the students aren't the only people suffering; the instructors are feeling the effects also. Their offices have ants crawling from various cracks in the walls. The dust in their offices is two inches thick. Spiders have woven cobwebs high in the windows and corners of the offices. Making both instructors and students wonder exactly where the insects hide during the day. Many light bulbs are broken near the offices, and the fluorescent bulbs flicker as if it is dancing to an unheard rhythm. The offices are as bad as the rest of the campus.

4

5　　The condition of the campus can hardly be blamed on the maintenance crew. They are constantly working and trying to keep up with the workload. The problem lies in the fact that by the time they finish one job, two or more weeks pass by before they can get back to that job. There just isn't enough money to hire the necessary personnel to cover the demands of the job. The college should put money into hiring more maintenance personnel before students transfer to other colleges because of the condition of this one. Why can't the college just spend the necessary money to make the campus beautiful again.

Discovering How the Essay Works

1. What is Jefferson analyzing in this essay?

   _____

2. Do Jefferson's facts, details, and reasons support his thesis statement? Explain your answer.

   _____

   _____

3. Does Jefferson confuse any coincidences with causes and effects? Explain your answer.

   _____

4. Do you feel that Jefferson gets to the real problems connected with his college's budget crisis? Explain your answer.

   _____

   _____

5. How does Jefferson organize the topics in his essay?

   _____

Revising and Editing the Student Essay

This essay is Jefferson's first draft, which now needs to be revised and edited. First, apply the Revising Checklist opposite to the content of Jefferson's draft. When you are satisfied that his ideas are fully developed and well organized, use the Editing Checklist on page 210 to correct his grammar and mechanics errors. Answer the questions after each checklist. Then write your suggested changes directly on Jefferson's draft.

REVISING CHECKLIST ✔

THESIS STATEMENT
✔ Does the thesis statement contain the essay's controlling idea?

✔ Does the thesis appear as the last sentence of the introduction?

BASIC ELEMENTS
✔ Does the title draw in the reader?

✔ Does the introduction capture the reader's attention and build up to the thesis statement effectively?

✔ Does each body paragraph deal with a single topic?

✔ Does the conclusion bring the essay to a close in an interesting way?

DEVELOPMENT
✔ Do the body paragraphs adequately support the thesis statement?

✔ Does each body paragraph have a focused topic sentence?

✔ Does each body paragraph contain *specific* details that support the topic sentence?

✔ Does each body paragraph include *enough* details to explain the topic sentence fully?

UNITY
✔ Do the essay's topic sentences relate directly to the thesis statement?

✔ Do the details in each body paragraph support its topic sentence?

ORGANIZATION
✔ Is the essay organized logically?

✔ Is each body paragraph organized logically?

COHERENCE
✔ Are transitions used effectively so that paragraphs move smoothly and logically from one to the next?

✔ Do the sentences move smoothly and logically from one to the next?

Thesis Statement

1. Put brackets around the last sentence in Jefferson's introduction. What does it say he is analyzing?

   _____

   _____

2. Rewrite Jefferson's thesis statement if necessary so that it states his purpose and introduces all his topics.

   _____

Basic Elements

1. Give Jefferson's essay an alternate title.

   _____

2. Rewrite Jefferson's introduction so that it captures the reader's attention and builds up to the thesis statement at the end of the paragraph.

   _____

   _____

   _____

3. Does each of Jefferson's body paragraphs deal with only one topic?

   _____

4. Rewrite Jefferson's conclusion using at least one suggestion from Part I.

   _____

   _____

   _____

Development

1. Write out Jefferson's thesis statement (revised, if necessary), and list his topic sentences below it.

   Thesis Statement:_____

   _____

   _____

   Topic 1: _____

   _____

   Topic 2: _____

   _____

   Topic 3: _____

   _____

2. Do the topics adequately develop the essay's thesis statement?

    _____

3. Does each body paragraph have a focused topic sentence?

    _____

4. Does Jefferson get to the *real* causes and effects in his essay?

    _____

5. Where do you need more information?

    _____

6. Make two of Jefferson's details more specific.
7. Add at least two new details to make his essay clearer.

Unity

1. Read each of Jefferson's topic sentences with his thesis statement. Do they go together?

    _____

2. Revise them if necessary so they are directly related.
3. Drop or rewrite the two sentences in paragraph 2 that are not directly related to their topic sentence.

Organization

1. Read Jefferson's essay again to see if all the paragraphs are arranged logically.
2. Move any paragraphs that are out of order.
3. Do you think his method of organization is the most effective one for his purpose? Explain your answer.

    _____

    _____

4. Look closely at Jefferson's body paragraphs to see if all his sentences are arranged logically within paragraphs.
5. Move the sentence in paragraph 2 that is out of order.

Coherence

For a list of transitions, see pages 70–71.

1. Add two transitions to Jefferson's essay.

2. Circle five pronouns Jefferson uses.

For a list of pronouns, see pages 381–382.

3. Explain how two of these make Jefferson's essay easier to read.

_____

_____

Now rewrite Jefferson's essay with your revisions.

EDITING CHECKLIST ✔

SENTENCES
- ✔ Does each sentence have a main subject and verb?
- ✔ Do all subjects and verbs agree?
- ✔ Do all pronouns agree with their nouns?
- ✔ Are modifiers as close as possible to the words they modify?

PUNCTUATION AND MECHANICS
- ✔ Are sentences punctuated correctly?
- ✔ Are words capitalized properly?

WORD CHOICE AND SPELLING
- ✔ Are words used correctly?
- ✔ Are words spelled correctly?

Sentences

Subjects and Verbs

For help with subjects and verbs, see Chapter 32.

1. Underline the subjects once and verbs twice in paragraphs 3 and 4 of your revision of Jefferson's essay. Remember that sentences can have more than one subject–verb set.

2. Does each of the sentences have at least one subject and verb that can stand alone?

_____

For help with fragments, see Chapter 33.

3. Did you find and correct Jefferson's two fragments? If not, find and correct them now.

Subject–Verb Agreement

1. Read aloud the subjects and verbs you underlined in your revision of Jefferson's essay.
2. Correct any subjects and verbs that do not agree.

For help with subject–verb agreement, see Chapter 36.

Pronoun Agreement

1. Find any pronouns in your revision of Jefferson's essay that do not agree with their nouns.
2. Did you find and correct the three pronoun agreement errors in Jefferson's essay? If not, find and correct them now.

For help with pronoun agreement, see Chapter 39.

Modifiers

1. Find any modifiers in your revision of Jefferson's essay that are not as close as possible to the words they modify.
2. Rewrite sentences if necessary so that modifiers are as close as possible to the words they modify.

For help with modifier errors, see Chapter 42.

Punctuation and Mechanics

Punctuation

1. Read your revision of Jefferson's essay for any errors in punctuation.
2. Find the two fragments you revised, and make sure they are punctuated correctly.
3. Did you find and correct Jefferson's two errors in end punctuation? If not, find and correct them now.

For help with punctuation, see Chapters 43–46.

Mechanics

1. Read your revision of Jefferson's essay for any errors in capitalization.
2. Be sure to check Jefferson's capitalization in the fragments you revised.

For help with capitalization, see Chapter 47.

Word Choice and Spelling

Word Choice

1. Find any words used incorrectly in your revision of Jefferson's essay.
2. Correct any errors you find.

For help with confused words, see Chapter 53.

Spelling

1. Use spell-check and a dictionary to check the spelling in your revision of Jefferson's essay.
2. Correct any misspelled words.

Now rewrite Jefferson's essay again with your editing corrections.

For help with spelling, see Chapter 54.

WORKING WITH YOUR OWN ESSAY

Returning to the cause/effect essay you wrote earlier in this chapter, revise and edit your own writing. The checklists above will help you apply what you have learned to your essay.

PRACTISING CAUSE/EFFECT

Reading Suggestions

In Chapter 30, you will find two essays that follow the guidelines you have studied in this chapter. "A Family Dilemma: To Scout or Not to Scout?" by Michael Alvear discusses the dilemma that the U.S. court ruling about gay scout leaders puts on one family, and "Too Much Self-Esteem: The Blight of Modern Times," by Johanna Schneller, discusses the effect of excessive positive reinforcement. You might want to read these selections before writing another cause/effect essay. As you read, notice how the writers make their points through well-thought-out, detailed reasoning.

Writing Workshop

Guidelines for Writing a Cause/Effect Essay

1. Write a thesis statement that tells what you are analyzing.
2. Choose facts, details, and reasons to support your thesis statement.
3. Do not mistake coincidence for cause or effect.
4. Search for the real causes and effects connected with your subject.
5. Organize your essay so that your readers can easily follow your analysis.

1. Explain how the scene above got started. What caused this reaction? Why did it happen? What were the results of the actions pictured here? Write an essay focusing on either the causes or the effects of this scene.

2. We all deal with change differently, but it is generally difficult to accept change in our lives. Think of a significant change in your life, and write about its causes and effects. What was the incident? What were the circumstances connected with the incident?

3. Write an essay that analyzes a current social problem—homelessness, drug abuse, environmental concerns—including the reasons for its existence.

4. Create your own cause/effect assignment (with the help of your instructor), and write a response to it.

Revising Workshop

Small Group Activity (5–10 minutes per writer)   Working in groups of three or four, each person should read his or her cause/effect essay to the other members of the group. Those listening should record their reactions on a copy of the Peer Evaluation Form (Appendix 1A). After your group goes through this process, give your evaluation forms to the appropriate writers so that each writer has two or three peer comment sheets for revising.

Paired Activity (5 minutes per writer)   Using the completed Peer Evaluation Forms, work in pairs to decide what you should revise in your essay. If time allows, rewrite some of your sentences, and have your partner look at them.

Individual Activity   Rewrite your paper, using the revising feedback you received from other students.

Editing Workshop

Paired Activity (5–10 minutes per writer)   Swap papers with a classmate, and use the editing portion of your Peer Evaluation Form (Appendix 1B) to identify as many grammar, punctuation, mechanics, and spelling errors as you can. If time allows, correct some of your errors, and have your partner look at them. Record your grammar, punctuation, and mechanics errors in the Error Log (Appendix 3) and your spelling errors in the Spelling Log (Appendix 4).

Individual Activity   Rewrite your paper again, using the editing feedback you received from other students.

ARGUING

Faced with the choice between changing one's
mind and proving that there is no need to do so,
almost everyone gets busy on the proof.

—JOHN KENNETH GALBRAITH

Argument may be our most important form of communication, because
it helps us get what we want in life. The main reason people argue is to persuade someone of something. When you want to get a certain job, sell your
car, or borrow some money, you need to present your request clearly and
convincingly. On the flip side, others try to persuade you to do things all the
time as well: Politicians make speeches trying to persuade you to vote for
them; your friends try to persuade you to go to a movie when you know you
should study for an exam; TV commercials, magazine ads, and billboards
everywhere try to persuade you to buy this cereal or that car.

As you might suspect, your ability to argue in writing is also important in
life. In fact, writing arguments is fundamental to your success on a personal
level, in school, and in the workplace:

The chairperson for your college reunion sends a letter with clear
reasons why everyone should attend this year.

A student writes an essay in an introductory composition course arguing for or against logging old growth forests.

A student writes a paper in a sociology course arguing that laws
against hate crimes need to be stronger.

A sales representative writes a letter arguing that customers should
order supplies from him rather than from his competitor.

A restaurant owner writes an advertisement to persuade people to
eat at her restaurant.

The purpose of **arguing** is to persuade someone to take a certain action
or to think or feel a specific way. You can use either logical arguments (based
on facts and reasoning) or emotional arguments (based on vivid description
and details) to achieve your purpose.

Some of the most important laws affecting people's lives in Canada are the result of arguments made to the Supreme Court. Lawyers argue such issues as child pornography, same sex marriage, aboriginal fishing rights, and drunk driving. If, for instance, lawmakers are trying to get stricter jail sentences for drunk driving, they might rely heavily on facts and statistics (logical evidence). But then they might add an emotional element by describing the mangled bike, the bloodstained clothes, and the grief in the faces of the parents of a 12-year-old girl killed by a drunk driver as she rode her bike home from school. Such an appeal to feelings would create a much stronger argument than statistics alone.

The better you become at arguing—in both thinking and writing—the more you will get what you want out of life (and out of your studies). Arguing effectively means a better chance of getting the pay raise you hope for, the refund you deserve, and the grades you've worked hard for. Argumentation is a powerful tool.

WRITING AN ARGUMENT ESSAY

The following argument, "Let Boys Be Boys" by Robert Sibley, tries to persuade its readers that the reason boys aren't doing as well as girls at school is the "crisis of masculinity" brought about by a society that is suppressing masculinity. Have you found that boys don't do as well at school as girls? Why do you think this is happening? Should boys and girls be educated separately?

LET BOYS BE BOYS
by Robert Sibley

An academic acquaintance once told me how silence comes over his male students when he lectures on Homer's *Odyssey* and describes how the character Telemachus was raised by his mother and grew up never knowing his father, Odysseus, the book's hero. "When I depict Telemachus as a boy from a broken home, forced at a too-early age to be his mother's protector, who has to bring himself up in a way that he hopes his absent father will be proud of," said my friend, "the young men in my undergraduate classes tend to become very quiet . . ." 1

I remembered this anecdote as I read Don Butler's insightful articles in the *Citizen's* series, "The Lost Boys," which concludes today. The series examined the demasculinization, as it were, of our universities, how women have become the majority on campuses. Mr. Butler cited various views on the phenomenon, but one in particular grabbed my attention: " 'Every mother on Earth knows from day one that little boys and little girls are completely different animals,' American academic Thomas Mortenson said. 2

'Wouldn't you expect our universities of education to be preparing our teachers to teach our little boys and little girls differently?' "

3   The answer, it seems, is no. The education system works well for girls, says Mr. Mortenson, but boys are "turned off." I'd like to suggest a connection between turned-off boys and the "crisis of masculinity." A spate of books—Waller Newell's *The Code of Man* and *What Is a Man?*; Leo Braudy's *From Chivalry to Terror: War and the Changing Nature of Masculinity*; Christina Hoff Summers's *The War Against Boys: How Misguided Feminism Is Harming Our Young Men*—testify to the fact of a crisis. (A crisis exists when once reliable ways of understanding the world no longer make sense.) But, as Mr. Mortenson suggests, we are now seeing its manifestations on the educational frontlines.

4   Indeed, Australian researchers report boys underachieving compared to girls. British social scientists say crime rates show men less inclined to adopt "social behaviour"—obeying the law, maintaining a job, supporting a family. American and Canadian studies find that, academically, boys are falling behind girls when, 30 years ago, they achieved top grades. Males drop out of school at a higher rate than females. Male teen suicides outnumber female suicides by five to one.

5   Some blame a "boy culture" and out-of-date ideas about masculinity for encouraging boys to live a slothful existence of television sports and computer games. I think not: It is not traditional maleness that is to blame for the "lost boys," but the debasement of masculinity. You might remember the movie *Fight Club*, starring Brad Pitt, in which young men relieve their boredom in basement fights. The film was denounced as a paean to fascism, but that judgment misses what's behind the nihilistic violence. The real "message" is delivered by Mr. Pitt's character, Tyler Durden: "I knew my dad for about six years, but I don't remember anything . . . What you see at fight club is a generation of men raised by women."

6   For four decades, our schools, courts and public institutions have engaged in a vast social experiment to effeminize society. This effort is rooted in the assumption that males are inherently violent and therefore "masculinity" must be suppressed. So the Boy Scouts are ordered by human rights tribunals to accept girls. The courts force little boys who sneak recess kisses to take sensitivity seminars. Drugs keep high-spirited boys in their seats.

7   The original goals of feminism—legal and political equality—were eminently reasonable. Today, though, the feminist agenda promotes a more extremist idea—eliminate all distinctions, psychological and physical, between men and women because the function and role of men and women, whether in the family or society, must be the same. Uproot traditional understandings of manhood, downgrade male virtues of courage, tenacity, pride and honour, and you'll produce "men" who have, well, "socially inclusive" habits. In other words, convert boys into girls, socially-speaking, and you'll have a kinder, gentler society.

It is a risky idea. Psychologically, young men need to undergo certain rites of passage to achieve a healthy maturity. Traditionally, these rites have been overseen by fathers or various father figures. But what happens to a society in which fatherhood is denigrated, where, in fact, many think fathers are no longer necessary for raising children? According to theorist Leon Podles, a society of absentee fathers leaves young males in a confused state of "hypermasculinity" in which they swing between the extremes of violence and hedonistic self-indulgence.   8

The ancient Greeks knew this, which was why they considered the education of young men so important. In the rush for the pacifist society, we have forgotten the Greek insight: The male instinct for violence has the same source as the impulse to protect children and rush into burning buildings. For the Greeks, a man's character was informed, for good and ill, by the spirited, or thymotic, part of his psyche. But *thymos* is not automatically rational; it has to be educated to reason. Hence, the central problem in Plato's *Republic*: Social order is at risk when the spirited psyches of young men are not directed to high purpose, so how do you educate young men to this purpose?   9

Homer certainly understood this, which is why in the Odyssey he sends Telemachus searching for his father to prevent his mother from marrying any of the evil suitors who want her to give up her husband for dead. As he wanders the world, Telemachus learns of Odysseus's struggles to return home, his fealty to home and hearth. Inspired by his father's example, Telemachus becomes a man himself.   10

What we see in *Fight Club* is young men who rightly don't want to be effeminized, but who lack worthy father figures to teach them about manhood. What we have in "The Lost Boys" series, perhaps inadvertently, is a consequence of the effeminization project—young men who lack healthy aggression and ambition, who've had their pride and sense of honour suppressed by their teachers. Barbarism, as Plato knew, can't be far behind.   11

PREPARING TO WRITE YOUR OWN ARGUMENT ESSAY

Choose a controversial issue on your campus or in the news that is important to you, and use one or more of the prewriting techniques that you learned in Chapter 2 to generate ideas on the issue. Consult your campus or local newspaper for ideas if you want. What is the exact issue? Why is it important? Why do people care about it? How do you think the issue should be resolved?

How to Write an Argument Essay

When you write an argument essay, choose a subject that matters to you. If you have strong feelings, you will find it much easier to gather evidence and convince your readers of your point of view. Keep in mind, however, that your readers might feel just as strongly about the opposite side of the issue. The following guidelines will help you write a good argument essay.

1. *State your opinion on your topic in your thesis statement.* To write a thesis statement for an argument essay, you must take a stand for or against an action or an idea. In other words, your thesis statement should be debatable—a statement that can be argued or challenged and will not be met with agreement by everyone who reads it. Your thesis statement should introduce your subject and state your opinion about that subject.

   Robert Sibley's thesis is in his third paragraph: "I'd like to suggest a connection between turned-off boys and the 'crisis of masculinity.'" He follows this statement with an explanation of what the crisis of masculinity is, and then restates the thesis more fully: "For four decades, our schools, courts and public institutions have engaged in a vast social experiment to effeminize society." This is a debatable thesis. Some other statements on the topic would not be good topics:

   Not debatable: More women are attending law school now than 20 years ago.

   Not debatable: More men are in prison for violent crimes than women.

   Sibley sets up his essay with an anecdote about an acquaintance's experiences when teaching *The Odyssey* to a university class. He writes about the reaction of the male students to the story of Telemachus, son of Odysseus.

2. *Find out as much as you can about your audience before you write.* Knowing your readers' background and feelings on your topic will help you choose the best supporting evidence and examples. Suppose you want to convince people in two different age groups to quit smoking. You might tell the group of teenagers that cigarettes make their breath rancid, their teeth yellow, and their clothes smell bad. But with a group of adults, you might discuss the horrifying statistics on lung and heart disease associated with long-term smoking.

   Sibley's essay was first published in *The Ottawa Citizen*, where he is a member of the editorial board. The essay addresses a fairly educated audience. Many people in his original audience would have disagreed with him, so he chooses support that will persuade an educated audience, such as studies and expert opinions. He also makes reference to writers such as Homer and Plato that educated readers could be expected to be familiar with.

3. ***Choose evidence that supports your thesis statement.*** Evidence is probably the most important factor in writing an argument essay. Without solid evidence, your essay is nothing more than opinion; with it, your essay can be powerful and persuasive. If you supply convincing evidence, your readers will not only understand your position but perhaps agree with it.

    Evidence can consist of facts, statistics, statements from authorities, and examples or personal stories. Examples and personal stories can be based on your own observations, experiences, and reading, but your opinions are not evidence. You can also develop your ideas by using the writing strategies you've learned in Chapters 9 through 16. Comparison/contrast, definition, and cause/effect can be particularly useful in building an argument. Use any combination of evidence and writing strategies that will help you support your thesis statement.

    In his essay, Sibley uses several different kinds of evidence. Here are some examples:

    Facts
    The Boy Scouts were ordered by human rights tribunals to accept girls.
    The ancient Greeks considered the education of young men important.

    Statistics
    Males drop out of school at a higher rate than females.
    Male teen suicides outnumber female suicides by five to one.

    Statements from Authorities
    American academic Thomas Mortenson
    Australian researchers
    Theorist Leon Podles

    Examples and Personal Stories
    The acquaintance telling the story of Telemachus
    The references to the movie *Fight Club*
    The references to *The Odyssey*

4. ***Anticipate opposing points of view.*** In addition to stating and supporting your position, anticipating and responding to opposing views is important. Presenting only your side of the argument leaves half the story untold—the opposition's half. If you admit that there are opposing arguments and answer them, you will move your reader further in your direction.

    In paragraph 7, Sibley describes his opposition, which is the modern "feminist agenda." He undercuts the opposition with his use of quotation marks—you'll produce "men" who have "socially inclusive" habits. Be careful of this ironic use of quotation marks. It works for a professional writer but may fall flat in a student essay. However, by stating the opinion of the opposition, Sibley does set up an opportunity to rebut the opposite opinion, which he does in the following paragraph, partly by quoting an expert.

5. ***Find some common ground.*** Pointing out common ground between you and your opponent is also an effective strategy. Common ground refers to points of agreement between two opposing positions. For example, one person might be in favour of the gun registry and another strongly opposed. But they might find common ground—agreement—in the need to keep guns out of teenagers' hands. Locating some common ground is possible in almost every situation. When you state in your essay that you agree with your opponent on certain points, your reader sees you as a fair person.

   Sibley knows he is writing for an audience who has first-hand experience with education. He can expect that most people will have noticed that girls are doing better than boys in many educational settings. He can also assume that his readers have been following the series of articles published in the newspaper that he mentions several times. His job is to show the connection between the change in the level of achievement of boys and what he calls the effeminization of society.

6. ***Maintain a reasonable tone.*** Just as you probably wouldn't be convinced by shouting or by nasty or sarcastic comments, don't expect your readers to respond well to such tactics. Keep the "voice" of your essay calm and sensible. Your readers will be much more open to what you have to say if they think you are a reasonable person.

   Sibley maintains a reasonable, if somewhat sarcastic, tone throughout the essay. The argument is intellectual rather than emotional, and he maintains the tone of an expert quoting experts.

7. ***Organize your essay so that it presents your position as effectively as possible.*** By the end of your essay, you want your audience to agree with you. So you want to organize your essay in such a way that your readers can easily follow it. The number of your paragraphs may vary, depending on the nature of your assignment, but the following outline shows the order in which the features of an argument essay are most effective:

   Outline
   Introduction
       Background information
       Introduction of subject
       Statement of your opinion
   Body Paragraphs
       Common ground
       Lots of evidence (logical and emotional)
       Opposing point of view
       Response to opposing point of view
   Conclusion

Restatement of your position
Call for action or agreement

The arrangement of your evidence in an argument essay depends to a great extent on your readers' opinions. Most arguments will be organized from general to particular, from particular to general, or from one extreme to another. When you know that your readers already agree with you, arranging your details from general to particular or from most to least important is usually most effective. With this order, you are building on your readers' agreement and loyalty as you explain your thinking on the subject.

If you suspect that your audience does not agree with you, reverse the organization of your evidence and arrange it from particular to general or from least to most important. In this way, you can take your readers step by step through your reasoning in an attempt to get them to agree with you.

Outline

Robert Sibley's essay follows the general outline just presented. Here is a skeleton of his essay.

Introduction

Related anecdote detailing the reaction of young men hearing the story of a fatherless boy who must act to save his family honour leads to a question and answer about educating boys and girls differently.

Body Paragraphs

Subject introduced

Examples: *Fight Club*

Opposing point of view

Theories, evidence, studies, statistics, and expert opinion

Traditions: Homer, Plato

Conclusion

Summary of argument

Reference to future

WRITING YOUR OWN ARGUMENT ESSAY

Write an essay that presents your opinion on the controversial issue you considered in your prewriting. Begin with a debatable thesis statement. Then follow the guidelines for writing an argument essay. As you write your essay, be sure you support your opinions with reasons. If a newspaper article inspired this assignment, attach it to your paper before you turn it in.

WORKING WITH A STUDENT ESSAY

Melinda Jackson, the student writer of the following essay, titled "A Call for Policies on Drinking," argues that drinking on college campuses is a serious problem. See if you can identify her main point and supporting evidence as you read this draft of her essay.

A Call for Policies on Drinking

1   College and drinking, drinking and college—most students believe the two go hand in hand. If asked, they would say that drinking in college is just a part of life, and it is not a major concern. However, when we examine drinking in college more closely, we see it is a serious problem that people on all levels are not facing. Drinking on college campuses is a bigger problem than parents and administrators realize, and something needs to be done about it—now.

2   No one would ever realistically believe that college students will never drink. In fact, most students, parents, and administrators are in favour of students taking a break and having fun. Studying during every available minute, parents and administrators realize the strain students are under. And they know that students will probably drink. What they don't understand is the trap students can fall into.

3   Jerry, a college student, explained how he got involved with alcohol and how it soon took over his life. Jerry went to a different fraternity party every weekend night, where his main goal was to get as drunk as possible. What he didn't know was that he was confrontational when he drank and that people didn't want to be around him. He didn't know his limit, so he often exceeded it. He usually passed out on someone's couch after drinking. In the morning he would wake up and find the next party. Jerry is just one of many students on every college campus.

4   Whereas most people think drinking occurs just during parties, it actually occurs for many students on a daily basis. Students like Jerry begin by drinking on weekends then they all too easily start drinking every day. They begin to need alcohol in order to feel normal. Once they fall into this pattern, several other serious problems can occur. Not only are they missing classes and falling behind in their coarses, but they are also endangering their lives. Drinking becomes the most important aspect in their lives. But it's not just the drinker who's life is effected. Drinkers disrupt their roommates, who are either distracted from their studying or awakened from their sleep. When the roommate complains about being disturbed. The drinker gets angry. And so the pattern repeats itself again and again.

5   According to our dean of students, students who drink often take risks that endanger their lives and the lives of others. The most obvious risk involves a drinker who gets behind the wheel of a car. Drinkers also tend to

get into more fights, because they mistakenly believe they are invincible. In this case, they risk harming the people they fight with and themselves, because they are in no condition to defend themselves. Everyone on the road is a potential victim of the drinker. Drinkers are also likely to have unprotected sex. This could lead to unwanted pregnancies, sexually transmitted diseases, or even AIDS. With the widespread drinking that occurs on college campuses, these consequences are very likely to occur to a student who drinks.

Drinking is a major problem on college campuses, but like every other   6
controversial issue, some people say it has been given too much publicity by overzealous worriers. They believe that the college knows light drinking occurs and that the administration has control of the students who drink. They believe that kids will be kids, students will drink no matter what. These people say that letting students have fun is what's important. But to adopt this attitude is possibly placing someone's life in danger. If even one person is in danger from a drunken student. Then the college must take action.

Drinking in college is definitely going to happen, but there are mea-   7
sures that can be taken to prevent serious harm to students who do decide to drink. Campuses could have alcohol awareness programs and give students easy access to condoms. Campuses could set up a response team that would pick up any student who was incapable of driving. They could require all student union pubs to confiscate keys before anyone is given a drink to ensure that a person who has been drinking won't drive. They can offer literature on organizations that can help students who become ad dicted to alcohol. Its time for students, parents, and administrators to see the problem before them and take steps to fix it before it's too late.

Discovering How the Essay Works

1A. What is Melinda's thesis statement?

_____

_____

1B. Does it state her opinion clearly? Explain your answer.

_____

_____

1C. Is it debatable? (Does it have more than one side?)

_____

_____

2. Who do you think Melinda is addressing in this essay? How did you come to this conclusion?

   _____

   _____

3. What evidence does the author use to support her thesis statement? Find an example of each type of evidence in her essay.

   Facts: _____

   Statistics: _____

   Statements from authorities: _____

   Examples and personal stories: _____

4. Does Melinda anticipate an opposing point of view? Explain your answer.

   _____

5. Did Melinda find some common ground with her readers? Explain your answer.

   _____

   _____

6. Does Melinda maintain a reasonable tone? Explain your answer.

   _____

7. How does Melinda organize the topics in her essay: general to particular, particular to general, or from one extreme to another?

   _____

Revising and Editing the Student Essay

This essay is Melinda's first draft, which now needs to be revised and edited. First, apply the Revising Checklist in Chapter 16 (page 207) to the content of Melinda's draft. When you are satisfied that her ideas are fully developed and well organized, use the Editing Checklist in Chapter 16 (page 210) to correct her grammar and mechanics errors. Answer the questions below. Then write your suggested changes directly on Melinda's draft.

Revision Questions

Thesis Statement

1. Put brackets around the last sentence in Melinda's introduction. Does it contain her opinion?

   _____

   Is it debatable?

   _____

2. Rewrite Melinda's thesis statement if necessary so that it states her opinion and is debatable.

   _____

Basic Elements

1. Give Melinda's essay an alternate title.

   _____

2. Rewrite Melinda's introduction so that it captures the reader's attention and builds up to the thesis statement at the end of the paragraph.

   _____

   _____

3. Does each of Melinda's body paragraphs deal with only one topic?

   _____

4. Rewrite Melinda's conclusion, using at least one suggestion from Part I.

   _____

   _____

   _____

Development

1. Write out Melinda's thesis statement (revised, if necessary), and list her topic sentences below it.

   Thesis Statement:_____

   _____

   _____

Topic 1: _____

_____

Topic 2: _____

_____

Topic 3: _____

_____

Topic 4: _____

_____

Topic 5: _____

_____

2. Do Melinda's topics adequately support her thesis statement?

_____

3. Does each body paragraph have a focused topic sentence?

_____

4. Does her evidence support her topic sentences?

_____

5. What type of evidence does Melinda provide in each body paragraph?

Paragraph 2: _____

Paragraph 3: _____

Paragraph 4: _____

Paragraph 5: _____

Paragraph 6: _____

What type of evidence does she use the most? _____

6. Is this a good choice for what she is trying to argue?

_____

7. Where do you need more information?

_____

Unity

1. Read each of Melinda's topic sentences with her thesis statement in mind. Do they go together?

_____

2. Revise them if necessary so they are directly related.
3. Drop or rewrite any sentences in her body paragraphs that are not directly related to their topic sentences.

Organization

1. Outline Melinda's essay to see if all her ideas are arranged logically.

_____

_____

_____

_____

_____

_____

_____

_____

2. Do you think her method of organization is the most effective one for her purpose? Explain your answer.

_____

_____

3. Move any paragraphs that are out of order.
4. Look closely at Melinda's body paragraphs to see if all her sentences are arranged logically within paragraphs.
5. Move any sentences that are out of order.

Coherence

1. Add two transitions to Melinda's essay.

For a list of transitions, see pages 70–71.

2. Circle five transitions, repetitions, synonyms, or pronouns Melinda uses.

For a list of pronouns, see pages 381–382.

3. Explain how two of these make Melinda's essay easier to read.

_____

_____

_____

Now rewrite Melinda's essay with your revisions.

Editing Questions

Sentences

Subjects and Verbs

For help with subjects and verbs, see Chapter 32.

1. Underline the subjects once and verbs twice in paragraphs 4 and 6 of your revision of Melinda's essay. Remember that sentences can have more than one subject–verb set.

2. Does each of Melinda's sentences have at least one subject and verb that can stand alone?

_____

For help with fragments and run-ons, see Chapters 33 and 34.

3. Did you find and correct Melinda's two fragments and two run-on sentences? If not, find and correct them now.

Subject–Verb Agreement

For help with subject–verb agreement, see Chapter 36.

1. Read aloud the subjects and verbs you underlined in your revision of Melinda's essay.

2. Correct any subjects and verbs that do not agree.

Pronoun Agreement

For help with pronoun agreement, see Chapter 39.

1. Find any pronouns in your revision of Melinda's essay that do not agree with their nouns.

2. Correct any pronouns that do not agree with their nouns.

Modifiers

For help with modifier errors, see Chapter 42.

1. Find any modifiers in your revision of Melinda's essay that are not as close as possible to the words they modify.

2. Did you find and correct Melinda's two modifier errors? If not, find and correct them now.

Punctuation and Mechanics

Punctuation

1. Read your revision of Melinda's essay for any errors in punctuation.
2. Find the two fragments and two run-on sentences you revised, and make sure they are punctuated correctly.

For help with punctuation, see Chapters 13–16.

Mechanics

1. Read your revision of Melinda's essay for any errors in capitalization.
2. Be sure to check Melinda's capitalization in the fragments and run-on sentences you revised.

For help with capitalization, see Chapter 47.

Word Choice and Spelling

Word Choice

1. Find any words used incorrectly in your revision of Melinda's essay.
2. Did you find and correct the four words Melinda used incorrectly? If not, find and correct them now.

For help with confused words, see Chapter 53.

Spelling

1. Use spell-check and a dictionary to check the spelling in your revision of Melinda's essay.
2. Correct any misspelled words.

Now rewrite Melinda's essay again with your editing corrections.

For help with spelling, see Chapter 54.

WORKING WITH YOUR OWN ESSAY

Returning to the argument essay you wrote earlier in this chapter, revise and edit your own writing. The checklists in Chapter 16 will help you apply what you have learned to your essay.

PRACTISING ARGUMENT

Reading Suggestions

In Chapter 31, you will find three examples of good argument essays: "We Are Training Our Kids to Kill" by Dave Grossman, which tries to persuade readers that our children are conditioned to kill from the violence they are exposed to through TV, movies, and video games, and two essays on spam, or junk e-mail: "Ban Spam: E-nough is E-nough" by Rick Broadhead; and "Ban Spam? What, and Banish All the World?" by Doug Saunders. You might want to read these selections before writing another argument essay. As you read, notice how the writers make their points through well-thought-out, detailed reasoning.

Writing Workshop

> **Guidelines for Writing an Argument Essay**
>
> 1. State your opinion on your topic in your thesis statement.
> 2. Find out as much as you can about your audience before you write.
> 3. Choose evidence that supports your thesis statement.
> 4. Anticipate opposing points of view.
> 5. Find some common ground.
> 6. Maintain a reasonable tone.
> 7. Organize your essay so that it presents your position as effectively as possible.

1. Explain what the photographer had in mind in creating this pictorial statement about littering. How does it appeal to its viewers? Write an essay explaining what the ad communicates.

2. Argue for or against a controversial political issue. Take a firm stand, and develop an essay supporting your position. You might want to look at some newspaper headlines to get ideas for this assignment.

3. Write a letter to a potential employer for the job of your dreams, arguing that you are the best candidate for the job. Try to convince the employer not only that you are the perfect person for the job but also that you can take the position forward in new directions. Follow the format for a well-developed argument essay.

4. Create your own argument essay assignment (with the help of your instructor), and write a response to it.

Revising Workshop

Small Group Activity (5–10 minutes per writer)   Working in groups of three or four, each person should read his or her argument essay to the other members of the group. Those listening should record their reactions on a copy of the Peer Evaluation Form (Appendix 1A0. After your group goes through this process, give your evaluation forms to the appropriate writers so that each writer has two or three peer comment sheets for revising.

Paired Activity (5 minutes per writer)   Using the completed Peer Evaluation Forms, work in pairs to decide what you should revise in your essay. If time allows, rewrite some of your sentences, and have your partner look at them.

Individual Activity   Rewrite your paper, using the revising feedback you received from other students.

Editing Workshop

Paired Activity (5–10 minutes per writer)   Swap papers with a classmate, and use the editing portion of your Peer Evaluation Form (Appendix 1B) to identify as many grammar, punctuation, mechanics, and spelling errors as you can. If time allows, correct some of your errors, and have your partner look at them. Record your grammar, punctuation, and mechanics errors in the Error Log (Appendix 3) and your spelling errors in the Spelling Log (Appendix 4).

Individual Activity   Rewrite your paper again, using the editing feedback you received from other students.

PART

III

THE ESSAY WITH SOURCES

In order to understand complex issues and situations and events,
we need to analyze them from multiple perspectives; every position
or every viewpoint ought to have reasons to support it; and the quality
of the conclusion is dependent on the quality of the reasoning that
went before it.

—JOHN CHAFFEE

Part III discusses the academic essay with sources from assignment to final draft. It explains not only what this type of essay is but also how to write one, step by step. It provides you with a student model of an essay with sources and then guides you through the process of writing one on a topic of your own.

CHAPTER 18

RECOGNIZING AN ESSAY WITH SOURCES

The content of an essay with sources is based mainly on facts, statistics, and the opinions of others. The main difference between an essay with sources and other essays is that writers use information from outside reading material when writing an essay with sources. In other words, writers consult books, periodicals, and the Internet to find facts, statistics, and other material or evidence to support their main point.

Just as you develop the body of most essays with common knowledge or personal experience, you develop this type of essay with trustworthy evidence from outside sources. To begin choosing appropriate sources, you must have a good sense of your thesis statement. Then you must set out to find information in various sources that will back up your thesis statement.

In an essay with sources, the title gives the reader a clue to the subject of the essay. The introduction gives some background for understanding the topic and states the purpose of the paper in a thesis statement. Body paragraphs provide evidence to back up the thesis statement. And the conclusion wraps up the essay by restating the thesis statement and bringing the paper to a close.

The following essay by Mary Minor, a student, is a good example of an essay with sources. She solidly proves her thesis statement using books and articles from many different sources as evidence in her supporting paragraphs. As you read the first paragraph of this draft of her essay, notice her thesis statement. Then, in each supporting paragraph that follows the introductory paragraph, be aware of how the author develops her essay and supports her thesis statement with material from outside sources.

Children as Robots

1   When children are infants, there are certain "norms" they are measured by to see if they are progressing through developmental stages at the rate of other infants their age. The "norms" are never clear-cut and leave room for individual differences. When a child hits the age of two or enters day care, "norms" become all-important. More than in any other time in history, the 1990s brought about a change in "norms" that left parents confused. The "terrible twos" and "trying threes" no longer seem to be

the best descriptions of toddlerhood. Today children who are "too" terrible at the age of two or "too" trying at the age of three are diagnosed with either "Attention Deficit Disorder (ADD) or its more severe variation, Attention Deficit Hyperactivity Disorder (ADHD). Both neurological conditions seem to be the childhood plague of the '90s" (Higdon 84). Children are often misdiagnosed with ADD or ADHD and suffer unnecessarily when medicated for a disorder they may not have.

Because medical professionals cannot agree on   2
"whether this is one disease with subcategories or two entirely different diseases" (Brink 80), the terms ADD and ADHD are often used interchangeably. Both terms, however, refer to "a short attention span" (Schmitt), with or without hyperactivity. The Diagnostic and Statistical Manual of Mental Disorders (DSM-IV) (American Psychiatric Association, 1994) defines ADHD as a "persistent pattern of inattention and/or hyperactivity-impulsivity that is more frequent and severe than typically observed in individuals at a comparable level of development" (Kendall 839). What's more, the disease ADD has become "one of the most commonly diagnosed" childhood diseases in the United States today (LeFever, Dawnson, and Morrow 1359), afflicting "approximately 4 to 7 percent" of American children (Durall 38). The National Institute of Mental Health (NIMH) claims that "differences do not a disorder make. The differences could simply be part of human variation. . . . We don't know if perhaps we shouldn't treat ADD as the far end of normal behaviour, just like height, weight, or muscle mass" (Koch 918). Given the fact that children are identified as having this disease based on what a person may consider "normal" behaviour, it is unfortunate for the children being diagnosed that nobody can agree on what "normal" means. So specialists need to be careful when recommending treatments for what could be everyday behaviour.

Many children today who do not fit the "norm" of   3
adult expectations may be diagnosed with ADD. Labelling a child's behaviour based on a set of "norms" is ludicrous since these qualities cannot accurately be measured, let alone defined. According to Thomas Armstrong, author of The Myth of the ADD Child, "Once the influential American Psychiatric Association (APA) declared ADD a disorder in 1980, the

DSM defined it more and more broadly. . . . Increasing numbers of children are caught in the ever-widening definition net and are then labeled ADD" (914). But even though we have a definition for this disorder, nobody really knows for sure what the disorder is. According to psychologist Stephen P. Hinshaw, "There's clearly not a single cause of all cases of well-diagnosed ADHD" (qtd. in Bower 343). Other professionals agree that accurate diagnosis "remains elusive and controversial" (Koch 907). If our leading professionals in the field don't know what a "well-diagnosed" case is, how can we be sure that they even know what any case of ADHD is?

4   Because there are no reliable tests for ADD, nobody is really able to tell if a child actually has the disorder. "Given the explosion in ADHD diagnoses . . . , the disorder is surprisingly ill defined. . . . There is no blood test, no PET scan, no physical exam that can determine who has it and who does not" (Gibbs 90). Professionals in the field argue over what the disease is, what causes it, how it should be treated, or whether it is a disease at all (Bower 343). Yet numerous children are diagnosed with this disease and are medicated because of it.

5   There are as many speculations about the causes of ADD and ADHD as there are experts. Unfortunately, the ones lost in the confusion are the children, and this is due to one fact: Ritalin, the most widely used method of treatment for this disorder, works so well that additional medical tests are not done. According to Dr. Sydney Walker, neither doctors nor insurance companies want to take the time or spend the money to track down the "real" cause of the problem. Instead, they mask the symptoms with Ritalin (Barkley and Walker 921). While Ritalin seems to work for many children, nobody knows why or how it works, not to mention what the long-term effects of the drug might be (Gibbs 89). We have no absolute information about ADD, only a set of symptoms, which include excessive talking, fidgeting, and similar behaviours. In other words, parents face the decision of whether or not to put their child on strong drugs when nobody has yet proved that a disorder exists.

6   Unfortunately, teachers are often the first to be involved in diagnosing a child, and "sometimes the school systems insist on a brain-disorder label" (Brink 81). One parent describes his experience and feelings about the matter in a U.S. News and World Report article:

First it was the teacher. Then the school counselor. Then the heavies in the school, the principal, start to show up. You go to meetings, and everybody thinks your child has a problem.... Doctors and therapists each had a different diagnosis—ADHD, anxiety disorder, obsessive-compulsive disorder, depression—and each diagnosis called for a different drug.... Social conformity and mental health are becoming the same terms.... The person with a different perspective is seen as a candidate for medication. (Brink 81)

Parents are often pressured into placing their children on drugs with the hope that their children will achieve "academic and social success" (Brink 76). However, this pressure may be unwarranted. "There is no solid evidence that stimulant medicine [such as Ritalin] has any impact on scholastic achievement. . . . Teachers and parents tend to approve of the drug because it makes unruly kids more manageable and more social" (Sheppard 46). So what may be disruptive to teachers or other students may simply be normal behaviour for some children.

Some children are so hard to control that mind-altering drugs such as Ritalin appear to be a blessing; but drugs, if used at all, should be used <u>only</u> for a short period of time—until the "real" cause of the problem behaviour is found. Pediatrician Lawrence Diller states his opinion on the subject well when he says, "I just don't believe a pill is the moral equivalent of good parenting and good schooling. . . . I prescribe it because . . . my job is to relieve suffering, and Ritalin, in the short term, will ease suffering" (qtd. in Brink 81). One must wonder, however, whose suffering this doctor is relieving; is it the teachers' and parents' or the children's? Diller's good intentions demonstrate why children should not be medicated for an ill-defined disease.

Despite major controversy in the medical field, however, there has been no proof that drugs are being overprescribed for children. Some experts even feel that children may be undertreated (Koch 912). No studies have been found that would prove one claim over the other, which again means that each child is treated according to the most popular opinion. As a result, "Students who were younger than their classmates were <u>21</u> times more likely to be medicated" for ADD or ADHD (920). With a statistic like this, it's astonishing that experts disagree on this subject.

9   Even if drugs can be beneficial in some instances, long-term usage is potentially dangerous because these drugs are presently "classified as 'having a high potential for abuse with severe liability for physical and/or psychic dependence'" (Morrow, Morrow, and Haislip 1121). Also, "a very small percentage of children treated at high doses have hallucinogenic responses" (Gibbs 90). To give a prescription for drugs to a child without comprehensive medical testing is, as Walker states, "inexcusable" (Barkley and Walker 921). Doctors need to agree that children are overmedicated for a disease that may not exist and find more acceptable ways to curb "disruptive behaviour." Many children exhibit the symptoms of ADHD due to family problems or other environmental factors. Diet may also play a major role in this scenario. The removal of certain foods, especially those containing "allergenic food additives and dyes" (Koch 916), may very well eliminate the symptoms. When doctors quote the Hippocratic Oath, they say these words: "I will apply dietetic measures for the benefit of the sick according to my ability and judgment; I will keep them from harm and injustice" ("Hippocratic Oath"). Sworn to dietetically treat their patients, doctors should remember this oath before prescribing drugs for a disease that nobody can prove exists.

10   Perhaps these "diseases" are nothing more than a belief system in an ever-increasing "conformist" society. Every effort should be made to find the cause of the "real" medical problems underlying ADD and ADHD before we even think about giving our children drugs. A doctor who doesn't order medical tests for a child with symptoms of ADD is negligent, to say the least, and the failure of a doctor to discuss alternatives to drug therapy with parents when diagnosing ADHD is more than "inexcusable"; it's unforgivable. More parents would seek alternative treatments if they knew that their child was diagnosed on the basis of nothing more than a list of symptoms that cannot be defined or measured. After all, most parents do not want their child placed on long-term stimulant drugs. It's time to say good-bye to "conformist" classrooms and diagnoses. People don't fit "norms"; they have personalities.

Works Cited

American Psychiatric Association. <u>The Diagnostic and Statistical Manual of Mental Disorders.</u> 4th ed. Washington: APA, 1994.

Armstrong, Thomas. <u>The Myth of the ADD Child: 50 Ways to Improve Your Child's Behavior and Attention Span Without Drugs, Labels, or Coercion.</u> New York: Dutton, 1995.

Barkley, Russell, and Sydney Walker III. "At Issue: Are Attention Deficit Disorder (ADD) and Attention Deficit Hyperactivity Disorder (ADHD) Legitimate Medical Diagnoses?" <u>CQ Researcher</u> 9 (1999): 921.

Bower, Bruce. "Kid's Attention Disorder Attracts Concern." <u>Science News</u> 154 (1998): 343.

Brink, Susan. "Doing Ritalin Right." <u>U.S. News and World Report</u> 23 Nov. 1998: 76–81.

Durall, John. "Toward an Understanding of ADHD: A Developmental Delay in Self-Control." <u>Camping Magazine</u> Jan. 1999: 38–41.

Gibbs, Nancy. "The Age of Ritalin." <u>Time</u> 30 Nov. 1998: 86–96.

Higdon, Hal. "Getting Their Attention." <u>Runner's World</u> July 1999: 84–87.

"Hippocratic Oath." <u>World Book Encyclopedia.</u> Vol. 9. 1999 ed.

Kendall, Judy. "Outlasting Disruption: The Process of Reinvestment in Families with ADHD Children." <u>Qualitative Health Research</u> 8 (1998): 839–857.

Koch, Kathy. "Rethinking Ritalin." <u>CQ Researcher</u> 9 (1999): 907–914+.

LeFever, Gretchen B., Keila V. Dawson, and Ardythe L. Morrow. "The Extent of Drug Therapy for Attention Deficit–Hyperactivity Disorder Among Children in Public Schools." <u>American Journal of Public Health</u> 89 (1999): 1359–1364.

Morrow, Robert C., Ardythe L. Morrow, and Gene Haislip.
"Methylphenidate in the United States, 1990–1995."
<u>American Journal of Public Health</u> 88 (1998): 1121.

Schmitt, B. D. "Attention Deficit Disorder (Short Attention
Span)." <u>Clinical Reference Systems</u> 1 July 1999. 17 Feb.
2000 <http://www.epnet.com/ehost/login.html>.

Sheppard, Robert. "Growing Up Hyperactive." <u>Maclean's</u>
7 Sept. 1998: 45–46.

Before continuing, choose one of the following topics for your own work in the rest of Part III:

Bias in the media	Censorship	Cloning
Spinal cord research	Government spending	Date rape
Herbal medicine	Performance enhancing drugs	Child abuse
Assisted suicide	Pollution	Alcohol and crime
Nursing homes	Drug treatment programs	Bilingual education

Avoiding Plagiarism

Plagiarism is using someone else's words or ideas as if they were your own. It is a serious offence in school and in life after school because it is dishonest. When you work with outside sources, you must give credit to them. In other words, if you quote, paraphrase, or summarize from another source, you must provide your reader with information about that source, such as the author's name, the title of the essay, and the identity of the publisher. If you use other people's words without giving them credit, you are plagiarizing.

When you don't cite your sources properly, your readers will think certain words and ideas are yours when they actually came from someone else. When you steal material in this way in college, you can get dismissed from school. When you commit the same offence in the professional world, you can end up in court. So make sure you understand what plagiarism is as you move through this chapter.

COMMON KNOWLEDGE

If you are referring to information such as historical events and known facts, like the effects of ultraviolet rays or smoking, you do not have to cite a source. This material is called *common knowledge* because it can be found in many different sources. You can use this information freely because you are not dealing with anyone's original words or ideas.

ORIGINAL IDEAS

If, however, you want to use someone's words or ideas, you must give that person credit by recording where you found this information. This process is called *citing* or *documenting* your sources, and it involves noting in your paper where you found the idea. Since essays based on sources are developed around sources that support your position, citations are an essential ingredient in any source paper.

As you can see in Mary Minor's paper in Chapter 18, every source is acknowledged at least twice in her paper: (1) in the paper right after a quotation or idea and then (2) at the end of the paper in a list of sources used in the paper. At the note-taking stage, you simply have to make sure that you have all the information on your sources that you need to acknowledge them in proper form in your paper. Having to track down missing details when you prepare your lists of works cited is frustrating and time-consuming.

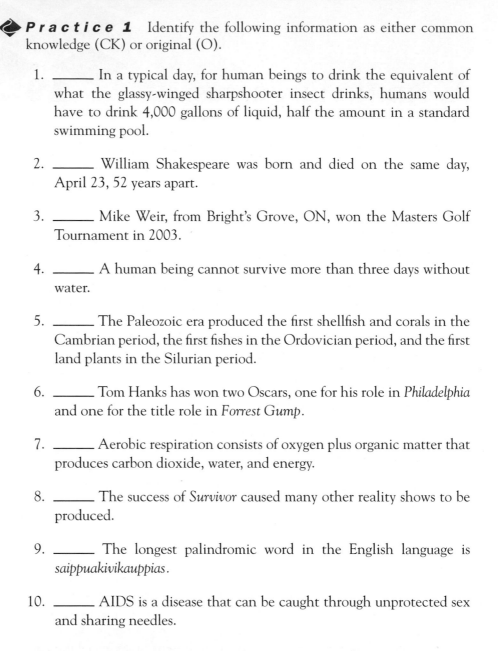 **Practice 1**   Identify the following information as either common knowledge (CK) or original (O).

1. _____ In a typical day, for human beings to drink the equivalent of what the glassy-winged sharpshooter insect drinks, humans would have to drink 4,000 gallons of liquid, half the amount in a standard swimming pool.

2. _____ William Shakespeare was born and died on the same day, April 23, 52 years apart.

3. _____ Mike Weir, from Bright's Grove, ON, won the Masters Golf Tournament in 2003.

4. _____ A human being cannot survive more than three days without water.

5. _____ The Paleozoic era produced the first shellfish and corals in the Cambrian period, the first fishes in the Ordovician period, and the first land plants in the Silurian period.

6. _____ Tom Hanks has won two Oscars, one for his role in *Philadelphia* and one for the title role in *Forrest Gump*.

7. _____ Aerobic respiration consists of oxygen plus organic matter that produces carbon dioxide, water, and energy.

8. _____ The success of *Survivor* caused many other reality shows to be produced.

9. _____ The longest palindromic word in the English language is *saippuakivikauppias*.

10. _____ AIDS is a disease that can be caught through unprotected sex and sharing needles.

USING AND SYNTHESIZING SOURCES

When writers use more than one source in an essay, they are *synthesizing* their sources. In other words, they are taking pieces of information from various sources and weaving them into an argument to form their own essay. If you've written any type of paper using outside sources, including a research paper, you were synthesizing material.

Once you have figured out your topics, you'll most likely start writing. You'll have done some prewriting to help you choose what method of organization to use. You may realize later that you'll have to change your organization around, but you can worry about that in revising.

Once you have written the introduction, ending with a thesis statement, you will probably begin working with your sources. This doesn't mean that you shouldn't use any sources in your introduction, but you'll want to save the majority of them for the body of your paper. As you write the paper, you want to make sure that you develop your argument and use sources as evidence for your claims. You should *not* write your paper around your sources. If you do this, you may end up with a disjointed argument, and your readers will not be able to determine what you really think about the issue. So when you write with sources, be sure to use them to back up your own argument and not the other way around.

Look at one of Mary Minor's paragraphs from her first draft:

> Many children today who do not fit the "norm" of adult expectations may be diagnosed with ADD. Labelling a child's behaviour based on a set of "norms" is ludicrous since these qualities cannot accurately be measured, let alone defined. According to Thomas Armstrong, author of <u>The Myth of the ADD Child</u>, "Once the influential American Psychiatric Association (APA) declared ADD a disorder in 1980, the DSM defined it more and more broadly. . . . Increasing numbers of children are caught in the ever-widening definition net and are then labeled ADD" (914). According to psychologist Stephen P. Hinshaw, "There's clearly not a single cause of all cases of well-diagnosed ADHD" (qtd. in Bower 343). Other professionals agree that accurate diagnosis "remains elusive and controversial" (Koch 907).

As Mary was revising this paragraph, she realized she was forcing the reader to make connections between her sources and her argument because she was not providing explanations that made those connections. So she revised her paragraph, connecting her sources to her own ideas and making her argument clearer.

> (1) Many children today who do not fit the "norm" of adult expectations may be diagnosed with ADD. (2) Labelling a child's behaviour based on a set of "norms" is ludicrous since these qualities cannot accurately be measured, let alone defined. (3) According to Thomas Armstrong, author of <u>The Myth of the ADD Child</u>, "Once the influential American Psychiatric Association (APA) declared ADD a disorder in 1980, the

DSM defined it more and more broadly. . . . (4) Increasing numbers of children are caught in the ever-widening definition net and are then labeled ADD" (914). (5) **But even though we have a definition for this disorder, nobody really knows for sure what the disorder is.** (6) According to psychologist Stephen P. Hinshaw, "There's clearly not a single cause of all cases of well-diagnosed ADHD" (qtd. in Bower 343). (7) Other professionals agree that accurate diagnosis "remains elusive and controversial" (Koch 907). (8) **If our leading professionals in the field don't know what a "well-diagnosed" case is, how can we be sure that they even know what any case of ADHD is?**

By adding the fifth sentence, "But even though we have a definition for this disorder, nobody really knows for sure what the disorder is," Mary explains the significance of the previous quotation and tells her readers what she wants them to be thinking about after they read it. Similarly, the last sentence in Mary's paragraph also clarifies the quotation before it. "If our leading professionals in the field don't know what a 'well-diagnosed' case is, how can we be sure that they even know what any case of ADHD is?" This sentence, which also acts as the paragraph's concluding sentence, shows readers that the professionals are arguing among themselves about the disease, so we should be careful about any diagnosis of it. Notice, also, how this last sentence provides a transition into Mary's discussion about the scarcity of reliable tests for ADHD.

To better understand how Mary's paragraph works, look at the following breakdown of her paragraph:

(1) Topic sentence

(2) Explanation of topic sentence

(3–4) Quotation from Source A, Thomas Armstrong
(with Source A Works Cited information at end)

(5) Statement explaining the significance of Source A

(6) Quotation from Source B, Stephen P. Hinshaw
(with Source B Works Cited information at end)

(7) Paraphrase and quotation from Source C, Kathy Koch
(with Source C Works Cited information at end)

(8) Concluding sentence showing relevance of Sources B and C and providing a transition into the next paragraph

This outline of Mary's paragraph should help you see how her paragraph works as one unit that supports her main argument. If you get stuck writing your own paragraphs, referring back to this outline might help you see where you need to add information.

Before you get to this stage, however, you must think about what information you want to use from your sources and how you might present that information. The most difficult task when writing an essay with sources is deciding what to quote directly, what to paraphrase, and what to summarize. Once you have a tentative thesis statement, you can start working with your outside sources.

DIRECT QUOTATION, PARAPHRASE, AND SUMMARY

Now that you know how to incorporate your sources, you need to decide whether you will directly quote, paraphrase, or summarize them. This section explains these three options to you. We will begin with an original source and show how to take and acknowledge material from the original in different ways.

The following paragraph is from "A Family Dilemma: To Scout or Not to Scout" by Michael Alvear. It was published in *Newsweek* magazine on November 6, 2000, on pages 12–13. The quoted passage is from page 12.

Original Source

> When my sister first called to tell me she was thinking of putting Ricky in the Cub Scouts (a program run by Boy Scouts of America), I could hear the torment in her voice. Ricky is a bright, athletic boy who suffers from a shyness so paralyzing he doesn't have any friends. The other day my sister asked who he had played with at recess. "Nobody," he mumbled, looking at the floor. "I just scratched the mosquito bites on my leg till it was time to go back to class."

Direct Quotation

If you use a direct quotation from another source, you must put the exact material you want to use in quotation marks:

Michael Alvear, in his essay "A Family Dilemma: To Scout or Not to Scout," states, "Ricky is a bright, athletic boy who suffers from a shyness so paralyzing he doesn't have any friends" (12).

Direct Quotation with Some Words Omitted

If you want to leave something out of the quotation, use three dots (with spaces before and after each dot). The omission of words is known as *ellipsis*.

Michael Alvear, in his essay "A Family Dilemma: To Scout or Not to Scout," states, "Ricky is a bright, athletic boy who . . . doesn't have any friends" (12).

Paraphrase

When you paraphrase, you are restating the main ideas of a quotation in your own words. *Paraphrase* literally means "similar phrasing," so it is usually about the same length as the original. Paraphrasing is one of the most difficult skills to master in college, but one trick you can use is to read the material, put it aside, and write a sentence or two about what you think it said. Then compare what you wrote with the original to make sure they are relatively the same. If you look at the source while you are trying to paraphrase it, you might inadvertently take a word or phrase from the original.

Then, even though this information is in your own words, you still need to let your readers know where you found it. A paraphrase of our original source might look like this:

> Michael Alvear, in his essay "A Family Dilemma: To Scout or Not to Scout," states that he could hear his sister's worry when he talked to her. She was thinking of putting her very shy son in the Cub Scouts. Even though his nephew, Ricky, was both athletic and intelligent, his shyness prevented him from making any friends (12).

Summary

When you summarize, you state the author's main idea in your own words. A summary is much briefer than the original or a paraphrase. As with a paraphrase, you need to cite in your paper where you found the information. Here is a summary of the original source:

> Michael Alvear, in his essay "A Family Dilemma: To Scout or Not to Scout," says his nephew, Ricky, was too shy to have any friends, so Alvear's sister was thinking of signing Ricky up for the Cub Scouts (12).

TAKING NOTES ON SOURCES

As you consider using your sources as direct quotations, paraphrases, and summaries, you will need to keep careful track of them. For your Works Cited page (Modern Language Association documentation style), References page (American Psychological Association documentation style), or Bibliography page (*Chicago Manual of Style*), you will need to provide your reader with several items of information for each source you use. The best time to start keeping track of this information is when you are taking notes.

When you take notes, notecards are an excellent tool because you can move them around as your paper takes shape. Put only one idea on a notecard. Taking notes this way will save you a lot of time in the future because you won't be scrambling around looking for the information on the source you just quoted. Taking notes electronically is another option. Whatever your choice, if you cannot find the original source for some information that you used in your paper and therefore cannot tell your reader where you found the quotation, then you cannot use the material.

As you read your sources, you should consider whether you might want to directly quote, paraphrase, or summarize the material. A general rule to follow is that you never want to use more than 10 percent of directly quoted information, which means 90 percent of the outside information you use in your essay should be paraphrased or summarized. The best way to determine whether you should use direct quotations or not is by asking yourself a question, "Is this the best possible way to relay this information?" If the answer is yes, then you should use a direct quotation. In most cases, however, you should try to put your sources in your own words. Only occasionally should you use the author's exact words in your paper. So when you are reading and taking notes on your sources, you should keep this in mind.

To avoid plagiarism when taking notes and when writing your paper, write down all the information you need to cite a source both in your paper and on the Works Cited page. For a book, you need the following information:

- Book title
- Author or authors
- City where published
- Publisher
- Year of publication

For an article, you must include the following:

- Article title
- Author or authors
- Title of the magazine or journal
- Date of issue (for a magazine)
- Year and volume and issue number (for a journal)
- Pages on which the article appeared

If you put all this information on one card, you can use just the author's last name on all other cards from that source. If an author has more than one book or article, add the source's date to the card. For both books and articles, you should also always record the page where you found the information. That way you can find it again or cite it in your paper. The format in which this information should be presented may depend on the field of study. A good handbook will help you with the formats of the various documentation styles; these include Modern Language Association (MLA) style for the humanities, American Psychological Association (APA) style for the social sciences, and *Chicago Manual of Style* (CMS) style for humanities and science.

Make sure you understand which documentation style your instructor wants you to use because they are all slightly different from each other.

In this book, we are using the Modern Language Association style of citation. The Alvear essay in the MLA format looks like this:

Alvear, Michael. "A Family Dilemma: To Scout or Not to Scout." <u>Newsweek</u> 6 Nov. 2000: 12–13.

◆ ***Practice 2***   Quote from, paraphrase, and summarize the following original sources. Document the source correctly in each case by looking up the MLA documentation style in a handbook.

1. The following paragraph is from "We Are Training Our Kids to Kill" by Dave Grossman. It was originally published in the *Saturday Evening Post* in July/August 1999 on pages 64–66, 68, 70, 72. The quoted paragraph appeared on page 65.

> This virus of violence is occurring worldwide. The explanation for it has to be some new factor that is occurring in all of these countries. There are many factors involved, and none should be discounted: for example, the prevalence of guns in our society. But violence is rising in many nations with Draconian gun laws. And though we should never downplay child abuse, poverty, or racism, there is only one new variable present in each of these countries that bears the exact same fruit: media violence presented as entertainment for children.

Quotation: _____

_____

_____

Paraphrase: _____

_____

_____

Summary: _____

_____

_____

Works Cited Citation: _____

_____

2. The following paragraph is from "Writer's Retreat" by Stan Higgins. It was originally published in *The Writer* in November 1991, volume 104, issue 11, on pages 21–23. The quoted paragraph appeared on page 21.

> During the day I wash dishes, clean tables, and mop floors. They call it Vocational Training. And today, as every day at three p.m., I return to my cozy, bathroom-size suite and drag out my tiny portable. We've all night, just the two of us, my blue typewriter that has been my steady cell-mate for six years, through seven facilities across two states, and I. Today's goal is three pages. I blow dust from the cover and clean the keys. The Muse calls. *Tack-tack. Tack. Tack-tack-tack.* My typewriter sings its staccato song as I search for a fertile word or idea, some harmonious junction of thought and paper. Locked in solitary combat with my machine, nothing exists outside my cell, or so I pretend. I type a line. My door opens. Two blue-uniformed guards stand there grinning. "Guess what?" one says. "Your number came up."

Quotation: _____

_____

_____

Paraphrase: _____

_____

_____

Summary: _____

_____

_____

Works Cited Citation: _____

_____

3. The following paragraph is from "Don't Be Cruel" by Dr. Roger Flax. It was originally published in *TWA Ambassador* in March 1992, on pages 49–51. The quoted paragraph appeared on page 49.

> Picture this scenario: Seymour Axshun (we'll call him), a terrific manager who has been a loyal employee for several years, messes up on an assignment. He misses a deadline on a proposal, and that three-day delay costs the company $9,100. Seymour's boss, Sy Kottick, has a near coronary over the incident, lashes out at Seymour, and criticizes him mercilessly. In front of four of Seymour's co-workers, Kottick shouts, "Axshun, how many times do I have to tell you to be more efficient with your planning? You blew it, and your mistake will cost us almost $10,000. I don't know what it takes to drill into your head that you must meet deadlines. It's disgusting, and I'm fed up. If you treated the money as if it were your own, you wouldn't be so careless."

Quotation: _____

_____

_____

Paraphrase: _____

_____

_____

Summary: _____

_____

_____

Works Cited Citation: _____

_____

4. The following paragraph is from "Healing Myself with the Power of Work" by Michael Norlen. It was originally published in *Newsweek*, on October 25, 1999, on page 12.

> It all changed 12 months ago. For the second time in six years, I abandoned my solo law practice. I stopped returning phone calls, forgot to pay bills, and ignored court dates. I began to sleep 16 hours a day. By July of last year I stopped coming into the office, leaving it to fill up with unopened mail and indignant phone messages. By August I was behind on my office rent, and by October my landlord asked me to leave. I ate, but nothing tasted good. I slept, but woke up tired. I felt like a stranger around my wife and two daughters. Thoughts of suicide shadowed me. And in the midst of all this, I knew. *It* had returned.

Quotation: _____

_____

_____

Paraphrase: _____

_____

Summary: _____

_____

Works Cited Citation: _____

_____

5. The following paragraph is from the essay "What Are Friends For?" by Marion Winik. It was originally published on pages 85–89 in a book titled *Telling: Confessions, Concessions, and Other Flashes of Light*, which was published by Villard Books in New York City in 1994. The quoted paragraph appeared on page 89.

> At the other end of the spectrum are Hero Friends. These people are better than the rest of us; that's all there is to it. Their career is something you wanted to be when you grew up—painter, forest ranger, tireless doer of good. They have beautiful homes filled with special handmade things presented to them by villagers in the remote areas they have visited in their extensive travels. Yet they are modest. They never gossip. They are always helping others, especially those who have suffered a death in the family or an illness. You would think people like this would just make you sick, but somehow they don't.

Quotation: _____

_____

_____

Paraphrase: _____

_____

_____

Summary: _____

_____

_____

Works Cited Citation: _____

_____

_____

FINDING SOURCES

No matter what you are studying, you should know how to find outside sources using the library through a computer. You can access an enormous amount of information that will help you generate paper topics, teach you new information, challenge your thinking, support your opinions, and make you smile. In today's electronic world, learning how to use the resources available through the library's services is a basic survival skill.

CREDIBILITY OF SOURCES

When you are looking for information to use in your essays, you must be careful about what you choose. Your sources must be relevant, reliable, and recent. This "three *Rs*" approach to finding sources will help you locate convincing evidence to support your argument.

Since anyone can put material on the Internet, you need to make sure you are not using biased or unreliable information in your academic papers. To use Web sites intelligently, follow these four guidelines.

1. *Check the end of a Web URL address.* It may be .com, .ca, .edu, .gov, or .org. The last four are generally reputable sources, but you must be very careful of .com sources because this stands for "communication," and anyone can purchase a .com site. For example, www.whitehouse.com is *not* a site for the U.S. president's home, as you might suspect. On the other hand, .edu stands for "education," .gov for "government," and .org for "organization." But any site has the potential for bias, and you should consider the material carefully.

2. *Pay attention to the argument a site makes.* Who is the author and what is his or her purpose for entering information on the site? If you log onto a Martin Luther King Jr. site and are inundated with racial slurs, chances are you've found a site that was created by a faction of the Ku Klux Klan. If the argument does not fit the site or if the author has an obvious agenda, avoid the site altogether.

3. *Make sure the site is providing fact and not opinion.* For academic purposes, facts and evidence are generally more useful than opinions. If you are looking for a site that deals with teen suicide, you'll want to avoid the site that tells you story after story about innocent children

dying, but fails to give you any specific information. Instead, you'll want to find a site that gives you examples that can be verified and supported with statistics.

4. ***Does the site provide any information about the other side of the argument?*** If a site provides you with details only about its own viewpoint, you should wonder why it is omitting information. If you find a site on breakfast in schools and see opinions only about why breakfast should be provided in schools, you should be curious about why they don't present the other side's argument. Will facts about the other side make you change your mind? The best sites provide both sides of an argument so the source can, in turn, show why one side is more valid than the other. If you find a Web site that does not offer balanced information, consider it biased, and avoid the site.

These four guidelines will help you determine whether or not you should use information you find on the Web. But if you want to be certain the information you are using will be acceptable to your instructor, you should stick with academic sources. These sources are different from other sources because they have been "refereed" or "reviewed." This means the authors of the essays send them to the publication and the editors of the publication send the essays anonymously to readers for review. If the readers accept the pieces for publication, they consider the essays to be well-researched and worth reading. If you can, you should use only these sources. The best place to find them is also online, as you will see in the following section.

CONSULTING ONLINE DATABASES, FULL-TEXT INDEXES, AND ELECTRONIC JOURNAL COLLECTIONS

The best places to begin searching for outside sources are online databases, full-text indexes, and electronic journal collections. You should have access to these services from home through your library's home page or from a computer in your library. We will discuss each type of source separately. You may need a reference librarian to help you find these for the first time.

Online Databases

Online databases can direct you to an incredible number of books and journals on a wide range of subjects. The following are some online indexes found in SilverPlatter's WebSPIRS database, which is an information retrieval system that contains indexes on many different subjects and is used by many libraries.

Index	Primary Use
Biological and Agriculture Index	Science
ERIC	Education
GeoRef	Geology
MLA	Literature, language, and linguistics
Philosopher's Index	Philosophy
Sociological Abstracts	Sociology

Full-Text Indexes

The following indexes take you directly to complete journal articles online. In other words, you can print out the journal articles you find, right from your own computer.

Index	Primary Use
ABI Inform	News and business
Dow Jones	News and business
EBSCOhost*	Many subject areas
Expanded Academic ASAP*	General information in several disciplines
HRAF	Ethnographies
Lexis-Nexis	News, business, and law
WilsonWeb*	Popular magazines and newspapers, social sciences, humanities, business, general science, and education journals

*Not all articles will be available in full text.

Electronic Journal Collections

Electronic journal collections are similar to online databases in that you can print out complete journal articles directly from your own computer. The following collections might help you find information on the topic you have chosen.

Collection	Primary Use
Academic Press's IDEAL	Articles published by academic publishers
American Chemical Society's Web Editions	American Chemical Society's 26 scientific journals
American Mathematical Journals	American Mathematical Society's proceedings and transactions

| JSTOR | Back issues of core journals in the humanities, social sciences, and sciences |
| Project Muse | Humanities, social sciences, and math |

Once you access an online database, index, or collection, you can easily find articles and books on your topic. You can do online searches by author, title, or subject; since you will most likely be looking for articles on a topic, you will use the subject function most often. When you are searching for a title by subject, you should be aware of *Boolean connectors* or *operators*, which are shortcuts to help you narrow the search field.

Using Boolean Connectors or Operators

The Boolean connectors or operators for requesting a search are *AND*, *OR*, and *NOT*. By using these words, you can limit the search and find information directly related to your topic. If you type "AND" between your key words (for example, *TV AND violence*), you are asking the computer to combine the key words for the search. If you put "OR" between the key words (*TV OR video games*), you are separating the words and asking the computer to find articles and books with either one of them. If you add "NOT" (*TV NOT video games*), you limit the search by excluding certain terms from the search.

Accessing Sources

Once you type your topic into the search function of a database, index, or journal collection, the computer will display the number of articles and books it has found in a "results list." Following are some examples of articles found on the topic of *television AND violence* in an online database, a full-text index, and an electronic journal collection.

From an Online Database

Record 40 of 313 in *Sociological Abstracts* [in WebSPIRS] 1986-2001/06

TI: The National Television Violence Studies

AU: Chaffee, -Steven

IN: Stanford U, CA 94305

SO: Journal of Communications; 1997, 47, 4, autumn, 170-173.

DT: aja Abstract-of-Journal-Article

AB: A review essay on books by four university research teams—U California (Santa Barbara), U North Carolina (Chapel Hill), U Texas (Austin), & U Wisconsin (Madison)—(1) National **Television Violence** Study, Vol. 1 (Thousand Oaks, CA: Sage, 1997); & National **Television Violence** Study, Vol. 1. & Vol. 2 (Thousand Oaks, CA: Sage, 1997 & 1998, respectively). These works report on recent university studies of TV **violence** in diverse sectors of the US. The Executive Summary provides an overview of the project & policy recommendations & is appropriate for parents & teachers. The two main volumes present the coding system for **violence,** the effects of ratings & antiviolence advertising, & content analysis based on earlier literature. It is concluded that this team effort offers much useful information for the study of TV **violence,** & presents the studies in such a way that they can be easily replicated. 3 References. M. Cella

DEM: ***Television** (D859500); *Mass-Media-**Violence** (D497700); *Communication-Research (D151900); *Programming-Broadcast (D668400)

AN: 9904482

From a Full-Text Index

Entry 17 of 99 (from the Social Science Index in WilsonWeb)
Formichelli, L. *Programming behavior* [restricting violent **television** programming during hours when children may be watching] *Psychology Today* v. 34 no. 1 (January/February 2001) p. 10

From an Electronic Journal Collection

2. Warning: The Surgeon General Has Determined That TV Violence Is Moderately Dangerous to Your Child's Mental Health

Leo Bogart
Public Opinion Quarterly, Vol. 36, No. 4. (Winter, 1972–1973), pp. 491–521.
[Citation/Abstract] [View Article] [Page of First Match] [Print] [Download]

Notice that these examples contain all of the information you need for citing those works in the text and at the end of your paper. So make sure you keep lists like this when you print them so that you can cite your sources correctly.

Practice 1   For each of the following topics, find a book from an online database, an article from a full-text index, and an article from an electronic journal source. Record the title and the database, index, or source where you found it.

Example: Topic: Violence and TV

Database: Sociological Abstracts—in WebSPIRS

Title: *The National Television Violence Studies*

Index: Social Science Index in WilsonWeb

Title: *Programming Behavior*

Electronic Journal: JSTOR

Title: Warning: *The Surgeon General Has Determined That TV Violence Is Moderately Dangerous to Your Child's Mental Health*

1. Topic: Drug testing in college sports

   Database: _____

   Title: _____

   Index: _____

   Title: _____

   Electronic journal: _____

   Title: _____

2. Topic: Overtime and the workforce

   Database: _____

   Title: _____

   Index: _____

   Title: _____

   Electronic journal: _____

   Title: _____

3. Topic: Fish farming

   Database: _____

   Title: _____

   Index: _____

   Title: _____

   Electronic journal: _____

   Title: _____

4. Topic: Women in combat

   Database: _____

   Title: _____

   Index: _____

Title: _____

Electronic journal: _____

Title: _____

5. Topic: Using animals for testing

Database: _____

Title: _____

Index: _____

Title: _____

Electronic journal: _____

Title: _____

SEARCHING FOR WEB SITES

To find a Web site related to your topic, you should go to the Internet through whichever browser you have (Netscape Communicator or Navigator, Microsoft Internet Explorer, etc.). Your browser probably has a search engine of its own that will let you search the Internet. Or you might want to use a search engine that automatically refers you to sites related to your topic: Both www.google.com and www.dogpile.com are examples of search engines that can save you a lot of time. For example, www.google.com searches millions of Web sites in mere seconds and is an excellent source for research.

Once you access a search engine, type in your topic as if you were searching a database. Most search engines will then begin helping you narrow your search and will provide a list of other possible topics. Here are some examples for the topic of *violence and television*.

Topic	Other Possible Topics
Violence and television	TV violence
	On TV violence
	Television violence
	TV violence and children
	Violence on television
	Causes of TV violence
	Media violence

When the search is complete, your search engine will list the different Web sites in the order it thinks they will be most helpful to you. It will also briefly describe each Web site. After the description, you will most often find the Web site address. The following are the first three "hits" or Web sites from www.dogpile.com for the topic *violence and television*.

1. National Coalition on TV Violence

   Learn about the effects of TV violence and facts about the V-Chip, and get ideas to help kids avoid violent entertainment.

   www.nctvv.org

2. American Psych. Association—Violence on Television

   Association investigates the effect of television violence on children and discusses ways parents can intervene to minimize its impact.

   www.apa.org

3. APA HelpCenter: Warning Signs of Teen Violence

   The American Psychological Association and MTV team up to get important information to the nation's youth about warning signs of violent behavior, including violence in schools. The Warning Signs site provides a violence prevention guide and resource.

   helping.apa.org

◆ *P r a c t i c e   2*   For each of the following topics, find a different Web page through a different search engine, and list the Web page title, the explanation, and the Web address.

> **Example:**   Topic: Violence and television
>
> Search engine: GoTo.com through dogpile.com
>
> Web page title: Center for Educational Priorities: Two Studies
>
> Explanation: Read brief overview of the 1996 National Violence Study and the 1995 UCLA Television Violence Monitoring Report
>
> Web address: www.cep.org

1. Topic: Bilingual education in Nunavut

   Search engine: _____

   Web page title: _____

   Explanation: _____

   _____

Web address: _____

2. Topic: Benefits of the Canadian space program

    Search engine: _____

    Web page title: _____

    Explanation: _____

    _____

    Web address: _____

3. Topic: Legalizing marijuana

    Search engine: _____

    Web page title: _____

    Explanation: _____

    _____

    Web address: _____

4. Topic: Homeopathic medicine

    Search engine: _____

    Web page title: _____

    Explanation: _____

    _____

    Web address: _____

5. Topic: Women's soccer

    Search engine: _____

    Web page title: _____

    Explanation: _____

    _____

    Web address: _____

USING THE LIBRARY

Once you have compiled a list of books and journals from databases and indexes or from Web sites, you should use your library to check out books or copy journal articles that were not available online. First, you need to access your library's online catalogue to see if your library has the book. (If your library does not have computers, use the traditional card catalogue.) Ask a librarian how to access your particular catalogue through your school. You might also ask if this information is available online. You can search for authors and subjects through your library's catalogue in much the same way as you would search online databases or program search engines. But since you have already done the preliminary research, all you have to do is search for the books and journals you need. Find the "title" section of the catalogue, and type in the title of the book or journal you need in this section. For help finding books and journals in the library, ask a librarian.

If you are searching for a chapter or an essay contained in a book, be sure to type in the main book title. For example, if you searched for "I Just Wanna Be Average" (by Mike Rose), your library computer will tell you that the library does not carry it. You must type in the title of the book it came from, *Lives on the Boundary*, to find the essay. Once you have located the titles of your books or journals in the library's catalogue, you should write down the call numbers so you can find the sources in your library. Then it's just a matter of finding the book itself in the stacks of your library.

Practice 3   Find five books from your research, and using the "title" portion of your library's catalogue, locate the call numbers.

> **Example:**   Title: *Youth Culture: Identity in a Postmodern World*
> Call number: HV 1431 Y684 1998

1. Title: _____

    Call number: _____

2. Title: _____

    Call number: _____

3. Title: _____

    Call number: _____

4. Title: _____

    Call number: _____

5. Title: _____

    Call number: _____

How to Write an Essay with Sources

An essay with sources is really just an essay with supporting material that comes from outside sources. This type of writing assignment has all the elements of a typical essay. The following chart compares a standard essay and an essay with sources.

Standard Essay		Essay with Sources
Introduction with thesis statement	⟷	Introduction with thesis statement
Body paragraphs with facts and personal experience to support thesis statement	⟷	Body paragraphs with documented evidence to support thesis statement
Concluding paragraph	⟷	Concluding paragraph

Keep this outline in mind as you read about how to construct a good essay with sources. Laying out some clear guidelines is the best place to start.

1. *Choose a subject.* You might be choosing a subject from infinite possibilities or working with an assigned topic. Doing some general reading online or in the library is often necessary to get you started. As you consider various topics, you must ask one very important question before you begin planning your essay: Will you be able to find enough information to back up your thesis statement? To make sure you will be able to find enough material to use as good evidence in the body paragraphs of your essay, you must do a good job of choosing a subject, narrowing down that subject, and then writing a working thesis statement. You will prove this thesis statement with the information you find when you search for sources on your topic. If you were writing an essay with sources on pursuing an applied degree in college, for example, your initial prewriting for the thesis statement might look like this:

> **General Subject:** College programs
> **More Specific:** Applied degree
> **More Specific:** Applied degree in land planning

This limited subject would be perfect for an essay with sources. You could search for books, catalogues, and periodicals on what it takes to earn a bachelor's degree in land planning from various colleges and universities. While you are looking, you could be thinking about how to narrow down your subject even further.

Mary Minor (in Chapter 18) might have started with a general topic like "childhood disorders," limited it to "childhood behavioural disorders," and finally settled on "ADD and ADHD as childhood behavioural disorders."

Practice 1 Choose a topic from the list on page 240. Why did you choose this topic?

Practice 2 Limit this topic so that you can write a paper about five pages long.

2. ***Write a good, clear thesis statement about your subject.*** Just as a thesis statement is the controlling idea of an essay, a thesis statement also provides the controlling idea for your argument in an essay with sources. This statement will guide the writing of your entire paper. Your course assignments will usually be broad topics. To compose a good essay with sources, you need to narrow a broad topic to an idea that you can prove within a limited number of pages. A working thesis statement will provide the direction for your essay, and the evidence you collect in your research is what proves the thesis statement.

A good way to start your first draft is to read some general sources on your topic. This reading will help you discover the range of your subject and will guide you toward a thesis. Before you start writing the first draft of your paper, make sure you write a sentence that clearly states your topic and your position on that topic. This is your working thesis statement and will be the controlling idea for your entire paper. Your thesis statement may change several times before your essay is finished, but making this statement and taking a position is a necessary first step. It will help you move from the broad subject of your assignment to your own perspective on the topic. This will also help you focus your essay and save you time in your search for good resources to back up your thesis statement.

Just as in a standard essay, the thesis statement in your essay with sources is a contract between you and your readers. The thesis statement tells your readers what the main idea of your essay will be and sets guidelines for the paragraphs in the body of your essay. If you don't deliver what your thesis statement promises, your readers will be disappointed. The thesis statement is usually the last sentence in the introduction. It outlines your purpose and position on the essay's general topic and gives the reader an idea of the type of resources that you will use to develop your essay.

Mary Minor's controlling idea or thesis statement appears at the end of her first paragraph:

> Children are often misdiagnosed with ADD or ADHD and suffer unnecessarily when medicated for a disorder they may not have.

Her entire essay is about children who are too readily diagnosed with ADD or ADHD simply because they do not fall into society's "norm" for children's behaviour. The paragraphs following this thesis statement supply evidence that proves that her claim is true.

◆ ***Practice 3***   List your thoughts and opinions on the topic you chose in Practice 1.

◆ ***Practice 4***   Put your topic and your position on that topic into a working thesis statement.

3. ***Find sources that are relevant, reliable, and recent to support your thesis statement.*** The thesis statement of an essay with sources is really only the beginning. To convince your readers that what you say in your essay is worth reading, you must support your thesis statement with evidence. The evidence of an essay with sources lies in the sources that you use to back up your thesis statement. The sources must be relevant, reliable, and recent. This "three *R*s" approach to supporting evidence in an essay with sources will help you write a solid essay with convincing evidence.

Mary's thesis statement suggests that young children are being too readily diagnosed with ADD and ADHD. To convince her readers that her thesis is correct, she uses a book, scientific journals, an encyclopedia, online journal articles, and general-circulation magazines as sources of evidence. Here is a breakdown of how she used her sources.

- **Book:** *The Myth of the ADD Child*
  This source provides well-researched information from an expert's point of view. Mary uses this source early in her paper to help define the scope of her study.
- **Scientific journals:** *CQ Researcher, Science News, Qualitative Health Research, American Journal of Public Health*
  These sources supply the reader with specific evidence put forth by experts in the field of ADD and ADHD research and diagnosis. Mary uses this information to prove that her thesis statement is true.
- **Encyclopedia:** *World Book Encyclopedia*
  Mary uses this source to provide the reader with an understandable definition of the Hippocratic Oath. This definition plays an important role in Mary's stance on her topic.

- **Online journal articles:** *Clinical Reference Systems*

    The article from this source was printed from WilsonWeb. The information in this article defines hyperactivity in children for the general reader.

- **General-circulation magazines:** *U.S. News and World Report, Camping Magazine, Time, Runner's World, Maclean's*

    These sources supply information readily available at a newsstand, yet highly informative and applicable to Mary's topic. Information from articles in these magazines speaks to the average citizen. Even though these magazines are not scientific journals, the evidence in them is extremely useful because it is intended to make specialized information understandable to the general reader.

Mary Minor uses sources in her essay that do a thorough job of supporting her thesis statement. The information from her chosen book, journals, encyclopedia, and magazines speaks to the average citizen. Even though they are not highly technical scientific sources, the evidence in them is relevant, reliable, and recent, which are the same guidelines you should use when looking for your sources.

◆ *Practice 5*   Review Chapter 20 to make sure that you understand the options available to you for finding sources to use in your essay.

◆ *Practice 6*   Find five sources that give you information about the limited topic that you chose. Make sure they are relevant, reliable, and recent.

4. *Take notes to avoid plagiarism.* Now is the time to read your sources and take careful notes—putting the ideas in your own words or putting the writer's words in quotation marks if you record the exact words. You should also note the page numbers of all information you take down. If you don't take notes carefully, you will never be able to trace information that you want to use in your paper to its original source. Also, trying to put someone's ideas into your own words is a very good skill that will help you as you are writing.

Taking notes on notecards will allow you to move your cards around and put ideas into different paragraphs. When you rearrange cards, you can work with them until you think the order will support what you are trying to prove. This notecard method saves you time in the long run.

Mary Minor had to read and take notes on all the sources she found. She first made a set of bibliography cards with a notecard for every source she found. For the books, she put book title, author, city where published, publisher, and year of publication on each card; for the articles, she recorded article title, author, title of the magazine or journal, date of issue or volume and issue numbers, and page numbers of the article on each card. Then she began to read her sources. She wrote only one idea or quotation on a notecard, and she remembered to record on each notecard the author's name and the page number on which she found the information. She also made sure, as she took notes, to restate information in her own words or else put the author's exact words in quotation marks.

◆ *P r a c t i c e   7*   Review Chapter 19 to make sure you understand what plagiarism is and how to avoid it.

◆ *P r a c t i c e   8*   Read and take notes on your sources using notecards. Make sure each of your cards has a source and page number on it.

5. *Make a working outline of your paper.* To do this, you just need to start re-arranging the notecards you have made. Start by putting all your notecards into small stacks of related ideas. Which ideas will work well together? Which should you put in the introduction? Which do you want to save for your conclusion? When you get all your notecards in stacks, label each group of cards according to its topic. These labels will then become the topics of your paper. You are now ready to start your working outline.

A good way to begin a working outline is to write your tentative thesis statement at the top of a page and then list the topics you have developed under that thesis. These topics should be arranged in some logical order that will help you prove your main point and is easy to follow. Each topic should also directly support your thesis statement. Leave room in your outline to add subtopics and details throughout the paper. This outline then becomes a guide for your writing. It will change and grow with every paragraph that you add to your paper.

Mary started developing her paper by putting related notecards into stacks. Next, she labelled her stacks of notecards and started organizing these topics in different ways until they started making sense to her. Her list of topics, with her thesis statement at the top, became the bulk of her working outline. She eventually turned these topics into topic sentences for her body paragraphs. The stack of cards for each topic became the content of her body paragraphs.

◆ *P r a c t i c e   9*   Divide your notecards into topics that logically support your thesis statement. Then label each stack of cards.

◆ *P r a c t i c e   1 0*   Start a working outline of your paper by listing your thesis statement and your supporting topics.

6. *Construct an introduction that leads up to your thesis statement.* The introduction to an essay with sources is your chance to make a great first impression. Just like a firm handshake and a warm smile in a job interview, an essay's introduction should capture your readers' interest, set the tone for your essay, and state your specific purpose. Introductions often have a

funnel effect. They typically begin with general information and then narrow the focus to your position on a particular issue. Regardless of your method, your introduction should "hook" your readers by grabbing their attention and letting them know what you are going to try to prove in your essay.

To lead up to the thesis statement, your introductory paragraph must stimulate your readers' interest. Some effective ways of capturing your audience's attention and giving necessary background information are (1) to use a quotation; (2) to tell a story that relates to your topic; (3) to provide a revealing fact, statistic, or definition; (4) to offer an interesting comparison; or (5) to ask an intriguing question. Be sure your introduction gives readers all the information they may need to follow your train of thought through the rest of your paper.

Mary's introduction starts out by noting the shifting "norms" that exist around early childhood development. The paragraph then discusses parents' confusion with their children's behaviour and introduces ADD and ADHD. The last sentence of the first paragraph contains Mary's thesis statement and ends the introduction.

◆ *Practice 11* Make a rough outline of your ideas for a possible introduction to your essay with sources.

◆ *Practice 12* Write a rough draft of your introduction, ending with your thesis statement.

7. ***Develop as many supporting paragraphs or body paragraphs as you think are necessary to explain your thesis statement.*** Following the introductory paragraph, an essay with sources includes several body paragraphs that support and explain the essay's thesis statement. Each body paragraph covers a topic that is directly related to the thesis statement.

Supporting paragraphs, or body paragraphs, usually include a topic sentence, which is a general statement of the paragraph's contents, and examples or details that support the topic sentence. (See Chapters 4 and 5 for methods to use when you develop and organize paragraphs.)

To write your supporting paragraphs, you should first organize your notecards within each of your stacks. Next, add the details from these cards to your working outline. Then write your supporting paragraphs by following your working outline and your notecards. Make adjustments in your outline as you write so that you can keep track of your ideas and make sure you are developing them in a logical order. The body of the paper and your outline should change and develop together with each sentence that you write.

After you write your body paragraphs, you should look at your thesis statement again to make sure it introduces what you say in the rest of your paper. Your thesis statement should refer to all of your topics, even if only indirectly, in the same order you discuss them in. It should also prepare your readers for the conclusions you are going to come to.

Mary's paper contains eight body paragraphs, each making a separate point that is directly related to her thesis:

Paragraph	Point
2	ADD and ADHD are defined as "a short attention span" and are the most commonly diagnosed childhood diseases.
3	Diagnosing children who do not fit a "norm" is ludicrous, especially since there is no accurate definition or diagnosis of ADD or ADHD.
4	No physical exam can determine that a child has ADD or ADHD.
5	There are as many theories about the causes of ADD as there are experts, so we are only treating the symptoms of these disorders.
6	Teachers, parents, and students get caught up in the diagnosis.
7	Drugs should only be a short-term answer to the hyperactive child.
8	No proof is available that says we overprescribe drugs for children.
9	Long-term use of drugs for ADD and ADHD is potentially dangerous.

Like the foundation of a solid building, these paragraphs provide support for the position Mary takes in her thesis statement. The stronger the supporting paragraphs are, the stronger the paper will be.

In addition to strong topic sentences, you should also use concluding sentences in your body paragraphs to help reinforce your thesis statement or build a transition to the next paragraph. Concluding sentences wrap up a paragraph just as a conclusion wraps up an essay, and using concluding sentences lets you remind your readers what you are arguing and where you are in your reasoning.

◆ *Practice 13*   Organize the notecards within each of your stacks so that they make sense. Add these details to your working outline.

◆ *Practice 14*   Write a rough draft of your body paragraphs. Remember that you will be revising and editing this draft a little later, so just concentrate on getting your ideas written up in an organized way. Revise your thesis statement, if necessary, to introduce all your body paragraphs.

8. ***Make sure you use your sources as evidence for your argument.*** Although your argument will evolve as you read your sources, you should decide on a general position on your topic before you begin to take notes. Don't write your essay around your sources, because your essay may become very disjointed and difficult to follow if you do. You should find appropriate sources to help you develop your argument. To heighten their effect, tell your reader the significance of the direct quotations, paraphrases, or summaries that you use. Look, for example, at one of the paragraphs in Mary's paper:

> Despite major controversy in the medical field, however, there has been no proof that drugs are being overprescribed . . . Some experts even feel that children may be undertreated (Koch 912). No studies have been found that would prove one claim over the other, which again means that each child is treated according to the most popular opinion. As a result, "Students who were younger than their classmates were <u>21</u> times more likely to be medicated" for ADD or ADHD (920). With a statistic like this, it's astonishing that experts disagree on this subject.

Notice how Mary does not stop with her source's remarks. Instead, she includes a point about the significance of what each source says. She reminds her readers that she is arguing against drugging young children unnecessarily.

If you simply provide a series of quotations and let them argue for you, you are not demonstrating your understanding of the quotations or showing how they fit into your argument. Make sure to use the quotations as support for your argument and not let them stand for the argument itself.

◆ ***Practice 15*** Consider the different ways your sources will support your argument. Organize them in a way that best helps you prove your main point.

◆ ***Practice 16*** Write your body paragraphs using your sources as evidence in your argument. Be careful not to choose sources haphazardly to include in your body paragraphs. You need to have a reason for using each of your sources.

9. ***Write a concluding paragraph.*** The concluding paragraph is the final paragraph of an essay. In its most basic form, it should summarize the main points of the essay and remind readers of the thesis statement.

The best conclusions expand on these two basic requirements and bring the essay to a close with one of these creative strategies: (1) Ask a question that provokes thought on the part of the reader, (2) predict the future, (3) offer a solution to a problem, or (4) call the reader to action. Each of these options sends a specific message and creates a slightly different effect at the end of the paper. The most important responsibility of the last paragraph is to bring the essay to an effective close. It is the last information that readers see before they form their own opinions or take action.

Mary's conclusion offers a solution to the problem raised in the second sentence of the paragraph:

> **Every effort should be made to find the cause of the "real" medical problems underlying ADD and ADHD before we even think about giving our children drugs.**

Toward the end of her conclusion, she calls the reader to action:

> **It's time to say good-bye to "conformist" . . . classrooms and diagnoses.**

She ends by reflecting on her thesis in one last, short line:

> **People don't fit "norms"; they have personalities.**

Her concluding paragraph refocuses the reader's attention on the problem, offers a solution to the problem, and then calls the reader to action.

◆ *Practice 17*   Make a rough outline of your ideas for a possible conclusion to your essay with sources. Choose a strategy that you want to use to bring your paper to a close.

◆ *Practice 18*   Write a rough draft of your conclusion, reminding your readers of your thesis statement.

10. ***Think of a catchy title.*** Your title is what readers see first in any essay. A title is a phrase, usually no more than a few words, placed at the beginning of your essay that suggests or sums up the subject, purpose, or focus of the essay. Some titles are very imaginative, drawing on different sources for their meaning. Others are straightforward, like the title of this chapter— "How to Write an Essay with Sources." These are just two of the many different approaches you can take to creating a title.

Besides suggesting an essay's purpose, a good title catches an audience's attention. For instance, Mary Minor's title, "Children as Robots," will catch most readers' attention because referring to children as "robots" is intriguing, and readers will want to find out just how and why this might occur. That's exactly what a title should do—make your readers want to read your paper.

◆ *Practice 19*   Jot down some catchy titles for your paper.

◆ *Practice 20*   Choose a title for your paper.

11. ***Check your sources and documentation format throughout your paper and at the end.*** Finding and using good, solid sources for evidence in an essay with sources is important, and equally important is the acknowledgment of those sources. If you use a source and do not cite it correctly or forget to cite it altogether, you are guilty of plagiarism, which can lead to a failing grade on the paper. So you need to learn when to cite a source (see Chapter 19), what documentation style to use (MLA, APA, or other appropriate format), and how to cite sources. You should check with your instructor to find out which format you should use in a particular course.

Citations are of two types: (a) The *in-text citation* indicates the source of a quotation or idea right after it appears in the essay; (b) then, at the end, a list of all the sources cited in the paper must appear on the *Works Cited* or *Reference* page. Many textbooks demonstrate the various forms of documentation, so you should look up the format that your instructor wants you to use. Then keep this text handy when you write papers with sources.

Mary uses the MLA format on her paper, which she wrote for an English class. Usually, English instructors ask their students to use the MLA format. Mary includes a variety of sources in her paper, which we can use to illustrate the two types of citations. Listed here are some sample entries at the end of Mary's paper, with the corresponding in-text citations in parentheses.

Book—name of author, title of book, city of publication, publisher, date of publication

> **Works Cited:**   Armstrong, Thomas. <u>The Myth of the ADD Child: 50 Ways to Improve Your Child's Behavior and Attention Span Without Drugs, Labels, or Coercion.</u> New York: Dutton, 1995.
>
> **In-Text Citation:**   (914)

Note: Notice how Mary introduced Armstrong before providing readers with this page number, so she doesn't have to repeat the author's name in the citation.

Journal—name of author, title of article, name of journal, volume number, year, page number

> **Works Cited:**   Bower, Bruce. "Kid's Attention Disorder Attracts Concern." <u>Science News</u> 154 (1998): 343.
>
> **In-Text Citation:**   (Bower 343)

Encyclopedia—name of author, title of article, name of encyclopedia, volume number, year

> **Works Cited:**   "Hippocratic Oath." <u>World Book Encyclopedia.</u> Vol. 9. 1999 ed.
>
> **In-Text Citation:**   ("Hippocratic Oath")

Note: If an article is unsigned, begin with the title of the article.

Online Database—name of author, title of article, name of database, date of publication, date you accessed the material, URL in angle brackets

> **Works Cited:** Schmitt, B. D. "Attention Deficit Disorder (Short Attention Span)." <u>Clinical Reference Systems.</u> 1 July 1999. 17 Feb. 2000 <http://www.epnet.com/ehost/login.html>.

> **In-Text Citation:** (Schmitt)

Note: If some information required in the citation is missing, include whatever is available.

General-Circulation Magazine—name of author, title of article, name of magazine, date of publication, page numbers

> **Works Cited:** Sheppard, Robert. "Growing Up Hyperactive." <u>Maclean's</u> 7 Sept. 1998: 45–46.

> **In-Text Citation:** (Sheppard 45)

Note: If an article is unsigned, begin with the title of the article.

These examples from Mary Minor's essay are just a few of the various types of sources that you will probably use in your essays with sources. Every source is cited in a slightly different way, depending on the type of source and the documentation style. Not even the best writers know the correct format for every source they use. So when you have chosen your sources and determined that they are relevant, reliable, and recent (the three *R*s), your last step is to consult an appropriate, current manual or Web site to make sure you cite each source correctly.

◆ *P r a c t i c e 21*   Make sure that the material from every source in your essay has an in-text citation. Then create a Works Cited, Reference, or Bibliography page, following an approved documentation format.

◆ *P r a c t i c e 22*   Check the format of your in-text citations and your list of works cited by consulting a current handbook.

CHAPTER 22

REVISING AND EDITING AN ESSAY WITH SOURCES

In this chapter, you will revise and edit a new student essay with sources and then revise and edit your own source essay. The checklists for this process are provided here, and the chapter will guide you through this process step by step.

REVISING CHECKLIST ✔

THESIS STATEMENT
✔ Does the thesis statement contain the essay's controlling idea and an opinion about that idea?
✔ Does the thesis appear as the last sentence of the introduction?

BASIC ELEMENTS
✔ Does the title draw in the reader?
✔ Does the introduction capture the reader's attention and build up to the thesis statement effectively?
✔ Does each body paragraph deal with a single topic?
✔ Does the conclusion bring the essay to a close in an interesting way?

DEVELOPMENT
✔ Do the body paragraphs adequately support the thesis statement?
✔ Does each body paragraph have a focused topic sentence?
✔ Does each body paragraph contain *specific* details that support the topic sentence?
✔ Does each body paragraph include *enough* details to explain the topic sentence fully?
✔ Are the sources relevant, reliable, and recent?
✔ Are references given for original sources to avoid plagiarism?
✔ Is the documentation format correct—in the paper and at the end?

UNITY

✔ Do the essay's topic sentences relate directly to the thesis statement?

✔ Do the details in each body paragraph support its topic sentence?

ORGANIZATION

✔ Is the essay organized logically?

✔ Is each body paragraph organized logically?

COHERENCE

✔ Are transitions used effectively so that paragraphs move smoothly and logically from one to the next?

✔ Do the sentences move smoothly and logically from one to the next?

EDITING CHECKLIST

SENTENCES

✔ Does each sentence have a main subject and verb?

✔ Do all subjects and verbs agree?

✔ Do all pronouns agree with their nouns?

✔ Are modifiers as close as possible to the words they modify?

PUNCTUATION AND MECHANICS

✔ Are sentences punctuated correctly?

✔ Are words capitalized properly?

WORD CHOICE AND SPELLING

✔ Are words used correctly?

✔ Are words spelled correctly?

REVISING AND EDITING A STUDENT ESSAY WITH SOURCES

Here is the first draft of an essay written by Rick Schroeder, a student. It demonstrates the guidelines for writing a successful essay with sources that you have learned in Chapters 18 through 21.

Space Bucks

1   Every year an enormous amount of money is poured into NASA for space exploration. Does this research justify the expense? Many people would gratefully sacrifice the money just to prove that Americans can compete in the space arena. An overwhelming force drives us into the unknown realms of our universe in the same way that Christopher Columbus was adventurously driven to search for what was once called the New World. On the other hand, many taxpayers believe that more justification is needed for the large amount of money put into NASA research. But what these "non-supporters" tend to overlook is NASA's chance "to lead the exploration and development of the space frontier, advancing science, technology, enterprise, and building institutions and systems that make accessible vast new resources" (United States). NASA is a worthwhile organization that many people benefit from.

2   Most significantly, technology research that results from space exploration greatly benefit the field of medicine. The International Space Station (ISS), which was built by 16 different nations, is one of the biggest and most costly projects that NASA has constructed and is essential for research in space technology. Scientists aboard the ISS have the opportunity to test various theories and conduct experiments in several different fields of science using the microgravity on this station in space (NASA *Space Station*). Some of the most important research that will be done onboard the ISS involves searching for cures for both osteoporosis and cancer (Von Brook, Siegel, and Foster 67). Also, according to Von Brook, Siegel, and Foster, the authors of <u>Space Exploration: The Dream and the Reality</u>, some additional examples of "space-pioneer medical technology include a cardiac pacemaker that can be automatically recharged without surgery, a human tissue simulator that relieves chronic pain, anti-contamination hospital garments, X-rays that can penetrate bone and produce pictures of body tissues and organs," and several other advances in autism, diabetes, heart disease, and premature birth (69). These are just a few of the contributions from space exploration that help improve the quality of life for humanity on a day-to-day basis. Without NASA's research, scientists would never have discovered these contributions. Therefore, we must continue to fund NASA and all its programs.

3   The vast number of effective medicines, treatments, and machines used to test for and treat illnesses would be enough to warrant the space exploration funds if they were the only benefits to society from the NASA research. But another benefit of NASA's research is their ability to monitor the environment to ensure continued life on Earth. Since the ISS is a permanent structure that will observe the earth for the next 30 years, scientists will be able to monitor the earth and distinguish changes that have been made over time to its environment (Von Brook, Siegel, and Foster 67). These studies could lead to more breakthroughs and solutions

for many environmental problems. For example, the balance between farming and water conservation will soon be made vastly more efficient due to advancements made by NASA using satellite imaging to determine watering priorities for irrigated farm lands (Rumsfeld 11). This information will help both the farmers and the general population—especially in a state like California where water rights are a volatile issue.

Not only can the space exploration program help solve environmental   4 problems, but it can also identify those problems. In fact, the space program gave us "our first real perspective on global warming, ozone layer depletion, deforestation, and other environmental scourges" (Von Brook, Siegel, and Foster 69). Yet not all environmental benefits are plans for the future. Von Brook, Siegel, and Foster state,

> we have already achieved very promising results with indoor air pollution and wastewater treatment using NASA technology. Today, NASA researchers are contributing steadily to our knowledge of landfill leachate treatment, hazardous waste disposal, tropical rainforest, and ground water pollution. (69)

Recently, astronauts aboard the space station spent ten days creating a topographic map of all locations on the world within 60 degrees of the equator. A topographic map of uniform scale circling the entire globe has never before been created, and NASA accomplished this feat in 10 days. This model of the Earth can now be used to monitor changes on the Earth's surface, providing a very useful tool humanity can use for many reasons, including fighting forest fires (Jet Propulsion Laboratory). The environment must be preserved, and since this task is made easier with the benefits of space exploration, we must continue to fund research for NASA.

Science, however, is not the only aspect of life that NASA affects, for   5 it also greatly influences the economy. According to Von Brook, Siegel, and Foster, "Space exploration . . . is the best investment for our future because it sharpens the skills and harnesses the talents of all Americans involved" (70). Sharpening the talents of Americans is important, yet the real question at hand is the economics of space exploration. A single space shuttle costs, for example, from $10,000–$20,000 per kilogram (Alpert 93). This is definitely a substantial amount of money to pay for a single launch. In 1975, NASA sponsored a study to design a space station it was never funded. A group of scientists created a plan for a circular station that would provide room for 10,000 colonists. The station would have cost $500 billion. However, the station would have paid for itself within 30 years because of enormous solar-power satellites that would be installed. A solar-energy-collection satellite would receive eight times as much energy as a collector on earth. The satellite would also produce five billion watts of electricity. Which is approximately five

6   times that of an average power plant (Alpert 93-94). The economic benefits of this power are enormous considering the energy crises that tend to afflict parts of the United States.

6   Given the proper chance, much of space exploration could pay for itself. Von Brook, Siegel, and Foster claim that "the Apollo mission yielded a 7-to-1 return of every dollar invested" (70). This does not suggest enormous waste. As Rumsfeld speculates, "An international space industry has developed, with revenues exceeding $80 billion in 2000. Industry forecasts project revenues will more than triple in the next decade" (11). Not only could a space project pay for itself, but the ISS will provide "50,000 jobs directly associated with spin-off technology," which "means greater national pride and fewer Americans that will require public support for basic needs like food and housing."

7   One major problem of NASA's budget, however, is the cuts it will cause for other programs. Unfortunately, NASA shares a budget with the Environmental Protection Agency (EPA), the Department of Housing and Urban Development (HUD), and the Veterans Administration (Von Brook, Siegel, and Foster 66). This means that budget cuts are mandatory for the other agencies if any one program requires more capital. Von Brook, Siegel, and Foster explain, "This puts some of the nation's most futuristic plans competing directly against some of America's most pressing social needs" (66). Nevertheless, Americans and humanity must look passed the present problems and see into the future for solutions. Social needs have plagued society for centuries. We have tried to throw money at these problems in the past, which has been ineffective, so new solutions must be sought. The answers can be found by looking beyond the problems that humanity faces today and into the future of space exploration.

8   NASA is an important and vital force in American society. As long as our desire to explore space continues to exist, advances and discoveries will follow. The benefits come not only in the form of space exploration, but also in medical, environmental, and economic advances that are necessary to the survival and progress of humanity. But NASA cannot continue to provide these major discoveries with a diminishing budget. In fact, NASA's 2002 budget allocation was less than the money it received in 1994 (NASA *FY 2003 Budget*). This budget desicion will affect all of American society for hundreds of years to come. An agency with the potential of NASA that has proven its usefulness time and time again should not be inadequately funded. It needs a generous budget that will let it continue to improve the quality of life for all Americans.

Works Cited

Alpert, Mark. "Making Money in Space." <u>The Future of Space Exploration</u>. 1 Jan. 1999: 92–95.

Jet Propulsion Laboratory. "Earth Has a New Look." NASA News. Jet Propulsion Laboratory, California Institute of Technology, Pasadena, California. News Release: 2003-116. August 22, 2003.

National Aeronautical and Space Agency (NASA). Chart: FY 2003 Budget vs. History and Background Material NASA FY 2003 Budget Briefing. 5 Sept. 2003 <http://www1.nasa.gov/audience/formediafeatures/ MP_Budget_Previous.html>.

Space Station Benefits. 4 Oct. 2003 <http://spaceflight.nasa.gov/station/benefits/index.html>.

Rumsfeld, Donald H. (chairman). Report of the Commission to Assess United States National Security Space Management and Organization. Pursuant to Public Law 106-65. January 11, 2001. 28 Sept. 2003 <www.defenselink.mil/pubs/ space20010111.html>.

United States. The Report of the National Commission on Space. Pioneering the Space Frontier. Toronto: Bantam Books, 1986.

Von Brook, Patricia, Mark A. Siegel, and Carol D. Foster. Space Exploration: The Dream and the Reality. Eds. Patricia Von Brook, Mark A. Siegel, and Carol D. Foster. Wylie, Texas: Information Plus, 1990.

Rick's first draft now needs to be revised and edited. First, apply the Revising Checklist (pages 274–275 at the beginning of this chapter) to the content of Rick's draft. When you are satisfied that his ideas are fully developed and well organized, use the Editing Checklist on page 275 to correct his grammatical and mechanical errors. The questions below will guide you through this process. Then rewrite the essay with your suggested changes.

Revision Questions

Thesis Statement

1. What is the main idea in Rick's essay with sources?

   _____

2. Put brackets around Rick's thesis statement. Does it introduce his main point?

   _____

3. Rewrite it to introduce all the topics in his essay.

   _____

   _____

Basic Elements

1. Give Rick's essay an alternate title.

    _____

2. Rewrite Rick's introduction so that it captures the reader's attention in a different way and builds up to the thesis statement at the end of the paragraph.

    _____

    _____

    _____

    _____

3. Does each of Rick's body paragraphs deal with only one topic?

    _____

4. Rewrite Rick's conclusion with a twist of your own.

    _____

    _____

    _____

    _____

Development

1. Do Rick's topic sentences support his thesis statement? Write out your revision of Rick's thesis statement, and list his six topic sentences.

    Thesis: _____

    _____

    Topics: _____

    _____

    _____

    _____

    _____

    _____

_____

_____

_____

_____

_____

_____

_____

_____

2. Does your revised thesis statement accurately introduce Rick's topic sentences?

_____

_____

3. Are Rick's examples specific?

_____

Add an even more specific detail to one of his paragraphs.

4. Does he offer enough examples or details in each paragraph?

_____

5. Are Rick's sources relevant, reliable, and recent?   For help, see Chapter 20.

_____

6. Does he give references for all original sources in his paper?   For help, see Chapter 19.

_____

Find the one sentence in paragraph 6 that is plagiarized and needs the reference "(Von Brook, Siegel, and Foster 68)."

_____

7. Is the documentation format correct in his paper?   For help, see Chapter 21.

_____

For help, see Chapter 21.

8. Is the format on his Works Cited page correct?

_____

Unity

1. Read each of Rick's topic sentences with his thesis statement in mind. Do they go together?

_____

2. Revise any topic sentences that are not directly related to his thesis.

3. Read each of Rick's paragraphs with its topic sentence in mind. Drop or rewrite any sentences that are not directly related to the paragraph's topic sentence.

Organization

1. Review your list of Rick's topics in item 1 under "Development," and decide if they are organized logically.

2. What is his method of organization?

_____

3. Read Rick's paper again to see if all his sentences are arranged logically.

4. Move any sentences that are out of order.

Coherence

For a list of transitions, see pages 70–71.

1. Circle five transitions that Rick uses.

2. Explain how three of these transitions make Rick's paper easier to read.

_____

_____

Now rewrite Rick's essay with your revisions.

Editing Questions

Sentences

Subjects and Verbs

For help with subjects and verbs, see Chapter 32.

1. Underline the subjects once and verbs twice in paragraph 4 of Rick's essay. Remember that sentences can have more than one subject–verb set.

2. Does each sentence have at least one subject and verb that can stand alone?

_____

3. Did you find and correct Rick's fragment in paragraph 5? If not, find and correct it now.

4. Did you find and correct Rick's run-on sentence in paragraph 5? If not, find and correct it now.

For help with fragments, see Chapter 33.

For help with run-ons, see Chapter 34.

Subject–Verb Agreement

1. Read aloud the subjects and verbs in paragraph 2 of Rick's revised essay.

2. Correct any subjects and verbs that do not agree.

3. Now read aloud the subjects and verbs in the rest of his revised essay.

4. Correct any subjects and verbs that do not agree.

For help with subject–verb agreement, see Chapter 36.

Pronoun Agreement

1. Find any pronouns in your revision of Rick's essay that do not agree with their nouns.

2. Correct any pronouns that do not agree with their nouns.

For help with pronoun agreement, see Chapter 39.

Modifier Errors

1. Find any modifiers in your revision of Rick's essay that are not as close as possible to the words they modify.

2. Rewrite sentences if necessary so that modifiers are as close as possible to the words they modify.

For help with modifier errors, see Chapter 42.

Punctuation and Mechanics
Punctuation

1. Read your revision of Rick's essay for any errors in punctuation.

2. Make sure any fragments and run-on sentences you revised are punctuated correctly.

For help with punctuation, see Chapters 43–46.

Mechanics

1. Read your revisions of Rick's essay for any errors in capitalization.

2. Be sure to check the capitalization in the fragments and run-on sentences you revised.

For help with capitalization, see Chapter 47.

Word Choice and Spelling
Confused Words

1. Find any words used incorrectly in your revision of Rick's essay.

For help with confused words, see Chapter 53.

2. Did you find and correct the confused word Rick used?

Spelling

For help with spelling, see Chapter 54.

1. Use spell-check and a dictionary to check the spelling in your revision of Rick's essay.

2. Did you find and correct his two misspelled words?

Now rewrite Rick's essay again with your editing corrections.

REVISING AND EDITING YOUR OWN ESSAY WITH SOURCES

Now revise and edit the essay that you wrote in Chapter 21. Use the techniques you used when revising and editing Rick's essay.

Guidelines for Writing an Essay with Sources

1. Choose a subject.
2. Do some general reading, and write a good, clear thesis statement about your subject.
3. Find sources that are relevant, reliable, and recent to support your thesis statement.
4. Take notes to avoid plagiarism.
5. Make a working outline of your paper.
6. Construct an introduction that leads up to your thesis statement.
7. Develop as many supporting paragraphs or body paragraphs as you think are needed to explain your thesis statement.
8. Make sure you use your sources as evidence for your argument.
9. Write a concluding paragraph.
10. Think of a catchy title.
11. Check your sources and documentation format throughout your paper and at the end.

1. As the photo on the facing page suggests, antidrug ads have changed over the past five years. How have they changed? Are they more or less effective now? Write an essay explaining these changes.

2. Research a controversial political issue of your choice. Then take a firm stand on the issue, and develop an essay supporting your position. You might want to look at newspaper headlines to get some ideas for this assignment.

3. Research a special trip that you want to take. Get all the information you need. Then write a letter to a close friend, inviting him or her to join you.

4. Create your own assignment (with the help of your instructor), and write a response to it.

Revising Workshop

Small Group Activity (10 minutes per writer)   In groups of three or four, each person should read his or her essay with sources to the other members of the group. The listeners should record their reactions on a copy of the Peer Evaluation Form (Appendix 1A). After your group goes through this process, give your evaluation forms to the appropriate writers so that each writer has two or three peer comment sheets for revising.

Paired Activity (5 minutes per writer)   Using the completed Peer Evaluation Forms, work in pairs to decide what you should revise in your essay. If time allows, rewrite some of your sentences, and have your partner check them.

Individual Activity   Rewrite your paper, using the revising feedback you received from other students.

Editing Workshop

Paired Activity (10 minutes per writer)   Swap papers with a classmate, and use the editing portion of your Peer Evaluation Forms (Appendix 1B) to identify as many grammar, punctuation, mechanics, and spelling errors as you can. Mark the errors on the student paper, using the correction symbols on the inside back cover. If time allows, correct some of your errors, and have your partner check them.

Individual Activity   Rewrite your paper again, using the editing feedback you received from other students. Record your grammar errors in the Error Log (Appendix 3) and your spelling errors in the Spelling Log (Appendix 4).

PART IV

FROM READING TO WRITING

To read without reflecting is like eating without digesting.

—EDMUND BURKE

Part IV is a collection of essays that demonstrate the rhetorical modes you are studying in this book. Each chapter focuses on a different rhetorical strategy and presents two essays that show the strategy at work with other strategies. After each essay you will find questions that check your understanding of the selection.

CHAPTER **23**

DESCRIBING

The first essay, "Underground Toronto," was written by journalist Allen Abel. In it he describes the diverse makeup of Toronto, as seen from its subway system. The second, "Dryden's Backyard," was written by Ken Dryden, ex-NHL goalie and current Member of Parliament. He describes playing hockey in his backyard as a child.

Allen Abel

UNDERGROUND TORONTO

Focusing Your Attention

1. Think of a place you have visited that has special meaning for you. Where was this place? Why was it special?

2. In the essay you are about to read, the author describes the sights, sounds, smells, tastes, and textures of the Toronto subway. What sights, sounds, smells, textures, and tastes do you remember of the place you have lived in or visited? Can you describe that place for someone who has never been there?

Expanding Your Vocabulary

The following words are important to your understanding of this essay:

archipelago: a large group of islands (paragraph 6)

bilious: sickly (paragraph 7)

Chinese *erhu*: two-stringed fiddle (paragraph 8)

reveries: dreams (paragraph 9)

patrician: aristocratic (paragraph 12)

deduce: conclude (paragraph 20)

utilitarian: plain, practical (paragraph 21)

evocative: bringing to mind, calling to mind (paragraph 22)

The slow train to China—and to Poland, Korea, Barbados, Greece, Peru 1
and the Azores—slides with a screech from a fluorescent terminus, north-
bound on a weekday noon.

With me in the long, steel car are about 70 other passengers, most of 2
them immigrants like me, strangers to each other and to this country, each
of us making up less than a millionth of the great lakeside city beneath
which we ride.

The car is rather crowded, yet nearly all of us today are riding alone. We 3
are solitary travellers on a two-dollar, round-the-world ticket, our skins and
stories far more colourful than the tired, tiled stations through which we
pass.

I look at the faces around me, and I wonder—who has just landed the 4
job of her dreams, and who has been let go? Who is newest to this cold, flat
city, farthest from his home, farthest from her children, closest to a dream?
Who is speeding toward a secret love affair, and who is running away?

But this is the subway. I keep my precious seat, flip through my paper, 5
count off the stations and dare not ask. And no one asks me.

What are we doing as we stutter from stop to stop, and from nation to 6
nation, below Toronto's ethnic archipelago? Drinking chocolate milk, studying *Parts of Speech* and the senior volleyball schedule of the Public School
Girls Athletic Association, making a quick phone call when the train leaps
from its tunnel for a two-stop breath of air. Or we are reading: Robert Hein-
lein, Ian McEwan, Mary Higgins Clark; *The Toronto Star*, *The Globe and
Mail*, *The Korea Times*; *Memoirs of a Geisha*, *The Wandering Fire*, *Introduction to Microsoft Exchange Server*, *Your Wedding File*, *Steps to Christ*.

The stations slip past in a blur of billboards: Jennifer Lopez's Still per- 7
fume, the ESP Psychic Expo, Parasuco Jeans. After a quarter-century on
these trains, I need only glimpse the station walls for an instant to know exactly where we are: the brown bricks at King Street; the bilious green of
Dundas; the murals of the Maple Leafs and Canadiens at College, where
big-league hockey was played (at least by the visitors) for nearly 70 years.

Then suddenly, amid the bustle of the transfer point, where the two 8
main lines meet at Bloor and Yonge streets, there is music—a two-stringed
Chinese *erhu*, haunting and high-pitched above the rumbling and squeal-
ing of the trains—crying out a melody familiar, I suspect, to half the people
in my car.

For me, this accidental concerto conjures other well-remembered 9
reveries: standing stock-still amid the rush-hour madness at Union Station
one winter morning, my eyes welling as a brilliant Russian violinist played
the sweet, sad "Meditation" from Massenet's *Thaïs*; a guitarist at the Bay
Street station one spring night singing Hank Williams' "I Saw the Light"
with such joy and spirit that I had to run to phone the woman I loved.

If this is your city, every stop of every ride returns a memory. (The den- 10
tist's office at Davisville? A court date at Osgoode?) If it is not, then each
opening of the doors invites the explorer to exit and taste what lies above.

11   So get out:

12   At patrician Rosedale, a neighbourhood so eager for its magnificence to be envied that it pulls the tracks out of the darkness and into the sun.

13   Or at Eglinton, where the smell of cinnamon buns from the bakery upstairs fills the cars with longing.

14   Or change trains with me at Bloor and Yonge, and head westward, just five stations, to another world—to Christie Street for a Korean lunch and the scorching stone bowl of rice and vegetables and chili paste that is known as bee-bim-bap.

15   For dessert, we can buy a bag of walnut cakes, tiny delights filled with sweet, creamy paste and baked on a long conveyor belt that passes through an oven imported, like almost everyone who gets off the train at Christie, from South Korea.

16   Then back on the subway:

17   "I'm hungry and you send me flowers. I cannot eat the iris."

18   "I wish I could walk around with my shirt off and feel comfortable."

19   I'm looking up at the advertising posters now and two quotations that face each other across the car. One is poetry ("Say It with Flowers" by Janice Kulyk Keefer) and the other is a placard for a hard-rock radio station that calls itself "The Edge."

20   I'll let you deduce which one is which.

21   Otherwise, there's not that much to see. There is no confusing Toronto's utilitarian tube with the grandeur of the Moscow subway, with its chandeliers and marble halls, or the silver-bullet rocketry of Hong Kong or the avant-garde (circa 1966) artistry of the Montréal Métro. Canada's oldest underground has been conveying commuters since 1954, which makes it far older than Toronto's new-found fascination with itself.

22   Newer stations such as Yorkdale, with an overarching rainbow of neon, and Eglinton West, with its giant murals of Toronto's beloved streetcars, offer some visual relief. There are a few open-cut stretches, including a simultaneous vista of the Davisville yards and Mount Pleasant Cemetery, allowing us to see the eventual destination of both the cars and the people who ride in them. But the evocative elevated tracks of my New York City childhood exist only on a rapid-transit branch line in the far northeastern suburbs. To wreak havoc on Toronto rapid transit, King Kong would have to ride all the way out to Scarborough and change trains at Kennedy Station.

23   This hardly matters—the passengers provide fascination enough. The racial and linguistic diversity is astonishing, especially at the extremities of the long east-west line, where the tracks stab deeply into the low-rent, high-rise immigrant quarters that orbit the city's leafy European core. Fittingly, the map of the system closely resembles the Chinese character for "world."

24   It is up to each rider to decide what part of that world he or she wants to devour. Korean bee-bim-bap at Christie or Greek souvlaki at Pape. Polish tripe soup at Dundas West or Portuguese pork and clams at Ossington. Don Mills or York Mills; High Park or Queen's Park; St. George or St. Clair or St. Patrick.

Nowhere in the world does a two-dollar ticket offer such an amazing   25
array. But there is one other station that the system serves. It is the most important destination of all, no matter where we board our train, no matter
how long we ride.

And that's the stop called Home.   26

Thinking Critically About Content

1. The article contains several metaphors. To what does the author
   compare the Toronto subway? What other metaphors can you find?

2. List as many sensory details as you can from the essay, including seeing, hearing, touching, feeling, smelling, and tasting.

3. How does the author capture the essence of Toronto without actually describing the city?

Thinking Critically About Purpose and Audience

4. What dominant impression does the author have of the city he describes? Does it sound like another city you have visited in Canada?
   How is it similar? How is it different?

5. Do you think it is necessary to have visited Toronto to enjoy the
   essay? Why or why not?

6. How does the author use figurative language in this essay?

Thinking Critically About Essays

7. If an essay is unified, all of its paragraphs are related to one central idea.
   Based on this explanation, is this essay unified? Explain your answer.

8. How does Abel organize his ideas and observations in this essay?
   (Refer to pages 37–47 for information on essay organization.) Make
   a rough outline of this essay.

9. The organization of this essay follows a journey Abel makes in the
   train. Many literary works (*The Adventures of Huckleberry Finn*, for
   example) follow the same pattern. How is this journey pattern effective in this essay?

10. Abel ends his essay with the words "And that's the stop called
    home." Is he referring literally to the stop where he is going to exit
    the train, or does he mean something more? What might he be try-
    ing to say? Explain your answer.

Ken Dryden

DRYDEN'S BACKYARD

Focusing Your Attention

1. Think of a place where you played as a child. Does thinking about
   that place evoke your childhood for you? In what way?

2. In the essay you are about to read, the author describes the feeling of playing hockey as a boy in his family's backyard. He remembers that as a child he really became the hockey heroes of his day, rather than thinking he would ever be one of them. Have you watched young children play? What kind of future life do they seem to imagine in their play?

Expanding Your Vocabulary

The following words are important to your understanding of this essay:

agility: nimbleness, quickness (paragraph 4)

billy boots: rubber boots (paragraph 4)

duffel coat: a hooded winter cloth coat with toggles for buttons (paragraph 12)

euphoria: a state of elation, a high (paragraph 14)

unseverable: unbreakable (paragraph 16)

1   I get out of bed and pull back the curtains. It has snowed overnight and traces are still gently falling. For several minutes I stand there, my forehead pressed to the window, watching the snow, looking out at the backyards of the houses behind, where the Pritchards, the McLarens, and the Carpenters lived, and down below at the winter's depth of snow, and at the backyard where I spent my childhood.

2   "Dryden's Backyard." That's what it was called in our neighborhood. It was more than 70 feet long, paved curiously in red asphalt, 45 feet wide at "the big end," gradually narrowing to 35 feet at the flower bed, to 25 feet at the porch—our center line—to 15 feet at "the small end." While Steve Shutt and Guy Lafleur were in Willowdale and Thurso on backyard rinks their fathers built, while Larry Robinson was on a frozen stream in Marvelville and Réjean Houle on a road in Rouyn under the only street light that his street had, I was here.

3   It was an extraordinary place, like the first swimming pool on the block, except there were no others like it anywhere. Kids would come from many blocks away to play, mostly "the big guys," friends of my brother, a year or two older than him, seven or eight years older than me. But that was never a problem. It was the first rule of the backyard that they had to let me play. To a friend who complained one day, Dave said simply, "If Ken doesn't play, you don't play."

4   We played "ball hockey" mostly, with a tennis ball, its bounce deadened by the cold. A few times, we got out a garden hose and flooded the backyard to use skates and pucks, but the big end was slightly lower than the small end, and the water pooled and froze unevenly. More important, we found that the more literal we tried to make our games, the less lifelike they became. We could move across the asphalt quickly and with great agility in rubber "billy" boots; we could shoot a tennis ball high and hard. But with skates on, with a puck, we were just kids. So after the first few weeks of the first year, we played only ball hockey.

Depending on the day, the time, the weather, there might be any num- 5
ber of kids wanting to play, so we made up games any number could play.
With four and less than nine, we played regular games, the first team scoring ten goals the winner. The two best players, who seemed always to
know who they were, picked the teams and decided on ends. First choice of
players got second choice of ends, and because the size of the big end
made it more fun to play in, the small end was the choice to defend. Each
team had a goalie—one with goalie pads, a catching glove, and a goalie
stick; the other with only a baseball glove and a forward's stick. When we
had more than eight players, we divided into three or more teams for a
round-robin tournament, each game to five. With fewer than four, it was
more difficult. Sometimes we attempted a regular game, often we just
played "shots," each player being both shooter and goalie, standing in
front of one net, shooting in turn at the other. Most often, however, we
played "penalty shots."

In the late 1950s, the CBS network televised NHL games on Saturday af- 6
ternoon. Before each game, there was a preview show in which a player
from each of the teams involved that day would compete in two contests,
one of which was a penalty-shot contest. The goalie they used each week
was an assistant trainer for the Detroit Red Wings named Julian Klymquiw.
Short and left-handed, Klymquiw wore a clear plexiglass mask that arched
in front of his face like a shield. None of us had ever heard of him, and his
unlikely name made us a little doubtful at first. But it turned out that he was
quite good, and most weeks he stopped the great majority of shots taken at
him. So, during backyard games of "penalty shots," we pretended to be Julian Klymquiw, not Terry Sawchuk or Glenn Hall. And before each of our
contests began, we would perform the ritual that Klymquiw and announcer
Bud Palmer performed each week:

"Are you ready, Julian?" 7

"Yes, Bud." 8

But the backyard also meant time alone. It was usually after dinner 9
when the "big guys" had homework to do and I would turn on the flood-
lights at either end of the house and on the porch, and play. It was a private
game. I would stand alone in the middle of the yard, a stick in my hands, a
tennis ball in front of me, silent, still, then suddenly dash ahead, stickhan-
dling furiously, dodging invisible obstacles for a shot on net. It was Maple
Leaf Gardens filled to wildly cheering capacity, a tie game, seconds re-
maining. I was Frank Mahovlich, or Gordie Howe, I was anyone I wanted
to be, and the voice in my head was that of Leafs broadcaster Foster Hewitt:
". . . there's ten seconds left, Mahovlich, winding up at his own line, at center, eight seconds, seven, over the blueline, six—he winds up, he shoots, *he
scores!*" The mesh that had been tied to the bottoms of our red metal goal-
posts until frozen in the ice had been ripped away to hang loose from the
crossbars, whipped back like a flag in a stiff breeze. My arms and stick flew
into the air, I screamed a scream inside my head, and collected my ball to
do it again—many times, for many minutes, the hero of all my own games.

10   It was a glorious fantasy, and I always heard that voice. It was what made my fantasy seem almost real. For to us, who attended hockey games mostly on TV or radio, an NHL game, a Leafs game, was played with a voice. If I wanted to be Mahovlich or Howe, if I moved my body the way I had seen them move theirs and did nothing else, it would never quite work. But if I heard the voice that said their names while I was playing out that fantasy, I could believe it. Foster Hewitt could make me them.

11   My friends and I played every day after school, sometimes during lunch and after dinner, but Saturday was always the big day. I would go to bed Friday night thinking of Saturday, waking up early, with none of the fuzziness I had other days. If it had snowed overnight, Dave and I, with shovels and scrapers, and soon joined by others, would pile the snow into flower beds or high against the back of the garage. Then at 9 A.M. the games would begin.

12   There was one team in the big end, another in the small; third and fourth teams sat like birds on a telephone wire, waiting their turn on the wall that separated the big end from Carpenter's backyard. Each team wore uniforms identical to the other. It was the Canadian midwinter uniform of the time—long, heavy duffel coats in browns, grays, or blues; tuques in NHL team colors, pulled snug over ears under the watchful eye of mothers, here rolled up in some distinctive personal style; leather gloves, last year's church gloves, now curling at the wrist and separating between fingers; black rubber "billy" boots over layers of heavy woolen socks for fit, the tops rolled down like "low cuts" for speed and style.

13   Each game would begin with a faceoff, then wouldn't stop again. Action moved quickly end to end, the ball bouncing and rolling, chased by a hacking, slashing scrum of sticks. We had sticks without tops on their blades—"toothpicks"; sticks with no blades at all—"stubs." They broke piece by heart-breaking piece, often quickly, but still we used them. Only at the start of a season, at Christmas (Dave and I routinely exchanged sticks until one year he gave me a stick and I gave him a pair of socks) and once or twice more, would we get new ones. All except John Stedelbauer. His father owned a car dealership and during the hockey season gave away hockey sticks to his customers as a promotion. Stedelbauer got all the new sticks he needed, fortunately, as they weren't very good. One year he broke nineteen of them.

14   A goal would be scored, then another, and slowly the game would leapfrog to five. Bodies grew warm from exertion, fingers and toes went numb; noses ran, wiped by unconscious sleeves; coats loosened, tuques fell off; steam puffed from mouths and streamed from tuqueless heads. Sticks hacked and slashed; tennis balls stung. But in the euphoria of the game, the pain disappeared. Sitting on the wall that overlooked his backyard, Rick "Foster" Carpenter, younger and not very athletic, gave the play-by-play, but no one listened. Each of us had his own private game playing in his head. A fourth goal, then a fifth, a cheer, and the first game was over. Quickly, four duffel coats, four tuques, four pairs of weathered

gloves and rubber "billy" boots would jump from the wall to replace the losers; and the second game would begin. We paused at noon while some went home and others ate the lunch that they had brought with them. At 6 P.M. the two or three who remained would leave. Eighteen hours later, after church, the next game would begin.

When I think of the backyard, I think of my childhood; and when I think 15 of my childhood, I think of the backyard. It is the central image I have of that time, linking as it does all of its parts: father, mother, sister, friends; hockey, baseball, and Dave—big brother, idol, mentor, defender, and best friend. Yet it lasted only a few years. Dave was already twelve when the backyard was built; I was six. He and his friends played for three or four years, then stopped; I played longer but, without them, less often. Yet until moments ago, I had never remembered that.

The backyard was not a training ground. In all the time I spent there, I 16 don't remember ever thinking I would be an NHL goalie, or even hoping I could be one. In backyard games, I dreamed I *was* Sawchuk or Hall, Mahovlich or Howe; I never dreamed I would be like them. There seemed no connection between the backyard and Maple Leaf Gardens; there seemed no way to get to there from here. If we ever thought about that, it never concerned us; we just played. It was here in the backyard that we *learned* hockey. It was here we got close to it, we got *inside* it, and it got inside us. It was here that our inextricable bond with the game was made. Many years have now passed, the game has grown up and been complicated by things outside it, yet still the backyard remains—untouched, unchanged, my unseverable link to that time, and that game.

Thinking Critically About Content

1. In paragraph 3, Dryden says that his backyard was "like the first swimming pool." In what way does the backyard resemble "the first swimming pool" on the block? Explain your answer.

2. List as many sensory details as you can from the essay, including seeing, hearing, touching, feeling, smelling, and tasting.

3. What role does "the voice" play in Dryden's childhood fantasy world? Explain your answer.

Thinking Critically About Purpose and Audience

4. What dominant impression does the author create in this description? Explain your answer in detail.

5. Who do you think Dryden's primary audience is?

6. Do the examples Dryden uses evoke memories of the games you played growing up? What details in the essay sound most like your own childhood?

Thinking Critically About Essays

7. If an essay is unified, all of its paragraphs are related to one central idea. Based on this explanation, is this essay unified? Explain your answer.

8. How does Dryden organize his ideas and observations in this essay? (Refer to pages 37–47 for information on essay organization.) Make a rough outline of this essay.

9. The essay begins with Dryden looking out the window at his old backyard as an adult. How does the window function metaphorically in the essay? How does the atmosphere he describes at the start help in the look backwards at his childhood?

10. Dryden ends his essay with the words "yet still the backyard remains." He has ended the essay physically where he started, but now he is referring to something that is inside him, and inside all Canadians. What is the effect of this change from external to internal in this essay? Explain your answer in detail.

Writing Topics: Describing

Before you begin to write, you might want to review the writing process in Part I.

1. In the first description essay, Allen Abel draws on impressions from many senses to describe the City of Toronto. Think of a place that is very important to you, a place that is a part of your life now or that was a part of your life in the past. Write a description of that place, drawing on as many of the senses as possible—seeing, hearing, touching, smelling, and tasting—so that your reader can experience it the way you did.

2. How well suited to you is the place where you live now? Write a description of the features of your house or apartment that make it most suitable or unsuitable for you.

3. What do you think are the most important features of a good description? Why are they important? What effect do they have on you?

NARRATING

The two essays included in this chapter should help you understand more clearly how to write narrative essays. In "The Worth of Women's Work," author Nina Lee Colwill recalls the wisdom of her grandmother. In the second essay, "Writer's Retreat" by Stan Higgins, the author tells a story about writing from a prison cell.

Nina Lee Colwill

THE WORTH OF WOMEN'S WORK

Focusing Your Attention

1. Can you recall visiting your grandparents when you were very young? Write down as many facts, impressions, and memories as you can of those visits.

2. In the essay you are about to read, the writer describes a person whose words stayed in her mind and shaped the way she thought. Has anyone had a similar impact on you? Have you found yourself, like the writer, thinking back to something someone said to you when you were younger and realizing how true it was?

Expanding Your Vocabulary

The following words are important to your understanding of this essay:

ruminating: thinking over (paragraph 6)

sombre: melancholy or sad (paragraph 8)

emulate: copy (paragraph 15)

lauded: praised (paragraph 18)

reconceptualized: formed a different concept or idea (paragraph 18)

derision: ridicule (paragraph 19)

1   I was born during World War II into a fatherless world. Daddy was in Belgium and the Netherlands, fighting the war that would bring worldwide peace forever. Mum and I lived with her parents and sisters and brothers in Gaspé, Québec, in the little farming village of Wakeham. Central to that life was Grandma—Grandma, who, then as now, personified strength and wisdom.

2   My earliest memory is of creeping downstairs in the morning and hugging Grandma's legs as she lit the fire in the kitchen stove. Her braids hung freely then, and I'd play with them while she rocked me in the old green wooden rocking chair, waiting for the kitchen to warm for the day. She would scold me: "You should be in bed where it's warm, Nina Lee, not down here in this cold kitchen." But I always knew I was right where she wanted me, curled up on her lap.

3   Grandma could do anything. She baked the most delicious of breads, drawing sifter after sifter of flour from the deep bin that Grandpa had built under the kitchen counter—soft white bread with thick, hard, brown crusts. She made the most comforting of bedtime snacks—dried bread and cream and brown sugar. She taught me to play solitaire when I was two. She taught me not to cheat at solitaire when I was four. She solved an architectural problem that had plagued my grandfather and the other carpenters in the village for years. And she could kill a chicken in a trice.

4   Grandma belonged to the Women's Institute. Every couple of weeks she'd change from her housedress into her church dress and set a hat on her head, and off she'd go to the mysterious WI.

5   I'll never forget the day I discovered the photograph. Actually, I'd seen that group of women every day of my life, standing in four neat rows in their flowered dresses, right there in a black wooden frame in the livingroom. But one day, playing alone with a puzzle on the chesterfield, I looked up and spied Grandma in that group. It was then that she showed me her name printed neatly on brown paper on the back of the photograph: Ruby Jane Patterson, Wakeham. As we sat at the kitchen table eating blueberries and cream, she told me how she'd taken a train to Montreal to represent her district at the WI Convention. It was, I believed, the most worldly and sophisticated work a person could possibly undertake.

6   When I was older and the war was no longer foremost in our thoughts, when my parents and I had moved to another life and our family had grown to four, then five, then six, I would often visit my grandparents in Gaspé. Sometimes I'd sit cross-legged on the painted wooden floor and study that photograph, ruminating about the women and imagining their lives. All those women, all over Québec, with their own families and their own work. And Grandma was part of this illustrious band.

7   No one ever told me about the value of women's work. No one ever said, "To love your work is to love life." Yet a sisterhood of women, a mysterious train trip to Montreal, a grandmother with grey braids wound around her head, humming as she kneaded bread—these pictures arranged themselves into a complex collage of women and work. Grandma never told me

that all work is a privilege, or that our integrity depends on the value we place on our work. But she treated her work as a calling, and silently she taught me that my work is a calling, too—that I've been chosen.

Yet there's a sombre side of work. To study women and work is to face   8 sadness, is to confront a belief shared by every culture in every country on this planet: the assumption that men, the things men do and all things masculine are more valuable than women, the things women do and all things feminine.

I remember the day it struck me, overwhelmed me: the work of women   9 is less valued than the work of men. I suppose I'd always known it at an intellectual level, for I'd studied women and work for half my life. But on the day I truly understood, with a logic beyond logic, that women's work is valued less than men's, I wasn't collecting a paycheque or reading in a library or consulting for some organization. I was in the Rijksmuseum in Amsterdam with my husband, Dennis, and we were viewing the work of the Dutch Masters for the first time.

The Rijksmuseum has erected a veritable shrine to the Dutch Masters,   10 where people the world over pay homage to the likes of Vermeer, de Hooch and Rembrandt. In every room is a guard, well-versed in the history of each painter and each painting, for many thousands of words have been written about these brilliant men and their work.

One passage leads from the chambers of the Dutch Masters into a quiet,   11 darkened room; eventually we found ourselves there, in the needlework gallery. There we could browse without attending to the explanations of guides or the murmurs of worshippers. We saw crocheting, needlepoint, quilting, embroidery. Ancient works—works from the days of the Dutch Masters. Exquisite works—works of brilliant artists. And no names.

You can imagine Dennis' shock when he found me in the corner sob-   12 bing over a tablecloth, weeping for the woman who designed and created it without recognition, for the woman who didn't sign her name.

Yet, I like to believe they created with joy, these women. I like to believe   13 their work was their calling, that they knew they'd been chosen. I hope their offerings were treated as precious, that people were generous with their praise and their payment. But most of all I hope they created with joy.

Because, when all is said and done, we must love our own work. If the   14 historical and universal belief that men's work is more important than women's work is not to be perpetuated to yet another generation, we must judge our own work to be worthy. And we must value it so highly that we value the men who choose to emulate us.

Because women and men, who have much to learn from each other, do   15 not imitate each other in equal numbers. For women to do the things men do, to do men's work, is for women to better themselves—a fine accomplishment in an achieving society. So women become ministers, fix their own cars and compete for Olympic medals in hockey, and most of us today consider such women to have achieved. But praise is not as loud for the men who become nurses or take on the family's housework and child care. To emulate one's superiors in an achieving society is to increase one's status. To emulate one's inferiors smacks of perversion.

16   No one ever told me that women would always be valued in proportion to the value we place on women's work. No one ever said that female physicians would never acquire the status of male physicians until secretaries are valued as highly as tool-and-die makers. No one ever explained that the father who needlepoints a birthday gift for his son must be accorded the same respect as the woman who wires her family cottage. But the status of women's work, I now know, is a measure of the value we place on women.

17   There's been monumental change in the past fifty years, in the past twenty years, even in the past year. It didn't occur because large groups of people decided simultaneously and unanimously that things must change. It occurred because you and I decided to change ourselves a little bit. We didn't change our spouses; we didn't change our children; we didn't change our co-workers. We addressed the only thing over which any of us has any direct control: we changed ourselves. We faltered, we backtracked and we hedged our bets, but we changed our beliefs about the worth of women and men. The rest followed.

18   We're placing higher value on women's traditional art forms, the fibre crafts: quilting, weaving, embroidery, smocking, tatting. Women's work. Honoured in ways it's never been honoured before in written history—in shops, in competitions, in art galleries, in homes. The entrepreneurial styles for which women have become famous are lauded today: start small, with as much of your own money as you can manage, and do what you love to do. As women feel free to be themselves, to lead as they are comfortable in leading, women's management styles are recognized and men are emulating those styles. More parents are steering their children away from violent, competitive sports and into lifetime, co-operative sports. And child care, the chronic issue of every employed mother, is slowly being reconceptualized as a family issue, a corporate issue, a community issue.

19   Of course there is more we can do. We can tell the world by word and by action that women and girls are valuable people and the things they do are valuable as well. We can refuse to participate in the derision of men and boys whose voices or gestures or interests are described as feminine. We can ensure that the family policies of our organizations and our governments are as supportive of fathers as they are of mothers. And if men who try to use these policies are ridiculed, we can be vocal in our protest of their treatment. For if we cannot imagine a world in which men choose to emulate women, we will never create a world in which women and men are equally valued.

20   When I finished my B.A. at the University of Western Ontario and was accepted into graduate school, Grandma sent me a note of praise and admiration—encouraging words, consistent with the support she'd given me all my life. But she closed her letter with a comment that enraged me:

"Remember your husband and children and home." Thirty years later, I think I understand what she was telling me, and I now count these words among her wisest: "Never undervalue the work that your foremothers carved out as their special domain, for in doing so, you undervalue yourself."

Thinking Critically About Content

1. Colwill refers to "the mysterious WI" (Women's Institute). Why is it mysterious? Does this organization stand for more than simply a social group in the author's mind?

2. Notice the way the writer describes her feelings when she suddenly discovers that her grandmother is one of the women in the black-framed group photo. What does this discovery represent for her? How does the discovery relate to the rest of the essay?

3. Colwill describes herself "sobbing over a tablecloth." Why is she sobbing? What has she realized?

4. The image at the beginning of the essay of the author cuddling on her grandmother's lap permeates the rest of the essay. Why do you think the author began the essay with that image? Explain your answer in detail.

Thinking Critically About Purpose and Audience

5. What do you think Colwill's purpose is in writing this narrative essay? Explain your answer.

6. Colwill asks us to "imagine a world in which men choose to emulate women." In your opinion, what reader does she have in mind when she asks this question? Is that the same reader she is writing for in the rest of the essay?

7. Colwill writes about her grandmother. Do you think that she might be imagining her grandmother as a possible reader of the piece? Is she to some extent apologizing to her grandmother? Should she in fact be apologizing to her grandmother, or is she trying to rationalize what her grandmother has said to her? Explain your answer.

Thinking Critically About Essays

8. How does Colwill organize the details in this essay? Is this an effective order?

9. What perspective is the author writing from when she says, "Daddy was in Belgium and the Netherlands, fighting the war that would bring worldwide peace forever." Do you sense an ironic adult presence in the comment, or is she writing from a child's point of view? At what points in the essay is she writing from a child's viewpoint, and when is she writing from an adult viewpoint?

10. Explain in detail how this essay would be different if it were written by Colwill's grandmother.

Stan Higgins

WRITER'S RETREAT

Focusing Your Attention

1. Can you remember a time in your life when you were frustrated in trying to meet a goal you had set for yourself? Write down as many facts, impressions, and memories as you can about this feeling.

2. In the essay you are about to read, the writer describes a person who is trying to write in prison. What do you think motivates him? Have you ever wanted to do something so much you would even do it in prison? Explain your answer.

Expanding Your Vocabulary

The following words are important to your understanding of this essay:

> **within a pole vault:** a few yards away (paragraph 1)
>
> **the Muse:** inspiration (paragraph 2)
>
> **staccato:** consisting of short, sharp sounds (paragraph 2)
>
> **ransacked:** torn apart (paragraph 3)
>
> **confiscated:** taken away (paragraph 3)
>
> **contraband:** prohibited items (paragraph 3)
>
> **lock down:** lock all prisoners in their cells (paragraph 4)
>
> **Bugler:** brand of tobacco (paragraph 7)
>
> **mud:** coffee (paragraph 16)
>
> **tier:** row of prison cells (paragraph 23)
>
> **persevere:** continue (paragraph 30)
>
> **tantamount:** equal (paragraph 32)
>
> **misdemeanors:** minor crimes (paragraph 32)
>
> **subsides:** decreases (paragraph 34)
>
> **nebulous:** vague, uncertain (paragraph 34)
>
> **girth:** size (paragraph 41)
>
> **obscenities:** offensive comments (paragraph 42)

1   Sandwiched between mountain snow and desert sand, hidden by sandstone walls 150 years old within a pole vault of the Arkansas River, it just doesn't get any better than this writer's retreat I call home. I write from a Colorado prison cell.

2   During the day I wash dishes, clean tables, and mop floors. They call it Vocational Training. And today, as every day at three P.M., I return to my

cozy, bathroom-size suite and drag out my tiny portable. We've all night, just the two of us, my blue typewriter that has been my steady cell-mate for six years, through seven facilities across two states, and I. Today's goal is three pages. I blow dust from the cover and clean the keys. The Muse calls. *Tack-tack. Tack. Tack-tack-tack.* My typewriter sings its staccato song as I search for a fertile word or idea, some harmonious junction of thought and paper. Locked in solitary combat with my machine, nothing exists outside my cell, or so I pretend. I type a line. My door opens. Two blue-uniformed guards stand there grinning. "Guess what?" one says. "Your number came up."

Somehow I know he doesn't mean the Lottery. One begins searching my cell. The other pats me down as I leave. I return twenty minutes later to find my house ransacked, my bed torn up, papers scattered, pencils and pens strewn about, sox, shorts, and typewriter piled in a heap on the floor. Taped to the shelf above my desk is a slip of yellow paper with a fancily scrawled list of books, magazines, and other confiscated contraband. I can't help but question their appreciation for the written word.   3

I put my house back in order. We lock down, and the guards count us. After ten minutes the Count is cleared. My hands tremble. I can't write, not now. It's time for the ultimate challenge to a prisoner's courage . . . Chow!   4

Buoyed at having survived another meal, I return to my cell and begin anew. *Tack-tack-tack.*   5

"Hey, Bro," a green-uniformed inmate named O'Neil hollers from my doorway. "Think I can get a pinch of tobacco?"   6

This, too, is part of the territory. I pause to hand him a can of Bugler. My attention returns to writing as I study the list of disjointed, unrelated words I have accumulated, but I see out of the corner of my eye that I still have company.   7

"Think I can get a rolling paper?" O'Neil asks as he pops the lid off the can.   8

With a deep breath I fish him a pack of papers from my pocket and hand them over. He fumbles with the paper as I reread my typed words.   9

"Think you could roll it for me, Bro?"   10

"What else, O'Neil?" I say whisking the paper and tobacco from his hands and rolling him a quick, crooked cigarette. He asks for a light as I usher him to the door.   11

Tack-tack-tack-tack, I resume. Just more words. I pinch my lips and study the nearly blank sheet of paper. *Write what you know*, memories of books past suggest. What do I know? Steel and concrete, jingling keys, and slamming doors. *Tack-tack-tack. Tack-tack.*   12

"M-m-Mr. Higgins?" another prisoner interrupts. It's a skinny kid in over-size greens, and his voice squeaks. "W-would you maybe have a dictionary I could, you know, sorta read, please?" He hesitates at the door in his stiff, fresh-out-of-the-package uniform that reminds me of pajamas, eyeing my bookshelf from a safe distance until I stand. I pull a *Webster's New Collegiate Dictionary* from my shelf above the desk and sit down again as he thumbs through it. He clears his throat. "Uh, excuse me, how do you spell *the*?"   13

14   "With two *r*'s instead of one," I tell him, shooing him away with the back of my hand.

15   *Tack-tack. Tack-tack, tack-tack-tack, tack.* Bones of steel, concrete skin, I type, and a soul as slippery as time.

16   Digger B. struts into my house. "Ya got a cup a mud I can get or what?" He pushes his empty cup in front of me, and as I fill it, he peers over my shoulder. "So what ya doin'?"

17   "Trying to write about trying to write."

18   "Man," he says and slurps coffee from his cup. "Whyn't ya write about somethin' interestin', know what I mean? Murder, war, sex, ya know—interestin'!"

19   I love encouragement. He wanders out.

20   I stare at my typewriter. I wait a few minutes. Nothing. My fingers creep back into place. *Tack-tack-tack.*

21   "Got a weed?" asks a gruff voice. It's Thunder. Six-foot-six and almost as wide, 300 pounds of beard and tattoo, he slides sideways into my cell. I quickly roll him a cigarette and light it.

22   "Anything else, Mr. Thunder?"

23   "Heared you typing clean down the tier," he grumbles. "What you doing?"

24   "Typing. Trying to type. Trying to write, I guess."

25   "You ain't writing 'bout me, are you?" He stares at me with eyes like rocks.

26   "No, sir, Mr. Thunder," I assure him, pointing to my almost blank paper. "Check it out."

27   He squints at it. "Don't like people writing 'bout me 'hind my back."

28   "I wouldn't do that, Mr. Thunder."

29   "Just so you ain't. 'At's all I care." He turns and sidles out the doorway. Thunder is unpredictable. Thunder hears voices. Thunder caught a guy in the shower once and stabbed him 53 times with a sharpened Number 2 pencil; he thought the man was talking about him. All in all, I figure it's not a bad idea to get along with Mr. Thunder.

30   The sun is setting. I've completed three sentences. My goal of three pages for the day is becoming as gray as my cell. At this rate I'm confident I can finish an 800-word article by my 2006 discharge date. *Persevere!* I get up and flip on the light.

31   Back to my typewriter; back on track. *Tack-tack-tack. Tack-tack, tack-tackity-tack.* I'm into it finally, my head is there, I'm on the verge of something . . . when Thunder stops at my door and pokes his woolly head in. "You sure you ain't writing things 'bout me?"

32   In prison, opening a can of tobacco, a bag of potato chips, or brewing a pot of coffee—like trying to type—is tantamount to throwing a side of beef into shark-infested waters. But these are minor distractions . . . misdemeanors. Prison overcrowding being what it is, Colorado officials have

on several occasions sent inmates to faraway places for temporary storage. Two years ago guards came to my door with a green duffel bag and ordered me to pack up. I surveyed my four-year accumulation of books, magazines, and notes that converted my six-by-ten-foot cell into a private classroom. Each book and magazine, then highlighted for frequent reference, had been a hard-collected treasure. There were works-in-progress scattered on my desk. "Now!" a guard encouraged. "You're going to Washington state. If your stuff don't all fit . . . ," he reassured me with a glint in his eye and a broad sweep of his arm, ". . . you don't need it!" A year later I was returned to sender. Back in Colorado, I set up housekeeping, mailed out another batch of address changes.

An aluminum trash can falls to the floor from an upper tier, perhaps   33
with a little help. I try to type. The cell block explodes in cheering and clapping. Pop cans rain from above. I hesitate at the keyboard. It might be boredom; it might be a fight or a stabbing. It might be a riot. Then again, it might be they just discovered what was for breakfast tomorrow.

It is dark outside. The noise subsides. I sit for a few minutes blissfully   34
alone, rescuing my thoughts, pondering my last sentence, imagining some nebulous, faraway, fairy tale future where everything is happily-ever-after. I imagine a steak dinner, the meat still sizzling, its pink and brown juice puddling the plate beneath a twice-baked potato and fresh asparagus, steam rising. . . .

"You ain't writing 'bout me!?" Thunder startles me. This time I didn't hear   35
or see him fill my doorway.

"No, sir," I tell him, cigarette smoke replacing the scent of steak. "Not one   36
word, Mr. Thunder."

He scratches his beard and stares. He steps in and looks over my shoul-   37
der. When he speaks again, after some moments, his voice is uncharacteristically soft and plaintive. "Not one word?"

I shake my head.   38

"Ain't I good enough to be in your stories?"   39

For a minute I think he is about to cry. I tell him I'll write something about   40
him if he likes. He reaches across the desk for the can of Bugler, rolls a cigarette, pats me on the back, and leaves.

I sigh into the typewriter keys and look up in time to see a couple of   41
guards making the rounds, parading their girth like badges of authority, jingling keys. "Attention on the Block! Attention on the Block!" blares the loudspeaker. "Five minutes to Count! Lock up now!"

Inmates shout obscenities, but they are just pretending. They filter off to   42
their cells. Visions of solitude dance in my head. Alone! Just me and my typewriter! Now I'll get something done. But maybe I am pretending also. Maybe we are all just pretending.

I get up and stretch, close my door, return to my desk, and wait.   43

"Count!" the loudspeaker squawks. "Count!"   44

45   Doors slam shut. Suddenly it is quiet. I pause to savor the silence. A plastic Salvation Army cup rests next to my typewriter, its contents cold, thick, and dark, but it is the best cup I've had all day. For a moment I think I hear crickets, distant, anonymous traffic, dogs barking, the hum of street lights.

46   *Tickticktickticktick . . .* complains my clock, its face turned away, hiding time.

47   This is it. I'm either going to write, or I'm not. I remove a three-by-five-inch wire-bound notebook: musings for the day, observations carried with me through the day. Flipped open and set on the desk beside my typewriter, it reminds me that place can also be irrelevant. I turn a page and begin typing. *Tack-tack, tack-tack, tack-tackity-tack. Tack-tack.* What is it like to write from a prison cell? I write. *Tack-tack.*

48   The glare of a flashlight hits me in the eyes. There is a pounding at my door. A guard is aiming his light in my face. "What're ya doing this time of night?" he asks.

49   I take a deep breath and count to ten before answering. Writing from prison, I tell myself, just ain't what it used to be. Maybe it never was. I count to twenty.

50   "Baking a cake," I finally answer.

51   He grins. "Yeah? Is it fun?"

52   "I don't know," I say. "I'll tell you when it's done."

Thinking Critically About Content

1. What characterizes this "writer's retreat"?
2. What is Higgins writing about on his typewriter?
3. How does Higgins deal with all the interruptions? In what ways are these incidents part of his writing process?

Thinking Critically About Purpose and Audience

4. Explain your understanding of the writer's main point in this essay.
5. Who do you think Higgins's primary audience is?
6. Why was Higgins frustrated trying to meet his goal of three pages of writing for the day?

Thinking Critically About Essays

7. Describe Higgins's point of view in this essay. Does it change throughout the essay? If so, in what ways?
8. Higgins uses many details to illustrate his frustration as he tries to write. Which details communicate his frustration most clearly to you?
9. Higgins talks about baking a cake in his conclusion. Is this an effective ending? Why or why not?
10. Tell this same story from Mr. Thunder's perspective.

Writing Topics: Narrating

Before you begin to write, you might want to review the writing process in Part I.

1. In "The Worth of Women's Work," Nina Lee Colwill writes of an epiphany she had when looking at pieces of embroidery and needlework in a Dutch museum. Many of us have had similar moments of enlightment. Write an essay in which you recall the details of such a moment. Write what you learned from the experience.

2. We all deal with frustration in different ways. Explain the coping strategies you have observed in friends and relatives. Do they work? Are they effective? Write a narrative essay focusing on various coping strategies that you have seen in action.

3. What do you think are the most important features of a good story? Why are they important? What effect do they have on you?

25

ILLUSTRATING

The two essays in this chapter show how the authors use examples, along with other strategies, to explain their main idea. The first essay, "I Just Wanna Be Average," written by Mike Rose, relates the author's experiences growing up labelled as a slow learner. The second essay, "Wild Weather," written by Chris Wood and published in *Maclean's* in January 1999, covers that favourite Canadian topic, bad weather. The article discusses the effects of global warming and illustrates these effects with several (at that time) recent examples of extreme weather.

Mike Rose

I JUST WANNA BE AVERAGE

Focusing Your Attention

1. What do you think about streaming, or separating students by ability level, in high school? What are the advantages and disadvantages of this system of teaching? Did your high school stream its students?

2. In the essay you are about to read, the writer claims that students use sophisticated defence mechanisms to get through high school. Have you ever used any defences in school? How did these defences make you act?

Expanding Your Vocabulary

The following words are important to your understanding of this essay:

vocational: focused on training for a job (paragraph 1)

Horace's Compromise: a novel by Theodore R. Sizer (paragraph 1)

hypotheses: educated guesses (paragraph 1)

disaffected: rebellious, uncooperative (paragraph 1)

skeletal: very basic (paragraph 1)

scuttling: moving quickly (paragraph 1)

somnambulant: walking while asleep (paragraph 2)

wherewithal: ability (paragraph 2)

prowess: strength (paragraph 3)

clique: exclusive social group (paragraph 3)

could care less: *slang for* could not care less (paragraph 3)

testament to: proof of (paragraph 3)

dearth: lack (paragraph 3)

much-touted: repeatedly praised (paragraph 4)

salubrious: socially or morally acceptable (paragraph 4)

equivocal: having two or more meanings (paragraph 4)

hit a chuckhole: stumbled (paragraph 4)

Argosy: a science-fiction magazine (paragraph 4)

Field and Stream: a hunting and fishing magazine (paragraph 4)

Daily Worker: a Socialist newspaper (paragraph 4)

The Old Man and the Sea: a novel by Ernest Hemingway (paragraph 4)

rough-hewn: unsophisticated, unpolished (paragraph 4)

apocryphal: a story that is not true but is believed by some people anyway (paragraph 4)

ducktail: a hairstyle in which the hair is swept back at the sides to meet in an upturned point at the back (paragraph 5)

parable of the talents: a story from the New Testament (paragraph 5)

restive: restless, fidgety (paragraph 5)

affect: emotion (paragraph 5)

laryngectomize: surgically remove a person's larynx (paragraph 5)

platitudinous: dull, boring, full of unoriginal thoughts (paragraph 5)

melee: battle (paragraph 5)

dissonant: nonconforming, disagreeing (paragraph 6)

elite: privileged individuals (paragraph 6)

constrained: kept within limits (paragraph 6)

liberate: free (paragraph 6)

gray matter: brain (paragraph 7)

diffuse: scatter (paragraph 7)

cultivate: encourage (paragraph 7)

malady: illness (paragraph 7)

Students will float to the mark you set. I and the others in the vocational classes were bobbing in pretty shallow water. Vocational education was aimed at increasing the economic opportunities of students who do not do well in our schools. Some serious programs succeed in doing that, and through exceptional teachers—like Mr. Gross in *Horace's Compromise*—students learn to develop hypotheses and troubleshoot, reason through a problem, and communicate effectively—the true job skills. The vocational track, however, is most often a place for those who are just not making it, a dumping ground for the disaffected. There were a few teachers who worked hard at education; young Brother Slattery, for example, combined a stern voice with weekly quizzes to try to pass along to us a skeletal outline of world history. But mostly the teachers had no idea of how to engage the imaginations of us kids who were scuttling along at the bottom of the pond.

2   And the teachers would have needed some inventiveness, for none of us was groomed for the classroom. It wasn't just that I didn't know things— didn't know how to simplify algebraic fractions, couldn't identify different kinds of clauses, bungled Spanish translations—but that I had developed various faulty and inadequate ways of doing algebra and making sense of Spanish. Worse yet, the years of defensive tuning out in elementary school had given me a way to escape quickly while seeming at least half alert. During my time in Voc. Ed., I developed further into a mediocre student and a somnambulant problem solver, and that affected the subjects I did have the wherewithal to handle: I detested Shakespeare; I got bored with history. My attention flitted here and there. I fooled around in class and read my books indifferently—the intellectual equivalent of playing with your food. I did what I had to do to get by, and I did it with half a mind.

3   But I did learn things about people and eventually came into my own socially. I liked the guys in Voc. Ed. Growing up where I did, I understood and admired physical prowess, and there was an abundance of muscle here. There was Dave Snyder, a sprinter and halfback of true quality. Dave's ability and his quick wit gave him a natural appeal, and he was welcome in any clique, though he always kept a little independent. He enjoyed acting the fool and could care less about studies, but he possessed a certain maturity and never caused the faculty much trouble. It was a testament to his independence that he included me among his friends—I eventually went out for track, but I was no jock. Owing to the Latin alphabet and a dearth of *R*'s and *S*'s, Snyder sat behind Rose, and we started exchanging one-liners and became friends.

4   There was Ted Richard, a much-touted Little League pitcher. He was chunky and had a baby face and came to Our Lady of Mercy as a seasoned street fighter. Ted was quick to laugh, and he had a loud, jolly laugh, but when he got angry he'd smile a little smile, the kind that simply raises the corner of the mouth a quarter of an inch. For those who knew, it was an eerie signal. Those who didn't found themselves in big trouble, for Ted was very quick. He loved to carry on what we would come to call philosophical discussions: What is courage? Does God exist? He also loved words, enjoyed picking up big ones like *salubrious* and *equivocal* and using them in our conversations—laughing at himself as the word hit a chuckhole rolling off his tongue. Ted didn't do all that well in school—baseball and parties and testing the courage he'd speculated about took up his time. His textbooks were *Argosy* and *Field and Stream*, whatever newspapers he'd find on the bus stop—from the *Daily Worker* to pornography—conversations with uncles or hobos or businessmen he'd meet in a coffee shop, *The Old Man and the Sea*. With hindsight, I can see that Ted was developing into

one of those rough-hewn intellectuals whose sources are a mix of the learned and the apocryphal, whose discussions are both assured and sad.

And then there was Ken Harvey. Ken was good-looking in a puffy way and had a full and oily ducktail and was a car enthusiast. . . . One day in religion class, he said the sentence that turned out to be one of the most memorable of the hundreds of thousands I heard in those Voc. Ed. years. We were talking about the parable of the talents, about achievement, working hard, doing the best you can do, blah-blah-blah, when the teacher called on the restive Ken Harvey for an opinion. Ken thought about it, but just for a second, and said (with studied, minimal affect), "I just wanna be average." That woke me up. Average?! Who wants to be average? Then the athletes chimed in with the clichés that make you want to laryngectomize them, and the exchange became a platitudinous melee. At the time, I thought Ken's assertion was stupid, and I wrote him off. But his sentence has stayed with me all these years, and I think I am finally coming to understand it.

Ken Harvey was gasping for air. School can be a tremendously disorienting place. No matter how bad the school, you're going to encounter notions that don't fit with the assumptions and beliefs that you grew up with—maybe you'll hear these dissonant notions from teachers, maybe from the other students, and maybe you'll read them. You'll also be thrown in with all kinds of kids from all kinds of backgrounds, and that can be unsettling—this is especially true in places of rich ethnic and linguistic mix, like the L.A. basin. You'll see a handful of students far excel you in courses that sound exotic and that are only in the curriculum of the elite: French, physics, trigonometry. And all this is happening while you're trying to shape an identity, your body is changing, and your emotions are running wild. If you're a working-class kid in the vocational track, the options you'll have to deal with this will be constrained in certain ways: You're defined by your school as "slow"; you're placed in a curriculum that isn't designed to liberate you but to occupy you, or, if you're lucky, train you, though the training is for work the society does not esteem; other students are picking up the cues from your school and your curriculum and interacting with you in particular ways. If you're a kid like Ted Richard, you turn your back on all this and let your mind roam where it may. But youngsters like Ted are rare. What Ken and so many others do is protect themselves from such suffocating madness by taking on with a vengeance the identity implied in the vocational track. Reject the confusion and frustration by openly defining yourself as the Common Joe. Champion the average. Rely on your own good sense. Fuck this bullshit. Bullshit, of course, is everything you—and the others—fear is beyond you: books, essays, tests, academic scrambling, complexity, scientific reasoning, philosophical inquiry.

The tragedy is that you have to twist the knife in your own gray matter to make this defense work. You'll have to shut down, have to reject intellectual stimuli or diffuse them with sarcasm, have to cultivate stupidity, have to convert boredom from a malady into a way of confronting the world. Keep your vocabulary simple, act stoned when you're not or act more stoned than you are, flaunt ignorance, materialize your dreams. It is a powerful and effective defense—it neutralizes the insult and the frustration of being a vocational kid and, when perfected, it drives teachers up the wall, a delightful secondary effect. But like all strong magic, it exacts a price.

Thinking Critically About Content

What Rose calls "tracking" is usually called "streaming" in Canada.

1. What was vocational education aimed at in Rose's school? Who is this stream for?

2. What examples from this essay illustrate most clearly what Rose's academic life involved?

3. Rose says the Voc. Ed. students "were bobbing in pretty shallow water" and then refers to them "scuttling along at the bottom of the pond" (paragraph 1). In these examples, he is comparing people trying to swim and stay above water to students in a vocational stream in high school. This comparison is called a *metaphor*. Find another comparison like this in paragraph 7.

Thinking Critically About Purpose and Audience

4. What do you think Rose's purpose is in this essay? Explain your answer.

5. What type of audience do you think would best understand and appreciate this essay?

6. What do you think Ken Harvey meant when he said, "I just wanna be average" (paragraph 5)?

Thinking Critically About Essays

7. Does Rose give enough examples for you to understand his learning environment in high school? Explain your answer.

8. Is this essay unified? Does each of the author's topic sentences support the essay's thesis statement? Explain your answer.

9. What is Rose's thesis in this essay? Where is it located?

10. Explain your opinion about streaming students. Is streaming a good idea? Does it help some students? Does it hurt anyone? Can you think of any alternatives to streaming? Respond to these questions in detail.

Chris Wood

WILD WEATHER

Focusing Your Attention

1. Think of your last experience with bad weather that broke records. What was it that made the weather so unusual? Was it the unusually high or low temperature, the amount of precipitation, or the inconvenience it caused?

2. In the essay you are about to read, the writer describes various cases of extreme weather. He points out that, according to experts, what is causing what we know as global warming is actually global wetting, as warm temperatures cause an increase in the amount of moisture the air can hold. Would you say that most of your experiences with extreme weather have involved an increase in either moisture or humidity? Did the extreme weather disrupt the way you worked or played?

Expanding Your Vocabulary

The following words are important to your understanding of this essay:

inundated: swamped, flooded (paragraph 2)

dislocation: put out of place (paragraph 2)

ratchets: increases incrementally (paragraph 4)

simulate: imitate (paragraph 5)

consensus: agreement (paragraph 5)

spawned: produced in large numbers (paragraph 9)

spate: sudden rush (paragraph 9)

wallop: punch (paragraph 13)

As a storm raged outside, the constantly ringing phones went unanswered at Environment Canada's Toronto offices last Thursday. Like many other workplaces in the city, it was shut down—by the worst series of blizzards ever to strike Toronto. As heavy snow and bitterly cold temperatures swept along a corridor from Windsor, Ont., to the Maritimes, they snarled traffic, crippled public transportation and stranded thousands of commuters in Canada's largest city. Toronto Mayor Mel Lastman called in the Canadian Forces. In the northeastern United States, where the storm delivered heavy snow and freezing rain, it established a record low temperature in the state of Maine: −48°C. 1

Even so, Canada's first great storm of '99 paled beside other recent examples of nature's fury—last January's ice storm in Quebec, eastern Ontario and parts of the Maritimes, in particular. In economic and human terms, that blast, which disrupted electric power supplies to three million 2 people and left more than 25 dead, was far more severe than last week's. Floods that inundated southern Manitoba in the spring of 1997 also produced greater dislocation—forcing 28,000 people from their homes and damaging hundreds of properties along the Red River. A year earlier, floods swept through Quebec's Saguenay region, leaving 10 dead and 2,000 families homeless.

3   Is it just our imaginations, or is the weather really getting worse? And if it is getting worse, just how bad can it get?

4   The answers, to the extent that science can provide them, are not comforting. For starters, it is not our imagination: the weather is indeed getting wilder. Researchers in the United States and Canada say extreme weather is not only becoming more frequent, it is getting more violent as well. The Ontario blizzard was typical, they say, of what Canadians can expect as Earth's temperature ratchets upward in the decades ahead.

5   As for how bad it could get, no one knows for sure. Computer models designed to simulate Earth's future climate hint at startling increases in snow and rainfall along with temperature shifts. But their reliability is unproven. And simulations designed to model large scale climate changes are unhelpfully imprecise about what may happen to local weather patterns in the 21st century. Still, there is a growing consensus among climate-watchers that worse, possibly far worse, weather lies ahead. As William Hsieh, head of the Climate Prediction Group at the University of British Columbia, put it: "You'll get more storms, and stronger storms."

6   The reason for that isn't the heat, it's the humidity. Along with global warming, scientists now forecast what might best be called global wetting. Warmer air is capable of holding more water vapour than cooler air. The warmth also increases the rate at which glaciers and polar ice melt, introducing yet more moisture into the environment. Taken together, the two effects will vastly increase the amount of water moving through the atmosphere, leading inevitably to heavier falls of both rain and snow. For Canadians there is an extra jolt in the global weather outlook. The greatest increases in precipitation are forecast to occur in the higher latitudes—those occupied by Canada—and in the winter.

7   Students of the world's climate have drawn another, sobering conclusion: the impact of global warming is already upon us. One of the world's most sophisticated computer models of Earth's atmosphere is at the Canadian Centre for Climate Modelling and Analysis in Victoria. "Changes," its researchers warned in a paper last September, "accelerate from the present into the next century."

8   In coming decades, their model suggests, Canada, and especially its central regions, can expect storms on the measure of last week's to become increasingly common. The number of extreme low pressure systems—the barometric engines that drive the most devastating storms—each winter could increase by more than 20 per cent by 2040. Precipitation—snow or ice in the winter and rain at other times—will become dramatically heavier. Other harsh weather patterns will also worsen: heat waves in some regions may become as much as 10 degrees hotter.

If human misery is the measure, the weather already seems bad   9
enough. The last few years have produced a long list of unusual weather
events:

- China's floods last summer, when the Yangtze River burst its banks
  and displaced millions of people from their homes, were some of the
  worst in that country's long history.
- The entire world sweltered through record heat last year—the hottest
  in 500 years.
- In Florida, forest fires during bone-dry heat last May destroyed
  200,000 hectares before they were finally brought under control in
  July. Ferocious fires in British Columbia bumped the cost of fighting
  them from $40 million to $100 million.
- A heat wave in the U.S. South in July killed more than 100 people, as
  temperatures simmered above 38°C for more than two weeks. Other
  hot spells killed more than 2,500 people in India and spawned raging
  brushfires in Australia.
- The most devastating storm to strike Central America in 200 years—
  Hurricane Mitch—killed an estimated 11,000 people in October. And
  in the U.S. Midwest, a spate of tornadoes left 129 people dead—more
  than the toll from the previous three years combined.

Although it is hard to say just how extreme the weather may become,   10
researchers at Environment Canada's Victoria Centre for Climate Modelling have some alarming predictions for the next half-century:

- Extremely violent winter storms that previously happened only once
  every 20 years will occur every 10 years, as the number of deep low-
  pressure systems generated each season increases.
- In some regions, including Canada's North, extreme daily maximum
  temperatures will peak at 10 Celsius degrees above present levels.
- Record rain and snow storms over Canada will deliver nearly 10 per
  cent more precipitation—and become more frequent. Vancouver's famous winter drizzle will become frequent torrential downpours. Blizzards in the East will last longer and dump more snow.

The changes, in fact, are already well under way. In a report released   11
last month, the U.S. National Oceanic and Atmospheric Administration
said the number of heat waves lasting three days or longer each summer
has jumped 88 per cent between 1949 and 1995. The same agency's National Climatic Data Center reported that extreme snow and rainstorms became 20 per cent more frequent over the last century.

New research at the University of Victoria's School of Earth and Ocean   12
Sciences points for the first time to similar findings for Canada. Graduate
student Daithi Stone, who is gathering data on extreme storms, has determined that current rain and snow falls are significantly heavier than those
of decades past, especially in Eastern Canada. "Precipitation has been increasing steadily," says the 24-year-old researcher, "in Ontario, Quebec
and the Maritimes for the last century, and in the North for about 40 years."

13   More snow means more avalanches like the one that killed nine people in a school gymnasium in Kangiqsualujjuaq, in northern Quebec, on New Year's Day. More winter precipitation will also mean more spring floods. And the presence of more heat and more water in the atmosphere means weather systems will hold more energy, giving them a bigger wallop when they touch down.

14   Some of the greatest changes will be felt in Central Canada, says Andrew Weaver, an atmospheric scientist at the University of Victoria's earth and ocean sciences school. "One of the misconceptions," he notes, "is that global warming means a slow, steady change in temperature. That is frankly not the issue. What will impact people most is the frequency of extreme events." Toronto's Storm of '99, like Montreal's Ice Storm of the Century and Winnipeg's Great Flood, could well turn out to be a mere overture to the far greater wrath of the weather to come.

Thinking Critically About Content

1. The author states that the weather is getting "wilder." Why does he use this word rather than saying it is getting worse? Explain.

2. What examples from this essay are the most persuasive? What makes an illustration persuasive?

3. In the opening of the essay, Wood describes the weather as moving along a corridor from Windsor to Toronto like a wild animal, snarling traffic and crippling transportation. This technique is a type of metaphor called a *personification*. Find other examples in the essay.

Thinking Critically About Purpose and Audience

4. What is Chris Wood's purpose in writing this essay? Why is the subject matter important?

5. Global warming is a popular topic, but global wettening may be a new term to many people. What are the effects of global wettening, and why is it important that Canadians, in particular, should be told about them?

6. You may have noticed that the essay was written in 1999 after a severe storm in Toronto. Is the essay still relevant today? Explain your answer. What examples would you use if you rewrote the essay today?

Thinking Critically About Essays

7. What is Wood's thesis in this essay? Where is it located?

8. Does Wood give enough examples to back up his thesis? Explain your answer. Are all the examples relevant? Why or why not?

9. The examples show what has happened in the past. What technique does the author use to relate these examples to future

changes? How does he convince the reader that these changes indicate that future weather will continue to be unusual? Give examples.

10 In the final paragraph the author mentions a "Storm of the Century" and a "Great Flood." Do the author's examples seem to get more and more extreme throughout the essay? Do they change geographically? Look at the examples and see if there is a pattern. Why might the author be using a pattern?

Writing Topics: Illustrating

Before you begin to write, you might want to review the writing process in Part I.

1. Contemporary North American society rewards students who fit into the educational system and can keep up. But some people just can't keep up with a course for a variety of reasons. Have you ever felt the way Mike Rose says he felt in his essay? What was your reason for not keeping up? Discuss any similarities you see between yourself and Mike Rose.

2. How do you think extremes in weather will affect Canadians, specifically those involved in farming and tourism? Can you think of other examples?

3. What do you think writers should consider first when choosing examples in an essay? How should the examples be related to the thesis statement? Why are these criteria important when working with examples?

26 ANALYZING A PROCESS

The essays in this chapter explain different events or processes. In other words, they tell you how to do something or why something happened the way it did. The first essay, "Don't Be Cruel" by Dr. Roger Flax, offers some guidelines for criticizing and motivating at the same time—at work, at home, at school. "Why We Have a Moon," written by David Levy, explains how the moon was formed and what its role is in relation to the earth.

Dr. Roger Flax

DON'T BE CRUEL

Focusing Your Attention

1. Think of a time when you had to explain to someone how to do something. Was it an easy or a difficult task? Did the person understand you? Was the person able to follow your directions?

2. In the process analysis essay you are about to read, the writer tells us how to criticize other people effectively. Have you ever wanted to tell someone about something he or she did wrong without ruining the relationship? What did you do to solve the problem?

Expanding Your Vocabulary

The following words are important to your understanding of this essay:

coronary: heart attack (paragraph 1)

mercilessly: cruelly (paragraph 1)

reprimands: expressions of disapproval (paragraph 4)

manager–subordinate scenarios: boss–employee situations (paragraph 4)

Project Management Work Teams: groups of individuals who work together in the workforce to improve their management style (paragraph 7)

rapport: sense of trust (paragraph 10)

repercussions: results or effects (paragraph 14)

malice: desire to cause harm or suffering (paragraph 16)

facilitate: guide (paragraph 20)

implementation: the act of putting something into practice (paragraph 21)

misconstrues: misunderstands (paragraph 21)

stroke: flatter, compliment (paragraph 22)

perennial: constant (paragraph 29)

belittle: say negative things about a person (paragraph 31)

Picture this scenario: Seymour Axshun (we'll call him), a terrific manager who has been a loyal employee for several years, messes up on an assignment. He misses a deadline on a proposal and that three-day delay costs the company $9,100. Seymour's boss, Sy Kottick, has a near coronary over the incident, lashes out at Seymour, and criticizes him mercilessly. In front of four of Seymour's co-workers, Kottick shouts, "Axshun, how many times do I have to tell you to be more efficient with your planning? You blew it, and your mistake will cost us almost $10,000. I don't know what it takes to drill into your head that you must meet deadlines. It's disgusting, and I'm fed up. If you treated the money as if it were your own, you wouldn't be so careless." 1

"Incidentally, Seymour, on another issue, don't you think you should come to work dressed a bit more professionally? That suit you wore yesterday was a bit outdated, especially since we had our big client, Meyer Fivis, here. And one more thing, while we're at it Seymour . . . " 2

Seymour shrinks from humiliation. He wishes he could push a button and disappear. He looks around him and sees four embarrassed colleagues. His boss storms out of the room and slams the door. 3

This thoughtless, but real-life, managerial scenario happens every minute of every day, in every city of every state. People insensitively and ruthlessly come down on others with reprimands and criticisms that leave permanent scars. And it happens not only in manager–subordinate scenarios, but in parent–child relationships, teacher–student interfaces, sports coach–player affairs, and friendships. 4

It's called *unconstructive, unmotivational criticism* or, in better words, *relationship breaking*. 5

Put yourself in Seymour Axshun's shoes. Would you ever want to work for that jerk again? And if you did, how dedicated would you really be? How motivated would you be to make him look good? 6

The two most critical assets of companies are people and time. Valuable people are hard to replace, and time is irreplaceable. With the evolution of Project Management Work Teams in companies throughout the world, it's absolutely imperative that team leaders and managers master the art of giving constructive, tactful, motivational criticism. After all, if the goal of the project group is to work as a team to attain a goal, unconstructive criticism 7 can destroy the group quickly. *Motivation magic*, as I call it, can only enhance the team.

8   You shouldn't be a robot when giving constructive criticism, but there is a human-relations approach that does work. Here's a several-step process to follow the next time you have to reprimand another person, but truly want to motivate that person and enhance the relationship.

9   1. *Always begin constructive criticism with a positive statement.* Open with an energizing comment that builds up the person's esteem and sincerely expresses your approval and support on a specific item. For example, in the Seymour Axshun incident, why not begin with, "Seymour, you've done an outstanding job in the Quality Improvement Program, and the results are quickly having an impact on our operation. Many people have commented to me about your great work."

10   2. *Never follow that complimentary opening remark with "but" or "however."* Those words immediately eliminate the good feeling and rapport initiated by the compliment. The person will quickly surmise that the opening statement was merely lip service—a manipulative tool geared to set up the reprimand or criticism. It's very natural, and even habitual, to say "but" or "however" after you open with a positive statement, but it will destroy the initial goodwill created and result in perceived insincerity.

11   3. *Use the acronym PEN to plan and verbalize the actual criticism.*

P—Problem. State the problem that exists. Be concise and to the point. Remember: Don't begin expressing the problem with "but" or "however."

E—Example. Give an example or two that clearly supports the problem or reason for criticism. Get your facts straight, and keep them brief. The lengthier the criticism is, the more painful it becomes.

N—Negative Impact. Let the person know what negative effects have resulted from the problem or action. It's important to do some planning before the criticism session. Think through your PEN before giving it. It will come across more concisely, smoothly, and convincingly.

12   4. *Avoid using the word "you" when giving the actual criticism.* This is definitely the most important rule to remember. Discipline yourself to criticize the object or the problem, not the person. Don't let yourself say "you"—it's accusatory, threatening and puts the criticism on a personal, emotional, confrontational level.

13   Example: "Seymour, you've done an outstanding job in the Quality Improvement Program, and the results are quickly having an impact on our operation. There's one situation that could be improved upon, and that is meeting deadlines. On one occasion this month, a deadline was missed by three days, and that has cost our company several

thousand dollars. The negative effects not only include a large dollar loss, but a potential loss in credibility for future dealings."

Now go back and read the opening example—the confrontational, insensitive way of criticizing. Notice in the second example that the criticizer avoided the word "you" (except for the opening praise) and dealt with the problem, not the person. You need to practice this technique over and over again. Don't just use it at work, but also use it with your spouse, children, friends, relatives—everyone. It goes a long way in relationship building and effective human relations, and it reduces the enormous repercussions that can occur from giving cutthroat criticism.   14

Of course, it's okay to use "you" when you're praising the person or engaging in a subsequent dialogue after the initial criticism has been communicated. However, the word "you" should be avoided when the actual bad news is being stated.   15

If husbands and wives disciplined themselves to avoid the word "you" during potential emotional outbursts, they wouldn't build up years of frustration and marital malice. If coaches stopped publicly criticizing their players and saying "you" every time the players made a mistake, there'd be many more motivated athletes exploiting and reaching their fullest potential.   16

5. *Ask for feedback.* After "PEN-ning" people, find out what their feelings or opinions are on the matter. Let them talk. Let them express their emotions, and don't interrupt. If they're looking to save a little face, go ahead and let them. Lose the battle, but win the war. Open the window of communication, and let the air flow in.   17

6. *Actively listen to their response.* Instead of just gazing at them as they speak, be an active, nonverbal listener. Show facial expressions, nod, react with sounds, such as "hmmm," "oh, I see," or "really." Show a genuine, caring interest.   18

When someone has a problem, active listening helps reduce the pain. That's what psychologists do every day. The client reveals painful experiences to the psychologist, and the psychologist uses active listening techniques to show support, concern, and empathy. It's also a technique used by successful sales pros who strive to develop relationships with customers.   19

7. *Discuss the situation in a low-key manner.* Your two-way communication, although unstructured, should remain focused on the problem. Facilitate the discussion to an agreed-upon action or solution. Clearly state what you want the person to do, if it's not clear, and make sure you obtain a mutual understanding. Don't dominate the communication. If the other person raises his or her voice, keep yours down. That will keep the discussion less emotional and more low-key.   20

8. *Mutually agree upon an action or next step.* It's always better this way. Forcing a person to do something usually produces substantially less long-term growth and relationship building. Both parties should   21

agree upon an action, set a date for its implementation, and end with a handshake. Try getting the person to verbalize what the action steps will be, thereby ensuring that both people are in sync. You'd be surprised how many times the criticized person misconstrues the next action step.

22   9. *End with a positive.* Now that the hard work is completed (and nobody likes giving criticism), go back and stroke the person a bit. Remind him or her that you greatly appreciate the person's effort and dedication and are very supportive of his or her performance. Make sure that no negative feelings exist, and if they do, probe and uncover them. You want to assure the person that this is a very correctable problem and that, in the big picture, you're a very satisfied manager.

23   Example: "Seymour, remember, I am extremely pleased with your performance. You are a valuable asset to our department."

24   A few musts to keep in mind when giving constructive, motivational criticism:

25   First, *always do it in private.* Nobody is proud of reprimands, so do it when you're alone with the person. It's humiliating when done in public.

26   Second, *limit the criticism session to one act.* If you bring up things from the past, you're turning the knife and potentially destroying the relationship. You should communicate criticism within a day or two of the occurrence; otherwise, drop it. Some people bring up events that occurred six months or even six years ago. That's a no-no.

27   Third, *criticize face-to-face, never over the phone.* You never know how the person is reacting. If you're criticizing over the phone, the other person might be dying inside, and you'll never know it. Even if it's timely to do it over the phone, hold it in. Set up an immediate meeting with the person.

28   Finally, *don't dig it in.* Statements such as "you see," "I told you so," or "you don't listen" are worthless. They might make you feel good, but they ruin relationships.

29   A great example of how *not* to criticize can be seen during a sports event—basketball, baseball, or football. How many times does a basketball coach yell at his point guard for missing the play and use the accusatory "you" over and over again? The coach raises his voice in frustration and does it in front of teammates and fans. The player feels abused, his confidence is shaken, and his motivation is drained from within. It's no wonder certain professional coaches go from team to team but continue to lose year after year. They might know the sport, but they know little about human motivation. A little motivational psychology would go a long way for these perennial losers.

30   How do you tie all these points together the next time you must criticize a person? Remember: The goal of motivational criticism should be to leave the person feeling helped, not hurt. So, the next time you're about to criticize a person, think it through before you do. Be tactful, firm, empathetic, and concise.

After all, you have to be little to belittle. You hold the key to motivational   31
magic.

Thinking Critically About Content

1. What does Dr. Roger Flax mean by "motivation magic" (paragraph 7)?
2. What are the nine main steps of Flax's method?
3. What does Flax say the main goal of motivational criticism is?

Thinking Critically About Purpose and Audience

4. What do you think Flax's purpose is in this essay?
5. Do you think that only businesspeople can benefit from this essay? Why? Explain your answer.
6. Which piece of Flax's advice do you feel you will find most useful for your own life?

Thinking Critically About Essays

7. Describe in a complete sentence Flax's point of view in his last paragraph.
8. How does Flax organize this essay? Write a rough outline to show his method of organization.
9. Choose a paragraph from his essay, and explain how it is developed.
10. Explain in detail whether or not you agree with Flax when he says that using "you" to criticize people makes them feel like they are being attacked.

David Levy

WHY WE HAVE A MOON

Focusing Your Attention

1. Astronomy is the study of planets and stars. What interests you about the world of astronomy?
2. In the essay you are about to read, the writer explains his research on how the moon was formed and what its role is in relation to the earth. Have you ever been interested enough in something that you took the time to look into its origins or related facts?

Expanding Your Vocabulary

The following words are important to your understanding of this essay:

orbit: the path of a planet, moon, or satellite (paragraph 3)

gravitational pull: the pull of a planet on an object near its surface (paragraph 3)

supercolossal: extremely large (paragraph 3)

plummeted: fell (paragraph 4)

devastation: severe damage (paragraph 4)

promontory: a piece of land that juts out into the sea (paragraph 7)

mottled: spotted (paragraphs 11 and 12)

exhalations: letting air out (paragraph 12)

meteors, comets, asteroids: bodies of rock and air in space (paragraph 13)

imminent: about to happen (paragraph 16)

carbon: a chemical element (paragraph 17)

hydrogen, nitrogen, oxygen: gases in the Earth's atmosphere (paragraph 17)

1   I remember the beautiful clear sky the day my granddaughter, then 14 months old, first fell under its spell. She called it the "oon." Soon, I knew, she'd be asking, "How did the Moon get there? Did people really walk on it? Will *I* someday?"—the same questions asked by Moonwatchers of all ages. So, how *did* the Moon get there?

2   About 4.5 billion years ago, the Earth had a bad day. The Sun was shining on our young world, which had no oceans yet and no life, but a surface filled with erupting volcanoes. The sky was awash with stars, though not the ones we see now. But the familiar planets were there—Venus, Jupiter, Saturn, Mars—and another planet the size of Mars but much closer.

3   Had we been alive back then, we would have noticed this other planet looping again and again around the Sun in an odd orbit that brought it very close to Earth, then farther away. On this day, that odd planet, approaching us again, became brighter than ever before, filling the sky and getting bigger by the minute, its gravitational pull now so great that rocks began to stretch and rumble. Then, with unimaginable energy and deafening noise, it sideswiped the Earth, bounced off and, seconds later, tore right back into our planet with a supercolossal force.

4   That Mars-size world broke apart, and huge chunks of Earth's crust flew off into space. Two rings of debris, their particles much larger than those in the fine-grained rings of Saturn, grew and circled the Earth. For many days, pieces of the inner ring plummeted down again, adding to the Earth's devastation. Pieces of the outer ring slowly gathered together around its largest chunks. In just a year, those pieces formed a large new world, a world that we can still see. That world we call the Moon.

5   So goes the prevailing theory, developed in the 1970s. In its earliest days, our Moon was probably no more than 10,000 miles away. The Earth

spun around faster then, in a 10-hour day. But over time the Moon slowly veered away from Earth, its gravity forever slowing Earth's rotation. By the time of the dinosaurs, more than 4 billion years after the Moon's formation, a day was about 22 hours long. With our day now at 24 hours, the Moon, still inching away at approximately 3 feet every century, is about 240,000 miles away. But even at this distance, it has a powerful influence on the Earth's waters.

The Moon and the Tides

We have tides on Earth because of the gravitational pull of the Moon (and the Sun, especially when the two are in alignment) across the diameter of the Earth. If you've ever been to an ocean beach, you have felt the Moon's whisper as its gravity brings the water in, then out, twice each day. One day in Nova Scotia, I felt the Moon roar.   6

At the eastern end of Canada's Bay of Fundy, a flow of water equal to the combined currents of all the rivers on Earth thunders through the Minas Channel into the Minas Basin twice a day for six hours. To see this marvelous sight, I traveled to a remote Nova Scotia promontory called Cape Split. I arrived as the incoming tidal flow was at its maximum.   7

A first-quarter Moon hung in the sky as a *million million* gallons of water poured into the Minas Basin. I found it incredible that the Moon, from a distance of 240,000 miles, was responsible for the tremendous noise in the channel below. After a few hours, the flow slowed, then stopped. For a half hour or so, the water was still. Then the huge basin began to empty, flowing *in reverse* like a movie running backward, the noise rising once again. Such is the power of the Moon's gravity.   8

The shape of the land makes the tides stronger. In midocean, the daily tidal bulge is about a yard. But at Minas Basin, it's 45 feet—the largest tidal flow on the planet—owing to the peculiar geography of the Gulf of Maine, the Bay of Fundy, the Minas Channel and basin. It's like a child playing in a bathtub, pushing the water to the front, then letting it flow back. A rhythm builds. If the child lifts up slightly each time, the water sloshes toward one end. Eventually, the water rides up the side of the tub and spills out. The child's movement is "in sync" with the natural motion of the water in the tub. The water's increased momentum, plus the confining shape of the tub, results in more force on the water—just as the Moon's gravity, aided by the shape of the land, strengthens the force of the Fundy tides.   9

The Moon Is a Mirror

When we look at the Moon, we see on its uneven surface a record of billions of years of bashing. The Moon's face is trying to tell us something about Earth's own past. If the Moon has been hit so often, the Earth, being a much bigger target, must have been struck even more often.   10

11   The first thing you notice about the Moon is its uneven, mottled surface. With binoculars, the unevenness appears more pronounced, with clear evidence of dark and bright spots. What are they?

12   To the ancient Greeks, the Moon's "spots" were exhalations from the Earth that rose all the way to the Moon. By the 1500s, it was common to compare the Moon to green cheese—not because of its mysterious color but because "green cheese" meant round, uncut cheese with a mottled surface. As recently as 1960, most scientists believed craters were the result of volcanic forces beneath the Moon's surface.

13   That was before Gene Shoemaker appeared on the scene. A young geologist, he was studying craters formed by underground nuclear testing near Las Vegas in the late 1950s. He noted that these craters, formed by far greater heat and pressure than a volcano could produce, resembled some of the great natural craters on Earth. Perhaps the latter—as well as the craters on the Moon—had resulted from impacts by meteors, comets or asteroids, whose energy would have been closer to that of an atomic bomb.

14   By 1960, Shoemaker had proved that a 1.2-mile-wide crater near Flagstaff, Ariz., was the result of the crash of an asteroid some 50,000 years ago. By studying detailed photographs of craters on the Moon, plus images taken by the *Ranger* and *Surveyor* spacecraft, Shoemaker established that the Moon's surface was a story of impacts over billions of years.

15   In 1972, the astronaut Harrison Schmidt went to the Moon on *Apollo 17* and confirmed Shoemaker's theory live on television. "Gene defined what the characteristics of the Moon's surface layer would be," Schmidt told me.

16   But the Moon's surface revealed a far more important story—that of the solar system's violent past, when the planets, including Earth, were bombarded by comets and meteors. On March 25, 1993, Shoemaker, his wife, Carol, and I discovered that a collision in the solar system was imminent. And 16 months later, as the world watched, comet Shoemaker-Levy 9 slammed into Jupiter at 37 miles per second—the equivalent of going from New York to Los Angeles *in 70 seconds.*

17   The spectacle of these comets hitting Jupiter was a replay of an ancient scenario in which comets—comprised of carbon, hydrogen, nitrogen, and oxygen—crashed into Earth, starting a slow process that eventually led to the earliest life here.

18   Is the Moon still being bombarded today? On July 10, 1941, Walter Haas, one of the world's most experienced observers, saw a speck of light move across Gassendi, a large lunar crater. Did Haas see a meteorite striking the Moon at enormous speed? Smaller particles did hit the Moon on Nov. 17, 1999, during the Leonid meteor shower.

19   If small objects still hit the Moon, can large ones? In 1178, some monks near Canterbury, England, reported a terrifying experience on a night of a crescent Moon: "Suddenly," the account reads, "the upper horn split in two. From the division, a flaming torch sprang up, spewing out, over a considerable distance, fire, hot coals, and sparks."

Could they have seen a major impact on the Moon? Conceivably, a   20
20-mile crater on the Moon's far side, called Giordano Bruno, was caused
by a large impact. We may never know the answer, but there's a clue.

In the 1970s, the McDonald Observatory in Texas, bouncing laser beams   21
off the Moon, found that it "sways" by a few yards about every three years.
Like a huge bell vibrating after being clanged, the Moon is acting as if it
had been struck by a large object within the last 1000 years. Perhaps, someday, my granddaughter, caught by the Moon's wondrous pull, will walk
there as others once did and find an answer.

Thinking Critically About Content

1. Writers often use personal stories to get the readers' attention or understanding. Where does Levy use stories in this essay? What effect
   do they have?

2. What were the steps in the moon's formation 4.5 billion years ago?

3. According to Levy, what is the relationship between the moon and
   the oceans?

Thinking Critically About Purpose and Audience

4. What do you think the purpose of this essay is?

5. How do you think a general audience would respond to the author's
   description of the moon as a mirror of the earth's past?

6. Levy often relates scientific information to everyday occurrences—
   like comparing the motion of the tides to a child playing in the
   bathtub (paragraph 9). Find one other example of this technique.
   How do you respond to this strategy as a reader?

Thinking Critically About Essays

7. Describe in a complete sentence the writer's point of view.

8. Why do you think Levy introduces current research on the moon in
   the last section of his essay?

9. What are the three main parts of Levy's essay? Why do you think he
   put these topics in this order?

10. If Levy were writing this essay for a publication to be read only by
    scientists, how might it be different? How might it be the same?
    Rewrite the introduction or the conclusion for an audience of
    scientists.

Writing Topics: Analyzing a Process

Before you begin to write, you might want to review the writing process in Part I.

1. In the first essay, Flax talks about motivating people by criticizing without using the word "you." Are you usually aware of your word choices as you talk? How can careful use of words help you get what you want in life? Explain a process that involved getting something you wanted by using words carefully.

2. Think of something in life that you want to study as much as Levy wants to study the moon and stars. Then discuss your plans for achieving your goals in this area of study.

3. Which type of process analysis do you find most interesting—the how-to essays or the background explanations? Explain your answer.

COMPARING AND CONTRASTING

The following essays use comparison and contrast to communicate and build on their central ideas. The first essay, written by Canadian Tom Hayden, a journalist who works for *U.S. News and World Report*, was published in *The Globe and Mail*. It compares and contrasts Washington, D.C., and Saskatoon to make a point about the need to discuss the problem of racism. The second essay is taken from *The Truth About Stories: A Native Narrative*, by Thomas King, which was originally presented as *The 2003 Massey Lecture*, sponsored by CBC Radio.

Tom Hayden
THAT IS NOT THE IMAGE WE HAVE OF CANADA

Focusing Your Attention

1. Do you feel that Native people are marginalized in Canadian society? How would you compare or contrast the way Canada has treated its earliest inhabitants with the way the United States has treated its African-American citizens?

2. In the essay you are about to read, the author compares and contrasts Saskatoon, the city he grew up in, with Washington, D.C., the city where he now lives. He looks at Saskatoon from an American point of view. What image do you think Americans might have of Canada? How accurate is that image, do you think? Explain.

Expanding Your Vocabulary

The following words are important to your understanding of this essay:

lynching: to execute without trial (paragraph 3)

marginalized: relegated to the outer edge of group (paragraph 7)

dilapidated: shabby and neglected (paragraph 8)

quadrant: one of four quarters (paragraph 8)

discourse: formal discussion (paragraph 9)

jibes: taunts (paragraph 12)

cacophony: harsh, discordant sounds (paragraph 12)

enclave: an enclosed area within another, larger area (paragraph 16)

1   When you live in Saskatoon, it's easy to forget how ugly it can be. The riverbank parks, tree-lined neighbourhoods and university campuses all are as lovely as any on the prairies, but drive in from Edmonton or the airport to the north and you get an entirely different impression. I prefer to just close my eyes as I pass the long, grey stretches of light industry and charmless cookie-cutter homes that crowd the city's flanks.

2   In the same way, it's all too easy to overlook the harder truths of life in Saskatoon. In the 11 years that I've lived in the United States, I've been a tireless, and sometimes I'm sure tiresome, booster of the city I left grudgingly and still consider home. But I'm finally opening my eyes more fully. Late last year the *Washington Post*, my new hometown newspaper, ran a front-page article datelined Saskatoon for the first time since the medicare debates of 1962: "Left for Dead in a Saskatchewan Winter." I knew immediately what it was about.

3   It's not hard to freeze to death in Saskatoon. When I was in high school there in the 1980s, we joked about who would get the yearbook dedication, a distinction too often claimed by a boozy grad who tried to wander home from a mid-winter party in only a jean jacket and running shoes. Easy enough to do, but from 1990 to 2000, several aboriginal men apparently had help from members of Saskatoon's police force—a particularly northern form of lynching.

4   With the final stage set to begin this week of a provincial inquiry into the death of Neil Stonechild, found frozen in a north Saskatoon industrial area in 1990, even the major American papers are starting to take notice.

5   "Okay, that is not the image we have of Canada," says Debra Dickerson, an American lawyer and journalist who writes regularly on race. She had never heard about the infamous "starlight tours" in which aboriginal men were abandoned on the city's outskirts by police officers, and was understandably shocked. The image was as foreign to me as it is to Ms. Dickerson. I thought I knew which side of the border had the real race problem. But living in Washington, D.C., at the very centre of America's racial discord, I'm no longer sure whether the bigger trouble is in my old home or my current one.

6   On the surface, Saskatoon and Washington could not be more different. Almost three times as many people call the District home, and 60 per cent of them are black; Saskatoon is as out of the way as D.C. is central, and 85 per cent white. People die of the heat in Washington's summer, and of cold in the prairie winter.

7   Still, there are similarities that go beyond the fact that both are long on leafy parks and short on movie theatres and interesting restaurants: Both cities are the murder capitals of their respective countries; while Saska-

toon's six homicides in 2002 can't compare to D.C.'s 264, the prairie town actually registered slightly more violent crimes per capita. And, most strikingly, much of Washington's African-American majority is as segregated and marginalized as Saskatoon's aboriginal minority is.

Like urban natives in Saskatoon's dilapidated core, working-class   8
blacks in Washington, Ms. Dickerson says, "are living in a different city and a different reality." A reality that white residents like me rarely visit. Like Washington's primarily black South East quadrant, which I've seen only from the safety of a Habitat for Humanity work site, I pass through Saskatoon's largely aboriginal west-side neighbourhoods only to visit St. Paul's Hospital.

Though I pride myself on knowing my hometown well, I grew up with-   9
out knowing a single aboriginal family. The geographical divide can be just as wide in American cities, but there's a critical difference. In the United States, race is a constant topic of conversation, and the discourse is opinionated, loud, and unmistakable. In the Saskatoon I grew up in, it simply didn't exist.

We didn't consider ourselves racist—who does?—but it can be tricky to   10
draw a line between active oppression and passive ignorance. Ms. Dickerson, who spent her 20s in the military before heading to Harvard Law School, says it took that long to understand that she could be doing the same things as the white students she went to high school with. "History is taught so poorly here that it took me a long time to realize that the condition of black people in this country was anything but accidental," she says.

And that too, sadly, is not so different from back home. "Indians should   11
just shut up" about treaty rights, I remember being told at the end of a heated argument in Saskatoon several years ago, "because we won the war." Maybe it was just the nearly empty beer keg between us, but I had no luck convincing my companion that the war he was thinking of happened in the country to the south. In high school, during a rare classroom discussion on racism, one student made the point that it was obviously unfair for Americans to be so racist against blacks. But here in Saskatoon, he said, it was another story. "It's different—Indians really are lazy."

Racism, it turns out, is easier to see from a distance. My first reaction to   12
the *Post* headline was horror, not at what happened—it was old news back home—but that word was getting out. We're a protective bunch, Saskatoonians, too used to the slights and jibes of our fellow Canadians, and my immediate impulse was to pray that no one would notice. But they did. I spent weeks fielding uncomfortable questions from friends and colleagues. And through the cacophony of racial dialogue in the States, I've seen a hint of what might come next for Saskatoon.

Yelling at each other across the racial divide isn't a solution, of course.   13
But that doesn't mean it can't be a promising sign. "Things are actually probably getting better" in Saskatoon, says John Lagimodiere, the Métis publisher and editor of *Eagle Feather News*, an aboriginal newspaper

based in Saskatoon. More natives are educating themselves and joining professions, he says. "There are still incredible problems to overcome, but I think we're at a real turning point," he says, noting that "times of change always get a little ugly."

14 And noisy. Perhaps the angry shouts of urban America are the soundtrack of racial divides being breached. Which would make the silence of Saskatoon the sound of living too comfortably with an uncomfortable truth.

15 In her classic 1990 impressionistic survey of Canadian cities, *O Canada: Travels in an Unknown Country*, travel writer Jan Morris called Saskatoon "Canada's best surprise." That's how I've always liked to think of it. But Ms. Morris also hit on a more painful reality—residents told her tales of narrow-mindedness, prejudice and inequality. "No city is without its seamy side, of course, but in Saskatoon . . . it seems unfairly incongruous, like a lump in a particularly well-made bed, or slugs in a salad."

16 Racial inequality in Saskatoon, a centre of community spirit and an enclave of culture and learning with a strong progressive heritage, is most painful of all. When I spoke with Saskatoon mayor Don Atchison this past Christmas, he emphasized the city's civic pride, the links between the university and the broader community, and its unparalleled levels of volunteerism. That's all true. But it's also true that extreme acts of racial brutality don't come out of a void.

17 Saskatoon is still a wonderful place, its people generous and caring. But it's not wonderful enough for too many of its citizens. The Stonechild inquiry is exposing the darker sides of our city, but it also gives us an opportunity. Having bit into the slug in our civic salad, we can now either swallow it down and force a grin, politely pretending it never was there at all. Or we can clear our throats and join in the messy, difficult business of trying to spit it out.

Thinking Critically About Content

1. Notice how in the opening passage the writer describes how he closes his eyes against the ugliness of the industrial outskirts of Saskatoon. How does this image foreshadow the article that follows? What does it tell you about him, and about the people of Saskatoon?

2. Why does the author describe the practice of dropping aboriginal men outside the city limits as a "particularly northern form of lynching"? How is it different from the southern version?

3. Does this essay make you think about your own home town and its prejudices? What kinds of prejudice exist? How are they evident? In what way is prejudice ignored?

Thinking Critically About Purpose and Audience

4. What do you think Hayden's purpose was in writing this essay? Give details from the article to back up your answer.

5. What readers might the essay affect? Would American readers and Canadian readers have something different to learn from the article? Explain your answer.

6. Should the writer have included a statement from the Saskatoon police? Why or why not?

Thinking Critically About Essays

7. Describe the writer's point of view in this essay. What comparison would you make between his physical and his emotional distance from the topic?

8. The comparison is confined to the centre of this essay. How is this effective in the development of the topic?

9. The title of the essay is taken from something someone said to the author. How is it effective?

10. Explain in detail how this essay might be different if it was written by someone who had not grown up in Saskatoon and moved away.

Thomas King

THE TRUTH ABOUT STORIES

Focusing Your Attention

1. Do you belong to a culture with a strong storytelling tradition? What kinds of stories does your family tell? How do the stories relate to cultural changes your family experienced?

2. The essay you are about to read begins with a reference to the Iroquoian story *The Woman Who Fell from the Sky*. As the story is not reproduced here due to lack of space, you might like to read it and other Iroquoian stories at http://iroquoisindians.freeweb-hosting.com/.

Expanding Your Vocabulary

The following words are important to your understanding of this essay:

decorum: appropriate behaviour (paragraph 1)

inherent: an essential part (paragraph 1)

exuberance: rich, excessive, usually applied to happiness (paragraph 1)

veracity: truthfulness (paragraph 1)

animism, polytheism, monotheism: types of religious beliefs (paragraph 3)

martial: warlike, from Mars, the Roman god of war (paragraph 9)

parlance: a manner of speaking, idiom (paragraph 9)

dichotomy: division into two opposing parts (paragraph 13)

> **honed:** sharpened or ground, like a knife edge (paragraph 15)
>
> **Silko's witches in the cave:** refers to *Ceremony*, a novel by Leslie Marmon Silko (paragraph 18)
>
> **rectitude:** moral uprightness (paragraph 22)
>
> **platitude:** trite or banal saying (paragraph 27)
>
> **insatiable:** impossible to satisfy (paragraph 35)

1   Okay. Two creation stories. One Native, one Christian. The first thing you probably noticed was that I spent more time with the Woman Who Fell from the Sky than I did with Genesis. I'm assuming that most of you have heard of Adam and Eve, but few, I imagine, have ever met Charm. I also used different strategies in the telling of these stories. In the Native story, I tried to recreate an oral storytelling voice and craft the story in terms of a performance for a general audience. In the Christian story, I tried to maintain a sense of rhetorical distance and decorum while organizing the story for a knowledgeable gathering. These strategies colour the stories and suggest values that may be neither inherent nor warranted. In the Native story, the conversational voice tends to highlight the exuberance of the story but diminishes its authority, while the sober voice in the Christian story makes for a formal recitation but creates a sense of veracity.

2   Basil Johnston, the Anishinabe storyteller, in his essay "How Do We Learn Language?" describes the role of comedy and laughter in stories by reminding us that Native peoples have always loved to laugh: "It is precisely because our tribal stories are comical and evoke laughter that they have never been taken seriously outside the tribe. . . . But behind and beneath the comic characters and the comic situations exists the real meaning of the story . . . what the tribe understood about human growth and development."[1]

3   Of course, none of you would make the mistake of confusing storytelling strategies with the value or sophistication of a story. And we know enough about the complexities of cultures to avoid the error of imagining animism and polytheism to be no more than primitive versions of monotheism. Don't we?

4   Nonetheless, the talking animals are a problem.

5   A theologian might argue that these two creation stories are essentially the same. Each tells about the creation of the world and the appearance of human beings. But a storyteller would tell you that these two stories are quite different, for whether you read the Bible as sacred text or secular metaphor, the elements in Genesis create a particular universe governed by a series of hierarchies—God, man, animals, plants—that celebrate law, order, and good government, while in our Native story, the universe is governed by a series of co-operations—Charm, the Twins, animals, humans— that celebrate equality and balance.

6   In Genesis, all creative power is vested in a single deity who is omnipotent, omniscient, and omnipresent. The universe begins with his thought,

and it is through his actions and only his actions that it comes into being. In the Earth Diver story, and in many other Native creation stories for that matter, deities are generally figures of limited power and persuasion, and the acts of creation and the decisions that affect the world are shared with other characters in the drama.

In Genesis, we begin with a perfect world, but after the Fall, while we gain knowledge, we lose the harmony and safety of the garden and are forced into a chaotic world of harsh landscapes and dangerous shadows. 7

In our Native story, we begin with water and mud, and, through the good offices of Charm, her twins, and the animals, move by degrees and adjustments from a formless, featureless world to a world that is rich in its diversity, a world that is complex and complete. 8

Finally, in Genesis, the post-garden world we inherit is decidedly martial in nature, a world at war—God vs. the Devil, humans vs. the elements. Or to put things into corporate parlance, competitive. In our Native story, the world is at peace, and the pivotal concern is not with the ascendancy of good over evil but with the issue of balance. 9

So here are our choices: a world in which creation is a solitary, individual act or a world in which creation is a shared activity; a world that begins in harmony and slides toward chaos or a world that begins in chaos and moves toward harmony; a world marked by competition or a world determined by co-operation. 10

And there's the problem. 11

If we see the world through Adam's eyes, we are necessarily blind to the world that Charm and the Twins and the animals help to create. If we believe one story to be sacred, we must see the other as secular. 12

You'll recognize this pairing as a dichotomy, the elemental structure of Western society. And cranky old Jacques Derrida notwithstanding, we do love our dichotomies. Rich/poor, white/black, strong/weak, right/wrong, culture/nature, male/female, written/oral, civilized/barbaric, success/failure, individual/communal. We trust easy oppositions. We are suspicious of complexities, distrustful of contradictions, fearful of enigmas. 13

Enigmas like my father. 14

I have a couple of old black-and-white pictures of him holding a baby with my mother looking on. He looks young in those photos. And happy. I'm sure he didn't leave because he hated me, just as I'm sure that my mother didn't stay because she loved me. Yet this is the story I continue to tell myself, because it's easy and contains all my anger, and because, in all the years, in all the tellings, I've honed it sharp enough to cut bone. 15

If we had to have a patron story for North America, we could do worse than the one about Alexander the Great, who, when faced with the puzzle of the Gordian knot, solved that problem with nothing more than a strong arm and a sharp sword. 16

Perhaps this is why we delight in telling stories about heroes battling the odds and the elements, rather than about the magic of seasonal 17 change. Why we relish stories that lionize individuals who start at the bottom and fight their way to the top, rather than stories that frame these forms of competition as varying degrees of insanity. Why we tell our children that life is hard, when we could just as easily tell them that it is sweet.

18   Is it our nature? Do the stories we tell reflect the world as it truly is, or did we simply start off with the wrong story? Like Silko's witches in the cave, conjuring up things to impress each other.

19   Making magic.

20   Making faces.

21   Making mistakes.

22   I'm dying to remind myself that the basis of Christian doctrine is rectitude and reward, crime and punishment, even though my partner has warned me that this is probably not a good idea. Tell a story, she told me. Don't preach. Don't try to sound profound. It's unbecoming, and you do it poorly. Don't show them your mind. Show them your imagination.

23   So am I such an ass as to disregard this good advice and suggest that the stories contained within the matrix of Christianity and the complex of nationalism are responsible for the social, political, and economic problems we face? Am I really arguing that the martial and hierarchical nature of Western religion and Western privilege has fostered stories that encourage egotism and self-interest? Am I suggesting that, if we hope to create a truly civil society, we must first burn all the flags and kill all the gods, because in such a world we could no longer tolerate such weapons of mass destruction?

24   No, I wouldn't do that.

25   Though certainly we understand that we clear-cut forests not to enrich the lives of animals but to make profit. We know that we dam(n) rivers not to improve water quality but to create electricity and protect private property. We make race and gender discriminatory markers for no other reason than that we can. And we maintain and tolerate poverty not because we believe adversity makes you strong, but because we're unwilling to share.

26   Ah. You've heard all this before, haven't you.

27   You may have already leaned over to a friend and whispered, Platitude. Platitude, platitude, platitude. Thomas King the duck-billed platitude.

28   But give this a thought. What if the creation story in Genesis had featured a flawed deity who was understanding and sympathetic rather than autocratic and rigid? Someone who, in the process of creation, found herself lost from time to time and in need of advice, someone who was willing to accept a little help with the more difficult decisions?

29   What if the animals had decided on their own names? What if Adam and Eve had simply been admonished for their foolishness?

30   I love you, God could have said, but I'm not happy with your behaviour. Let's talk this over. Try to do better next time.

31   What kind of a world might we have created with that kind of story?

Unfortunately, by the time we arrived in the wilderness, broke and homeless, the story of being made in God's image, of living in paradise, of naming the animals must have gone to our heads, for while we weren't the strongest or the fastest or the fiercest creatures on the planet, we were, certainly, as it turned out, the most arrogant.   32

God's Chosen People. The Alpha and the Omega. Masters of the Universe.   33

It is this conceit we continue to elaborate as we fill up our tanks at the gas station, the myth we embrace as we bolt our doors at night, the romance we pursue as we search our guidebooks for just the right phrase. The lie we dangle in front of our appetites as we chase progress to the grave.   34

Or as Linda McQuaig so delightfully puts it in her book *All You Can Eat: Greed, Lust and the New Capitalism*, "The central character in economics is Homo Economicus, the human prototype, who is pretty much just a walking set of insatiable material desires. He uses his rational abilities to ensure the satisfaction of all his wants, which are the key to his motivation. And he isn't considered some weirdo; the whole point of him is that he represents traits basic to all of us—Homo Economicus 'R' Us, as it were."[2]   35

It was Sir Isaac Newton who said, "To every action there is always opposed an equal reaction." Had he been a writer, he might have simply said, "To every action there is a story."   36

Take Charm's story, for instance. It's yours. Do with it what you will. Tell it to friends. Turn it into a television movie. Forget it. But don't say in the years to come that you would have lived your life differently if only you had heard this story.   37

You've heard it now.   38

References

[1] Basil Johnston, "How Do We Learn Language?" in *Talking on the Page: Editing Aboriginal Oral Texts*, eds. Laura Murray and Keren Rice (Toronto: University of Toronto Press, 1999), 14.

[2] Linda McQuaig, *All You Can Eat: Greed, Lust and the New Capitalism* (Toronto: Viking, 2001), 12.

Thinking Critically About Content

1. Explain the major differences between the two creation myths.

2. Why does King interject the story of his father into his discussion of the two creation myths? Is he momentarily getting off track, or is there a specific purpose to his use of this story? Explain.

3. According to King, "If we had to have a patron story for North America, we could do worse than the one about Alexander the Great." Why does King think the story of Alexander and the Gordian knot is appropriate for North America?

Thinking Critically About Purpose and Audience

4. What do you think Thomas King's purpose is in this essay?

5. Why do you think the writer phrases his comments in paragraph 23 in the form of questions? What effect might this form have on the reader?

6. The essay was originally delivered as a lecture. What elements of the essay do you think would work well in a lecture? Explain and illustrate your answer from the essay.

Thinking Critically About Essays

7. Can you locate a thesis statement in this essay? Where is it? How does the author lead up to the thesis?

8. Name three points of similarity and three points of contrast in this essay.

9. Is the essay organized by point, by subject, or by a combination of the two? Is the style he has chosen the most effective for this material? Explain your answer.

10. Are the details King uses persuasive? Does it matter that all of the details of the stories of Charm and Genesis are not given here? What did you feel you had learned when you had finished reading? Did you find yourself questioning previously held assumptions? Write a detailed response to the essay.

Writing Topics: Comparing and Contrasting

Before you begin to write, you might want to review the writing process in Part I.

1. Tom Hayden's article compares and contrasts Washington, D.C., and Saskatoon as part of an investigation of racism. Thomas King's essay compares Judeo-Christian creation myths with Native ones. Both, however, ultimately ask us to take a serious look at our attitude towards Native peoples. Write a comparison of the two essays, focusing on attitudes.

2. What process do you have to go through to come up with an interesting comparison or contrast? How is it different from the process you go through for other rhetorical modes?

3. Compare Canadian culture to that of another country you know well. Begin by creating a list of similarities and differences.

DIVIDING AND CLASSIFYING

CHAPTER

28

The essays in this chapter show division and classification at work. The first, "Bad Boys" by Mordecai Richler, divides and classifies male losers in the dating world of Montreal in the thirties and forties. The second essay, "What Are Friends For?" by Marion Winik, divides and classifies various types of friends.

◆◆━━━━━━━━━━◆◆

Mordecai Richler

BAD BOYS

Focusing Your Attention

1. What dating fiascos have you heard about, or experienced yourself? What is your definition of a bad date? What are the female equivalents of the categories the author covers?

2. In the essay you are about to read, the writer divides and classifies young men for women to watch out for when they are dating. Do all bad dates fall into particular categories? What are they? Are there particular new problems with dating now that the Internet is so prevalent? Could you classify the problems that might happen to someone using an online dating service?

Expanding Your Vocabulary

The following words are important to your understanding of this essay:

loping: running with a steady even gait (paragraph 1)

seminal: the original basis for development, the seed (paragraph 2)

prescient: knowing what is coming (paragraph 3)

braggart: boaster (paragraph 3)

cherished: beloved (paragraph 7)

When we were horny teenagers, me and my bunch dreaded the coming of Saturday nights. Our anxieties, such as they were, struck as we left high school on Friday afternoons, loping home to begin to work the phones. Would we manage to get a date for the following night or would we be   1 humiliated yet again? We were sixteen years old at the time, grade 11 students in Montreal, and the ungrateful girls we had invested in selflessly for years—treating them to double features at the Rialto, followed by toasted tomato and mayo sandwiches, washed down with Cokes or milkshakes at Ben Ash's, never mind the cost—had suddenly turned against us. Upwardly mobile in their nifty sweaters, tight skirts, nylons, and high heels, reeking of some cheap perfume shoplifted at Woolworth's, they now preferred the company of older guys, later to prosper as dentists or accountants, who were already at McGill. This being the case, we often had to put up with being men without women, as Mr. Hemingway had it, on Saturday nights, settling for going out together to shoot pool at the Park Billiards. However, there were Saturday nights when we did make out, repairing to neck on a bench in Outremont Park after the movie.

2   Be that as it may, I'm glad dating is no longer a problem for me and my bunch, because we would now all be classified as either the Show-Off, Know-It-All, Cheater, Sex Guzzler, Mr. Ego, Bug-Eyed Boy, or Boozer, dismissed as Losers to Watch Out For. I am indebted for this information to a fascinating book which recently came my way, *RED FLAGS! How to Know When You're Dating a LOSER*, published by Plume, the down-market imprint of Penguin Books. It is the seminal work of two eminent shrinks, doctors Gary S. Aumiller and Daniel A. Goldfarb. Aumiller is an "internationally known" lecturer and Goldfarb serves as Webmaster to several psychology self-help sites on the Internet. Both authors have put in time as the prez of the Society of Police and Criminal Psychology and helped some 4,000 patients solve problems and make better decisions before combining to warn women about the 25 Losers to Watch Out For and How to Dump Them and Move On.

3   Consider, for instance, the Show-Off. In an idiom refreshingly free of academic prose, the authors warn, "If the man you are dating does more strutting than a rooster on Viagra in a brand-new hen house," this guy's a turkey. Cook his goose. The Show-Off, according to the prescient authors, can easily be recognized. He is a braggart, and a sharp dresser, who flexes his muscles a lot, and looks at himself frequently in the mirror, and, um, "other reflective substances" but is very insecure underneath his plumage. Reminds me of Hershel Greenbaum. Show him the Red Flag, girls.

4   "The Game for the Know-It-All is *Jeopardy!* Beat Him to the Buzzer," say Aumiller and Goldfarb. Signals to watch out for: his eyes dart, he name-drops, puts his friends down, and insists on ordering dinner for you. Yes, but like Arnie Debrofsky of blessed memory, he also showers a lot, and reads lots of non-fiction, which don't strike me as such bad things. But the doctors also adjudge him a Loser and highly recommend a clean break, goodbye: "Then go home and turn on the Discovery Channel and learn about the mating rituals of the giant Galapagos turtles. You too can know it all."

5   The Sex-Guzzler, as you might have expected, is very bad news. "The Way to Your Heart is Not Through Your Pants." Happily such villains can be

easily spotted. They tend to wear gold jewellery, neck chains, bracelets, touch you very quickly on the first date, and talk about life being an adventure and about the need to take risks. Watch out, girls. If the sex is great, you could end up a Guzzler yourself.

With equal ease the doctors dispose of Mr. Ego ("If He Thinks He's God's 6 Gift, Exchange Him!"); the Cheater, who tends to look at your breasts or legs and to invade personal space; the Bug-Eyed Boy, yet another eye-darter, who looks at body parts, not faces, when he is talking to you or other women (gosh, I used to know guys like that); and the Boozer, no eye-darter he, but he does tend to be restless, and at times has a rumpled look. Worse news. He has more than two drinks on the first date. Aumiller and Goldfarb recommend boozers to rely on the three Ms: meetings with Alcoholics Anonymous, meditation, and masturbation, "because he should not have a woman around."

RED FLAGS! takes no prisoners. It provides women with further good 7 advice against Neglecters, Pleasers, Possessors, Abusers, and Loners, taking in just about all of my cherished male friends. Girls, beware of these two shrinks. Dump Them. Cook Their Goose. Lest you end up old maids.

Thinking Critically About Content

1. Richler divides and classifies dating losers into several categories. What are these categories?

2. What are the main differences in these categories? What phrase ties the categories together?

3. In the final paragraph, the author tells girls to beware of "these two shrinks." What indications has he given throughout the essay that he might disagree with the authors he is reviewing? Give examples.

Thinking Critically About Purpose and Audience

4. The essay is written as if it is a book review. Is this its main purpose?

5. Who do you think is Richler's main audience?

6. Is the author asking "girls" to accept any loser rather than "end up an old maid"? Is this a valid observation? Why or why not?

Thinking Critically About Essays

7. The paragraphs describing the different types of dating losers are organized in a similar pattern. Outline the pattern.

8. How do the descriptions of Richler's friends in the opening paragraph and the reference to "my cherished friends" in the last paragraph work in this essay?

9. Choose one of the central paragraphs from the essay and decide whether it is unified or not. Explain why.

10. Write a detailed description of one of the dating losers described in the final paragraph of the essay.

Marion Winik

WHAT ARE FRIENDS FOR?

Focusing Your Attention

1. Who do you rely on to talk out your problems with? To confide in? To tell secrets to? How do these people fit into your life? How do you fit into theirs?

2. In the essay you are about to read, the author divides and classifies the types of friends people generally have. What do you think these types are?

Expanding Your Vocabulary

The following words are important to your understanding of this essay:

half-slip: undergarment worn by women (paragraph 1)

innumerable: too many to count (paragraph 2)

Aquarena Springs: a theme park in San Marcos, Texas, that is now a preservation and education centre (paragraph 2)

infallible: unfailing (paragraph 6)

indispensable: absolutely necessary (paragraph 8)

wistful: nostalgic (paragraph 10)

ill-conceived: poorly planned (paragraph 10)

inopportune: inconvenient (paragraph 11)

tonic: boost (paragraph 14)

1   I was thinking about how everybody can't be everything to each other, but some people can be something to each other, thank God, from the ones whose shoulders you cry on to the ones whose half-slips you borrow to the nameless ones you chat with in the grocery line.

2   Buddies, for example, are the workhorses of the friendship world, the people out there on the front lines, defending you from loneliness and boredom. They call you up, they listen to your complaints, they celebrate your successes and curse your misfortunes, and you do the same for them in return. They hold out through innumerable crises before concluding that the person you're dating is no good, and even then understand if you ignore their good counsel. They accompany you to a movie with subtitles or to see the diving pig at Aquarena Springs. They feed your cat when you are out of town and pick you up from the airport when you get back. They come over to help you decide what to wear on a date. Even if it is with that creep.

3   What about family members? Most of them are people you just got stuck with, and though you love them, you may not have very much in common. But there is that rare exception, the Relative Friend. It is your cousin, your

brother, maybe even your aunt. The two of you share the same views of the other family members. Meg never should have divorced Martin. He was the best thing that ever happened to her. You can confirm each other's memories of things that happened a long time ago. Don't you remember when Uncle Hank and Daddy had that awful fight in the middle of Thanksgiving dinner? Grandma always hated Grandpa's stamp collection; she probably left the windows open during the hurricane on purpose.

While so many family relationships are tinged with guilt and obligation, a relationship with a Relative Friend is relatively worry-free. You don't even have to hide your vices from this delightful person. When you slip out Aunt Joan's back door for a cigarette, she is already there.

Then there is that special guy at work. Like all the other people at the job site, at first he's just part of the scenery. But gradually he starts to stand out from the crowd. Your friendship is cemented by jokes about co-workers and thoughtful favors around the office. Did you see Ryan's hair? Want half my bagel? Soon you know the names of his turtles, what he did last Friday night, exactly which model CD player he wants for his birthday. His handwriting is as familiar to you as your own.

Though you invite each other to parties, you somehow don't quite fit into each other's outside lives. For this reason, the friendship may not survive a job change. Company gossip, once an infallible source of entertainment, soon awkwardly accentuates the distance between you. But wait. Like School Friends, Work Friends share certain memories which acquire a nostalgic glow after about a decade.

A Faraway Friend is someone you grew up with or went to school with or lived in the same town as until one of you moved away. Without a Faraway Friend, you would never get any mail addressed in handwriting. A Faraway Friend calls late at night, invites you to her wedding, always says she is coming to visit but rarely shows up. An actual visit from a Faraway Friend is a cause for celebration and binges of all kinds. Cigarettes, Chips Ahoy, bottles of tequila.

Faraway Friends go through phases of intense communication, then may be out of touch for many months. Either way, the connection is always there. A conversation with your Faraway Friend always helps to put your life in perspective: When you feel you've hit a dead end, come to a confusing fork in the road, or gotten lost in some crackerbox subdivision of your life, the advice of the Faraway Friend—who has the big picture, who is so well acquainted with the route that brought you to this place—is indispensable.

Another useful function of the Faraway Friend is to help you remember things from a long time ago, like the name of your seventh-grade history teacher, what was in that really good stir-fry, or exactly what happened that night on the boat with the guys from Florida.

Ah, the Former Friend. A sad thing. At best a wistful memory, at worst a dangerous enemy who is in possession of many of your deepest secrets. But what was it that drove you apart? A misunderstanding, a betrayed confidence, an unrepaid loan, an ill-conceived flirtation. A poor choice of spouse can do in a friendship just like that. Going into business together can be a serious mistake. Time, money, distance, cult religions: all noted friendship killers. You quit doing drugs, you're not such good friends with your dealer anymore.

11   And lest we forget, there are the Friends You Love to Hate. They call at inopportune times. They say stupid things. They butt in, they boss you around, they embarrass you in public. They invite themselves over. They take advantage. You've done the best you can, but they need professional help. On top of all this, they love you to death and are convinced they're your best friend on the planet.

12   So why do you continue to be involved with these people? Why do you tolerate them? On the contrary, the real question is, What would you do without them? Without Friends You Love to Hate, there would be nothing to talk about with your other friends. Their problems and their irritating stunts provide a reliable source of conversation for everyone they know. What's more, Friends You Love to Hate make you feel good about yourself, since you are obviously in so much better shape than they are. No matter what these people do, you will never get rid of them. As much as they need you, you need them too.

13   At the other end of the spectrum are Hero Friends. These people are better than the rest of us, that's all there is to it. Their career is something you wanted to be when you grew up—painter, forest ranger, tireless doer of good. They have beautiful homes filled with special handmade things presented to them by villagers in the remote areas they have visited in their extensive travels. Yet they are modest. They never gossip. They are always helping others, especially those who have suffered a death in the family or an illness. You would think people like this would just make you sick, but somehow they don't.

14   A New Friend is a tonic unlike any other. Say you meet her at a party. In your bowling league. At a Japanese conversation class, perhaps. Wherever, whenever, there's that spark of recognition. The first time you talk, you can't believe how much you have in common. Suddenly, your life story is interesting again, your insights fresh, your opinion valued. Your various shortcomings are as yet completely invisible.

15   It's almost like falling in love.

Thinking Critically About Content

1. How many types of friends does Winik introduce? What are they?

2. On what basis does Winik create these categories?

3. In what ways is a new friend "a tonic" (paragraph 14)?

Thinking Critically About Purpose and Audience

4. Why do you think Winik wrote this essay?

5. Who would be most interested in this essay?

6. How does this essay make you feel about the role of friends in your life?

Thinking Critically About Essays

7. How does Winik organize her essay? Why do you think she puts her categories in this order?

8. How does the author develop each category? Use one paragraph to explain your answer.

9. Explain Winik's title.

10. Write a detailed description of one of your friends. Why is this person a friend of yours?

Writing Topics: Dividing and Classifying

Before you begin to write, you might want to review the writing process in Part I.

1. In the first essay, Richler writes about losers to avoid dating. Divide and classify classmates you have encountered in your courses.

2. Divide and classify your friends into meaningful categories, and write an essay explaining your classification system.

3. What process do you have to go through to come up with an interesting classification essay? How is it different from the process you go through for other rhetorical modes?

29

DEFINING

Here are two essays that show how definition works in two completely different contexts: "Ways to Ai" by Wang Ping defines "love" from the point of view of her Chinese heritage. The second essay, "Healing Myself with the Power of Work" by Michael Norlen, explains how work has been a form of lifesaving therapy for the author.

Wang Ping

WAYS TO AI—爱

Focusing Your Attention

1. How many different kinds of love do you know about? How many have you experienced?

2. The essay you are about to read defines love. What does *love* mean to you? What emotions do you associate with this word?

Expanding Your Vocabulary

The following words are important to your understanding of this essay:

faction: political group (paragraph 3)

filial: involving a son or daughter (paragraphs 4 and 5)

1   "Love? Can love buy you a decent meal with rice and meat? Can it keep you warm in snow? Safe in a storm?" my paternal grandma would answer whenever I asked about her arranged marriage, her long widowed life.

2   "Don't even think about 'talking love' before you turn 25, before you join the Communist Party and have made something of life!" my father warned when I left home at 15.

3   "There's no such thing as love without a reason, just as there is no such thing as hate without a reason." We chanted Mao's words as we spat and kicked at the teachers we had once adored, broke windows, burnt books, beat up Red Guards from a different faction who were once our best friends.

My grandma's favorite dinner story is about a widow who cut chunks of   4
flesh from her arms and thighs to make broth for her dying mother-in-law.
Such a filial deed moved the gods so much that they let the old woman re-
vive and live another ten years. As the story proceeded, my mother would
bang her chopsticks and rice bowl louder and louder on the table and finally stomp out. "Have you heard a better love story than that?" my
grandma would ask, her cheeks sunk deep in a toothless mouth.

"This is for the burnt rice," my mother said as she whipped us with   5
her bamboo stick. "And this is for the bowl you broke, the corner you
didn't sweep, the dirty words that slipped out of your mouth." She aimed at
our thighs, where the meat was the thickest, the pain unforgettable. "A filial
son comes from under a rod. I want you to remember this, with your flesh.
You'll be grateful when you grow up, and you'll pass it on to your children,
and next, and next. And this is the best love a mother can give you, kiddos."

I've never written a love poem, nor said the word love—*ai*—in Chinese.   6
When pressed by my Chinese boyfriend, I'd say it in English and French
only. (He found it cute in the beginning, but later used it as an excuse to
dump me.) The word sounds like bad luck, too much like a sigh—*ai*. It
makes me feel like an old man bent with heavy loads. We say *teng ai* (pain
love) to our children, *eng ai* (gratitude love), or *ai qing* (love emotion) between husband and wife, *lian ai* (pity love) to a mistress or a child. Love is
conditioned, heavily.

I trace the word on paper. First is the hand, then the roof of a house. This   7
makes sense. You want to keep a firm hand on your shelter, your safety, before you can even start talking about love. Is that why my father warned me
over and over again not to "talk love" before I've established myself? Then
comes the part "friend." I open my biggest dictionary, *Ocean of Words*. 17
years away from China, and I'm losing my mother tongue. It's a complicated system, each word made with two, three, even six different compo-
nents. No, I'm not wrong; the word does end with a friend, a friend holding
up the roof of a house with an assuring hand. So what does it have to do
with love? I look back into the dictionary again. It says "love among brothers." Ok, brotherly love, love of the same sex before it extends to the other.
Then it says "love − adultery." I squirm in my chair. That explains why I've
been so reluctant to say "I love you" in my mother tongue. The third item:
"love = penny-pinch = greed."

My palms get clammy with cold sweat. The definitions of love in my   8
Chinese dictionary don't seem friendly, and I can't discard them as rubbish,
for they are all backed up by Confucius' writing, history, famous poets and
politicians. All of them seem to say: love is a wild animal. Control it or it will
tear you apart, drag you into the abyss.

"Don't talk love before you turn 25." How the father knows!   9

And the companion words—gratitude, respect, duty, pain, pity, addic-   10
tion, treasure, and many many others—that go side by side with the taboo
word *ai*. Are they meant to tame this beast deep in our hearts? Does it mean

we Chinese can't love for the sake of love? And if we do, we must love with all the pain, all the duties, all the consequences? Is this how my grandmas, my ancestors, women of my race find their happiness, though they never met their men before wedding nights, though their husbands may beat them up, sell them to redeem a debt, take in as many concubines as they could afford, whenever they wanted?

11   Does it mean I'm hopeless?

12   "Love?" poofed my mother. "Love is puffed rice. It satisfies you for five minutes. That's all. And men. You can't believe a word they say, they're like commercials. So when you choose a husband, no need to look at his face or crotch, just look into his checking account."

13   "Love is a wild deer in the forest. It won't return no matter how you call it," my twice-divorced sister said on the phone.

14   When pressed to remarry, she replied, "Men are like parking lots. All the good ones are taken, and the rest are handicapped."

15   "It's possible to bear fruit before blossom," my grandma insisted. "Children first, then respect, then love."

16   I suppose, I suppose, I mutter to myself as my index finger goes up and down the dictionary. Security, responsibility, control, all wise and sound. But something is missing. Suddenly my eyes pop wide. At the bottom is the traditional version of the character *ai:* a hand, a roof, a friend, the usual stuff. Then in the middle, between the friend and roof, stands a heart. It was taken out by the government in the 50s to make Chinese words easier to use.

17   "That's it!" I shout out loud. That's what's been missing, the heart—心—*xin.*

18   Dot by dot, I try out the newly found character, adding the heart. Memories rush to me from all sides: first crush, first fight, first betrayal, the whipping, the cursing, my mother and grandmas barking their stories to my ears, my ancestors, their ways of love, of hatred, cunning and twisted, with its own wisdom and truth. I thought I'd buried them, to make my life easier, more modern, more western, but they've been living with me, all these years, waiting to come out.

19   爱—the hand comes first, then the roof, then the heart—心. Its three dots spurt and drip like blood over a standing leg. For decades, the heart has been erased from books, papers, magazines. But its pulse has never stopped. It's been pulsing in my grandmas' stories, my sister's waiting for the reunion with her long lost daughter, in the shafts of sunlight, moon rise, fallen leaves, in the whip my mother carefully placed behind the bedroom door.

20   "*Ai,*" I sigh as I complete the last stroke. The heart looks a bit squashed between the house and people, a bit fragile under the weight of the roof. But it's there, beating with its own rhythm, its own rules of law. Someday, when the heart takes root again, I'll learn how to say the word, in my native tongue, a sound that can also mean a sigh, an obstacle, a sound soaked with pain and joy.

Thinking Critically About Content

1. Restate Wang Ping's definition of *love* in your own words.

2. What was the missing element the author discovered about the Chinese word for love?

3. What does Wang Ping mean when she says, "Love is a wild animal. Control it or it will tear you apart, drag you into the abyss" (paragraph 8)?

Thinking Critically About Purpose and Audience

4. What is Wang Ping's purpose in writing this essay?

5. Who do you think is her primary audience?

6. Does Wang Ping capture the essence of love in her essay? Which details communicate this message most effectively?

Thinking Critically About Essays

7. The author uses similes and metaphors (comparisons of two unlike items) to help her explain love. One example is in paragraph 13: "Love is a wild deer in the forest." Explain this comparison, and find one other example of this technique.

8. How does Wang Ping organize her definition? Is this the most effective arrangement for her ideas?

9. Choose three transitions in Wang Ping's essay that you think work well. Explain why they are effective.

10. Write a response to this essay titled "Love in [another language]."

Michael Norlen

HEALING MYSELF WITH THE POWER OF WORK

Focusing Your Attention

1. As a student or as an employee in the job market, what advantages do you get from your work? Are these rewards mostly physical or emotional?

2. The essay you are about to read defines *depression*. Have you ever been depressed? How did you manage your daily responsibilities? How did you pull yourself out of your depression?

Expanding Your Vocabulary

The following words are important to your understanding of this essay:

Kansas City Star: a daily newspaper published in Missouri (paragraph 1)

perfunctory: indifferent (paragraph 2)

indignant: angry (paragraph 3)

despondency: sadness (paragraph 4)

night-dwellers: people who are active at night (paragraph 6)

Patsy Cline: country singer who died in a plane crash at age 30 in 1963 (paragraph 6)

insidious: slowly destructive (paragraph 8)

neurons: nerve endings (paragraph 8)

synapses: spaces between nerve endings (paragraph 8)

serotonin: a substance that transmits impulses between nerves (paragraph 8)

dopamine: a substance that transmits impulses between nerves (paragraph 8)

manifest: become noticeable (paragraph 8)

dispiriting: depressing (paragraph 8)

regimen: systematic plan, such as a diet (paragraph 9)

antidepressants: medications to fight depression (paragraph 9)

tolerance: resistance, lack of response (paragraph 9)

Jim Beam: a brand of bourbon (paragraph 10)

Coors: a brand of beer (paragraph 10)

introverted: focused on oneself (paragraph 10)

psychotherapy: professional counselling (paragraph 11)

arsenal: collection of weapons (paragraph 12)

satiated: no longer hungry (paragraph 12)

1   "The paper guy's here!" Every Monday morning a cashier at Eckerd's drugstore greets me with these words. A manager gives her a key, and she fishes $3 and change from the cash drawer and pays me for the copies of the *Kansas City Star* sold the previous week. I pick up the 10 or 12 unsold papers and throw them in my car, next to the returns from the supermarket, the doughnut shop, and the Texaco station.

2   Quite a difference from a year ago. Then, I would announce myself in response to a judge's perfunctory order: "Counsel, state your appearance." Instead of delivering papers from 1:30 a.m. to 6 a.m., I spent my nights sleeping and my days in an office, a courtroom, or a library.

3   It all changed 12 months ago. For the second time in six years, I abandoned my solo law practice. I stopped returning phone calls, forgot to pay bills, and ignored court dates. I began to sleep 16 hours a day. By July of last year, I stopped coming into the office, leaving it to fill up with unopened mail and indignant phone messages. By August I was behind on my office

rent, and by October my landlord asked me to leave. I ate, but nothing tasted good. I slept, but woke up tired. I felt like a stranger around my wife and two daughters. Thoughts of suicide shadowed me. And in the midst of all this, I knew. *It* had returned.

Tracy Thompson, the journalist, calls *It* "The Beast." To Winston   4
Churchill, *It* was his "Black Dog." To me, it is both of these: a nameless, face-less thing that infects me with a despondency so bleak I fear that I will never feel joy again. It is depression. Twice now *It* has laid me low.

Trying to throw me a lifeline, a friend offered me a job delivering news-   5
papers. To my great surprise, I found myself almost enjoying the job. Con-trasted to the stresses of maintaining a law practice, this mindless work of assembling and bundling papers in a dimly lit warehouse was a welcome distraction. When I left the warehouse to deliver the papers, to vending ma-chines, gas stations, and supermarkets, I began to catch glimpses of small joys.

After months of hiding from people and avoiding conversation, little by   6
little I got to know some of the night-dwellers. The clerk at the Phillip's station who plays country music and seems to have an obsession with Patsy Cline. The jogger I always pass at 4 a.m. With friendly greetings and idle conversation, these people, whose names I still don't know, began to draw me out of my darkness.

At the end of each night, I look down at my hands, stained with ink from   7
handling 450 newspapers. I stretch and feel a tightness in my shoulders from lifting the 40- or 50-pound bundles into and out of my car. The grime and the pain serve as wake-up calls for my tired body and mind. And every Sunday morning, when my friend hands me a modest check, I begin to feel just a bit more confident.

Depression is an insidious disease. On one level, it is about neurons and   8
synapses, seratonin levels, and dopamine readings. On another level, it is memories of trauma stashed in dusty corners of the mind that manifest years later in fear and anxiety. And on yet another level, it is a crippling, dispiriting mind-set that convinces me I am worthless and helpless.

For almost five years, I have been on a steady regimen of antidepres-   9
sants, from Prozac to Serzone. When I build up a tolerance to one drug, my doctor simply switches me to another. Except for some inconvenient side ef-fects, they have been my safety net, stopping my free fall into madness.

For most of the same period, I have been in individual or group therapy.   10
I've learned how some of the difficult periods of my life have shaped me and contributed to my depression. The memories of my drunken mother and the Jim Beam and Coors bottles strewn around our rented houses help me understand why I'm so fearful of failure, so introverted and so reluctant to trust others.

For all the insight and help I've received from drug therapy and psy-   11
chotherapy, I still have feelings of worthlessness. Every bout of depression eats away at my self-esteem, and no amount of drugs or talking can restore

it. That restoration has to come through a different vehicle. For me, that vehicle is physical work. Every time I look at the calluses on my hands, I realize that this job provides me with a reason to get out of bed.

12   One day soon I'll be ready to leave this job behind, but I'll never again view work as just a paycheck or a daily obligation. It will always be a part of my therapy, my healing. I don't know where my next job will be; in the courtroom, the classroom, or the office. But wherever it is, my work will be a weapon in my arsenal against the attacks I know will come again and again, because the Beast will not be satiated, and the Dog will never be securely leashed.

Thinking Critically About Content

1. Restate Norlen's definition of depression in your own words. Does Norlen's definition make sense to you?

2. How does the author say he is digging himself out of his depression?

3. What does Norlen mean when he says, "I'll never again view work as just a paycheck or a daily obligation" (paragraph 12)?

Thinking Critically About Purpose and Audience

4. Why do you think Norlen wrote this essay?

5. Who do you think is his primary audience?

6. Have you ever helped someone who was depressed? What did you do? Explain your answer.

Thinking Critically About Essays

7. Paragraph 7 ends rather than begins with its controlling idea. Explain how Norlen develops this particular paragraph.

8. How is paragraph 3 organized? Why do you think Norlen puts these facts in this particular order?

9. Choose one paragraph, and explain its tone or mood.

10. Write a summary of this essay for your English class.

Writing Topics: Defining

Before you begin to write, you might want to review the writing process in Part I.

1. In the first essay, Wang Ping defines *love*. Write your own definition of another state of mind, such as *joy*, *fear*, *loneliness*, or *stress*.

2. Using Norlen's method of development through personal narrative, define *work* for your class.

3. Now that you have studied different approaches to the process of definition, what makes a definition effective or useful for you? Apply what you have studied about definition to your answer.

30

ANALYZING CAUSES AND EFFECTS

In the essays in this chapter, the writers analyze the causes and effects related to their topics. "A Family Dilemma: To Scout or Not to Scout?" by Michael Alvear openly discusses the issue of gay Boy Scout leaders. The second essay, "Too Much Self-Esteem: The Blight of Modern Times" by Johanna Schneller, looks at one result of parents reinforcing self-esteem at any cost.

Michael Alvear

A FAMILY DILEMMA: TO SCOUT OR NOT TO SCOUT?

Focusing Your Attention

1. Think of the last time you had a moral dilemma. What caused the dilemma? How did you handle it?

2. In the essay you are about to read, Michael Alvear looks at the effect on his family of the U.S. Supreme Court ruling that the Scouts have a constitutional right to fire gay Scout leaders. What has the greatest impact on your life—your family or your peers? Analyze the effect one of these groups has on your life.

Expanding Your Vocabulary

The following words are important to your understanding of this essay:

backlash: strong negative reaction (paragraph 3)

municipal: owned and operated by the town (paragraph 3)

unsettling: disturbing (paragraph 5)

ethical: moral (paragraph 5)

quandary: dilemma (paragraph 7)

ironically: surprisingly (i.e., opposite of what would have been expected) (paragraph 10)

inconceivable: impossible to imagine (paragraph 11)

My sister constantly tells me how much her 6-year-old son Ricky (not his real name) adores me. So when he came home with a flier about joining a fun and exciting group for kids his age, she had a tough decision to make. Should she let him join a group that doesn't like his beloved uncle Michael?

When the Supreme Court ruled that the Boy Scouts have the constitutional right to fire Scout leaders for being gay, my sister was caught in an agonizing moral dilemma: allowing her son to become a member of America's most family-friendly group meant dishonoring part of her family.

The political backlash since the ruling against the Boy Scouts is clear to anyone who reads the local papers. Many cities, believing the Scouts are engaging in discrimination, have told local Scout troops that they can't use parks, schools, and other municipal sites. Companies and charities have withdrawn hundreds of thousands of dollars in support. But what isn't so easy to see is the division the Supreme Court ruling created in millions of families like mine.

When my sister first called to tell me she was thinking of putting Ricky in the Cub Scouts (a program run by the Boy Scouts of America), I could hear the torment in her voice. Ricky is a bright, athletic boy who suffers from a shyness so paralyzing he doesn't have any friends. The other day my sister asked who he had played with during recess. "Nobody," he mumbled, looking at the floor. "I just scratched the mosquito bites on my leg till it was time to go back to class."

It breaks my sister's heart to see what Ricky's shyness is doing to him. Karate, softball, and soccer leagues helped, but not nearly enough. In another age, my sister wouldn't have thought twice about letting him join the Scouts. But now the decision has taken on an unsettling ethical dimension.

"I don't understand why they're making me take sides in my own family," she said about the Boy Scout policy. "In order to help my son I have to abandon my brother."

My sister was up against some disturbing questions. Should she violate her sense of family loyalty for the social needs of her son? Or keep her values intact and deny her son the possibility of overcoming his shyness? By saying that troops have the right to fire gay leaders, the Boy Scouts created the unimaginable: a moral quandary about joining the most wholesome group in America.

My sister was afraid she'd be doing the same thing many parents did a generation ago when they joined country clubs that didn't allow blacks and Jews. They, too, must have rationalized their membership by saying the clubs' wholesome activities would be good for their kids.

There was one thing my sister and her husband were not conflicted about: me. "No way are we putting Ricky in the Scouts if this is an issue for you," she said. "Blood is thicker than camping." Still, she wanted to know how I'd feel if my nephew became a Scout.

I felt completely torn, but I answered with as much certainty as I could muster. "I am not getting in the way of what's best for a 6-year-old," I told her. Ironically, I found myself trying to persuade her to let Ricky join the Scouts. It's families that teach morality, I argued, not after-school groups. Besides, I added, it's not like the issue will come up during any of the Scouting activities.

11   Or will it? Is it really inconceivable that kids who know why the president of the United States was impeached would ask their Scout leader why gay people aren't allowed in the organization? And what would the scoutmaster's response be? I was shaken by the possibility of my nephew hearing a trusted grown-up trying to convince him that his uncle Michael is someone to be scared of.

12   One night I had a terrible dream of a Boy Scout official pointing me out to Ricky and saying, "See that guy? The one you love more than any other man except your father? He's not allowed in here."

13   I woke up feeling a kind of enraged helplessness. How could I mean so much to my family and so little to so many outside it? Ultimately, I knew I could live with the indignity of my nephew belonging to a group that discriminates against his uncle; what I couldn't live with was the guilt of denying Ricky a chance to improve his life.

14   How can Ricky's parents know what the right thing to do is in this situation? For starters, they plan to get more information before they make a decision. And so my sister, a mom torn between her devotion to her brother and concern for her son, will go to next month's Scout meeting with her husband.

15   Will they put Ricky in the Scouts? I don't know. But as the date of the meeting approaches, I can't help thinking how unfair it is that my sister will have to pass under that imaginary sign that hangs over every Scout gathering: YOUR SON IS WELCOME, BUT YOUR BROTHER IS NOT.

Thinking Critically About Content

1. What is Alvear analyzing in this essay?

2. What are the causes and effects of the moral dilemma Alvear's sister is struggling with?

3. What is Alvear referring to when he says, "I was shaken by the possibility of my nephew hearing a trusted grown-up trying to convince him that his uncle Michael is someone to be scared of" (paragraph 11)?

Thinking Critically About Purpose and Audience

4. What do you think Michael Alvear's purpose is in this essay?

5. Who do you think would find this essay most interesting? Explain your answer.

6. What emotions do you think Alvear is trying to evoke in his readers as he analyzes his family's moral dilemma?

Thinking Critically About Essays

7. Describe this writer's point of view toward this moral dilemma.

8. The author sets the scene for his essay by explaining his close relationship with his sister's son. Is this an effective beginning? Why or why not?

9. How does Alvear organize his essay? List his main points to answer this question.

10. Analyze your reactions to this situation as Ricky's dad. How would you feel? Why would you feel that way?

Johanna Schneller

TOO MUCH SELF-ESTEEM: THE BLIGHT OF MODERN TIMES

Focusing Your Attention

1. What gives you a sense of self-esteem? Are you able to feel good about yourself without being told you are doing well?

2. In the essay you are about to read, Johanna Schneller writes about the effect the excessive reinforcement of self-esteem by baby-boomer parents has had on a generation of young people. Do you think that self-esteem should always be based on actual achievements? Is a sense of self-esteem necessary for happiness?

Expanding Your Vocabulary

The following words are important to your understanding of this essay:

chagrined: embarrassed (paragraph 2)

sashayed: flounced or strutted (paragraph 2)

fogey: an old-fashioned person (paragraph 2)

smitten: hit by a deep emotion (paragraph 3)

accolades: approval, praise (paragraph 3)

gorgons: ugly, like Medusa, the mythological woman with snakes for hair (paragraph 6)

angst: anxiety (paragraph 8)

ilk: kind (paragraph 17)

simulacrum: a mockery or sham (paragraph 20)

travails: hard work (paragraph 24)

synapses: the pathway between nerves (paragraph 25)

1   Earlier this season on *American Idol*, 19-year-old contestants were dolled up like children dressed as hookers for Halloween. Sometimes they sang, but sometimes their caterwauling was earsplitting. When the latter occurred, the show's three judges, music professionals all, proffered their opinions: "You are screaming, not singing," they said, again and again.

2   Were the children chagrined to be humiliated on TV? Did they vow to improve, sign up for singing lessons? No. Semi-nude, they sashayed straight up to the cameras, tossed their manes of hair and told those fogey judges, "You don't know anything about singing."

3   In the current reality movie *The Real Cancun*, a film spinoff of MTV's *Real World* series, fourteen 21-year-olds share a Mexican beach house for a week while cameras film their every move. "I am a very observant person," one young woman announces. Another says, "I am so good at figuring out people," while failing to pick up obvious signals from a smitten housemate. "You are so hot!" a boy says to a girl. "Thank you," she replies flatly, clearly accustomed to (and bored by) such accolades.

4   Remarkably, in the course of the entire week, only three of the 14 admit to any self-doubt. The rest are stunningly sure of themselves, particularly one young woman who is being pursued avidly by one of the guys.

5   On the dance floor, she gyrates her fanny against his crotch for hours. Clad in a minuscule bikini, she swims all over him in the pool. At the bar, she downs an oil drum's worth of tequila with him while discussing what she likes in bed. But she refuses his advances for five days. Finally, he has sex with someone else. She is furious. "I can do what I want," she shrieks at him. "The guys who like me are persistent. I play hard to get. I'm a mystery. It's your job to figure me out." He apologizes to her. Then she sleeps with him. Holy moly.

6   Watching these children—and the twentysomething contestants on *Survivor*, who are perfectly at ease telling the whole world that they don't have to collect firewood because they're too good-looking to have to; the young women on *The Bachelor* who hurl insults at one another and then explain blithely, "I know it's hurtful, but it's the way I feel, and I have to get my feelings out"; and the teenage clerk who recently waited on me at a gas station, overcharged me by $30, and then refused to apologize, because "it was the computer's fault for adding your bill wrong, and my manager's fault for programming the computer wrong"—what I want to know is, from where did these gorgons of self-confidence spring? How can they be so self-satisfied, so sure of themselves? Especially when their level of self-love appears to be in inverse proportion to their level of accomplishment?

7   Not all twentysomethings are egomaniacs, of course.

8   I know plenty who are plagued by anxiety, anorexia, alienation, angst; who are overwhelmed by how big and brutal this world of ours can be.

9   Hard as life is for them, they are my kind of kids. I can relate to them. I was them. But I'm fascinated by their opposite, this new breed of youth—ill-mannered, obnoxious, happy—that seems to be the unholy offspring of self-help books and shopping networks.

Their "issue" is to me unfathomable. They suffer from too much self-esteem. 10

Years ago, I attended a dinner party with old, very close friends. None of 11 us had children yet. After a (large) number of bottles of wine, we went around the table and confessed the one thing we wished we could change about ourselves.

For all eight of us, it was some variation on our lack of self-confidence, 12 our excess of self-loathing. Perhaps we—and our entire, therapy-happy generation—made the same silent vow: Whatever else we did to our kids, they would not hate themselves.

"We went to the other extreme," says Barbara Coloroso, the child-rearing 13 expert and author (*Kids Are Worth It*).

"Instead of finding the middle ground, where a kid can genuinely as 14 sess herself, can strive to accomplish things, can make mistakes, admit them and learn from them, we went to the other extreme."

We told our kids that they are great no matter what they do. We hesi- 15 tated to correct them for fear of damaging their fragile egos. We never wanted them to feel bad about anything, even if they did bad things.

And to our horror, we produced a population who cannot make change 16 or point to Chad on a map, but who, when offered the slightest correction or criticism, turn away with a look of scorn which says, "We pity you—and we hate that."

The would-be Idols and their ilk think they deserve to be famous, feted 17 and lauded, without bothering to actually do anything first. In fact, they think accomplishment is a chump's game.

"Earning money is good," goes the lottery ad pitched at twentysome- 18 things. "Winning is better."

They don't want to be Mozart, writing symphonies at the age of 14. They 19 want to go on the MuchMusic show *Becoming*, in which young adults recreate their favourite music videos shot by shot, move by move, sock by sock, hair by hair.

The perverse goal is to achieve a perfectly soulless copy, a simulacrum 20 in which nothing is genuine or original. (An original moment would be a glitch, it would be wrong.)

The young girl who recreates Avril Lavigne's video for "Complicated"— 21 ironically, the song repeats the line, "Promise me I'm never going to find you faking" several times—is pampered, primped and puffed up, for doing nothing other than taking orders and accepting favours.

At the show's end, she says, "I'm so proud of myself, I really did it." She 22 really means it too—but what is it that she really thinks she did?

"Our original intent, to give our kids a strong sense of self, was good," 23 Coloroso says.

"But self-esteem should be a by-product of other traits, of integrity, civil- 24 ity, compassion. Instead, we made self-esteem a goal. Now, we have a gen-eration of big egos without a real sense of self, whose only question is, 'What's in it for me?' " My question is, where do the too-confident go from here? Will the travails of their 30s eventually humble them?

25 Or is humility, like language, something that has to be woven into one's brain while young or it's too late, the necessary synapses just aren't there? Will their children (if they can spare the time to birth and tend to them) rebel by becoming modest in the extreme?

26 "I now stay away from the word self-esteem in my lectures," Coloroso says.

27 "Instead, I say, 'We have to teach kids to have a strong sense of self.' If ever I do slip and say, 'We have to teach them self-esteem,' every parent in the place rolls their eyes."

Thinking Critically About Content

1. What is Schneller analyzing in this essay? How does the title help focus her analysis?

2. Name three possible effects of unearned positive reinforcement on a young person.

3. How does Schneller suggest parents change the way they speak to kids?

Thinking Critically About Purpose and Audience

4. Why do you think Schneller wrote this article?

5. Considering that this article was originally published in the newspaper *The Globe and Mail*, who do you think Schneller's intended audience is? Explain your answer.

6. Did you expect praise from your parents regardless of whether you had been successful at an activity? Were you ever told that all that was important was that you did your best? If so, how did that affect you?

Thinking Critically About Essays

7. The author of this article quotes expert Barbara Coloroso. Are you convinced by what Coloroso says?

8. Which of Schneller's paragraphs deal primarily with causes? Which with effects? Do you think this is a reasonable balance? Explain your answer.

9. Find five transitions in Schneller's article that work well, and explain why they are effective.

10. Discuss the effect of constant positive reinforcement on your generation. Did it affect everybody the same way? Will it affect your expectations of school and work?

Writing Topics: Analyzing Causes and Effects

Before you begin to write, you might want to review the writing process in Part I.

1. Are you currently dealing with any moral dilemmas? What are they? Does one bother you more than the others? Write an essay analyzing the causes and effects of this particular dilemma.

2. In "Too Much Self-Esteem: The Blight of Modern Times," Johanna Schneller writes about the dangers of boosting self-esteem without achievement. The same generation has been subject to zero tolerance for violence in school. How has that affected them? Write an essay analyzing the effects of zero tolerance policies.

3. How would looking closely at causes and effects help you live a better life? How would the process of discovering causes and effects help you think through your decisions and problems more logically? Explain your answer.

ARGUING

In all three essays in this chapter, the writers state their evidence clearly and convincingly. In the first essay, "We Are Training Our Kids to Kill," Dave Grossman tries to persuade his readers of the dangers for children witnessing violence on TV.

The next two essays in this chapter deal with a problem that has reached annoying proportions in the past five years: junk e-mail, or spam. The first essay, "Ban Spam: E-nough is E-nough," written by Rick Broadhead, states what most of us feel about the e-mail that is flooding our In boxes: "Make it stop!" The opposite side is expressed in an article by Doug Saunders of *The Globe and Mail*: "Ban Spam? What, and Banish All the World?"

Dave Grossman

WE ARE TRAINING OUR KIDS TO KILL

Focusing Your Attention

1. At what age or in what situation do you think children can handle violence in the media?

2. In the essay you are about to read, the writer discusses the dangers connected with violence on TV for children. What do you think some of these issues are?

Expanding Your Vocabulary

The following words are important to your understanding of this essay:

averted: avoided (paragraph 4)

phenomenally: amazingly (paragraph 6)

Draconian: harsh (paragraph 7)

indiscriminately: casually (paragraph 8)

pervasively: universally (paragraph 9)

anomaly: an exception from the normal (paragraph 15)

desensitized: numbed (paragraph 15)

epidemiological: referring to childhood behaviours (paragraph 25)

variable: element being compared (paragraph 25)

bayonet: stab (paragraph 28)

dismay: fear, dread (paragraph 32)

benign: good (paragraph 34)

I am from Jonesboro, Arkansas. I travel the world training medical, law enforcement, and U.S. military personnel about the realities of warfare. I try to make those who carry deadly force keenly aware of the magnitude of killing. Too many law enforcement and military personnel act like "cowboys," never stopping to think about who they are and what they are called to do. I hope I am able to give them a reality check.

So here I am, a world traveler and an expert in the field of "killology," when the (then) largest school massacre in American history happens in my hometown of Jonesboro, Arkansas. That was the March 24, 1998, school-yard shooting deaths of four girls and a teacher. Ten others were injured, and two boys, ages 11 and 13, were jailed, charged with murder.

Virus of Violence

To understand the why behind Littleton, Jonesboro, Springfield, Pearl, and Paducah, and all the other outbreaks of this "virus of violence," we need to first understand the magnitude of the problem. The per capita murder rate doubled in this country between 1957—when the FBI started keeping track of the data—and 1992. A fuller picture of the problem, however, is indicated by the rate at which people are attempting to kill one another—the aggravated assault rate. That rate in America has gone from around 60 per 100,000 in 1957 to over 440 per 100,000 in 2002. As bad as this is, it would be much worse were it not for two major factors.

The first is the increased imprisonment of violent offenders. The prison population in America nearly quintupled between 1975 and 2002. According to criminologist John A. DiIulio, "dozens of credible empirical analyses . . . leave no doubt that the increased use of prisons averted millions of serious crimes." If it were not for our tremendous imprisonment rate (the highest of any industrialized nation), the aggravated assault rate and the murder rate would undoubtedly be even higher.

The second factor keeping the murder rate from being even worse is medical technology. According to the U.S. Army Medical Service Corps, a wound that would have killed nine out of ten soldiers in World War II, nine out of ten could have survived in Vietnam. Thus, by a very conservative estimate, if we still had a 1940-level medical technology today, our murder rate would be ten times higher than it is. The murder rate has been held down by the development of sophisticated lifesaving skills and techniques, such as helicopter medevacs, 911 operators, paramedics, CPR, trauma centers, and medicines.

6   Today, both our assault rate and murder rate are at phenomenally high levels. Both are increasing worldwide. In Canada, according to their Centre for Justice, per capita assaults increased almost fivefold between 1964 and 2002, attempted murder increased nearly sevenfold, and murders doubled. Similar trends can be seen in other countries in the per capita violent crime rates reported to Interpol between 1977 and 2002. In Australia and New Zealand, the assault rate increased approximately fourfold, and the murder rate nearly doubled in both nations. The assault rate tripled in Sweden and approximately doubled in Belgium, Denmark, England and Wales, France, Hungary, the Netherlands, and Scotland. Meanwhile, all these nations had an associated (but smaller) increase in murder.

7   This virus of violence is occurring worldwide. The explanation for it has to be some new factor that is occurring in all of these countries. There are many factors involved, and none should be discounted: for example, the prevalence of guns in our society. But violence is rising in many nations with Draconian gun laws. And though we should never downplay child abuse, poverty, or racism, there is only one new variable present in each of these countries that bears the exact same fruit: media violence presented as entertainment for children.

Killing Is Unnatural

8   Before retiring from the military, I spent almost a quarter of a century as an army infantry officer and a psychologist, learning and studying how to enable people to kill. Believe me, we are very good at it. But it does not come naturally; you have to be taught to kill. And just as the army is conditioning people to kill, we are indiscriminately doing the same thing to our children, but without the safeguards.

9   After the Jonesboro killings, the head of the American Academy of Pediatrics Task Force on Juvenile Violence came to town and said that children don't naturally kill. It is a learned skill. And they learn it from abuse and violence in the home and, most pervasively, from violence as entertainment in television, the movies, and interactive video games.

10   Killing requires training because there is a built-in aversion to killing one's own kind. I can best illustrate this fact by drawing on my own military research into the act of killing.

11   We all know how hard it is to have a discussion with a frightened or angry human being. Vasoconstriction, the narrowing of the blood vessels, has literally closed down the forebrain—that great gob of gray matter that makes one a human being and distinguishes one from a dog. When those neurons close down, the midbrain takes over and your thought processes and reflexes are indistinguishable from your dog's. If you've worked with animals, you have some understanding of what happens to frightened human beings on the battlefield. The battlefield and violent crime are in the realm of midbrain responses.

Within the midbrain there is a powerful, God-given resistance to killing   12
your own kind. Every species, with a few exceptions, has a hardwired resistance to killing its own kind in territorial and mating battles. When animals with antlers and horns fight one another, they head-butt in a nonfatal
fashion. But when they fight any other species, they go to the side to gut
and gore. Piranhas will turn their fangs on anything, but they fight one another with flicks of the tail. Rattlesnakes will bite anything, but they wrestle
one another. Almost every species has this hard-wired resistance to killing
its own kind.

When we human beings are overwhelmed with anger and fear, we   13
slam head-on into that midbrain resistance that generally prevents us from
killing. Only sociopaths—who by definition don't have that resistance—
lack this innate violence immune system.

Throughout all human history, when humans have fought each other,   14
there has been a lot of posturing. Adversaries make loud noises and puff
themselves up, trying to daunt the enemy. There is a lot of fleeing and sub-
mission. Ancient battles were nothing more than great shoving matches. It
was not until one side turned and ran that most of the killing happened,
and most of that was stabbing people in the back. All of the ancient military
historians report that the vast majority of killing happened in pursuit when
one side was fleeing.

In more modern times, the average firing rate was incredibly low in   15
Civil War battles. British author Paddy Griffith demonstrates in his book
The Battle Tactics of the Civil War that the killing potential of the average
Civil War regiment was anywhere from five hundred to a thousand men
per minute. The actual killing rate was only one or two men per minute per
regiment. At the Battle of Gettysburg, of the 27,000 muskets picked up from
the dead and dying after the battle, 90 percent were loaded. This is an
anomaly, because it took 90 percent of their time to load muskets and only
5 percent to fire. But even more amazing, of the thousands of loaded muskets, only half had multiple loads in the barrel—one had 23 loads in the
barrel.

In reality, the average man would load his musket and bring it to his   16
shoulder, but he could not bring himself to kill. He would be brave, he
would stand shoulder to shoulder, he would do what he was trained to do;
but at the moment of truth, he could not bring himself to pull the trigger.
And so he lowered the weapon and loaded it again. Of those who did fire,
only a tiny percentage fired to hit. The vast majority fired over the enemy's
head.

During World War II, U.S. Army Brig. Gen. S. L. A. Marshall had a team   17
of researchers study what soldiers did in battle. For the first time in history,
they asked individual soldiers what they did in battle. They discovered that
only 15 to 20 percent of the individual riflemen could bring themselves to
fire at an exposed enemy soldier.

18   That is the reality of the battlefield. Only a small percentage of soldiers are able and willing to participate. Men are willing to die. They are willing to sacrifice themselves for their nation; but they are not willing to kill. It is a phenomenal insight into human nature; but when the military became aware of that, they systematically went about the process of trying to fix this "problem." From the military perspective, a 15 percent firing rate among riflemen is like a 15 percent literacy rate among librarians. And fix it the military did. By the Korean War, around 55 percent of the soldiers were willing to fire to kill. And by Vietnam, the rate rose to over 90 percent.

19   The method in this madness: desensitization.

20   How the military increases the killing rate of soldiers in combat is instructive because our culture today is doing the same thing to our children. The training methods militaries use are brutalization, classical conditioning, operant conditioning, and role modeling. I will explain each of these in the military context and show how these same factors are contributing to the phenomenal increase of violence in our culture.

21   Brutalization and desensitization are what happens at boot camp. From the moment you step off the bus, you are physically and verbally abused: countless push-ups, endless hours at attention or running with heavy loads, while carefully trained professionals take turns screaming at you. Your head is shaved; you are herded together naked and dressed alike, losing all individuality. This brutalization is designed to break down your existing mores and norms, and force you to accept a new set of values that embraces destruction, violence, and death as a way of life. In the end, you are desensitized to violence and accept it as a normal and essential survival skill in your brutal new world.

22   Something very similar to this desensitization toward violence is happening to our children through violence in the media—but instead of 18-year-olds, it begins at the age of 18 months when a child is first able to discern what is happening on television. At that age, a child can watch something happening on television and mimic that action. But it isn't until children are six or seven years old that the part of the brain kicks in that lets them understand where information comes from. Even though young children have some understanding of what it means to pretend, they are developmentally unable to distinguish clearly between fantasy and reality.

23   When young children see somebody shot, stabbed, raped, brutalized, degraded, or murdered on TV, to them it is as though it were actually happening. To have a child of three, four, or five watch a "splatter" movie, learning to relate to a character for the first 90 minutes and then in the last 30 minutes watch helplessly as that new friend is hunted and brutally murdered, is the moral and psychological equivalent of introducing your child to a friend, letting her play with that friend, and then butchering that friend in front of your child's eyes. And this happens to our children hundreds upon hundreds of times.

Sure, they are told, "Hey, it's all for fun. Look, this isn't real; it's just TV." 24
And they nod their little heads and say OK. But they can't tell the difference.
Can you remember a point in your life or in your children's lives when
dreams, reality, and television were all jumbled together? That's what it is
like to be at that level of psychological development. That's what the media
are doing to them.

The *Journal of the American Medical Association* published the defini- 25
tive epidemiological study on the impact of TV violence. The research
demonstrated what happened in numerous nations after television made
its appearance as compared to nations and regions without TV. The two
nations or regions being compared are demographically and ethnically
identical; only one variable is different: the presence of television. In every
nation, region, or city with television, there is an immediate explosion of
violence on the playground, and within 15 years there is a doubling of the
murder rate. Why 15 years? That is how long it takes for the brutalization of
a three-to five-year-old to reach the "prime crime age." That is how long it
takes for you to reap what you have sown when you brutalize and desensi-
tize a three-year-old.

Today the data linking violence in the media to violence in society are 26
superior to those linking cancer and tobacco. Hundreds of sound scientific studies demonstrate the social impact of brutalization by the media.
The *Journal of the American Medical Association* concluded that "the introduction of television in the 1950s caused a subsequent doubling of the
homicide rate, i.e., long-term childhood exposure to television is a causal
factor behind approximately one half of the homicides committed in the
United States, or approximately 10,000 homicides annually." The article
went on to say that "if, hypothetically, television technology had never
been developed, there would today be 10,000 fewer homicides each year
in the United States, 70,000 fewer rapes, and 700,000 fewer injurious
assaults" (June 10, 1992).

Classical Conditioning

Classical conditioning is like the famous case of Pavlov's dogs they 27
teach in Psychology 101. The dogs learned to associate the ringing of the
bell with food, and once conditioned, the dogs could not hear the bell without salivating.

The Japanese were masters at using classical conditioning with their 28
soldiers. Early in World War II, Chinese prisoners were placed in a ditch on
their knees with their hands bound behind them. And one by one, a select
few Japanese soldiers would go into the ditch and bayonet "their" prisoner
to death. This is a horrific way to kill another human being. Up on the bank,
countless other young soldiers would cheer them on in their violence. Com-
paratively few soldiers actually killed in those situations, but by making the
others watch and cheer, the Japanese were able to use these kinds of atrocities to classically condition a very large audience to associate pleasure

with human death and suffering. Immediately afterwards, the soldiers who had been spectators were treated to sake, to the best meal they had in months, and to so-called comfort girls. The result? They learned to associate committing violent acts with pleasure.

29   The Japanese found these kinds of techniques to be extraordinarily effective at quickly enabling very large numbers of soldiers to commit atrocities in the years to come. Operant conditioning (which we will look at shortly) teaches you to kill, but classical conditioning is a subtle but powerful mechanism that teaches you to like it.

30   This technique is so morally reprehensible that there are very few examples of it in modern U.S. military training, but there are some clear-cut examples of it being done by the media to our children. What is happening to our children is the reverse of the aversion therapy portrayed in the movie *A Clockwork Orange*. In *A Clockwork Orange*, a brutal sociopath, a mass murderer, is strapped to a chair and forced to watch violent movies while he is injected with a drug that nauseates him. So he sits and gags and retches as he watches the movies. After hundreds of repetitions of this, he associates violence with nausea. And it limits his ability to be violent.

31   We are doing the exact opposite: Our children watch vivid pictures of human suffering and death, and they learn to associate it with their favorite soft drink and candy bar or their girlfriend's perfume.

32   After the Jonesboro shootings, one of the high-school teachers told me how her students reacted when she told them about the shootings at the middle school. "They laughed," she told me with dismay. A similar reaction happens all the time in movie theaters when there is bloody violence. The young people laugh and cheer and keep right on eating popcorn and drinking pop. We have raised a generation of barbarians who have learned to associate violence with pleasure, like the Romans cheering and snacking as the Christians were slaughtered in the Colosseum.

33   The result is a phenomenon that functions much like AIDS, a phenomenon I call AVIDS—Acquired Violence Immune Deficiency Syndrome. AIDS has never killed anybody. It destroys your immune system, and then other diseases that shouldn't kill you become fatal. Television violence by itself does not kill you. It destroys your violence immune system and conditions you to derive pleasure from violence. And once you are at close range with another human being, and it's time for you to pull that trigger, Acquired Violence Immune Deficiency Syndrome can destroy your midbrain resistance.

Operant Conditioning

34   The third method the military uses is operant conditioning, a very powerful repetitive procedure of stimulus-response, stimulus-response. A benign example is the use of flight simulators to train pilots. An airline pilot in training sits in front of a flight simulator for endless hours; when a particular warning light goes on, he is taught to react in a certain way. When another warning light goes on, a different reaction is required. Stimulus-

response, stimulus-response, stimulus-response. One day the pilot is actually flying a jumbo jet; the plane is going down, and 300 people are screaming behind him. He is wetting his seat cushion, and he is scared out of his wits; but he does the right thing. Why? Because he has been conditioned to respond reflexively to this particular crisis.

When people are frightened or angry, they will do what they have been   35
conditioned to do. In fire drills, children learn to file out of the school in orderly fashion. One day there is a real fire, and they are frightened out of their wits; but they do exactly what they have been conditioned to do, and it saves their lives.

The military and law enforcement community have made killing a   36
conditioned response. This has substantially raised the firing rate on the modern battlefield. Whereas infantry training in World War II used bull's-eye targets, now soldiers learn to fire at realistic, man-shaped silhouettes that pop into their field of view. That is the stimulus. The trainees have only a split second to engage the target. The conditioned response is to shoot the target, and then it drops. Stimulus-response, stimulus-response, stimulus-response—soldiers or police officers experience hundreds of repetitions. Later, when soldiers are on the battlefield or a police officer is walking a beat and somebody pops up with a gun, they will shoot reflexively and shoot to kill. We know that 75 to 80 percent of the shooting on the modern battlefield is the result of this kind of stimulus-response training.

Now, if you're a little troubled by that, how much more should we be   37
troubled by the fact that every time a child plays an interactive point-and-shoot video game, he is learning the exact same conditioned reflex and motor skills?

I was an expert witness in a murder case in South Carolina offering mit-   38
igation for a kid who was facing the death penalty. I tried to explain to the jury that interactive video games had conditioned him to shoot a gun to kill. He had spent hundreds of dollars on video games learning to point and shoot, point and shoot. One day he and his buddy decided it would be fun to rob the local convenience store. They walked in, and he pointed a snub-nosed .38 pistol at the clerk's head. The clerk turned to look at him, and the defendant shot reflexively from about six feet. The bullet hit the clerk right between the eyes—which is a pretty remarkable shot with that weapon at that range—and killed this father of two. Afterward, we asked the boy what happened and why he did it. It clearly was not part of the plan to kill the guy—it was being videotaped from six different directions. He said, "I don't know. It was a mistake. It wasn't supposed to happen."

In the military and law-enforcement worlds, the right option is often not   39
to shoot. But you never, ever put your money in that video machine with the intention of not shooting. There is always some stimulus that sets you off. And when he was excited, and his heart rate went up, and vasoconstriction closed his forebrain down, this young man did exactly what he was conditioned to do: he reflexively pulled the trigger, shooting accurately just like all those times he played video games.

40   This process is extraordinarily powerful and frightening. The result is ever more "homemade" sociopaths who kill reflexively. Our children are learning how to kill and learning to like the idea of killing; and then we have the audacity to say, "Oh my goodness, what's wrong?"

41   One of the boys involved in the Jonesboro shootings (and they are just boys) had a fair amount of experience shooting real guns. The other one, to the best of our knowledge, had almost no experience shooting. Between them, those two boys fired 27 shots from a range of over 100 yards, and they hit 15 people. That's pretty remarkable shooting. We run into these situations often—kids who have never picked up a gun in their lives pick up a real gun and are incredibly accurate. Why? Video games.

Thinking Critically About Content

1. According to Grossman, what is the "virus of violence" (paragraph 3)?
2. What three methods does the military use to train its soldiers to kill?
3. What does Grossman mean when he claims that the media are presenting violence "as entertainment for children"?

Thinking Critically About Purpose and Audience

4. What do you think Grossman's purpose is in this essay?
5. Who do you think would be most interested in this essay?
6. What effect do you think this essay would have on parents?

Thinking Critically About Essays

7. Describe in a complete sentence the writer's argument.
8. Grossman's statistics on violent assaults and murders in Canada are not accurate. Knowing this, how convinced are you by the essay as a whole?
9. Explain the title of this essay.
10. This essay discusses the sensitive issues related to children and violence in the media and then ends abruptly. Add a paragraph to the essay making some concrete suggestions for solving the problem the author poses.

ARGUING A POSITION

Focusing Your Attention

1. If you were asked to take a position for or against a topic that you knew people held a strong opinion on, what are some of the topics you would consider?

2. In the two essays you will be reading, the writer of the first claims that we should not tolerate junk e-mail arriving in our e-mail boxes. The other writer claims that banning spam would cut people off from the world.

Rick Broadhead

BAN SPAM: E-NOUGH IS E-NOUGH

Expanding Your Vocabulary

The following words are important to your understanding of this essay:

proliferators: those who cause growth to increase rapidly (paragraph 2)

purveyors: those who provide supplies (paragraph 7)

cocoon: provide protective covering (paragraph 9)

concoctions: mixtures (paragraph 9)

Imagine if a quarter of all the voice-mail messages left in homes and businesses across North America never reached their intended recipients. Imagine if mail delivered through Canada Post had only a one-in-five chance of getting to its destination. Would we tolerate such a ridiculous state of affairs? Absolutely not. 1

But on the Internet, we have let proliferators of electronic junk mail control our lives and wreak havoc with the economy. That's why, last week, the four biggest e-mail providers—Microsoft, Yahoo, America Online and Earthlink—filed lawsuits in the United States against hundreds of individuals (including several Canadians) for sending unsolicited e-mails and swamping strangers' mailboxes. 2

The extent of the problem has become evident with recent revelations that roughly one out of every five e-mail messages sent over the Internet never gets to its intended recipient. Thanks to the increasing usage of junk-mail filters, which have become a necessity for businesses and Internet service providers these days, there's a roughly 20-per-cent chance that your next e-mail message will mistakenly get tagged as spam and never reach its final destination. It's a shocking situation that should make every lawmaker and politician sit up and take notice. 3

I've experienced this new reality first-hand. In the past few weeks, I've received multiple calls from colleagues who have been unable to e-mail me because their messages were classified as junk mail and rejected by my Internet service provider. The only alternative was to have the filter turned off completely. A flood of junk mail now pours into my e-mail box every day, but at least I'm no longer missing any vital communications. 4

The writing is on the wall: If we continue on this dangerous path, sending an e-mail message on the Internet and hoping for a successful delivery will be no better than rolling the dice at a Las Vegas casino. 5

During the past decade, we've made real progress at transforming the Internet into a powerful tool that is responsible for substantial economic 6 growth. But all that progress will quickly evaporate if the Internet becomes an anarchic frontier controlled by unapologetic e-mail bandits. According to recent estimates, spam now accounts for as much as 60 per cent of global e-mail traffic. America Online and Microsoft are fending off more than four billion spam messages a day. And the global cost of spam to businesses has reached a staggering $20 billion (U.S.). How did we ever let it get this bad?

7   Purveyors of electronic junk mail are winning the war and sadly, we're going out of our way to accommodate them. In an attempt to communicate with business colleagues on-line, I'm now encountering people who require me to go to a website and identify myself as a real person (as opposed to a computer sending junk mail) before my electronic mail message can be granted safe passage.

8   Users of this new technology automatically quarantine messages from unfamiliar recipients and presume them to be junk e-mail unless the senders prove otherwise. The technology obviously works, but it's brought a disturbing chill to the Internet reminiscent of crime-plagued neighbourhoods where fearful citizens lock their doors, pull down their shutters and retreat indoors.

9   The Internet is supposed to make it easier for us to communicate—not force people to cocoon themselves from a hurricane of unwanted e-mail. E-mail marketers are controlling the Internet's streets, while we shield ourselves behind spam filters and other high-tech concoctions. It's time to take back our streets from the e-mail thugs who control them.

10   Immediate action is needed and it requires our lawmakers to recognize that spam is no longer just a nuisance—it's a serious threat to the vitality of our economy. As long as peddlers of junk e-mail continue to believe they're safe from prosecution, they'll have the upper hand.

11   Critics argue that legislation is an ineffective weapon against senders of spam, and they have a point. In the U.S., previous attempts to sue senders of spam at the state level have failed miserably. More tellingly, the amount of spam on the Internet has increased, not decreased, despite dozens of lawsuits filed in recent years by legal heavyweights such as Microsoft.

12   But one only need look at the recent lawsuits filed by the Recording Industry Association of America as proof that the threat of legal action does act as an effective deterrent. The amount of file-sharing on file-sharing networks such as Kazaa dropped by 50 per cent after the music industry began suing people who were illegally swapping music on-line. Now that the United States has federal anti-spam legislation in place, spam distributors will have fewer places to hide.

13   It is appalling that the Canadian government has continued to sit on the sidelines while other nations, most noticeably the United States, are cracking down on spam with renewed vigour.

14   The very nature of our global, interconnected economy means that the United States cannot win this war on its own. Indeed, one of the U.S. law-

suits filed last week alleges that a father and two sons from Kitchener, Ont., were responsible for disseminating an astonishing 94 million junk e-mail messages to Internet users—and that's just in the month of January. The story made headlines around the world, casting a black eye on Canada as a breeding ground for spam.

It is time for Canadian legislators to act swiftly and forcefully to send a strong message to the global community that Canada is not a safe haven for spam. The world is watching.   15

Doug Saunders

BAN SPAM? WHAT, AND BANISH ALL THE WORLD?

Expanding Your Vocabulary

The following words are important to your understanding of this essay:

pariahs: social outcasts (paragraph 2)

hapless: unfortunate (paragraph 4)

teeming: overflowing, abounding (paragraph 5)

souk: a market in an Arab city (paragraph 5)

interlopers: intruders (paragraph 6)

snake oil: a worthless or fraudulent cure (paragraph 6)

embellish: enhance (paragraph 6)

Amazon.com: an online bookstore (paragraph 8)

ad-hoc: formed for one purpose—a committee, for example (paragraph 8)

insidious: spreading harm stealthily (paragraph 9)

lumpen class: underclass of society (paragraph 10)

dubious: uncertain or questionable (paragraph 15)

pungent: sharp or biting (paragraph 16)

dissolute: lacking moral restraint (paragraph 16)

Since nobody else appears willing to do it, I have taken it upon myself, ladies and gentlemen of the jury, to come to the defence of junk e-mail.   1

These poor Canadians you see before you, fellow citizens, have become pariahs, all because their London, Ont., "spam factory" helped make our country the world's second-largest exporter of unsolicited e-mail.   2

Now, I am fully aware of the pain and unease inflicted by their acts. The e-mail address at the bottom of this column is attached to a spam-catcher program that currently has 2,276 items in its box. Sorry, it just grew to 2,310.   3

4   Yet I am not defending these hapless individuals out of sympathy for abstract principle or for personal gain. I am defending them because I have become a spam believer.

5   My life has been improved by its teeming souk of goods and services, much as my diet has been vastly improved by the flyers that arrive in my mailbox, much as my house is being expertly and affordably painted by the student who knocked on my door.

6   What should offend us about junk e-mail, my friends, is not its existence, but its quality. The spam that bothers you is the spam that sells plain old fraud, like those polite interlopers from Nigeria, or snake oil, like the folks who promise to embellish your privates. I implore you all to put this corruption to an end, to shut down the illegitimate voices. But please, ignore the calls of those like Rick Broadhead, who asked the government in these pages the other day to "ban all spam." By doing that, you are cutting yourself off from the world.

7   By banning all spam, look what you are doing:

8   **You're a corporate clone.** There is a scent of hypocrisy here: Many of the people who oppose spam most aggressively are those who frequent a community java shop and wouldn't be caught dead in a Starbucks, who prefer poky local bookshops to Amazon.com. Yet unsolicited e-mail is the electronic equivalent of that local coffee shop: It is an ad-hoc, community alternative to the monolithic, homogenizing voices of big-corporation marketing.

9   If you're against the corporatization of society, you should be in favour of junk mail. The big companies reach you in far more insidious, unavoidable ways. The spammers are the entrepreneurs who are trying to give you an alternative. In fact, even if you're fully opposed to capitalism, you should be for spam. These people are merchants, not capitalists. They are engaged in the ancient craft of buying low and selling high—the heart of any system, even collective utopias.

10   Capital, and labour exploitation, is not involved. These folks are not, to put it in Marxist terms, engaging in the extraction of surplus value from alienated labour—they are the lumpen class, exploiting nobody but themselves.

11   **You're racist.** One thing unites the people putting the flyers in your mailbox and the people sending spam to your inbox: Many of them (the London case notwithstanding) are recent immigrants, pulling themselves up by their bootstraps and DSL lines, struggling in a minority culture.

12   The guy who sold me the $104 computer router the other day, because I had noticed his appealing pitch in my spam-catcher box, had moved here from India two years ago. The man in Quebec who sold me the excellent Roland Kirk recordings, after pitching them to my home e-mail address (which gets a better class of spam because of its relative secrecy) was a first-generation Russian Jew. All the scores of people who have sold me

things through flyers and spam letters have been new Canadians, whose entrepreneurial spirit has got me good stuff and cheap prices.

The "no flyers" signs that have polluted mailboxes in better-heeled   13 neighbourhoods are essentially shouting "no truck nor trade with immigrants." Is it any coincidence that the people who put up those signs are usually white and well-established? They are the same ones calling for a ban on spam. It is their way of keeping their people in, and the horde of newcomers with their low-priced goods and handshake deals and neighbourly banter out.

"Our people do not do business that way. We keep to our own. Get the   14 hell off my doorstep." That is what "ban all spam" means.

You're boring. Yes, I know. Most spam is garbage. Of course it is. That is   15 why it is a true human venture. Pick a dozen recordings, at random, from a CD store and the whole idea of music will seem dubious. Pull a few random books from random shelves in a library, and you'll conclude that the printed word is a dull and wasteful enterprise. It is the one in a thousand that has any value—a truth that we are willing to accept about other human beings (in love, employment and friendship)—so why can't we say it about their electronic output?

What kind of street do you want to live on? The one in the all-white,   16 gated community, where the only merchants allowed are the Roto-Rooter guy and the Sears truck? Or the one with the colourful storefronts, the streetside stalls full of pungent scents and surprising deals in imported goods and, yes, the occasional obnoxious beggar or dissolute old perv? I've always chosen to live on those streets, because they offer real human life.

I would rather we all lived on that street. It would make us better people.   17 We can police the content and legality of those market stalls, but not their very presence here. That street, my friends, is called spam.

The defence rests.   18

Thinking Critically About Content

1. Make a list of the reasons, evidence, and statistics each writer uses to convince the reader of his position.

2. Explain how each writer uses analogies.

3. Which essay contains the most convincing evidence in your opinion? Why is it so convincing to you?

Thinking Critically About Purpose and Audience

4. What do you think the writers' purposes are in these essays?

5. What type of audience would be most interested in the subject of these two essays? Explain your answer.

6. If you changed your mind as the result of reading one of these essays, what in the essay caused the change?

Thinking Critically About Essays

7. State both writers' point of view in a single sentence.

8. How have both writers organized their essays? Make a rough outline to demonstrate your answer. What is the effect of the three words at the end of the second article: "The defence rests."

9. Which points, if any, do the two writers agree on? Which points do they disagree on? Explain your answer.

10. Both writers use physical analogies in their discussions. Write your own argument based on the similarities between real and virtual mail.

Writing Topics: Arguing and Persuading

Before you begin to write, you might want to review the writing process in Part I.

1. In "We Are Training Our Kids to Kill," Grossman tries to convince his readers that various forms of violence in the media teach our kids to kill. Argue for or against government control of violence on TV, in movies, and/or in video games.

2. The pro and con essays deal with the annoyances or the usefulness of junk e-mail. Many young people now communicate with instant messaging programs. Write an argument for or against banning instant messaging on school computers. Gather as much evidence as you can before you begin to write.

3. How can being able to develop good arguments and persuade people of your point of view help you in life? How might this ability give you the edge over other people on the job market?

P
A
R
T

V

THE HANDBOOK

This part of *Mosaics* provides you with a complete handbook for editing your writing. You can use it as a reference tool as you write or as a source of instruction and practice in areas where you need work.

This handbook consists of an Introduction and eight units:

The chapters in each unit start with a self-test to help you identify your strengths and weaknesses in that area. Then the chapter teaches specific sentence skills and provides exercises so you can practise what you have learned. Each chapter also asks you to write your own sentences and then work with another student to edit each other's writing.

The Editing Symbols on the inside back cover will give you marks for highlighting errors in your papers. In addition, the Error Log (Appendix 3) and Spelling Log (Appendix 4) will help you tailor the instruction to your own needs and keep track of your progress.

INTRODUCTION: PARTS OF SPEECH, PHRASES, AND CLAUSES

This handbook uses very little terminology. But sometimes talking about the language and the way it works is difficult without a shared understanding of certain basic grammar terms. For that reason, your instructor may ask you to study parts of this introduction to review basic grammar—parts of speech, phrases, and clauses. You might also use this introduction for reference. You can refer to the Web site for practice exercises.

This section has three parts:

Parts of Speech
Phrases
Clauses

PARTS OF SPEECH

Test Yourself

In the following paragraph, label the parts of speech listed here:

2 verbs (v)	2 adverbs (adv)
2 nouns (n)	2 prepositions (prep)
2 pronouns (pro)	2 conjunctions (conj)
2 adjectives (adj)	2 interjections (int)

Professional basketball is definitely one of the best spectator sports. The talented players move around the court so quickly that the audience never has a chance to become bored. Boy, I'll never forget that Saturday night last February when my favourite uncle took me to see the Raptors game against the Trailblazers. It was an important home game for Toronto, so the SkyDome was packed. The Raptors were behind throughout most of the game, but they pulled through and won with a three-pointer in the last few seconds. Wow! I have never seen so many people on their feet, screaming at the top of their lungs.

(Answers are in Appendix 8 on the Web site.)

Every sentence is made up of a variety of words that play different roles. Each word, like each part of a coordinated outfit, serves a distinct function. These functions fall into eight categories:

1. Verbs
2. Nouns
3. Pronouns
4. Adjectives
5. Adverbs
6. Prepositions
7. Conjunctions
8. Interjections

Some words, such as *is*, can function in only one way—in this case, as a verb. Other words, however, can serve as different parts of speech, depending on how they are used in a sentence. For example, look at the different ways the word *show* can be used:

Verb:	The artists **show** their work at a gallery. (*Show* is a verb here, telling what the artists do.)
Noun:	The **show** will start in 10 minutes. (*Show* functions as a noun here, telling what will start in 10 minutes.)
Adjective:	My aunt loves to sing **show** tunes. (*Show* is an adjective here, modifying the noun *tunes*.)

Verbs

The **verb** is the most important word in a sentence because every other word depends on it in some way. Verbs tell what's going on in the sentence.

There are three types of verbs: action, linking, and helping. An **action verb** tells what someone or something is doing. A **linking verb** tells what someone or something is, feels, or looks like. Sometimes an action or linking verb has **helping verbs**—words that add information, such as when an action is taking place. A **complete verb** consists of an action or linking verb and all the helping verbs.

Action:	The girl **wandered** too far from the campsite.
Action:	Luca **ran** to the bus stop.
Linking:	He **looks** very tired.
Linking:	It **was** a real surprise to see you.
Helping:	My aunt and uncle **will be** arriving tomorrow.
Helping:	My grandmother **has** been very ill lately.

Complete Verb:	My aunt and uncle **will be arriving** tomorrow.
Complete Verb:	My grandmother **has been** very ill lately.

Nouns

People often think of **nouns** as "naming words" because they identify—or name—people (*student, Susan, mom, pilot*), places (*city, ocean, Kingston*), or things (*bush, airplane, chair, shirt*). Nouns also name ideas (*peace, justice*), qualities (*bravery, patience*), emotions (*sadness, happiness*), and actions (*challenge, compromise*). A **common noun** names something general (*singer, hill, water, theatre*). A **proper noun** names something specific (*Avril Lavigne, Niagara Falls, Canada Dry, The Bay*).

Hint: To test whether a word is a noun, try putting *a, an,* or *the* in front of it:

Nouns:	a squirrel, an orange, the hope
NOT Nouns:	a funny, an over, the eat

This test does not work with all proper nouns:

NOT	a Natalie, the Winnipeg
BUT	the Raptors

Pronouns

Pronouns can do anything nouns can do. In fact, pronouns can take the place of nouns. Without pronouns, you would find yourself repeating nouns and producing boring sentences. Compare the following sentences, for example:

George drove **George's** car very fast to **George's** house because **George** had to get home early.

George drove **his** car very fast to **his** house because **he** had to get home early.

There are many different types of pronouns, but you only need to focus on the following four types for now.

Most Common Pronouns

Personal (refer to people or things)

Singular:	First person:	*I, me, my, mine*
	Second person:	*you, your, yours*
	Third person:	*he, she, it, him, her, hers, his, its*
Plural:	First person:	*we, us, our, ours*
	Second person:	*you, your, yours*
	Third person:	*they, them, their, theirs*

Demonstrative (point out someone or something)

Singular: *this, that*

Plural: *these, those*

Relative (introduce a dependent clause)

   who, whom, whose, which, that

Indefinite (refer to someone or something general, not specific)

Singular: *another, anybody, anyone, anything, each, either, everybody, everyone, everything, little, much, neither, nobody, no one, nothing, one, other, somebody, someone, something*

Plural: *both, few, many, others, several*

Either Singular or Plural: *all, any, more, most, none, some*

Hint: When any of these words are used with nouns, they become adjectives instead of pronouns.

Adjective:	He can have **some candy.**
Pronoun:	He can have **some.**
Adjective:	The baby wants **that toy.**
Pronoun:	The baby wants **that.**

Adjectives

Adjectives modify—or describe—nouns or pronouns. Adjectives generally make sentences clear and vivid.

Without Adjectives:	She took an umbrella, a towel, and an Ipod to the beach.
With Adjectives:	She took a **bright orange** umbrella, a **striped blue** towel, and a **waterproof** Ipod to the beach.

Adverbs

Adverbs modify—or describe—adjectives, verbs, and other adverbs. They do *not* modify nouns. Adverbs also answer the following questions:

How?	thoughtfully, kindly, briefly, quietly
When?	soon, tomorrow, late, now

Where?	inside, somewhere, everywhere, there
How often?	daily, always, annually, rarely
To what extent?	generally, specifically, exactly, very

Hint: Notice that adverbs often end in *-ly*. That might help you recognize them.

Prepositions

Prepositions indicate relationships among the ideas in a sentence. Something is *at*, *in*, *by*, *next to*, *behind*, *around*, *near*, or *under* something else. A preposition is always followed by a noun or a pronoun, which is called the **object of the preposition.** Together, they form a **prepositional phrase.**

Preposition	+	Object	=	Prepositional Phrase
near		the beach		near the beach
for		the party		for the party

Here is a list of some common prepositions.

Common Prepositions

about	beside	into	since
above	between	like	through
across	beyond	near	throughout
after	by	next to	to
against	despite	of	toward
among	down	off	under
around	during	on	until
as	except	on top of	up
at	for	out	upon
before	from	out of	up to
behind	in	outside	with
below	in front of	over	within
beneath	inside	past	without

Hint: *To* + a verb (as in *to go, to come, to feel*) is not a prepositional phrase. It is a verb phrase, which we will deal with later in this unit.

Conjunctions

Conjunctions connect groups of words. Without conjunctions, most of our writing would be choppy and boring. The two types of conjunctions are easy to remember because their names state their purpose: *Coordinating conjunctions* link equal ideas, and *subordinating conjunctions* make one idea subordinate to—or dependent on—another.

Coordinating conjunctions connect parts of a sentence that are of equal importance or weight. Among other things, these parts can be **independent clauses,** a group of words with a subject and verb that can stand alone as a sentence (see page 386). There are only seven coordinating conjunctions:

Coordinating Conjunctions

and, but, or, nor, for, so, yet

Coordinating:	Melvin's parents arrived late **and** left early.
Coordinating:	My sister wanted to go shopping **or** see a movie.
Coordinating:	The teacher was very demanding, **but** I learned a lot from him.

Subordinating conjunctions join two ideas by making one dependent on the other. The idea introduced by the subordinating conjunction becomes a **dependent clause,** a group of words with a subject and a verb that cannot stand alone as a sentence (see page 386). The other part of the sentence is an independent clause.

Dependent Clause

Subordinating: I won't leave **until he comes home.**

Dependent Clause

Subordinating: **Unless you study more,** you won't get a scholarship.

Common Subordinating Conjunctions

after	*because*	*since*	*until*
although	*before*	*so*	*when*
as	*even if*	*so that*	*whenever*
as if	*even though*	*than*	*where*
as long as	*how*	*that*	*wherever*
as soon as	*if*	*though*	*whether*
as though	*in order that*	*unless*	*while*

Interjections

Interjections are words that express strong emotion, surprise, or disappointment. An interjection is usually followed by an exclamation point or a comma.

Interjection: **Whoa!** You're going too fast.

Interjection: **Ouch,** that hurt!

Other common interjections include *aha, alas, great, hey, neat, oh, oops, yay, well, wow,* and *yippee*.

PHRASES

Test Yourself

Underline the phrases in the following sentences.

- Using the computer, I got most of the research done for my report.
- To be totally confident, I checked for spelling and grammar errors twice.
- Susan lives in the grey house at the end of Maple Avenue behind the bank.
- Tess is going to be a ballet dancer when she gets older.
- Do you want to join us for dinner this evening?

(Answers are in Appendix 8 on the Web site.)

A **phrase** is a group of words that function together as a unit. Phrases cannot stand alone, however, because they are missing a subject, a verb, or both.

Phrases: the silver moon, a boneless fish

Phrases: threw out the trash, navigated the river, floated to the top

Phrases: after piano lessons, in the crowded boat, by the beach

Phrases: jumping into the water, to be smart

Notice that all these groups of words are missing a subject, a verb, or both.

CLAUSES

Test Yourself

Underline the clauses in the following sentences.

- Magdalena will make a great attorney because she argues so well.
- You don't understand the math concept, so I will keep going over it with you.
- If Shane is going to drive, he must have car insurance.
- We finished the big test, and then we all went out for pizza.
- I enjoyed the vacation even though I had one really bad seafood dinner.

(Answers are in Appendix 8 on the Web site.)

Like phrases, **clauses** are groups of words. But unlike phrases, a clause always contains a subject and a verb. There are two types of clauses: *independent* and *dependent*.

An **independent clause** contains a subject and a verb and can stand alone and make sense by itself. Every complete sentence must have at least one independent clause.

Independent Clause: The doctor held the baby very gently.

Now look at the following group of words. It is a clause because it contains a subject and a verb. But it is a **dependent clause** because it is introduced by a word that makes it dependent, *because*.

Dependent Clause: Because the doctor held the baby very gently.

This clause cannot stand alone. It must be connected to an independent clause in order to make sense. Here is one way to finish the dependent clause and form a complete sentence.

Dependent   Independent

Because the doctor held the baby very gently, the baby stopped crying.

Hint: Subordinating conjunctions (such as *since, although, because, while*) and relative pronouns (*who, whom, whose, which, that*) make clauses dependent. (For more information on subordinating conjunctions, see page 384, and on relative pronouns, see page 382.)

SUBJECTS AND VERBS

CHAPTER 32

✔ CHECKLIST for Identifying Subjects and Verbs

> ✔ Does each sentence contain a subject?
> ✔ Does each sentence contain a verb?

Test Yourself

Underline the subjects once and the verbs twice in the following sentences.

- You are my best friend.
- Hang up your clothes.
- They really wanted to be here tonight.
- He made a sandwich and put it in a brown paper bag.
- Susie and Tom went to the dance.

(Answers are in Appendix 8 on the Web site.)

A sentence has a message to communicate, but for that message to be meaningful, the sentence must have a subject and a verb. The subject is the topic of the sentence, what the sentence is about. The verb is the sentence's motor or action. It moves the message forward to its destination. Without these two parts, the sentence is not complete.

SUBJECTS

To be complete, every sentence must have a subject. The **subject** tells who or what the sentence is about.

Subject
↓
He   always came home on time.
Horror **movies**   appeal to teenagers.

Compound Subjects

When two or more separate words tell what the sentence is about, the sentence has a **compound subject.**

> Compound Subject: **Painting** and **sewing** are my hobbies.
>
> Compound Subject: **My brother** and **I** live with my grandmother.

Hint: Note that *and* is not part of the compound subject.

Unstated Subjects

Sometimes a subject does not actually appear in a sentence but is understood. This occurs in commands and requests. The understood subject is always *you,* meaning either someone specific or anyone in general.

> Command: Get up now or you'll be late.
>
>   s
> Unstated Subject: **(You)** get up now or you'll be late.
>
> Request: Write me an e-mail soon, please.
>
>   s
> Unstated Subject: **(You)** write me an e-mail soon, please.

Subjects and Prepositional Phrases

The subject of a sentence cannot be part of a prepositional phrase. A **prepositional phrase** is a group of words that begins with a **preposition,** a word like *in, on, under, after, from,* or *with.* Here are some examples of prepositional phrases:

in the yard	**next to** it	**before** supper
on the plane	**behind** the chair	**instead of** me
under the rug	**around** the circle	**across** the road
after school	**into** the boat	**for** the family
from the grocery store	**during** the storm	**at** school

(See page 383 for a more complete list of prepositions.)

If you are looking for the subject of a sentence, first cross out all the prepositional phrases. Then figure out what the sentence is about.

>   s   s
> ~~During the game,~~ the coaches and the players had a fight ~~with the other team.~~

>   s
> The new store ~~around the corner~~ sells designer jeans.

                s
Some ~~of our luggage~~ was lost ~~on the trip~~.

REVIEWING SUBJECTS

What is a subject?

_____

What is a compound subject?

_____

_____

What is an unstated subject?

_____

How can you find the subject of a sentence?

_____

_____

◆ *P r a c t i c e   1*   **Identifying** Cross out the prepositional phrases in each of the following sentences, and then underline the subjects.

1. The golfer stood quietly in front of the ball.

2. Marty and Mike gave a presentation at the big convention.

3. Two of the graduates had perfect grade point averages.

4. Before I go to the store, I need to put on a jacket.

5. Get the mayonnaise out of the refrigerator.

◆ *P r a c t i c e   2*   **Completing** Fill in each blank in the following sentences with a subject without using a person's name.

1. _____ was voted the best restaurant in this area.

2. Walking to class, _____ thought seriously about changing his major.

3. Sometimes, _____ is a great bargain.

4. _____ and _____ are two very positive personality traits.

5. _____ was late for work again.

◆ *P r a c t i c e 3* **Writing Your Own** Write five sentences of your own, and underline the subjects.

VERBS

To be complete, a sentence must have a verb as well as a subject. A **verb** tells what the subject is doing or what is happening.

Verb
↓

He   always **came** home on time.
Horror movies   **appeal** to teenagers.

Action Verbs

An **action verb** tells what a subject is doing. Some examples of action verbs are *skip*, *ski*, *stare*, *flip*, *breathe*, *remember*, *restate*, *sigh*, *cry*, *decrease*, *write*, and *pant*.

Action Verb: The children **laughed** at the clown.
Action Verb: The car **crashed** into the tree.

Linking Verbs

A **linking verb** connects the subject to other words in the sentence that say something about it. Linking verbs are also called **state-of-being verbs** because they do not show action. Rather, they say that something "is" a particular way. The most common linking verb is *be* (*am*, *are*, *is*, *was*, *were*).

Linking Verb: The horses **are** in the stable.
Linking Verb: I **am** unhappy with the results.

Other common linking verbs are *remain*, *act*, *look*, *grow*, and *seem*.

Linking Verb: Ian **remains** enthusiastic about school.
Linking Verb: I **act** happy even when I'm not.
Linking Verb: The yard **looks** neglected.
Linking Verb: She **grew** fonder of her aunt.
Linking Verb: Nala **seems** happy with her new house.

Some words, like *smell* and *taste*, can be either action verbs or linking verbs.

Action Verb: I **smell** smoke.
Linking Verb: This house **smells** like flowers.

Action Verb: She **tasted** the soup.
Linking Verb: It **tasted** too salty.

Compound Verbs

Just as a verb can have more than one subject, some subjects can have more than one verb. These are called **compound verbs.**

Compound Verb: She **cooks** and **cleans** every day.

Compound Verb: He **runs** and **swims** twice a week in the summer.

Hint: A sentence can have both a compound subject and a compound verb.

s   s   v   v

Joe and **Philip jumped** into the water and **swam** to the raft.

Helping Verbs

Often the **main verb** (the action verb or linking verb) in a sentence needs help to convey its meaning. **Helping verbs** add information, such as when an action took place. The **complete verb** consists of a main verb and all its helping verbs. Here, the helping verb is underlined.

Complete Verb: The children <u>will</u> **return** tomorrow.

Complete Verb: It <u>might</u> **rain** this weekend.

Complete Verb: We <u>should have</u> **gone** to the concert.

Complete Verb: My uncle <u>has</u> **given** me money for Christmas.

Complete Verb: My sister <u>will be</u> **coming** home for my wedding.

Complete Verb: You <u>should</u> not **go** home with them.

Hint: Note that *not* isn't part of the helping verb. Similarly, *never, always, only, just,* and *still* are never part of the verb.

Complete Verb: I <u>have</u> always **liked** history classes.

The most common helping verbs are

be, am, is, are, was, were
have, has, had
do, did

Other common helping verbs are

may, might
can, could
will, would
should, used to, ought to

REVIEWING VERBS

What is a verb?

_____

What is the difference between action verbs and linking verbs?

_____

_____

Give an example of a compound verb. _____

Give an example of a helping verb. _____

What is the difference between a subject and a verb?

_____

_____

◆ *P r a c t i c e* **4** **Identifying** Underline the complete verbs in each of the following sentences.

1. The students seemed tired in class Monday morning.
2. One of my professors is a popular public speaker.
3. High school students must read *Who Has Seen the Wind?*
4. Timothy will go to the championships.
5. Get out of the rain.

◆ *P r a c t i c e* **5** **Completing** Fill in each blank in the following sentences with a verb. Avoid using *is*, *are*, *was*, and *were* except as helping verbs.

1. Brendan _____ extreme pain after falling from the ladder and landing on his back.
2. The specialist _____ her client about the different options.
3. Both the parents and the teachers _____ about the need for more meetings.
4. My ill child _____ throughout the night.
5. Red stickers on the price tags _____ the sale items.

♦ *P r a c t i c e 6* **Writing Your Own** Write five sentences of your own, and underline all the verbs in each.

CHAPTER REVIEW

Terms and Definitions

Subject: who or what the sentence is about

Compound Subject: two or more separate words that tell who or what the sentence is about

Unstated Subject: The subject does not appear in the sentence. It is implied or understood.

Preposition: a word such as *in, on, under, after, from,* or *with*

Prepositional Phrase: a phrase beginning with a preposition

Verb: tells what the subject is doing or what action is happening

Linking Verb: connects the subject to other words in the sentence

State-of-Being Verb: does not show action, but shows that something "is" a particular way (*am, are, is, was, were*)

Compound Verb: more than one verb for one or more subjects

Helping Verb: adds information, such as when the action took place

Complete Verb: includes the main verb and all its helping verbs

♦ *Review P r a c t i c e 1* **Writing Your Own** Write a paragraph about a major decision you made within the past three years. How has it affected your life? What did you learn from the process?

♦ *Review P r a c t i c e 2* **Editing Your Writing** Exchange paragraphs from Review Practice 1 with another student, and do the following:

1. Underline the subjects once.

2. Underline the verbs twice.

Then return the paragraph to its writer, and edit any sentences in your own paragraph that do not have both a subject and a verb. Record your errors on the Error Log in Appendix 3.

CHAPTER 33

FRAGMENTS

✅ CHECKLIST for Identifying and Correcting Fragments

> ✔ Does each sentence have a subject?
> ✔ Does each sentence have a verb?

Test Yourself

Put an X by the sentences that are fragments.

- _____ I wanted to go to the gym yesterday.
- _____ Whose tie doesn't match his suit.
- _____ Giving up his seat for an elderly woman.
- _____ Paul asked for the most popular menu item.
- _____ While the captain was away from the cockpit.

(Answers are in Appendix 8 on the Web site.)

One of the most common errors in student writing is the fragment. A fragment is a piece of a sentence that is punctuated as a complete sentence, but does not express a complete thought. Once you learn how to identify fragments, you will be able to avoid them in your writing.

ABOUT FRAGMENTS

A complete sentence must have both a subject and a verb. If one or both are missing, or if the subject and verb are introduced by a dependent word, you have only part of a sentence, a **fragment.** Even if it begins with a capital letter and ends with a period, it cannot stand alone and must be corrected in your writing. The five most common types of fragments are explained in this chapter.

Type 1: Afterthought Fragments

He goes to school during the day. **And works at night.**

Type 2: *-ing* Fragments

Finding no one at the house. Kenny walked back home.

Type 3: *to* Fragments

The school started a tutoring program. **To help improve math results.**

Type 4: Dependent-Clause Fragments

Because I decided to go back to school. My boss fired me.

Type 5: Relative-Clause Fragments

Last summer I visited Winnipeg. **Which is a beautiful city.**

Ways to Correct Fragments

Once you have identified a fragment, you have two options for correcting it. You can connect the fragment to the sentence before or after it or make the fragment into an independent clause.

Correction 1:   *Connect the fragment to the sentence before or after it.*

Correction 2:   *Make the fragment into an independent clause:*

(a) either add the missing subject and/or verb, or

(b) drop the subordinating word before the fragment.

We will discuss these corrections for each type of fragment.

REVIEWING FRAGMENTS

What is a sentence fragment?

_____

_____

What are the five types of fragments?

_____   _____

_____   _____

_____

What are the two ways to correct a fragment?

1. _____

2. _____

IDENTIFYING AND CORRECTING FRAGMENTS

The rest of this chapter discusses the five types of fragments and the ways to correct each type.

Type 1: Afterthought Fragments

Afterthought fragments occur when you add an idea to a sentence but don't punctuate it correctly.

> **Fragment:** He goes to school during the day. **And works at night.**

The phrase *And works at night* is punctuated and capitalized as a complete sentence. Because this group of words lacks a subject, however, it is a fragment.

> **Correction 1:**   *Connect the fragment to the sentence before or after it.*
>
> **Example:**   He goes to school during the day **and** works at night.

> **Correction 2:**   *Make the fragment into an independent clause.*
>
> **Example:**   He goes to school during the day. **He** works at night.

The first correction connects the fragment to the sentence before it. The second correction makes the fragment into an independent clause with its own subject and verb.

REVIEWING AFTERTHOUGHT FRAGMENTS

What is an afterthought fragment?

_____

Give an example of an afterthought fragment.

_____

What are the two ways to correct an afterthought fragment?

1. _____

2. _____

  _____

◆ *P r a c t i c e   1 A*   **Identifying** Underline the afterthought fragments in each of the following sentences.

1. The men on the opposing team were very strong. Everyone was scared to play them. Especially me.

2. Mark peered into the window of his locked car and saw his keys. Stuck in the ignition.

3. I am thinking about buying a really special car next year. For example, a Chevy Tahoe.

4. Carlene turned in her paper on time and knew she would get a good grade. Because she really liked her topic.

5. "He shoots. He scores!" is an expression. That my friends use.

◆ *P r a c t i c e   1 B*   **Correcting** Correct the fragments in Practice 1A by rewriting each sentence.

◆ *P r a c t i c e   2*   **Completing** Correct the following afterthought fragments using both correction 1 and correction 2. Rewrite any corrected sentences that you think could be smoother.

1. The child drew in a colouring book. With brand new crayons.

2. I am going to buy some new books to read. For example, the Harry Potter books.

3. Jennifer usually drives very fast. Sometimes running stop signs.

4. My friends are going to the beach. In Grand Bend for the weekend.

5. He walked over to my desk very slowly. And smiled in a friendly way.

◆ *P r a c t i c e   3*   **Writing Your Own** Write five afterthought fragments of your own, and correct them.

Type 2: *-ing* Fragments

Words that end in *-ing* are forms of verbs that cannot be the main verbs in their sentences. For an *-ing* word to function as a verb, it must have a helping verb with it (*be*, *do*, or *have*; see page 391).

Fragment: Finding no one at the house. Kenny walked back home.

Finding is not a verb in this sentence because it has no helping verb. Also, this group of words is a fragment because it has no subject.

Correction 1:   *Connect the fragment to the sentence before or after it.*

Example: **Finding no one at the house, Kenny walked home.**

Correction 2:   *Make the fragment into an independent clause.*

Example: **He found no one at the house.** Kenny walked home.

Hint: When you connect an *-ing* fragment to a sentence, insert a comma between the two sentence parts. You should insert the comma whether the *-ing* part comes at the beginning or the end of the sentence.

Kenny walked home, **finding no one at the house.**
Finding no one at the house, Kenny walked home.

REVIEWING *-ing* FRAGMENTS

How can you tell if an -ing word is part of a fragment or is a main verb?

_____

_____

Give an example of an -ing fragment.

_____

What are the two ways to correct an -ing fragment?

1. _____

2. _____

_____

What kind of punctuation should you use when you join an -ing fragment to another sentence?

_____

◆ **P r a c t i c e   4 A   Identifying** Underline the *-ing* fragments in each of the following sentences.

1. Driving to the store. I thought about all the things I needed to buy.

2. The baseball player dropped the ball. Tripping over his shoelaces while running to make the catch.

3. Mr. Holland was the best music teacher I ever had. Treating everyone with respect.

4. I plan to read at least one book each month. Challenging my brother to do the same.

5. Wanting to leave her parents' house. Marissa got married when she was 18 years old.

◆ *P r a c t i c e*   **4 B**   **Correcting** Correct the fragments in Practice 4A by rewriting each sentence.

◆ *P r a c t i c e*   **5**   **Completing** Correct each of the following *-ing* fragments using both methods. Remember to insert a comma when using correction 1.

1. Making the best grade in the class. Pasquale was excited to tell his parents about it.

2. I think I hurt my back. Trying to move the desk.

3. Looking back at my last year of high school. I can't believe I dated that guy.

4. Wondering whether he had left his car windows down. Julio saw the rain begin to fall.

5. Jamar was glad he had survived the accident. Seeing the damage to his car.

◆ *P r a c t i c e*   **6**   **Writing Your Own** Write five *-ing* fragments of your own, and correct them.

Type 3: *to* Fragments

When *to* is added to a verb (*to see*, *to hop*, *to skip*, *to jump*), the combination cannot be a main verb in its sentence. As a result, this group of words is often involved in a fragment.

> **Fragment:**   The school started a tutoring program. **To improve math results.**

Because *to* + a verb cannot function as the main verb of its sentence, *to improve math results* is a fragment as it is punctuated here.

> **Correction 1:**   *Connect the fragment to the sentence before or after it.*
>
> Example: The school started a tutoring program **to improve math results.**

> **Correction 2:**   *Make the fragment into an independent clause.*
>
> Example: The school started a tutoring program. **It wanted to improve math results.**

Hint: A *to* fragment can also occur at the beginning of a sentence. In this case, insert a comma between the two sentence parts when correcting the fragment.

To improve math results, the school started a tutoring program.

REVIEWING *to* FRAGMENTS

What does a to fragment consist of?

_____

Give an example of a to fragment.

_____

What are the two ways to correct a to fragment?

1. _____

2. _____

_____

◆ *P r a c t i c e   7 A*   **Identifying** Underline the *to* fragments in each of the following sentences.

1. To make the crowd more excited. The rodeo clown came out and chased the bull around the arena.

2. To grow perfect roses. You should attend free classes at The Garden Centre.

3. The baby screamed loudly. To tell his parents he was hungry.

4. We stopped eating fried foods and sweets. To lose weight before summer.

5. To improve their chances at winning the Stanley Cup. The Toronto Maple Leafs signed Mats Sundin.

◆ *P r a c t i c e   7 B*   **Correcting** Correct the fragments in Practice 7A by rewriting each sentence.

◆ *P r a c t i c e   8*   **Completing** Correct the following *to* fragments using both correction 1 and correction 2. Try putting the fragment at the beginning of the sentence instead of always at the end. Remember to insert a comma when you add the *to* fragment to the beginning of a sentence.

1. Avoid driving faster than the posted speed limit. To get the best gas mileage.

2. He wanted to buy a new suit. To impress his boss.

3. Amber told Warren that she had a boyfriend. To avoid hurting his feelings.

4. The bank is closed on Labour Day. To give the employees time with their families.

5. I put the names and addresses in a mail merge. To make it easier to print labels.

◆ *Practice 9* **Writing Your Own** Write five *to* fragments of your own, and correct them.

Type 4: Dependent-Clause Fragments

A group of words that begins with a **subordinating conjunction** (see the list below) is called a **dependent clause** and cannot stand alone. Even though it has a subject and a verb, it is a fragment because it depends on an independent clause to complete its meaning. An **independent clause** is a group of words with a subject and a verb that can stand alone. (See page 386 for help with clauses.)

Here is a list of some commonly used subordinating conjunctions that create dependent clauses.

Subordinating Conjunctions

after	because	since	until
although	before	so	when
as	even if	so that	whenever
as if	even though	than	where
as long as	how	that	wherever
as soon as	if	though	whether
as though	in order that	unless	while

Fragment: <u>Because</u> **I decided to go back to school.** My boss fired me.

This sentence has a subject and a verb, but it is introduced by a subordinating conjunction, *because*. As a result, this sentence is a dependent clause and cannot stand alone.

Correction 1:   *Connect the fragment to the sentence before or after it.*

Example: **Because I decided to go back to school,** my boss fired me.

Correction 2:   *Make the fragment into an independent clause.*

Example: ~~Because~~ I decided to go back to school. My boss fired me.

Hint: If the dependent clause comes first, put a comma between the two parts of the sentence. If the dependent clause comes second, the comma is not needed.

Because I decided to go back to school, my boss fired me.

My boss fired me **because I decided to go back to school.**

REVIEWING DEPENDENT-CLAUSE FRAGMENTS

What is a dependent-clause fragment?

_____

What type of conjunction makes a clause dependent?

_____

What is an independent clause?

_____

Give an example of a dependent-clause fragment.

_____

What are the two ways to correct a dependent-clause fragment?

1. _____

2. _____

_____

◆ *P r a c t i c e   1 0 A*   **Identifying** Underline the dependent-clause fragments in each of the following sentences.

1. I love to eat sushi. Although it's sometimes very expensive.

2. It is good to know some trivia. So that you can participate in lots of conversations.

3. After the child finished riding on it. The rocking horse stood in the corner.

4. I will have Thanksgiving dinner at my house again. As long as my parents get along with my in-laws.

5. Before she goes to work in the morning. Margaret takes her children to school.

◆ *P r a c t i c e   1 0 B*   **Correcting** Correct the fragments in Practice 10A by rewriting each sentence.

◆ *P r a c t i c e   1 1*   **Completing** Correct the following dependent-clause fragments, using both correction 1 and correction 2. When you use correction 1, remember to add a comma if the dependent clause comes first.

1. Manny takes his basketball with him. Wherever he goes.
2. While I'm out of town. My mother will take care of my house.
3. The power bill is higher this month. Though we didn't run the air conditioner very often.
4. When she got home from work. Jamie made green beans for dinner.
5. Jean-Pierre always watches TV for an hour. After he finishes studying.

◆ *P r a c t i c e   1 2*   **Writing Your Own** Write five dependent-clause fragments of your own, and correct them.

Type 5: Relative-Clause Fragments

A **relative clause** is a dependent clause that begins with a relative pronoun: *who, whom, whose, which,* or *that*. When a relative clause is punctuated as a sentence, the result is a fragment.

Fragment: Last summer I visited Winnipeg. **Which is a beautiful city.**

Which is a beautiful city is a clause fragment that begins with the relative pronoun *which*. This word automatically makes the words that follow it a dependent clause, so they cannot stand alone as a sentence.

Correction 1:   *Connect the fragment to the sentence before or after it.*

Example: Last summer I visited Winnipeg, **which is a beautiful city.**

Correction 2:   *Make the fragment into an independent clause.*

Example: Last summer I visited Winnipeg. **It is a beautiful city.**

REVIEWING RELATIVE-CLAUSE FRAGMENTS

How is a relative-clause fragment different from a dependent-clause fragment?

_____

_____

Give an example of a relative-clause fragment.

_____

What are the two ways to correct a relative-clause fragment?

1. _____

2. _____

◆ **Practice 13A** **Identifying** Underline the relative-clause fragments in the following sentences.

1. I made an appointment with the doctor. Whom my cousin recommended.

2. The child ate the pills. That the father left on the bathroom counter.

3. The fire station got a new captain. Who transferred from another department.

4. At the car wash, I talked to the man. Whose name tag said "Sylvester."

5. Karen got a job at the bakery. Which makes fresh doughnuts every morning.

◆ **Practice 13B** **Correcting** Correct the fragments in Practice 13A by rewriting each sentence.

◆ **Practice 14** **Completing** Correct the following relative-clause fragments, using both correction 1 and correction 2.

1. Paul studied for the midterm with Charlotte. Who scored the highest on the first exam.

2. My girlfriend works at the bank. That is located on the corner of Front Street and Market Avenue.

3. I put more memory in my computer. Which cost me about $70.

4. My boss is the man with the goatee. Whose ties are usually very colourful.

5. Penny shops only at grocery stores. That offer double coupons.

◆ **Practice 15** **Writing Your Own** Write five relative-clause fragments of your own, and correct them.

CHAPTER REVIEW

Terms and Definitions

Fragment: an incomplete sentence. It is missing a subject or a verb. It cannot stand alone as a complete thought.

Afterthought Fragment: an added idea that is not punctuated properly

-ing Fragment: An *-ing* verb must have a helping verb with it; otherwise, it will be a sentence fragment.

to Fragment: When *to* is added to the verb, it cannot be the main verb.

Dependent-Clause Fragment: It cannot stand alone as a complete thought or sentence. It depends on a complete sentence for more information.

Independent Clause: a complete sentence. It has a subject and a verb and stands on its own as a complete thought.

Relative Pronouns: *who, whom, whose, which, that*

◆ *Review P r a c t i c e 1*   **Writing Your Own** Write a paragraph about your dream vacation. Where would you go? How long would you stay? Who would go with you, or would you go alone?

◆ *Review P r a c t i c e 2*   **Editing Your Writing** Exchange paragraphs from Review Practice 1 with another student, and do the following:

1. Put brackets around any fragments that you find.

2. Identify the types of fragments that you find.

Then return the paper to its writer, and use the information in this chapter to correct any fragments in your own paragraph. Record your errors on the Error Log in Appendix 3.

CHAPTER 34

FUSED SENTENCES AND COMMA SPLICES

✅ CHECKLIST for Identifying and Correcting Fused Sentences and Comma Splices

> ✔ Are any sentences run together without punctuation?
> ✔ Are any sentences incorrectly joined with only a comma?

Test Yourself

Mark any incorrect sentences here with a slash between the independent clauses that are not joined properly.

- The rainstorm washed out my garden, I had just planted spring bulbs.
- When we cleaned the house, we found the TV remote control it was between the couch cushions.
- People in authority are often criticized and seldom thanked.
- The kids didn't find all of the Easter eggs during the hunt, when we finally found them, they were rotten.
- You should ask Aubri to cut your hair she's been cutting mine for four years.

(Answers are in Appendix 8 on the Web site.)

When we cram two separate statements into a single sentence without correct punctuation, we create what are called *fused sentences* and *comma splices*. These run-on sentences generally distort our message and cause problems for our readers. In this chapter, you will learn how to identify and avoid these errors in your writing.

IDENTIFYING FUSED SENTENCES AND COMMA SPLICES

Whereas a fragment is a piece of a sentence, **fused sentences** and **comma splices** are made up of two sentences written as one. In both cases, the first sentence runs into the next without the proper punctuation between the two.

Fused Sentence: The bus stopped we got off.

Comma Splice: The bus stopped, we got off.

Both of these sentences incorrectly join two independent clauses. The difference between them is one comma.

A **fused sentence** is two sentences "fused" or jammed together without any punctuation. Look at these examples:

Fused Sentence: Rosa's favourite subject is math she always does very well on her math tests.

This example consists of two independent clauses with no punctuation between them:

1. Rosa's favourite subject is math.
2. She always does very well on her math tests.

Fused Sentence: My grandfather likes to cook his own meals he doesn't want anyone to do it for him.

This example also consists of two independent clauses with no punctuation between them:

1. My grandfather likes to cook his own meals.
2. He doesn't want anyone to do it for him.

Like a fused sentence, a **comma splice** incorrectly joins two independent clauses. However, a comma splice puts a comma between the two independent clauses. The only difference between a fused sentence and a comma splice is the comma. Look at the following examples:

Comma Splice: Rosa's favourite subject is math, she always does very well on her math tests.

Comma Splice: My grandfather likes to cook his own meals, he doesn't want anyone to do it for him.

Both of these sentences consist of two independent clauses—but a comma is not the proper punctuation to use to separate these two clauses.

REVIEWING FUSED SENTENCES AND COMMA SPLICES

What are the two types of run-on sentences?

_____   _____

What is the difference between them?

_____

_____

◆ *Practice 1* **Identifying** Put a slash between the independent clauses that are not joined correctly.

1. Paul plays hockey every Thursday he usually gets home after dark.

2. My mom always tucked me into bed at night, that's what I remember most about her.

3. Toni borrowed my pencil yesterday then she lost it.

4. My boyfriend made my favourite cake for my birthday, I had to eat the whole thing.

5. The child needed a bone marrow transplant, we raised $10,000 last night for her cause.

◆ *Practice 2* **Identifying** For each incorrect sentence in the following paragraph, put a slash between the independent clauses that are not joined properly.

The fitness craze is sweeping across Canada, it seems like everyone has a gym membership. The best-selling food items have "light," "lite," or "fat free" on the packaging, and people are watching their cholesterol and counting calories. Only the thinnest models are shown in food advertisements they symbolize good health, responsible eating habits, and overall physical attractiveness. Ironically, thin people are even used in ads for unhealthy food items, like candy and soft drinks, this sends a very confusing message to the consumer. The stereotypes are not fair not everyone can have the "perfect" body seen in the ads. Some people are just born with bigger body shapes, and there is nothing wrong or unattractive about that. These people should learn to eat healthy foods, they should not try to be unnaturally thin.

◆ *Practice 3* **Writing Your Own** Write five fused sentences. Then write the same sentences as comma splices.

CORRECTING FUSED SENTENCES AND COMMA SPLICES

You have four different options for correcting your fused sentences and comma splices.

1. Separate the two sentences with a period, and capitalize the next word.
2. Separate the two sentences with a comma, and add a coordinating conjunction (*and, but, for, nor, or, so,* or *yet*).
3. Change one of the sentences into a dependent clause with a subordinating conjunction (such as *if, because, since, after,* or *when*) or a relative pronoun (*who, whom, whose, which,* or *that*).
4. Separate the two sentences with a semicolon.

Correction 1: Use a Period

Separate the two sentences with a period, and capitalize the next word.

> Rosa's favourite subject is math**.** **She** always does very well on her math tests.
>
> My grandfather likes to cook his own meals**.** **He** doesn't want anyone to do it for him.

◆ *P r a c t i c e **4*** **Correcting** Correct all the sentences in Practice 1, using correction 1.

◆ *P r a c t i c e **5*** **Correcting** Correct the paragraph in Practice 2, using correction 1.

◆ *P r a c t i c e **6*** **Writing Your Own** Correct the sentences you wrote in Practice 3, using correction 1.

Correction 2: Use a Coordinating Conjunction

Separate the two sentences with a comma, and add a coordinating conjunction (*and, but, for, nor, or, so,* or *yet*).

> Rosa's favourite subject is math**, so** she always does very well on her math tests.
>
> My grandfather likes to cook his own meals**, and** he doesn't want anyone to do it for him.

◆ *P r a c t i c e **7*** **Correcting** Correct all the sentences in Practice 1, using correction 2.

◆ *Practice 8* **Correcting** Correct the paragraph in Practice 2, using correction 2.

◆ *Practice 9* **Writing Your Own** Correct the sentences you wrote in Practice 3, using correction 2.

Correction 3: Create a Dependent Clause

Change one of the sentences into a dependent clause with a subordinating conjunction (such as *if, because, since, after,* or *when*) or a relative pronoun (*who, whom, whose, which,* or *that*).

> Rosa's favourite subject is math **because** she always does very well on her math tests.
>
> **Since** my grandfather likes to cook his own meals, he doesn't want anyone to do it for him.

For a list of subordinating conjunctions, see page 384.

Hint: If you put the dependent clause at the beginning of the sentence, add a comma between the two sentence parts.

> **Because** she always does very well on her math tests, Rosa's favourite subject is math.

◆ *Practice 10* **Correcting** Correct all the sentences in Practice 1, using correction 3.

◆ *Practice 11* **Correcting** Correct the paragraph in Practice 2, using correction 3.

◆ *Practice 12* **Writing Your Own** Correct the sentences you wrote in Practice 3, using correction 3.

Correction 4: Use a Semicolon

Separate the two sentences with a semicolon.

> Rosa's favourite subject is math; she always does very well on her math tests.
>
> My grandfather likes to cook his own meals; he doesn't want anyone to do it for him.

You can also use a **transition**, a word or an expression that indicates how the two parts of the sentence are related, with a semicolon. A transition often makes the sentence smoother. It is preceded by a semicolon and followed by a comma.

Rosa's favourite subject is math; **as a result,** she always does very well on her math tests.

My grandfather likes to cook his own meals; **therefore,** he doesn't want anyone to do it for him.

Here are some transitions commonly used with semicolons.

Transitions Used with a Semicolon Before and a Comma After

also	*however*	*furthermore*	*instead*
meanwhile	*consequently*	*for example*	*similarly*
in contrast	*therefore*	*for instance*	*otherwise*
of course	*finally*	*in fact*	*nevertheless*

◆ *P r a c t i c e* **1 3**   **Correcting** Correct all the sentences in Practice 1, using correction 4.

◆ *P r a c t i c e* **1 4**   **Correcting** Correct the paragraph in Practice 2, using correction 4.

◆ *P r a c t i c e* **1 5**   **Writing Your Own** Correct the sentences you wrote in Practice 3, using correction 4.

REVIEWING METHODS OF CORRECTING FUSED SENTENCES
AND COMMA SPLICES

What are the four ways to correct a fused sentence or comma splice?

1. _____

2. _____

3. _____

4. _____

Why is correcting fused sentences and comma splices important?

_____

CHAPTER REVIEW

Fused Sentences: two or more separate sentences put into a single sentence without proper punctuation. A fused sentence is also called a run-on sentence.

Comma Splice: two or more separate sentences joined together with a comma. A comma splice is also called a run-on sentence.

Correct run-on sentences by using a period, a coordinating conjunction, or a semicolon.

Coordinating Conjunction: Words such as *and, but, for, nor, so,* or *yet* can join two complete sentences. A comma comes before the conjunction.

◆ *Review P r a c t i c e 1*   **Writing Your Own** Write a paragraph about your favourite season of the year. Why do you enjoy it? What do you do during this time of year?

◆ *Review P r a c t i c e 2*   **Editing Through Collaboration** Exchange your paragraph from Review Practice 1 with another student, and do the following:

1. Put brackets around any sentences that have more than one independent clause.

2. Circle the words that connect these clauses.

Then return the paper to its writer, and use the information in this chapter to correct any run-on sentences in your own paragraph. Record your errors on the Error Log in Appendix 3.

REGULAR AND IRREGULAR VERBS

☑ CHECKLIST for Using Regular and Irregular Verbs

> ✔ Are regular verbs in their correct forms?
>
> ✔ Are irregular verbs in their correct forms?

Test Yourself

Underline the complete verb in each of the following sentences. Then mark an X if the form of the verb is incorrect.

- _____ The pipe has bursted.
- _____ Sim reacted to the scene calmly.
- _____ I bought my car at an auction.
- _____ We had hid in the basement.
- _____ Sorry, I eated all the cookies.

(Answers are in Appendix 8 on the Web site.)

All verbs are either regular or irregular. *Regular verbs* form the past tense and past participle by adding *-d* or *-ed* to the present tense. If a verb does not form its past tense and past participle this way, it is called an *irregular verb*.

REGULAR VERBS

Here are the principal parts (present, past, and past participle forms) of some regular verbs. **Regular verbs** form the past tense and past participle by adding *-d* or *-ed*. The past participle is the verb form often used with helping verbs like *have*, *has*, or *had*.

Some Regular Verbs

PRESENT TENSE	PAST TENSE	PAST PARTICIPLE (USED WITH HELPING WORDS LIKE *HAVE, HAS, HAD*)
talk	talked	talked
sigh	sighed	sighed
drag	dragged	dragged
enter	entered	entered
consider	considered	considered

The different forms of a verb tell when something happened—in the *present* (I *talk*) or in the *past* (I *talked*, I *have talked*, I *had talked*).

REVIEWING REGULAR VERBS

What is a regular verb?

_____

Identify three forms of a regular verb.

_____   _____   _____

♦ *P r a c t i c e   1*   **Identifying** Put an X to the left of the incorrect verb forms in the following chart.

Present Tense	**Past Tense**	**Past Participle**
1. _____ clap	_____ clapped	_____ clapped
2. _____ help	_____ helpt	_____ helped
3. _____ watched	_____ watched	_____ watched
4. _____ gaze	_____ gazed	_____ gazd
5. _____ reclined	_____ reclined	_____ reclined

◆ *P r a c t i c e* **2** **Completing** Write the correct forms of the following regular verbs.

	Present Tense	Past Tense	Past Participle
1. smoke	_____	_____	_____
2. create	_____	_____	_____
3. paste	_____	_____	_____
4. buzz	_____	_____	_____
5. pick	_____	_____	_____

◆ *P r a c t i c e* **3** **Writing Your Own** Write five sentences using variations of the verbs in Practice 1.

IRREGULAR VERBS

Irregular verbs do not form their past tense and past participle with *-d* or *-ed*. That is why they are irregular. Some follow certain patterns (*spring, sprang, sprung; ring, rang, rung; drink, drank, drunk; sink, sank, sunk*). But the only sure way to know the forms of an irregular verb is to spend time learning them. As you write, you can check a dictionary or the following list.

Common Irregular Verbs

PRESENT TENSE	PAST TENSE	PAST PARTICIPLE (USED WITH HELPING WORDS LIKE *HAVE, HAS, HAD*)
am	*was*	*been*
are	*were*	*been*
begin	*began*	*begun*
bring	*brought* (not *brang*)	*brought* (not *brung*)
build	*built*	*built*
burst	*burst* (not *bursted*)	*burst*
buy	*bought*	*bought*
choose	*chose*	*chosen*
come	*came*	*come*
deal	*dealt*	*dealt*

do	*did* (not *done*)	*done*
draw	*drew*	*drawn*
drink	*drank*	*drunk*
drive	*drove*	*driven*
eat	*ate*	*eaten*
fall	*fell*	*fallen*
get	*got*	*got, gotten*
go	*went*	*gone*
is	*was*	*been*
know	*knew*	*known*
lay	*laid*	*laid*
leave	*left*	*left*
lie[1]	*lay*	*lain*
lose	*lost*	*lost*
meet	*met*	*met*
pay	*paid*	*paid*
prove	*proved*	*proved, proven*
ride	*rode*	*ridden*
ring	*rang*	*rung*
rise	*rose*	*risen*
run	*ran*	*run*
see	*saw* (not *seen*)	*seen*
shake	*shook*	*shaken*
shine[2] (*a light*)	*shone*	*shone*
shrink	*shrank*	*shrunk*
sink	*sank*	*sunk*
spring	*sprang* (not *sprung*)	*sprung*
stand	*stood*	*stood*
steal	*stole*	*stolen*
stick	*stuck*	*stuck*
stink	*stank* (not *stunk*)	*stunk*
strike	*struck*	*struck, stricken*
strive	*strove*	*striven, strived*
swear	*swore*	*sworn*
swell	*swelled*	*swelled, swollen*
swim	*swam*	*swum*
swing	*swung*	*swung*

take	*took*	*taken*
throw	*threw*	*thrown*
write	*wrote*	*written*

[1]*Lie* meaning "tell a lie" is regular: *lie, lied, lied.*
[2]*Shine* meaning "brighten by polishing" is regular: *shine, shined, shined.*

REVIEWING IRREGULAR VERBS

What is the difference between regular and irregular verbs?

_____

What is the best way to learn how irregular verbs form their past tense and past participle?

_____

◆ *P r a c t i c e*   **4**   **Identifying** Put an X to the left of the incorrect verb forms in the following chart.

Present Tense	**Past Tense**	**Past Participle**
1. _____ bear	_____ beared	_____ borne
2. _____ shrink	_____ shrank	_____ shrank
3. _____ swing	_____ swung	_____ swang
4. _____ dcal	_____ dealed	_____ dealt
5. _____ chose	_____ chose	_____ chosen

◆ *P r a c t i c e*   **5**   **Completing** Write the correct forms of the following irregular verbs.

	Present Tense	**Past Tense**	**Past Participle**
1. am	_____	_____	_____
2. write	_____	_____	_____
3. sweep	_____	_____	_____
4. fall	_____	_____	_____
5. swell	_____	_____	_____

◆ ***P r a c t i c e 6*** **Writing Your Own** Write five sentences using at least five of the words from the chart in Practice 5.

USING *LIE/LAY* AND *SIT/SET* CORRECTLY

Two pairs of verbs are often used incorrectly—*lie/lay* and *sit/set*.

Lie/Lay

	Present Tense	Past Tense	Past Participle
lie (recline or lie down)	lie	lay	(have, has, had) lain
lay (put or place down)	lay	laid	(have, has, had) laid

The verb *lay* always takes an object. You must lay something down:

Lay down *what?*

Lay down *your books*.

Sit/Set

	Present Tense	Past Tense	Past Participle
sit (get into a seated position)	sit	sat	(have, has, had) sat
set (put or place down)	set	set	(have, has, had) set

Like the verb *lay*, the verb *set* must always have an object. You must set something down:

Set *what?*

Set *the presents* over here.

REVIEWING *Lie/Lay* AND *Sit/Set*

What do lie and lay mean?

_____

What are the principal parts of lie and lay?

_____

What do sit and set mean?

_____

What are the principal parts of sit and set?

_____

Which of these verbs always take an object?

_____

◆ **P r a c t i c e 7 Identifying** Choose the correct verb in the following sentences.

1. After I (sat, set) down, I felt much better.
2. All day I have (lain, laid) in my room watching TV.
3. He has (lay, laid) the blanket down for our picnic.
4. We had to (sat, set) our watches to exactly the same time.
5. (Lie, Lay) the pieces of the puzzle out on the table, please.

◆ **P r a c t i c e 8 Completing** Fill in each blank in the following sentences with the correct form of *lie/lay* or *sit/set*.

1. Suzy has _____ in the bathtub for so long that her skin has wrinkled.
2. I could have _____ in the moonlight looking at the stars all night.
3. The cook _____ out all the ingredients.
4. Please _____ those heavy boxes down before you strain your back.
5. I think I will go and _____ down for a while.

◆ **P r a c t i c e 9 Writing Your Own** Write five sentences using variations of *lie/lay* or *sit/set*.

CHAPTER REVIEW

Regular Verbs: form the past tense and past participle by adding *-d* or *-ed*.

Past Participle: verb form often used with helping verbs like *have*, *has*, or *had*

Irregular Verbs: do not form the past tense or past participle by adding *-d* or *-ed*.

◆ **Review P r a c t i c e 1 Writing Your Own** Write a paragraph explaining the most important parts of your daily routine. Be sure to explain why each activity is important.

Review Practice 2 **Editing Your Writing** Exchange paragraphs from Review Practice 1 with another student, and do the following:

1. Circle any verb forms that are not correct.
2. Suggest a correction for these incorrect forms.

Then return the paper to its writer, and use the information in this chapter to correct the verb forms in your own paragraph. Record your errors on the Error Log in Appendix 3.

Subject–Verb Agreement

✅ CHECKLIST for Correcting Subject–Verb Agreement Problems

> ✔ Do all subjects agree with their verbs?

Test Yourself

Underline the subjects once and the complete verbs twice in the following sentences. Put an X by the sentence if its subject and verb do not agree.

- _____ Neither the shorts nor the shirt fit me.
- _____ Chips and dip is my favourite snack.
- _____ There were a large storm last night.
- _____ Some of the soil along with the fertilizer are for the orchard.
- _____ Cotton and silk is more comfortable than wool.

(Answers are in Appendix 8 on the Web site.)

Almost every day, we come across situations that require us to reach an agreement with someone. For example, you and a friend might have to agree on which movie to see, or you and your manager might have to agree on how many hours you'll work in the coming week. Whatever the issue, agreement is essential in most aspects of life—including writing. In this chapter, you will learn how to resolve conflicts in your sentences by making sure your subjects and verbs agree.

SUBJECT–VERB AGREEMENT

Subject–verb agreement simply means that singular subjects must be paired with singular verbs and plural subjects with plural verbs. Look at this example:

Singular: **She works** in Halifax.

The subject *she* is singular because it refers to only one person. The verb *works* is singular and matches the singular subject. Here is the same sentence in plural form:

Plural: **They work** in Halifax.

The subject *they* is plural, referring to more than one person, and the verb *work* is also plural.

REVIEWING SUBJECT–VERB AGREEMENT

What is the difference between singular and plural?

_____

What kind of verb goes with a singular subject?

_____

What kind of verb goes with a plural subject?

_____

◆ *P r a c t i c e   1*   **Identifying** Underline the verb that agrees with its subject in each of the following sentences.

1. In her free time, Cassie (are, is) a volunteer nurse.
2. The girls usually (store, stores) their gear in the lockers.
3. Rocky, my 80-pound dog, (eat, eats) more food in a day than I do.
4. I (do, does) all my reading for my classes at least a week ahead of time.
5. You (has, have) something green in your hair.

◆ *P r a c t i c e   2*   **Completing** Fill in each blank in the following sentences with a present-tense verb that agrees with its subject.

1. Every evening, Michael _____ by the fire.
2. They _____ many questions.
3. Neil _____ everything chocolate.
4. We rarely _____ down that path, for it is always dark and eerie.
5. He _____ to only classical music.

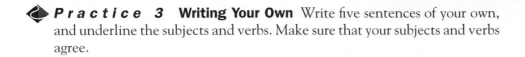
◆ *P r a c t i c e 3* **Writing Your Own** Write five sentences of your own, and underline the subjects and verbs. Make sure that your subjects and verbs agree.

WORDS SEPARATING SUBJECTS AND VERBS

With sentences that are as simple and direct as *She works in Halifax*, checking that the subject and verb agree is easy. But problems can arise when words come between the subject and the verb. Often the words between the subject and verb form a prepositional phrase. If you follow the advice given in Chapter 32, you will be able to find the subject and verb: *Cross out all the prepositional phrases in a sentence. The subject and verb will be among the words that are left.* Here are some examples:

s   v

Prepositional Phrases: The **notebook** ~~for history class~~ **is** ~~in my backpack~~.

When you cross out the prepositional phrases, you can tell that the singular subject, *notebook*, and the singular verb, *is*, agree.

s   v

Prepositional Phrases: The **roses** ~~in my garden~~ **bloom** ~~in April~~.

When you cross out the prepositional phrases, you can tell that the plural subject, *roses*, and the plural verb, *bloom*, agree.

REVIEWING WORDS SEPARATING SUBJECTS AND VERBS

What words often come between subjects and verbs?

_____

What is an easy way to identify the subject and verb in a sentence?

_____

◆ *P r a c t i c e 4* **Identifying** Cross out the prepositional phrase and underline the subject once and the verb twice in each of the following sentences. Cross out the prepositional phrases first. Put an X to the left of any sentence in which the subject and verb do not agree.

1. _____ Cindy, unlike many people today, do so much for others.

2. _____ That man in the blue pants think a lot about his social life.

3. _____ Frog legs, in spite of what most people say, tastes like frog legs.

4. _____ The flowers in the garden smell nice.

5. _____ The economy in Canada seem to be getting stronger.

◆ *Practice* **5**   **Completing** Fill in each blank in the following sentences with a present-tense verb that agrees with its subject.

1. My little brother, despite being told otherwise, still _____ in Santa Claus.

2. The train for Regina _____ in the station at 7:45 p.m.

3. MuchMusic _____ to air more music videos.

4. The boxes in the hallway _____ in the moving van.

5. The wind during a thunderstorm always _____ me.

◆ *Practice* **6**   **Writing Your Own** Write five sentences of your own with at least one prepositional phrase in each, and underline the subjects and verbs. Make sure that your subjects and verbs agree.

MORE THAN ONE SUBJECT

Sometimes a subject consists of more than one person, place, thing, or idea. These subjects are called **compound** (as discussed in Chapter 32). Follow these three rules when matching a verb to a compound subject:

1. When compound subjects are joined by *and,* use a plural verb.

   Plural: **Thursday and Friday were** hot days.

   The singular words *Thursday and Friday* together make a plural subject. Therefore, the plural verb *were* is needed.

2. When the subject appears to have more than one part but the parts refer to a single unit, use a singular verb.

   Singular: **Macaroni and cheese is** Eli's favourite food.

   Macaroni is one item and *cheese* is one item, but Eli does not eat one without the other, so they form a single unit. Because they are a single unit, they require a singular verb—*is.*

3. When compound subjects are joined by *or* or *nor,* make the verb agree with the subject closest to it.

   Singular: Neither hot dogs nor **chicken was** on the menu.

   The part of the compound subject closest to the verb is *chicken,* which is singular. Therefore, the verb must be singular—*was.*

   Plural: Neither chicken nor **hot dogs were** on the menu.

This time, the part of the compound subject closest to the verb is *hot dogs*, which is plural. Therefore, the verb must be plural—*were*.

REVIEWING SUBJECT–VERB AGREEMENT
WITH MORE THAN ONE SUBJECT

Do you use a singular or plural verb with compound subjects joined by and?

_____

Why should you use a singular verb with a subject like macaroni *and* cheese?

_____

If one part of a compound subject joined by or *or* nor *is singular and the other is plural, how do you decide whether to use a singular or plural verb?*

_____

Practice 7 Identifying Cross out the prepositional phrases and underline the verb that agrees with its subject in each of the following sentences.

1. You and I (was, were) going the wrong way down a one-way street.
2. Chicken and dumplings (taste, tastes) better with a little salt and pepper.
3. Either the mosquitoes or the wind (cause, causes) my skin problems.
4. Celery and peanut butter (is, are) my favourite snack.
5. Neither the professor nor the students (knows, know) the answer to this question.

Practice 8 Completing Cross out the prepositional phrases and fill in each blank in the following sentences. Use a present-tense verb that agrees with its subject. Don't use *is*, *are*, *was*, or *were*.

1. Either lilies or tulips _____ well in the spring.
2. Pie and ice cream _____ the best dessert.
3. The ants and flies in the house _____ me.
4. The train and the passengers _____ sometime this evening.
5. Neither the entrees nor the dessert _____ appetizing tonight.

◆ *P r a c t i c e 9* **Writing Your Own** Write a sentence of your own for each of the following compound subjects. Make sure that your subjects and verbs agree.

1. either the handouts or the manuscript _____

2. brooms and brushes _____

3. neither the nurses nor the doctor _____

4. ham and cheese _____

5. the horse and her foal _____

VERBS BEFORE SUBJECTS

When the subject follows its verb, the subject may be hard to find, so making the subjects and verbs agree becomes more difficult. Subjects come after verbs in two particular situations—when the sentence begins with *here* or *there* and when a question begins with *Who, What, Where, When, Why,* or *How.* Here are some examples:

Verb Before Subject: Here **come** the **guests** for the party.

Verb Before Subject: There **is iced tea** in the refrigerator.

In sentences that begin with *here* or *there*, the verb always comes before the subject. Don't forget to cross out prepositional phrases to help you identify the subject or is split by the subject. One of the words that's left will be the subject, and then you can check that the verb agrees with it.

Verb Before Subject: Who **is** that tall **man** in the blue suit?

Verb Before Subject: Where **are** the watercolour **paintings kept**?

Verb Before Subject: When **are you flying** to Whitehorse?

In questions that begin with *Who, What, When, Where, Why,* and *How*, the verb comes before the subject or is split by the subject, as in the last two examples.

REVIEWING VERBS BEFORE SUBJECTS

Where will you find the verb in sentences that begin with here *or* there?

_____

Where will you find the verb in questions that begin with who, what, where, when, why, *and* how?

_____

◆ **P r a c t i c e 1 0 Identifying** Cross out the prepositional phrases and underline the subject once and the verb twice in each of the following sentences.

1. Here lies the cause of the problem despite the evidence.

2. Who is the leader of your group?

3. How do you feel after your recent operation?

4. Where in the world are my keys?

5. There on the table are your books.

◆ **P r a c t i c e 1 1 Completing** Cross out the prepositional phrases in each sentence. Fill in each blank in the following sentences with a verb that agrees with its subject.

1. Where _____ the rest of the rhubarb pie?

2. Over the hill, there _____ a great swimming hole.

3. Why _____ their dirty clothes on the bathroom floor?

4. How many times _____ your sister asked you to fix that hair dryer?

5. What _____ this mess in the front yard?

◆ **P r a c t i c e 1 2 Writing Your Own** Write a sentence of your own for each of the following words and phrases. Make sure that your subjects and verbs agree.

1. there may be _____

2. what has been _____

3. how did he _____

4. when is _____

5. here is _____

COLLECTIVE NOUNS

Collective nouns name a group of people or things. Examples include such nouns as *army, audience, band, class, committee, crew, crowd, family, flock, gang, jury, majority, minority, orchestra, senate, team,* and *troupe.* Collective nouns can be singular or plural. They are singular when they refer to a group as a single unit. They are plural when they refer to the individual actions or feelings of the group members.

                                           s   v

Singular: The string **quartet performs** three times a year.

Quartet refers to the entire unit or group. Therefore, it requires the singular verb *performs.*

                                           s   v

Plural: The string **quartet get** their new instruments on Monday.

Here *quartet* refers to the individual members, who will each get a new instrument, so the plural verb *get* is used.

REVIEWING COLLECTIVE NOUNS
....

When is a collective noun singular?

_____

When is a collective noun plural?

_____

◆ *P r a c t i c e   1 3*   **Identifying** Underline the correct verb in each of the following sentences. Cross out the prepositional phrases.

1. The audience (listen, listens) intently to the guest speaker.

2. The majority (have, has) voted at different polling booths.

3. The orchestra (play, plays) different selections, depending on the concert.

4. Our high school cheerleading squad (is, are) all going to different colleges.

5. The litter of puppies (get, gets) a bath today.

◆ *P r a c t i c e 1 4* **Completing** Fill in each blank in the following sentences with a present-tense verb that agrees with its subject. Cross out the prepositional phrases.

1. A flock of geese always _____ south for the winter.

2. The crew _____ trouble making sure everyone has a good time.

3. The school orchestra _____ this competition every year.

4. The army _____ students who have degrees as officers.

5. The House of Commons _____ according to individual beliefs.

◆ *P r a c t i c e 1 5* **Writing Your Own** Write a sentence of your own using each of the following words as a plural subject. Make sure that your subjects and verbs agree.

1. committee _____

2. gang _____

3. class _____

4. minority _____

5. group _____

INDEFINITE PRONOUNS

Indefinite pronouns do not refer to anyone or anything specific. Some indefinite pronouns are always singular, and some are always plural. A few can be either singular or plural, depending on the other words in the sentence. When an indefinite pronoun is the subject of a sentence, the verb must agree with the pronoun. Here is a list of indefinite pronouns.

Indefinite Pronouns

ALWAYS SINGULAR		ALWAYS PLURAL	EITHER SINGULAR OR PLURAL
another	*neither*	*both*	*all*
anybody	*nobody*	*few*	*any*
anyone	*no one*	*many*	*more*
anything	*nothing*	*others*	*most*
each	*one*	*several*	*none*
either	*other*		*some*

everybody	somebody
everyone	someone
everything	something
little	
much	

Singular: **No one** ever **changes** at work.

        s   v

Everybody refuses to work harder.

Plural: **Many take** long lunches and **go** home early.

Others stay late but **are** tired and unmotivated.

The pronouns that can be either singular or plural are singular when they refer to singular words and plural when they refer to plural words.

Singular: **Some** of Abby's *day* **was** hectic.

Some is singular because it refers to *day*, which is singular. The singular verb *was* agrees with the singular subject *some*.

Plural: **Some** of Abby's *co-workers* **were** late.

Some is plural because it refers to *co-workers*, which is plural. The plural verb *were* agrees with the plural subject *some*.

REVIEWING INDEFINITE PRONOUNS

What is an indefinite pronoun?

_____

When are all, any, more, most, none, and some singular or plural?

_____

_____

◆ *Practice 16* **Identifying** Underline the verb that agrees with its subject in each of the following sentences. Cross out the prepositional phrases first.

1. All of my money (is, are) gone.

2. Both of the pools (was, were) treated with chlorine.

3. No one (do, does) more work than Pam.

4. Something (fly, flies) into my window every night and (buzz, buzzes) around my head.

5. Most of Omar's friends (seem, seems) friendly.

◆ *Practice 17* **Completing** Fill in each blank in the following sentences with a present-tense verb that agrees with its subject. Cross out the prepositional phrases.

1. Most of the people _____ to work in the mornings.

2. No one really _____ if he will accept the job.

3. Both _____ the consequences of their actions.

4. None of the fake contestants _____ it was a joke.

5. Somebody _____ moving my things off my desk.

◆ *Practice 18* **Writing Your Own** Write a sentence of your own using each of the following words as a subject, and combining it with one of the following verbs: *is, are, was, were*. Make sure that your subjects and verbs agree.

1. anything _____

2. others _____

3. some _____

4. any _____

5. several _____

CHAPTER REVIEW

Subject–Verb Agreement: Singular subjects must be paired with singular verbs. Plural subjects must be paired with plural verbs.

Prepositional Phrase: a group of words that begins with a preposition (*in, on, after, under, with*). The subject of a sentence cannot be in the prepositional phrase.

Compound Subject: a subject that consists of more than one person, place, thing, or idea.

Verbs Before Subjects: Place the verb before the subject in sentences that begin with *here, there, who, what, where, when, why,* or *how*.

Collective Nouns: a group of people or things

Indefinite Pronouns: do not refer to anyone or anything specific

◆ *Review P r a c t i c e 1* **Writing Your Own** Write a paragraph explaining why you did or did not join a committee, team, or other group. Make sure that your subjects and verbs agree.

◆ *Review P r a c t i c e 2* **Editing Through Collaboration** Exchange paragraphs from Review Practice 1 with another student, and do the following:

1. Underline the subject once in each sentence.
2. Underline the verb twice.
3. Put an X by any verbs that do not agree with their subjects.

Then return the paper to its writer, and use the information in this chapter to correct any subject–verb agreement errors in your own paragraph. Record your errors on the Error Log in Appendix 3.

PRONOUN PROBLEMS

✅ CHECKLIST for Using Pronouns

> ✔ Are all subject pronouns used correctly?
>
> ✔ Are all object pronouns used correctly?
>
> ✔ Are all possessive pronouns used correctly?
>
> ✔ Are pronouns used in *than* or *as* comparisons in the correct form?
>
> ✔ Are the pronouns *this, that, these,* and *those* used correctly?

Test Yourself

Correct the pronoun errors in the following sentences.

- The ball was their's to begin with.
- Tom told Valerie and I the most exciting story.
- James can type a lot faster than me.
- Those there running shoes are Kim's.
- Me and Julio are going to the movies tonight.

(Answers are in Appendix 8 on the Web site.)

Pronouns are words that take the place of nouns. They help us avoid repeating nouns. In this chapter, we'll discuss five types of pronoun problems: (1) using the wrong pronoun as a subject, (2) using the wrong pronoun as an object, (3) using an apostrophe with a possessive pronoun, (4) misusing pronouns in comparisons, and (5) misusing demonstrative pronouns.

PRONOUNS AS SUBJECTS

Single pronouns as subjects usually don't cause problems.

Subject Pronoun: **I** attended the opera with my aunt and uncle.

Subject Pronoun: **They** relocated to Calgary.

You wouldn't say "*Me* attended the game" or "*Them* went to Nunavut." But an error often occurs when a sentence has a compound subject and one or more of the subjects is a pronoun.

NOT   **The boys and us** competed all the time.

Correct: **The boys and we** competed all the time.

Correct: **We and the boys** competed all the time.

NOT   **Her and me** decided to go to Paris.

Correct: **She and I** decided to go to Paris.

To test whether or not you have used the correct form of the pronoun in a compound subject, try each subject alone.

Subject Pronoun?   **The boys and us** competed for the trophy.

Test: **The boys** competed for the trophy. **YES**

Test: **Us** competed for the trophy. **NO**

Test: **We** competed for the trophy. **YES**

Correction: **The boys and we** competed for the trophy.

Correction: **We and the boys** competed for the trophy.

Here is a list of subject pronouns.

Subject Pronouns

Singular	Plural
I	*we*
you	*you*
he, she, it	*they*

REVIEWING PRONOUNS AS SUBJECTS

Name two subject pronouns.

_____

How can you test whether you are using the correct pronoun as the subject of a sentence?

_____

◆ *P r a c t i c e* *1*   **Identifying** Underline the pronouns used as subjects in each of the following sentences.

1. Diane and he will be gone for at least a week.
2. He is going to have to work faster if he wants to meet the deadline.
3. "I really don't want to go," he said.
4. We cannot use the elevator because it is not working.
5. She and I have been best friends since I can remember.

◆ *P r a c t i c e* *2*   **Completing** Fill in each blank in the following paragraph with a subject pronoun.

      At first, my friends had me convinced that (1) _____ should

go on the annual deep-sea fishing trip. (2) _____ spoke on and

on about how much fun the last trip was. But before long, Brian

admitted that (3) _____ got sick once the boat was out at sea.

Then Misty described how the captain of the boat cut off the

heads of the fish and gutted them. (4) _____ found the whole

process exciting. (5) _____ can just imagine my reaction! I

don't think I'll be joining my friends on their fishing trip.

◆ *P r a c t i c e* *3*   **Writing Your Own** Write a sentence of your own for each of the following subject pronouns.

1. they _____

2. you _____

3. he _____

4. it _____

5. I _____

PRONOUNS AS OBJECTS

    One of the most frequent pronoun errors is using a subject pronoun when the sentence calls for an object pronoun. The sentence may require an object after a verb, showing that someone or something receives the action of the verb. Or it may be an object of a preposition that is required (see page 383 for a list of prepositions).

NOT	She gave **Kenisha and I** some money.
Correct:	She gave **Kenisha and me** some money.

NOT	The secret is between **you and I.**
Correct:	The secret is between **you and me.**

Like the subject pronoun error, the object pronoun error usually occurs with compound objects. Also like the subject pronoun error, you can test whether you are using the correct pronoun by using each object separately.

Object Pronoun?	She gave **Kenisha and I** some money.
Test:	She gave **Kenisha** some money. **YES**
Test:	She gave **I** some money. **NO**
Test:	She gave **me** some money. **YES**
Correction:	She gave **Kenisha and me** some money.

Here is a list of object pronouns:

Object Pronouns

Singular	Plural
me	us
you	you
him, her, it	them

REVIEWING PRONOUNS AS OBJECTS

In what two places are pronouns used as objects?

_____

How can you test whether you have used the correct pronoun as the object in a sentence?

_____

◆ *P r a c t i c e 4* **Identifying** Underline the correct object pronoun in each of the following sentences.

1. Natalie's grandmother had raised (her, she) since she was five.

2. The wonderful neighbours welcomed (we, us) to the community with a chocolate cake.

3. Corrina accidentally sprayed my sister and (I, me) with the hose.

4. All are going on the trip except for you and (him, he).

5. For (her, she), I will sit through this awful movie.

◆ *P r a c t i c e* 5 Completing Fill in each blank in the following sentences with an object pronoun.

1. Between the two of _____, we should be able to fix the problem.

2. He asked you and _____ to the same dance.

3. Unlike _____, I am going to take emergency gear on this hiking trip.

4. According to you and _____, the test will take one hour.

5. The priest took _____ on a tour of the temple.

◆ *P r a c t i c e* 6 Writing Your Own Write a sentence of your own for each of the following object pronouns.

1. us _____

2. him _____

3. me _____

4. them _____

5. her _____

POSSESSIVE PRONOUNS

   Possessive pronouns show ownership (**my** *house,* **her** *hat,* **our** *family*). (See pages 381–382 for a list of pronouns.) An apostrophe is used with nouns to show ownership (**Jack's** *dog, the* **farmer's** *barn, the* **people's** *opinions*). But an apostrophe is never used with possessive pronouns.

Possessive Pronouns

Singular	Plural
my, mine	*our, ours*
your, yours	*you, yours*
his, her, hers	*their, theirs*

NOT	That house is **their's**.
Correct:	That house is **theirs**.

NOT	The book on the table is **your's**.
Correct:	The book on the table is **yours**.

NOT	The dog chased **it's** tail.
Correct:	The dog chased **its** tail.

REVIEWING POSSESSIVE PRONOUNS

When do you use an apostrophe with a noun?

_____

Do possessive pronouns take apostrophes?

_____

◆ *P r a c t i c e 7* **Identifying** Underline the correct possessive pronoun in each of the following sentences.

1. The computer needs its monitor fixed.
2. Both of my aunts live in New Brunswick.
3. That piece of cake on the counter is hers.
4. The children left their toys in the driveway.
5. Hey! That was his.

◆ *P r a c t i c e 8* **Completing** Fill in each blank in the following sentences with a possessive pronoun.

1. These books aren't _____, so they must be _____.
2. _____ dogs bothered the neighbours so much that we had to move away.
3. The film crew left _____ equipment on the set.
4. Look at John's dog carrying _____ bowl in his mouth.
5. The car won't start because three of _____ tires are flat.

◆ *P r a c t i c e 9* **Writing Your Own** Write a sentence of your own for each of the following possessive pronouns.

1. mine _____

2. theirs _____

3. his _____

4. its _____

5. our _____

PRONOUNS IN COMPARISONS

Sometimes pronoun problems occur in comparisons with *than* or *as*. An object pronoun may be mistakenly used instead of a subject pronoun. To find out if you are using the right pronoun, you should finish the sentence as shown here.

NOT   She can analyze poems better than **me.**

Correct: She can analyze poems better than **I** [can analyze poems].

NOT   Lilly is not as good a piano player as **him.**

Correct: Lilly is not as good a piano player as **he** [is].

Hint: Sometimes an object pronoun is required in a *than* or *as* comparison. But errors rarely occur in this case because the subject pronoun sounds so unnatural.

NOT   Kay dislikes him more than she dislikes **I.**

Correct: Kay dislikes him more than she dislikes **me.**

REVIEWING PRONOUNS IN COMPARISONS

What causes pronoun problems in comparisons?

_____

_____

How can you test whether to use a subject pronoun or an object pronoun in a than *or* as *comparison?*

_____

_____

◆ *Practice 10* **Identifying** Underline the correct pronoun in each of the following comparisons.

1. Mark is much neater than (I, me).
2. Cindy, the head majorette at our high school, can twirl a baton as well as (we, us).
3. Simone is not as talented an artist as (him, he).
4. Those other puppies are much fatter than (they, them).
5. Tony is just as happy as (she, her).

◆ *Practice 11* **Completing** Fill in each blank in the following sentences with an appropriate pronoun for comparison.

1. After he appeared in *Star Wars*, Harrison Ford became a bigger star than _____.
2. Joey can throw a ball as far as _____.
3. My friends managed to stay longer in the haunted house than _____ did.
4. He makes you just as mad as he makes _____.
5. Julia, whose parents are well-known artists, is a more talented painter than _____.

◆ *Practice 12* **Writing Your Own** Write a sentence of your own using each of the following pronouns in *than* or *as* comparisons.

1. I _____
2. she _____
3. they _____
4. we _____
5. he _____

DEMONSTRATIVE PRONOUNS

There are four demonstrative pronouns: *this, that, these,* and *those.* **Demonstrative pronouns** point to specific people or objects. Use *this* and *these* to refer to items that are near and *that* and *those* to refer to items farther away. Look at the following examples.

Demonstrative (near):	**This** is my room.
Demonstrative (near):	**These** are yesterday's notes.

Demonstrative (farther):   **That** is the town hall.

Demonstrative (farther):   **Those** are the cheerleaders for the other team.

Sometimes demonstrative pronouns are not used correctly.

	Incorrect	Correct
NOT	this here, that there	this, that
NOT	these here, these ones	these
NOT	them, those there, those ones	those

NOT   **Them** are the clothes she bought.

Correct: **Those** are the clothes she bought.

NOT   I'd like to have **these here** books.

Correct: I'd like to have **these** books.

NOT   I found **those ones** in the attic.

Correct: I found **those** in the attic.

NOT   **Those there** are the ones I like.

Correct: **Those** are the ones I like.

When demonstrative pronouns are used with nouns, they become adjectives.

Pronoun: **That** is mine.

Adjective: **That computer** is hers.

Pronoun: **Those** are actions you may regret.

Adjective: You may regret **those actions.**

The problems that occur with demonstrative pronouns can also occur when these pronouns act as adjectives.

NOT   Please give me **that there** paper.

Correct: Please give me **that** paper.

REVIEWING DEMONSTRATIVE PRONOUNS

Name the four demonstrative pronouns.

_____

Give two examples of errors with demonstrative pronouns.

_____

_____

♦ *P r a c t i c e 1 3 A* **Identifying** Underline the demonstrative pronoun errors in each of the following sentences.

1. The babies usually play with those there toys.

2. This here test is just too difficult.

3. I believe that there pair of shoes will do nicely for this outfit.

4. These ones should be brought in out of the rain.

5. I can carry this here if you'll take that there.

♦ *P r a c t i c e 1 3 B* **Correcting** Correct the demonstrative pronoun errors in Practice 13A by rewriting the incorrect sentences.

♦ *P r a c t i c e 1 4* **Completing** Fill in each blank in the following sentences with a logical demonstrative pronoun.

1. _____ are the skates he wanted.

2. Would you like _____ curtains for your house?

3. _____ Corvette belongs to my uncle.

4. She baked _____ cookies herself.

5. I want _____ for my bathroom.

♦ *P r a c t i c e 1 5* **Writing Your Own** Write four sentences of your own, using each demonstrative pronoun. Be sure you don't use these pronouns as adjectives in your sentences.

CHAPTER REVIEW

Pronouns: take the place of nouns in a sentence

Subject Pronouns: take the place of the subject (*I, he, she, it, they*)

Object Pronouns: take the place of the object. One of the most frequent errors in pronoun usage is using a subject pronoun instead of an object pronoun (*him, her, me, them*).

Possessive Pronouns: show ownership. Never use an apostrophe with a possessive pronoun (*his, hers, ours, theirs, its, mine, yours*).

Demonstrative Pronouns: point to specific people or objects (*this, that, these, those*)

◆ *Review P r a c t i c e   1* **Writing Your Own** Write a short paragraph about your most treasured object. Why is it your favourite possession?

◆ *Review P r a c t i c e   2* **Editing Through Collaboration** Exchange paragraphs from Review Practice 1 with another student, and do the following:

1. Circle all pronouns.
2. Check that all the subject and object pronouns are used correctly. Also check that possessive pronouns, pronouns used in comparisons, and demonstrative pronouns are used correctly. Put an X through any that are not in the correct form.

Then return the paper to its writer, and use the information in this chapter to correct the pronoun errors in your own paragraph. Record your errors on the Error Log in Appendix 3.

CHAPTER 38

PRONOUN REFERENCE AND POINT OF VIEW

✔ CHECKLIST for Correcting Problems with Pronoun Reference and Point of View

> ✔ Does every pronoun have a clear antecedent?
> ✔ Are pronouns as close as possible to the words they refer to?
> ✔ Do you maintain a single point of view?

Test Yourself

Underline the pronouns in these sentences. Then put an X over any pronouns that are confusing or unclear.

- It says to schedule your own appointments.
- Millie and Tanya were planning to go to Montreal, but her car broke down.
- I created a backup plan because you should always be prepared for the unexpected.
- You know they are covering up evidence of alien beings.

(Answers are in Appendix 8 on the Web site.)

Anytime you use a pronoun, it must clearly refer to a specific word in the sentence. The word it refers to is called its **antecedent.** Two kinds of problems occur with pronoun references: The antecedent may be unclear, or the antecedent may be missing altogether. You should also be careful to stick to the same point of view in your writing. If, for example, you start out talking about "I," you should not shift to "you" in the middle of the sentence.

PRONOUN REFERENCE

Sometimes a sentence is confusing because the reader can't tell what a pronoun is referring to. The confusion may occur because the pronoun's antecedent is unclear or is completely missing.

Unclear Antecedents

In the following examples, the word each pronoun is referring to is unclear.

Unclear:	A bucket and an oar lay in the boat. As Rachel reached for **it,** the boat moved.
	(Was Rachel reaching for *the bucket* or *the oar*? Only Rachel knows for sure.)
Clear:	A bucket and an oar lay in the boat. As Rachel reached for **the bucket,** the boat moved.
Clear:	A bucket and an oar lay in the boat. As Rachel reached for **the oar,** the boat moved.

Unclear:	Michael told Oliver that **he** should change jobs.
	(Does *he* refer to *Michael* or *Oliver*? Only the writer knows.)
Clear:	Michael told Oliver that **Oliver** should change jobs.
Clear:	Talking with Oliver, **Michael** said that **he** should change jobs.

How can you be sure that every pronoun you use has a clear antecedent? First, you can proofread carefully. Probably an even better test, though, is to ask a friend to read what you have written and tell you if your meaning is clear or not.

Missing Antecedents

Every pronoun should have a clear antecedent, the word it refers to. But what happens when there is no antecedent at all? The writer's message is not communicated. Two words in particular should alert you to the possibility of missing antecedents: *it* and *they*.

The following sentences have missing antecedents:

Missing Antecedent:	In a recent political poll, **it** shows that many people consider their votes unimportant.
	(What does *it* refer to? It has no antecedent.)
Clear:	A **recent political poll** shows that many people consider their votes unimportant.

Missing Antecedent:	**They** say that a fool and his money are soon parted.
	(Who is *they*?)
Clear:	**An old saying** states that a fool and his money are soon parted.

REVIEWING PRONOUN REFERENCE

What is an antecedent?

_____

How can you be sure every pronoun you use has a clear antecedent?

_____

_____

What two words warn you that an antecedent may be missing?

_____   _____

◆ *P r a c t i c e   1 A*   **Identifying** Underline the pronouns in each of the following sentences. Then put an X next to any sentences with missing or unclear antecedents.

1. _____ According to recent surveys, it says that more people are walking to work.

2. _____ My red pen should be in my purse, but I can't find it.

3. _____ The sitting room must have its baseboards cleaned.

4. _____ Talking with Katrina and Mindy, I learned that she is moving to Saskatchewan!

5. _____ They say you can catch more flies with honey than with vinegar.

◆ *P r a c t i c e   1 B*   **Correcting** Correct the sentences with pronoun errors in Practice 1A by rewriting them.

◆ *P r a c t i c e   2*   **Completing** Correct the unclear or missing pronoun references in the following sentences by rewriting them. Pronouns that should be corrected are underlined.

1. <u>It</u> says that we are all required to be at the meeting.

2. <u>They</u> always told me to treat people the way I want to be treated.

3. According to Sue and Hannah, <u>she</u> has been accepted into Lakehead University.

4. We have chocolate and vanilla ice cream, but <u>it</u> tastes better.

5. <u>It</u> indicates that we should have turned left at the first light.

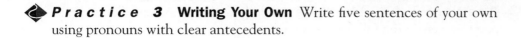

◆ *P r a c t i c e   3* **Writing Your Own** Write five sentences of your own using pronouns with clear antecedents.

SHIFTING POINT OF VIEW

Point of view refers to whether a statement is made in the first person, the second person, or the third person. Each person—or point of view—requires different pronouns. The following chart lists the pronouns for each point of view.

Point of View

First Person:	*I, we*
Second Person:	*you, you*
Third Person:	*he, she, it, one, they*

If you begin writing from one point of view, you should stay in that point of view. Do not shift to another point of view. For example, if you start out writing "I," you should continue with "I" and not shift to "you." Shifting point of view is a very common error in writing assignments.

Shift:	If **a person** doesn't study, **you** will not do well in school.
Correct:	If **a person** doesn't study, **he or she** will not do well in school.
Shift:	I changed jobs because **you** have more opportunities here.
Correct:	I changed jobs because **I** have more opportunities here.

REVIEWING POINT OF VIEW

What is point of view?

_____

_____

What does it mean to shift point of view?

_____

◆ *P r a c t i c e   4 A*   **Identifying** Underline the pronouns that shift in point of view in the following sentences.

1. If you don't eat a good diet, they may find their health suffering.

2. One can always find unique merchandise at the more exclusive stores, but you have to be willing to pay the price.

3. I hinted that I didn't want to take part in the play, but you never know if you've gotten the message across.

4. I see a couple of concerts a year because everyone needs a little culture in his or her life.

5. I've already started writing my research paper because you should never wait until the last minute.

◆ *P r a c t i c e   4 B*   **Correcting** Correct the point-of-view errors in Practice 4A by rewriting the incorrect sentences.

◆ *P r a c t i c e   5*   **Completing** Complete the following sentences with pronouns that stay in the same point of view.

1. I decided to pack lightly and carry my luggage on board the airplane, so _____ know my luggage will arrive when I do.

2. I should taste these dishes since _____ never know if I'm going to like them until I try them.

3. A person is expected to follow the rules of the road; otherwise, _____ may cause an accident.

4. I always wear a smile on my face since _____ never know who might be around.

5. One should pay attention; then _____ might not feel so confused.

◆ *P r a c t i c e   6*   **Writing Your Own** Write a sentence of your own for each of the following pronouns. Be sure the pronouns have clear antecedents and do not shift point of view.

1. they _____

2. you _____

3. I _____

4. it _____

5. we _____

CHAPTER REVIEW

Antecedent: the word that the pronoun refers to in the sentence.

Unclear Antecedent: the word each pronoun is referring to is unclear.

Missing Antecedent: If there is no word for the pronoun to refer to, then the meaning of the sentence will be unclear.

Point of View: refers to whether a statement is in first person (*I, we*), second person (*you*), or third person (*he, she, it, one, they*) point of view. Keep point of view consistent throughout your writing.

◆ *Review P r a c t i c e 1* **Writing Your Own** Write a paragraph about a new experience you have had. Include at least six different pronouns.

◆ *Review P r a c t i c e 2* **Editing Through Collaboration** Exchange paragraphs from Review Practice 1 with another student, and then do the following:

1. Underline all pronouns.

2. Draw arrows to the words they modify.

3. Put an X through any pronouns that do not refer to a clear antecedent or that shift point of view.

Then return the paper to its writer, and use the information in this chapter to correct any pronoun reference and point-of-view errors in your own paragraph. Record your errors on the Error Log in Appendix 3.

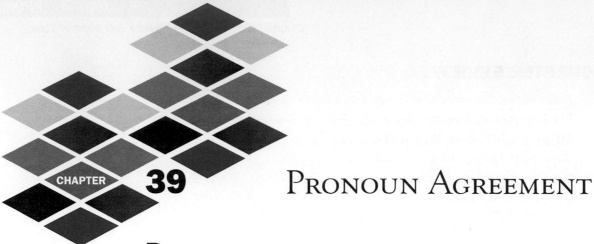

CHAPTER 39

PRONOUN AGREEMENT

☑ CHECKLIST for Correcting Pronoun Agreement Problems

> ✔ Do all pronouns and their antecedents agree in number (singular or plural)?
> ✔ Do any pronouns that refer to indefinite pronouns agree in number?
> ✔ Are any pronouns used in a sexist way?

Test Yourself

Underline the pronoun in each sentence, and draw an arrow to its antecedent. Put an X over any pronouns that do not agree with their antecedents.

- Somebody left his lights on in his car.
- A judge must put aside her bias.
- Each of the children needs their permission slip signed.
- None of the fans could keep their voices quiet.
- A motorcyclist must take care of her gear.

(Answers are in Appendix 8 on the Web site.)

As you learned in Chapter 36, subjects and verbs must agree for clear communication. If the subject is singular, the verb must be singular; if the subject is plural, the verb must be plural. The same holds true for pronouns and the words they refer to—their *antecedents*. They must agree in number—both singular or both plural. Usually, pronoun agreement is not a problem, as these sentences show:

Singular: **Dr. Wu** told **his** patient to stop smoking.

Plural: **Carlos** and **Gina** took **their** children to Canada's Wonderland.

INDEFINITE PRONOUNS

Pronoun agreement may become a problem with indefinite pronouns. Indefinite pronouns that are always singular give writers the most trouble.

NOT	**One** of the students finished **their** test early. (How many students finished early? Only one, so use a singular pronoun.)
Correct:	**One** of the students finished **her** test early.
Correct:	**One** of the students finished **his** test early.

NOT	**Somebody** just drove **their** new car into a ditch. (How many people just drove a car into a ditch? One person, so use a singular pronoun.)
Correct:	**Somebody** just drove **her** new car into a ditch.
Correct:	**Somebody** just drove **his** new car into a ditch.

Here is a list of indefinite pronouns that are always singular.

Singular Indefinite Pronouns

another	*either*	*much*	*one*
anybody	*everybody*	*other*	*neither*
anyone	*everyone*	*nobody*	*somebody*
anything	*everything*	*no one*	*someone*
each	*little*	*nothing*	*something*

 Hint: A few indefinite pronouns can be either singular or plural, depending on their meaning in the sentence. These pronouns are *any*, *all*, *more*, *most*, *none*, and *some*.

Singular:	**Some** of the money was left over, so we gave **it** to charity.
Plural:	**Some** of the donations were left over, so we gave **them** to charity.

In the first sentence, *money* is singular, so the singular pronoun *it* is used. In the second sentence, *donations* is plural, so the plural pronoun *them* is used.

> REVIEWING INDEFINITE PRONOUNS
>
> *Why should a pronoun agree with the word it refers to?*
>
> _____
>
> *Name five indefinite pronouns that are always singular.*
>
> _____   _____   _____   _____   _____

◆ ***Practice 1*** **Identifying** Underline the correct pronoun from the choices in parentheses, and be prepared to explain your choices.

1. All of the infants had (his or her, their) footprints and handprints recorded at the hospital.
2. None of the cars needs (its, their) tires changed.
3. Anyone can get (his or her, their) high school diploma.
4. Before anybody can join the club, (he or she, they) must fill out an enrollment form.
5. The farmers and the farmworkers want (his or her, their) work hours reduced.

◆ ***Practice 2*** **Completing** Fill in each blank in the following sentences with a pronoun that agrees with its antecedent.

1. Fabiola and Fabian asked _____ questions at the same time.
2. Everyone should listen more closely to _____ teacher.
3. Matt lost _____ backpack at the park.
4. Anyone who could do a thing like that should have _____ head examined.
5. Something in the car leaked all _____ fluids onto the driveway.

◆ ***Practice 3*** **Writing Your Own** Write a sentence of your own for each of the following pronouns.

1. none _____
2. other _____
3. no one _____
4. everything _____
5. someone _____

AVOIDING SEXISM

In the first section of this chapter, you learned that you should use singular pronouns to refer to singular indefinite pronouns. For example, the indefinite pronoun *someone* requires a singular pronoun, *his* or *her*, not the plural *their*. But what if you don't know whether the person referred to is male or female? Then you have a choice: (1) you can say "he or she" or "his or her"; (2) you can make the sentence plural; or (3) you can rewrite the sentence to avoid the problem altogether. What you should not do is ignore half the population by referring to all humans as males.

NOT	If **anyone** wants to go, **they** are welcome to do so.
NOT	If **anyone** wants to go, **he** is welcome to do so.
Correct:	If **anyone** wants to go, **he or she** is welcome to do so.
Correct:	**People** who want to go are welcome to do so.

NOT	**Everyone** remembered to bring **their** lunch.
NOT	**Everyone** remembered to bring **his** lunch.
Correct:	**Everyone** remembered to bring **his or her** lunch.
Correct:	**All** the students remembered to bring **their** lunch.

Sexism in writing can also occur in ways other than with indefinite pronouns. We often assume that doctors, lawyers, and bank presidents are men and that nurses, schoolteachers, and secretaries are women. But that is not very accurate.

NOT	Ask a **fireman** if **he** thinks the wiring is safe. (Why automatically assume that the person fighting fires is a male instead of a female?)
Correct:	Ask a **firefighter** if **he or she** thinks the wiring is safe.

NOT	The **mailman** delivered my neighbour's mail to my house by mistake. (Since both men and women deliver mail, the more correct term is *mail carrier.*)
Correct:	The **mail carrier** delivered my neighbour's mail to my house by mistake.

NOT	An **assistant** cannot reveal **her** boss's confidential business. (Why leave the men who are assistants out of this sentence?)
Correct:	An **assistant** cannot reveal **his or her** boss's confidential business.

Correct: **Assistants** cannot reveal **their** bosses' confidential business.

REVIEWING SEXISM IN WRITING

What is sexism in writing?

_____

What are two ways to get around the problem of using male pronouns to refer to both women and men?

_____   _____

Give two other examples of sexism in writing.

_____   _____

◆ **P r a c t i c e   4 A**   **Identifying** Underline the sexist references in the following sentences.

1. The chairperson should keep his board informed of new developments.

2. A nurse gives her time and patience freely.

3. Each person is responsible for make-up work if they miss an assignment.

4. Everybody must bring food if they plan to eat.

5. A good sailor knows his knots.

◆ **P r a c t i c e   4 B**   **Correcting** Correct the sexist pronouns in Practice 4A by rewriting the incorrect sentences.

◆ **P r a c t i c e   5**   **Completing** Fill in each blank in the following sentences with an appropriate pronoun.

1. A technician might become frustrated with _____ job.

2. A hairdresser who attracts celebrity customers can name _____ price.

3. An accountant needs help with _____ accounts.

4. Somebody wrote _____ phone number on the washroom wall.

5. Another child has forgotten _____ lunch.

◆ *P r a c t i c e 6* **Writing Your Own** Write a sentence of your own for each of the following antecedents. Include at least one pronoun in each sentence.

1. doctor _____

2. politician _____

3. police officer _____

4. spokesperson _____

5. astronaut _____

CHAPTER REVIEW

Pronoun Agreement: Pronouns must agree in number. The pronouns must be consistently singular or plural throughout the sentence.

Avoiding Sexism: Be aware of leaving out half the population by assuming the pronoun is only masculine or feminine. Don't forget that men can be nurses and women can be firefighters.

◆ *R e v i e w P r a c t i c e 1* **Writing Your Own** Write a paragraph describing your favourite type of music. Why is it your favourite?

◆ *R e v i e w P r a c t i c e 2* **Editing Through Collaboration** Exchange paragraphs from Review Practice 1 with another student, and then do the following:

1. Underline any pronouns.

2. Circle any pronouns that do not agree with the words they refer to.

Then return the paper to its writer, and use the information in this chapter to correct any pronoun agreement errors in your own paragraph. Record your errors on the Error Log in Appendix 3.

CHAPTER 40

ADJECTIVES

✔ CHECKLIST for Using Adjectives Correctly

> ✔ Are all adjectives that show comparison used correctly?
> ✔ Are the forms of *good* and *bad* used correctly?

Test Yourself

Underline the adjectives in the following sentences. Then put an X over the adjectives that are used incorrectly.

- The kites were very colourful.
- She has the worstest hair colour that I have ever seen.
- We were more busier this week than last week.
- He is the oldest of the two brothers.
- The Ford Mustang is more better than the Nissan Sentra.

(Answers are in Appendix 8 on the Web site.)

Adjectives are modifiers. They help us communicate more clearly (I have a *green* car; I want a *red* one) and vividly (the movie was *funny* and *romantic*). Without adjectives, our language would be drab and boring.

USING ADJECTIVES

Adjectives are words that modify—or describe—nouns or pronouns. Adjectives often tell how something or someone looks: *dark, light, tall, short, large, small.* Most adjectives come before the words they modify, but with linking verbs (such as *is, are, look, become,* and *feel*), adjectives follow the words they modify.

Adjectives Before a Noun:	We felt the **cold, icy** snow.
Adjectives After a Linking Verb:	The snow was **cold** and **icy.**

REVIEWING ADJECTIVES

What are adjectives?

_____

Where can you find adjectives in a sentence?

_____

◆ *P r a c t i c e* **1** **Identifying** In the following sentences, underline the adjectives, and circle the words they modify.

1. Michael left a shiny red apple on the wooden desk on Monday morning.
2. Mrs. Johnson gave the two-year-old boy a piece of hard candy.
3. Our family doctor wants us to come in for our annual checkups.
4. I read a great book by Rohinton Mistry last week.
5. Grandma's beautiful garden is a quiet place for me to read, draw, or take a quick nap.

◆ *P r a c t i c e* **2** **Completing** Fill in each blank in the following sentences with logical adjectives.

During my (1) _____ year of high school, I asked the head cheerleader to go to the prom with me. I was (2) _____ when she agreed to be my date, and I really wanted to impress her. I rented an expensive tuxedo, bought a (3) _____ corsage for her to wear on her wrist, and made sure to pick her up on time. The (4) _____ price was worth it because when we arrived at the dance, all of my buddies patted me on the back and said, "You two look (5) _____ together!"

◆ *P r a c t i c e* **3** **Writing Your Own** Write a sentence of your own for each of the following adjectives.

1. curious _____

2. durable _____

3. thirteen _____

4. helpful _____

5. short-tempered _____

COMPARING WITH ADJECTIVES

Most adjectives have three forms: a **basic** form, a **comparative** form (used to compare two items or indicate a greater degree), and a **superlative** form (used to compare three or more items or indicate the greatest degree).

For positive comparisons, adjectives form the comparative and superlative in two different ways.

1. For one-syllable adjectives and some two-syllable adjectives, use *-er* to compare two items and *-est* to compare three or more items.

Basic	Comparative (used to compare two items)	Superlative (used to compare three or more items)
bold	bolder	boldest
warm	warmer	warmest
foggy	foggier	foggiest
cozy	cozier	coziest

2. For some two-syllable adjectives and all longer adjectives, use *more* to compare two items and *most* to compare three or more items.

Basic	Comparative (used to compare two items)	Superlative (used to compare three or more items)
friendly	more friendly	most friendly
peaceful	more peaceful	most peaceful
wonderful	more wonderful	most wonderful
appropriate	more appropriate	most appropriate

For negative comparisons, use *less* to compare two items and *least* to compare three or more items.

Basic	Comparative (used to compare two items)	Superlative (used to compare three or more items)
loud	less loud	least loud
funny	less funny	least funny

popular   less popular   least popular

Hint: Some adjectives are not usually compared. For example, one person cannot be "more dead" than another. Here are some more examples.

broken	*final*	*square*	*unique*
empty	*impossible*	*supreme*	
equal	*singular*	*unanimous*	

REVIEWING ADJECTIVE FORMS

When do you use the comparative form of an adjective?

_____

When do you use the superlative form of an adjective?

_____

How do one-syllable and some two-syllable adjectives form the comparative and superlative in positive comparisons?

_____

How do some two-syllable adjectives and all longer adjectives form the comparative and superlative in positive comparisons?

_____

How do you form negative comparisons?

_____

◆ *P r a c t i c e 4* **Identifying** Underline the adjectives, and note whether they are basic (B), comparative (C), or superlative (S).

1. _____ The most logical decision would be to appoint Sam to the position.

2. _____ Today the students showed how dedicated they can be.

3. _____ Mila was happier about the engagement than her father was.

4. _____ The strongest students always score the highest on the exam.

5. _____ The food Nora and Richard ate on vacation was less healthy than what they eat at home.

> ◆ *P r a c t i c e 5* **Completing** Fill in each blank in the following para-
> graph with the correct basic, comparative, or superlative form of the adjec-
> tive in parentheses.

One summer afternoon, I was hiking high in the mountains when
the sky above me grew suddenly (1) _____ (dark) than I
have ever seen it. It looked like rain was going to fall soon, and I happened to be in an (2) _____ (unsheltered) place on the
mountain. I looked around to find the (3) _____ (suitable)
tree to sit under, but there weren't any that would protect me. Even
the (4) _____ (thick) tree was very puny and wouldn't
keep the rain off of my head. Quickly, I realized I had no option but
to run (5) _____ (fast) than the rain to find shelter farther
down the hill.

> ◆ *P r a c t i c e 6* **Writing Your Own** Write a sentence of your own for
> each of the following adjectives.

1. a superlative form of *pretty* _____

2. the basic form of *sensible* _____

3. a comparative form of *talented* _____

4. a superlative form of *disgusting* _____

5. a comparative form of *tall* _____

COMMON ADJECTIVE ERRORS

Two types of problems occur with adjectives used in comparisons.

1. Instead of using one method for forming the comparative or superlative, both are used. That is, both *-er* and *more* or *less* are used to
   compare two items or both *-est* and *most* or *least* are used to compare
   three or more items.

   NOT   My youngest son is **more taller** than his brothers.
   Correct: My youngest son is **taller** than his brothers.

   NOT   This is the **most happiest** day of my life.
   Correct: This is the **happiest** day of my life.

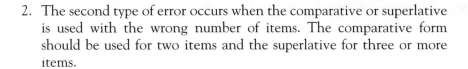

2. The second type of error occurs when the comparative or superlative is used with the wrong number of items. The comparative form should be used for two items and the superlative for three or more items.

NOT   Marina is the **smartest** of the two sisters.

Correct: Marina is the **smarter** of the two sisters.

NOT   History is the **harder** of my four classes this semester.

Correct: History is the **hardest** of my four classes this semester.

REVIEWING COMMON ADJECTIVE ERRORS

Can you ever use -er + more or -est + most?

_____

When do you use the comparative form of an adjective?

_____

When do you use the superlative form of an adjective?

_____

◆ *P r a c t i c e 7 A*   **Identifying** Underline the adjectives in the following sentences that are used incorrectly in comparisons. Mark sentences that are correct C.

1. _____ The most rudest customers are usually the ones who are trying to get something for free.

2. _____ Bob and Chad are both good-looking, but Bob is smartest.

3. _____ This class would be more fun if we could meet outside sometimes.

4. _____ The most rainiest day of the year was April 15.

5. _____ The bigger house in town is at 1859 King Street.

◆ *P r a c t i c e 7 B*   **Correcting** Correct the adjective errors in Practice 7A by rewriting the incorrect sentences.

◆ *P r a c t i c e 8*   **Completing** Choose the correct adjective forms in the following paragraph to complete the sentences.

Giving the dog a bath is the (1) _____ (more difficult, most difficult) chore in our house, and somehow it always seems to be my job. My sister Stephanie and I share most of the chores, but I am definitely (2) _____ (more responsible, most responsible) than she is. Usually, I do my chores without complaining, but bathing the dog is just unfair. We have an Australian sheepdog, and he is the (3) _____ (clumsiest, most clumsiest) thing alive. He seems to find every puddle of mud and sticky stuff to step in, and it quickly gets all over his fur. Unfortunately, though, he has a great dislike for baths, so the struggle to wash him is (4) _____ (trickiest, trickier) than it should be. And Stephanie is no help at all. While I'm fighting to hose him down, she just stands back and laughs at me, which makes me even (5) _____ (madder, more madder).

◆ *P r a c t i c e 9*   **Writing Your Own** Write a sentence of your own for each of the following adjectives.

1. strongest _____

2. more truthful _____

3. most gracious _____

4. larger _____

5. most frightening _____

USING *GOOD* AND *BAD* CORRECTLY

The adjectives *good* and *bad* are irregular. They do not form the comparative and superlative like most other adjectives. Here are the correct forms for these two irregular adjectives:

Basic	Comparative (used to compare two items)	Superlative (used to compare three or more items)
good	better	best
bad	worse	worst

Problems occur with *good* and *bad* when writers don't know how to form their comparative and superlative forms.

NOT   more better, more worse, worser, most best, most worst, bestest, worstest

Correct: better, worse, best, worst

These errors appear in sentences in the following ways:

NOT   That is the **worstest** food I've ever tasted.

Correct: That is the **worst** food I've ever tasted.

NOT   Air pollution is getting **more worse** every year.

Correct: Air pollution is getting **worse** every year.

REVIEWING *Good* AND *Bad*

What are the three forms of good?

_____

What are the three forms of bad?

_____

◆ *P r a c t i c e   1 0 A*   **Identifying** In the following sentences, underline the forms of *good* and *bad* used correctly, and circle the forms of *good* and *bad* used incorrectly.

1. Both options are good, but getting a raise is more better than getting time off from work.

2. Giving that presentation in my psychology class was the worstest experience of my college career.

3. Giving your time to a charity is more good than just giving your money.

4. Sean wanted to go to the University of Western Ontario, but his grades were worse than he thought.

5. Doing the laundry is more worse than getting a root canal.

◆ *P r a c t i c e   1 0 B*   **Correcting** Correct the errors with *good* and *bad* in Practice 10A by rewriting the incorrect sentences.

◆ *P r a c t i c e   1 1*   **Completing** Using the correct forms of *good* or *bad*, complete the following paragraph.

The (1) _____ day of my life was July 8, 2001. I will always remember it (2) _____ than any other. I had just bought a brand new convertible and was taking it to the beach for a couple of days of fun in the sun. Fortunately, my (3) _____ friend, Tara, was with me, because just 60 kilometres outside town, the engine of my dream car overheated! What was (4) _____ was neither of us had a cell phone, and the closest pay phone was more than three kilometres away. We finally found a phone and called another friend, and then we waited and waited for a tow truck. After spending more than $3,000 on repairs, I found that my dream car had become my (5) _____ nightmare.

◆ *P r a c t i c e   1 2*   **Writing Your Own** Write a sentence of your own for each of the following forms of *good* and *bad*.

1. best _____

2. bad _____

3. worse _____

4. better _____

5. worst _____

CHAPTER REVIEW

Adjective: words that modify or describe the noun or pronoun

Basic Adjective: the adjective in its original form

Comparative Adjective: used to compare two items or indicate a greater degree

Superlative Adjective: used to compare three or more items or indicate the greatest degree

◆ *R e v i e w   P r a c t i c e   1*   **Writing Your Own** Write a paragraph describing the first pet you ever owned. What kind of animal was it? What did it look like? How did it act? What did you name it, and why did you choose that name?

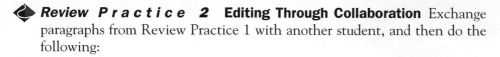 *Review P r a c t i c e 2* **Editing Through Collaboration** Exchange paragraphs from Review Practice 1 with another student, and then do the following:

1. Underline all the adjectives.

2. Circle those that are not in the correct form.

Then return the paper to its writer, and use the information in this chapter to correct any adjective errors in your own paragraph. Record your errors in the Error Log in Appendix 3.

CHAPTER 41

ADVERCS

(image contains "ADVERBS")

✅ CHECKLIST for Using Adverbs

> ✔ Are all adverbs that show comparison used correctly?
> ✔ Are *good/well* and *bad/badly* used correctly?

Test Yourself

Underline the adverbs in the following sentences. Then put an X over the adverbs that are used incorrectly.

- The pants fit me too loose, so I returned them to the store.
- Tori wasn't never so happy as after she won the lottery.
- When Madeline returned from Paris, she said she'd had a real good time.
- We happily made more ice cream when our first supply ran out.
- I wanted so bad to win the race, but I couldn't catch up.

(Answers are in Appendix 8 on the Web site.)

Like adjectives, adverbs help us communicate more clearly (she talked *slowly*) and more vividly (he sang *beautifully*). They make their sentences more interesting.

USING ADVERBS

Adverbs modify verbs, adjectives, and other adverbs. They answer the questions *How? When? Where? How often?* and *To what extent?* Look at the following examples.

How:	My grandfather walked **slowly** up the stairs.
When:	Classes **always** begin after Labour Day.
Where:	Music lessons are held **here**.

How often: I shop at The Bay **regularly.**

To what extent: The airport is **extremely** busy during the holidays.

Some words are always adverbs, including *here, there, not, never, now, again, almost, often,* and *well.*

Other adverbs are formed by adding *-ly* to an adjective:

Adjective	Adverb
dim	dimly
soft	softly
careless	carelessly

Hint: Not all words that end in *-ly* are adverbs. Some, such as *friendly, early, lonely, chilly,* and *lively,* are adjectives.

REVIEWING ADVERBS

What are adverbs?

_____

What five questions do adverbs answer?

_____ _____ _____ _____ _____

List four words that are always adverbs.

_____ _____ _____ _____

How do many adverbs end?

_____

◆ *P r a c t i c e 1* **Identifying** In the following sentences, underline the adverbs, and circle the words they modify.

1. We drove quickly to Toronto so that we wouldn't miss the concert.

2. I never saw that girl again.

3. Alex suddenly changed his mind and agreed to host the party.

4. Stephen successfully completed the nursing program.

5. When the children became impatient during the drive, we continually told them, "We're almost there."

◆ *P r a c t i c e 2*   **Completing** Fill in each blank in the following sentences with an adverb that makes sense.

Sam's mom (1) _____ drove him to the airport, where he caught a plane to Winnipeg, Manitoba. He was going to visit his grandparents (2) _____. Sam was only 10 years old, but he had (3) _____ flown alone before. When the plane landed in Winnipeg, Sam (4) _____ grabbed his carry-on luggage and (5) _____ ran to meet "Papa" and "Nonny."

◆ *P r a c t i c e 3*   **Writing Your Own** Write a sentence of your own for each of the following adverbs.

1. now _____

2. briskly _____

3. innocently _____

4. lazily _____

5. often _____

COMPARING WITH ADVERBS

Like adjectives, most adverbs have three forms: a **basic** form, a **comparative** form (used to compare two items), and a **superlative** form (used to compare three or more items).

For positive comparisons, adverbs form the comparative and superlative forms in two different ways.

1. For one-syllable adverbs, use *-er* to compare two items and *-est* to compare three or more items.

Basic	Comparative (used to compare two items)	Superlative (used to compare three or more items)
soon	sooner	soonest
fast	faster	fastest

2. For adverbs of two or more syllables, use *more* to compare two items and *most* to compare three or more items.

Basic	Comparative (used to compare two items)	Superlative (used to compare three or more items)
strangely	more strangely	most strangely
carefully	more carefully	most carefully
happily	more happily	most happily

For negative comparisons, adverbs, like adjectives, use *less* to compare two items and *least* to compare three or more items.

Basic	Comparative (used to compare two items)	Superlative (used to compare three or more items)
close	less close	least close
quickly	less quickly	least quickly
creatively	less creatively	least creatively

Hint: Like adjectives, certain adverbs are not usually compared. Something cannot last "more eternally" or work "more invisibly." The following adverbs cannot logically be compared.

endlessly	*eternally*	*infinitely*
equally	*impossibly*	*invisibly*

REVIEWING ADVERB FORMS

When do you use the comparative form of an adverb?

_____

When do you use the superlative form of an adverb?

_____

How do one-syllable adverbs form the comparative and superlative in positive comparisons?

_____

How do adverbs of two or more syllables form the comparative and superlative in positive comparisons?

_____

How do you form negative comparisons with adverbs?

_____

◆ *P r a c t i c e*   **4**   **Identifying** Underline the adverbs, and note whether they are basic (B), comparative (C), or superlative (S).

1. _____ When Jack joined the gym, he began to lose weight more quickly.

2. _____ The sun shone more brightly after the rain stopped.

3. _____ London is the most rapidly growing city in southern Ontario.

4. _____ People enroll less often in the morning classes than the afternoon classes.

5. _____ Priscilla rudely interrupted her mother and walked out of the room.

◆ *P r a c t i c e*   **5**   **Completing** Fill in each blank in the following paragraph with the correct comparative or superlative form of the adverb in parentheses.

At one time, *Owl* was the (1) _____ (widely) read children's magazine. It had (2) _____ (simply) written stories for the younger readers and (3) _____ (intellectually) challenging games for the older kids than any other magazine. Because of the wide variety of material in each issue, *Owl* was the (4) _____ (highly) acclaimed publication for Canadian youth. Now, though, *Owl* has lots of competition, and big publishers are creating magazines for young readers (5) _____ (often) than they used to.

◆ *P r a c t i c e 6* **Writing Your Own** Write a sentence of your own for each of the following adverbs.

1. a superlative form of *readily* _____

2. a comparative form of *eagerly* _____

3. the basic form of *unhappily* _____

4. a superlative form of *angrily* _____

5. a comparative form of *honestly* _____

ADJECTIVE OR ADVERB?

One of the most common errors with modifiers is using an adjective when an adverb is called for. Keep in mind that adjectives modify nouns and pronouns, whereas adverbs modify verbs, adjectives, and other adverbs. Adverbs *do not* modify nouns or pronouns. Here are some examples.

NOT   She spoke too **slow.** [adjective]

Correct: She spoke too **slowly.** [adverb]

NOT   We were **real** sorry about the accident. [adjective]

Correct: We were **really** sorry about the accident. [adverb]

REVIEWING THE DIFFERENCE
BETWEEN ADJECTIVES AND ADVERBS

How do you know whether to use an adjective or an adverb in a sentence?

_____

_____

Give an example of an adverb in a sentence.

_____

Give an example of an adjective in a sentence.

_____

◆ *P r a c t i c e   7 A*   **Identifying** Underline the adverbs in the following sentences. Write C next to the sentences that are correct.

1. _____ Mike Myers' character laughed loud in the movie *Austin Powers*.

2. _____ I rocked the baby gently to put her to sleep.

3. _____ Mr. Simpson talked too quick, and I didn't understand the assignment.

4. _____ Before we left the zoo, we checked the map careful to make sure we'd seen everything.

5. _____ Cook the beans slow so they don't burn.

◆ *P r a c t i c e   7 B*   **Correcting** Correct the adverb errors in Practice 7A by rewriting the incorrect sentences.

◆ *P r a c t i c e   8*   **Completing** Choose the correct adverb to complete the sentences in the following paragraph.

Zack and I went to Canada's Wonderland last weekend and had a (1) _____ (real, really) good time. When we pulled into the parking lot, we could hear the roller coasters zooming (2) _____ (loudly, loud) overhead, and we could smell the yummy junk food. After we got through the gates, we ran (3) _____ (quick, quickly) to the line for the Ghoster Coaster. The line moved along (4) _____ (smoothly, smooth), and we were on the ride within 20 minutes. When the ride was over, we (5) _____ (glad, gladly) got in line to go on it again.

◆ *P r a c t i c e   9*   **Writing Your Own** Write a sentence of your own for each of the following adverbs.

1. specifically _____

2. tightly _____

3. greatly _____

4. sadly _____

5. coldly _____

DOUBLE NEGATIVES

Another problem that involves adverbs is the **double negative**—using two negative words in one clause. Examples of negative words include *no, not, never, none, nothing, neither, nowhere, nobody, barely,* and *hardly.* A double negative creates the opposite meaning of what is intended.

Double Negative: She **never** had **no** time to rest.

The actual meaning of these double negatives is "She did have time to rest."

Correction: She had **no** time to rest.

Double Negative: My brother does **not** give me **nothing.**

The actual meaning of these double negatives is "My brother does give me something."

Correction: My brother does **not** give me **anything.**

Double negatives often occur with contractions.

Double Negative: There **aren't hardly** any apples left.

The actual meaning of these double negatives is "There are plenty of apples left."

Correction: There are **hardly** any apples left.

Using two negatives is confusing and grammatically wrong. Be on the lookout for negative words, and use only one per clause.

REVIEWING DOUBLE NEGATIVES

What is a double negative?

_____

List five negative words.

_____   _____   _____   _____   _____

Why should you avoid double negatives?

_____

◆ *P r a c t i c e 1 0 A* **Identifying** Mark each of the following sentences either correct (C) or incorrect (X).

1. _____ He didn't never study, but he always passed the tests.

2. _____ Tabitha wasn't hardly four years old when her mother passed away.

3. _____ Nobody showed up for none of the practices last week.

4. _____ Hawkins doesn't really know what he wants to do.

5. _____ I wouldn't go nowhere with him.

◆ *P r a c t i c e 1 0 B* **Correcting** Correct the double negatives in Practice 10A by rewriting the incorrect sentences.

◆ *P r a c t i c e 1 1* **Completing** Choose the correct negative modifiers to complete the following paragraph.

Last summer, I went to the beach and (1) _____ (was hardly, wasn't hardly) prepared for the sunshiny weather. I didn't buy (2) _____ (any, no) sunscreen before I left because I had a decent tan already. To my surprise, I started to burn after only three hours on the beach, and there (3) _____ (wasn't nothing, wasn't anything) I could do about it. I thought the burning feeling wouldn't (4) _____ (ever, never) go away. And no matter what lotions and ointments I put on, I couldn't get (5) _____ (no, any) relief. Next time, I'll remember to take along an umbrella.

◆ *P r a c t i c e 1 2* **Writing Your Own** Write a sentence of your own for each of the following negative adverbs.

1. never _____

2. not _____

3. barely _____

4. nobody _____

5. nowhere _____

USING *GOOD/WELL* AND *BAD/BADLY* CORRECTLY

The pairs *good/well* and *bad/badly* are so frequently misused that they deserve special attention.

Good is an adjective; *well* is an adverb.
Use *good* with a noun (n) or after a linking verb (lv).

                            n

Adjective: Brian is a **good** boy.

                    lv

Adjective: She looks **good.**

Use *well* for someone's health or after an action verb (av).

               lv

Adverb: He is **well** again. [health]

                   av

Adverb: The baby sleeps **well** at night.

Bad is an adjective; *badly* is an adverb.
Use *bad* with a noun (n) or after a linking verb (lv). Always use *bad* after *feel* if you're talking about emotions.

                       n

Adjective: He seems like a **bad** person.

                 lv

Adjective: I feel **bad** that I got a ticket.

Use *badly* with an adjective (adj) or after an action verb (av).

                         adj

Adverb: The house was **badly** burned.

               av

Adverb: He swims **badly.**

REVIEWING *Good/Well* AND *Bad/Badly*

When should you use the adjective good?

_____

When should you use the adverb well?

_____

> *When should you use the adjective* bad?
>
> _____
>
> *When should you use the adverb* badly?
>
> _____

◆ **P r a c t i c e   1 3 A   Identifying** Label each of the following sentences either correct (C) or incorrect (X).

1. _____ I want to do good in this job so my boss will like me.

2. _____ My favourite team is playing bad this week.

3. _____ Vilma sings well and is pursuing a career in opera.

4. _____ Rachel said she felt bad about Mr. Brown's accident.

5. _____ I wanted so bad to go diving, but I couldn't.

◆ **P r a c t i c e   1 3 B   Correcting** Correct the adverb errors in Practice 13A by rewriting the incorrect sentences.

◆ **P r a c t i c e   1 4   Completing** Choose the correct modifiers to complete the following paragraph.

When Scott was in high school, there was only one thing he could do really (1) _____ (good, well). He struggled with academics, he played most sports very (2) _____ (bad, badly), and he was never popular with the girls. But his one strength was music. From the moment he picked up his first guitar, he was always (3) _____ (good, well) at creating songs. Fortunately, his natural talent earned him several (4) _____ (good, well) scholarship offers from big-name universities. Unfortunately, his (5) _____ (bad, badly) study habits in high school made university more difficult for him, but he survived.

◆ *P r a c t i c e   1 5* **Writing Your Own** Write a sentence of your own for each of the following modifiers.

1. well _____

2. badly _____

3. good _____

4. bad _____

5. well _____

CHAPTER REVIEW

Adverbs: words that modify verbs, adjectives and other adverbs. They answer the questions *How? When? Where? How often?* and *To what extent?*

Comparative Adverb: used to compare two items

Superlative Adverb: used to compare three or more items

◆ *Review P r a c t i c e   1* **Writing Your Own** If you could prepare anything you wanted for dinner tonight, what would you make? Write a paragraph about this meal. How would you prepare it? How would you serve it? How many courses would it consist of?

◆ *Review P r a c t i c e   2* **Editing Through Collaboration** Exchange paragraphs from Review Practice 1 with another student, and then do the following:

1. Underline all the adverbs.

2. Circle those that are not in the correct form.

3. Put an X above any double negatives.

Then return the paper to its writer, and use the information in this chapter to correct any adverb errors in your own paragraph. Record your errors on the Error Log in Appendix 3.

42

MODIFIER ERRORS

✅ CHECKLIST for Identifying and Correcting Modifier Problems

> ✔ Are modifiers as close as possible to the words they modify?
> ✔ Are any sentences confusing because the words that the modifiers refer to are missing?

Test Yourself

Underline the modifier problem in each sentence.

- After studying together, his grades really improved.
- Before doing the laundry, the car needed to be washed.
- To get a good job, the interview must go well.
- The professor told the class he was retiring before he dismissed them.
- I wrote a letter to the newspaper that complained about rising power bills.

(Answers are in Appendix 8 on the Web site.)

As you know, a modifier describes another word or group of words. Sometimes, however, a modifier is too far from the words it refers to (*misplaced modifier*), or the word it refers to is missing altogether (*dangling modifier*). As a result, the sentence is confusing.

MISPLACED MODIFIERS

A modifier should be placed as close as possible to the word or words it modifies, but this does not always happen. A **misplaced modifier** is too far from the word or words it refers to, making the meaning of the sentence unclear. Look at these examples.

Misplaced: The instructor explained why plagiarism is wrong **on Friday.**

(Is plagiarism wrong only on Friday? Probably not. So the modifier *on Friday* needs to be moved closer to the word it actually modifies.)

Correct: The instructor explained **on Friday** why plagiarism is wrong.

Correct: **On Friday** the instructor explained why plagiarism is wrong.

Misplaced: In Ontario, it is illegal to carry liquor in a car **that has been opened.**

(It is the liquor, not the car, that must not have been opened. So the modifier *that has been opened* needs to be moved closer to the word it modifies.)

Correct: In Ontario, it is illegal to carry liquor **that has been opened** in a car.

Certain modifiers that limit meaning are often misplaced, causing problems. Notice how the meaning changes by moving the limiting word *only* in the following sentences:

Only Aunt Emily says that Lilly was a bad cook.
(Aunt Emily says this, but no one else does.)

Aunt Emily **only** says that Lilly was a bad cook.
(Aunt Emily says this, but she doesn't really mean it.)

Aunt Emily says **only** that Lilly was a bad cook.
(Aunt Emily says this but nothing more.)

Aunt Emily says that **only** Lilly was a bad cook.
(Lilly—and no one else—was a bad cook.)

Aunt Emily says that Lilly **only** was a bad cook.
(Aunt Emily says that there were some who were good cooks and Lilly was the only bad one.)

Aunt Emily says that Lilly was **only** a bad cook.
(Lilly was a bad cook, but she wasn't bad at other things.)

Aunt Emily says that Lilly was a bad cook **only.**
(Lilly was a bad cook, but she wasn't bad at other things.)

Here is a list of common limiting words.

almost	*hardly*	*merely*	*only*
even	*just*	*nearly*	*scarcely*

REVIEWING MISPLACED MODIFIERS

What is a misplaced modifier?

_____

How can you correct a misplaced modifier?

_____

◆ *P r a c t i c e   1 A*   **Identifying** Underline the misplaced modifiers in the following sentences.

1. Tina told Tom that to win the lottery she had a great chance.
2. The car leaked all its oil by the time I called a mechanic in the driveway.
3. Brittany went to the mall with Jim wearing her new hat.
4. I sold Luigi my old watch after I bought an expensive new one for $10.
5. We made a pie in the kitchen with lots of blueberries.

◆ *P r a c t i c e   1 B*   **Correcting** Correct the misplaced modifiers in Practice 1A by rewriting the incorrect sentences.

◆ *P r a c t i c e   2*   **Completing** Fill in each blank in the following paragraph with a modifier that makes sense. Include at least two phrases.

Several years ago, Rodger owned a (1) _____ farm in Saskatchewan where he grew corn and wheat. He also had (2) _____ orchards of apples that he (3) _____ harvested every September. His children had (4) _____ the farm. Shortly before Rodger died, he trained his children (5) _____ the family business.

◆ *P r a c t i c e   3*   **Writing Your Own** Write a sentence of your own for each of the following modifiers.

1. before summer _____

2. since the company hired him _____

3. while driving to the store _____

4. after she bought the car _____

5. though no one was there _____

DANGLING MODIFIERS

Modifiers are "dangling" when they have nothing to refer to in a sentence. **Dangling modifiers** (starting with an *-ing* word or with *to*) often appear at the beginning of a sentence. Here is an example.

> **Dangling:** **Reaching the top of the hill,** the view was beautiful.

A modifier usually modifies the words closest to it. So the phrase *Reaching the top of the hill* modifies *view*. But it's not the view that reaches the top of the hill. In fact, there is no logical word in the sentence that the phrase modifies. It is left dangling. You can correct a dangling modifier in one of two ways—by inserting the missing word that is being referred to, or by rewriting the sentence.

> **Correct:** **Reaching the top of the hill,** we saw a beautiful view.
> **Correct:** **When we reached the top of the hill,** the view we saw was beautiful.

> **Dangling:** **To get into the movie,** an ID must be presented.
> **Correct:** **To get into the movie,** you must present an ID.
> **Correct:** You must present an ID **to get into the movie.**

> **Dangling:** The garage was empty **after moving the tools.**
> **Correct:** **After moving the tools,** we had an empty garage.
> **Correct:** The garage was empty **after we moved the tools.**

REVIEWING DANGLING MODIFIERS

What is a dangling modifier?

_____

How do you correct a dangling modifier?

_____

_____

◆ Practice 4A   **Identifying**   Underline the dangling modifiers in the following sentences.

1. To get a good deal, time must be spent comparing prices.
2. Screaming for help, the chair fell over with the little boy in it.
3. As an only daughter with four brothers, there was never enough food in the house.
4. To get a driver's licence, two tests must be passed.
5. Giving the dog a bath, the bathroom floor became flooded.

◆ Practice 4B   **Correcting**   Correct the dangling modifiers in Practice 4A by rewriting the incorrect sentences.

◆ Practice 5   **Completing**   Fill in each blank in the following paragraph with a modifier that makes sense. Include at least two phrases.

(1) _____ professional baseball teams begin spring training. The coaches plan on (2) _____ weight lifting and lots of running. Hundreds of (3) _____ athletes begin training each season, but within days, many get cut from the major league teams. These men usually get placed on (4) _____ teams. These men hope to play well throughout the season and (5) _____ move up.

◆ Practice 6   **Writing Your Own**   Write a sentence of your own for each of the following phrases.

1. warm and bright _____

2. shaking my hand _____

3. to understand the opposite sex _____

4. getting a chance to see the ocean _____

5. to win an argument _____

CHAPTER REVIEW

Modifier: describes another word or group of words

Misplaced Modifier: The modifier is placed too far away from the word it is modifying, causing confusion in the meaning of the sentence.

Dangling Modifier: The modifier has nothing to refer to, or modify, in the sentence.

◆ *Review Practice 1* **Writing Your Own** Write a paragraph about your greatest accomplishment. What did you do? How hard did you work for it? What was your reward?

◆ *Review Practice 2* **Editing Through Collaboration** Exchange paragraphs from Review Practice 1 with another student, and then do the following:

1. Underline any misplaced modifiers.

2. Put brackets around any dangling modifiers.

Then return the paper to its writer, and use the information in this chapter to correct any modifier problems in your own paragraph. Record your errors on the Error Log in Appendix 3.

CHAPTER **43**

COMMAS

✓ CHECKLIST for Using Commas

- ✔ Are commas used to separate items in a series?
- ✔ Are commas used to set off introductory material?
- ✔ Is there a comma before *and, but, for, nor, or, so,* and *yet* when they are followed by an independent clause?
- ✔ Are commas used to set off interrupting material in a sentence?
- ✔ Are commas used to set off direct quotations?
- ✔ Are commas used correctly in numbers, dates, addresses, and letters?

Test Yourself

Add commas to the following sentences.

- We drove to the beach and we had a picnic.
- Before I eat breakfast I take a multivitamin.
- "This is my favourite restaurant" said Matt.
- E-mail though makes corresponding easy and fast.
- They were married on May 26 2004 in Bright's Grove Ontario.

(Answers are in Appendix 8 on the Web site.)

The **comma** is the most frequently used punctuation mark, but it is also the most often misused. Commas make reading sentences easier because they separate the parts of sentences. Following the rules in this chapter will help you write clear sentences that are easy to read.

COMMAS WITH ITEMS IN A SERIES

Use commas to separate items in a series.

This means that you should put a comma between all items in a series.

Series: The house had three bedrooms, two bathrooms, and a pool.

Series: She caught the fish, cleaned it, and then cooked it.

Series: William can have a new car if his grades improve, if he gets a job, and if he does his chores at home.

Sometimes this rule applies to a series of adjectives in front of a noun, but sometimes it does not. Look at these two examples.

Adjectives with Commas: The **foggy, cold** weather is finally over.

Adjectives Without Commas: The **loose bottom** knob fell off my TV.

Both of these examples are correct. So how do you know whether or not to use commas? You can use one of two tests. One test is to insert the word "and" between the adjectives. If the sentence makes sense, use a comma. Another test is to switch the order of the adjectives. If the sentence still reads clearly, use a comma between the two words.

Test 1: The **foggy and cold** weather is finally over. **OK, so use a comma**

Test 2: The **cold, foggy** weather is finally over. **OK, so use a comma**

Test 1: The **loose and bottom** knob fell off my TV. **NO comma**

Test 2: The **bottom loose** knob fell off my TV. **NO comma**

REVIEWING COMMAS WITH ITEMS IN A SERIES

Why use commas with items in a series?

_____

Where do these commas go?

_____

♦ *P r a c t i c e   1*   **Identifying** In the following sentences, circle the commas that are used incorrectly, and add any commas that are missing.

1. In my free time, I like to read sew, and make jelly.

2. My girlfriend is very good, at tennis volleyball and golf.

3. The best things, about gardening are the relaxation, the sense of ac-complishment, and the feeling of being at one with nature.

4. To play professional basketball, one must practise regularly, play com-petitively and get a big break.

5. The couch the footstool and the computer desk are going to be donated to Goodwill.

♦ *P r a c t i c e   2*   **Completing** Add the missing commas to the follow-ing paragraph.

We are flying to Halifax this weekend to attend a friend's wedding. Before we leave, I need to do the laundry pay the bills and arrange for a house sitter. My husband's childhood friend is the one getting married, so he also hopes to see some of his other friends there—especially Gene Brad and Dwayne. During the past two months, we bought airline tickets arranged for a rental car and reserved a hotel room. Now all we have to do is make it to the airport on time! I'm also trying to decide whether to wear navy pink or grey, and my husband is getting his best suit altered. Though it has required lots of time energy and money, we are really looking forward to this trip.

♦ *P r a c t i c e   3*   **Writing Your Own** Write a sentence of your own for each of the following sets of items.

1. three things to do at the mall _____

2. three sports you like to play _____

3. three items on a to-do list _____

4. three popular magazines _____

5. three of your favourite snack foods _____

COMMAS WITH INTRODUCTORY WORDS

Use a comma to set off an introductory word, phrase, or clause from the rest of its sentence.

If you are unsure about whether to add a comma, try reading the sen-tence with your reader in mind. If you want your reader to pause after the in-troductory word or phrase, you should insert a comma.

Introductory Word:	**No,** it didn't rain.
Introductory Word:	**Really,** the weather wasn't as bad as we thought it would be.
Introductory Phrase:	**On the whole,** this is a great town to live in.
Introductory Phrase:	**To prove this to my relatives,** I took them for a tour of the town.
Introductory Clause:	**As the doors opened,** the light poured in.
Introductory Clause:	**When the movie was over,** everyone was silent.

REVIEWING COMMAS WITH INTRODUCTORY WORDS

Why use commas with introductory words, phrases, and clauses?

_____

How can you tell if a comma is needed?

_____

_____

◆ *P r a c t i c e*   **4**   **Identifying** In the following sentences, circle the commas that are used incorrectly, and add any commas that are missing.

1. Three years, ago, we lived in Red Deer.
2. As the fire continued, to burn the firefighters feared it would get out of control.
3. Sure I can take you to the store.
4. After spilling the water the little boy began to cry.
5. The next time you go, to Chapters would you pick up a gift certificate for me?

◆ *P r a c t i c e*   **5**   **Completing** Add the missing commas to the following paragraph.

When Terina was 7 years old we took her to Disneyland. Since she was tall enough to ride all of the rides she really enjoyed herself. First we had to take pictures with Mickey and Minnie. Of course we couldn't miss them! Next we got in line for Space Mountain, which turned out to be her favourite ride. By the end of the day we had ridden Space Mountain five times.

◆ *P r a c t i c e   6*   **Writing Your Own** Write a sentence of your own for each of the following introductory words, phrases, or clauses.

1. well _____

2. when we thought it was almost over _____

3. yes _____

4. as the mail carrier arrived _____

5. wanting to win the lottery _____

COMMAS WITH INDEPENDENT CLAUSES

Use a comma before *and, but, for, nor, or, so,* and *yet* when they join two independent clauses. (Remember that an independent clause must have both a subject and a verb.)

Independent Clauses:	The boy flew to London, **and** he took a boat to France.
Independent Clauses:	He enjoyed the flight, **but** he liked the boat ride more.

Hint: Do not use a comma when a single subject has two verbs.

                        no
  s   v   comma   v
The **boy flew** to London and **left** for France the next day.

Adding a comma when none is needed is one of the most common errors in college writing assignments. Only when the second verb has its own subject should you add a comma.

        s   v   comma   s   v
The **boy flew** to London, and **he left** for France the next day.

REVIEWING COMMAS WITH COORDINATING CONJUNCTIONS

Name three coordinating conjunctions.

_____   _____   _____

When should you use a comma before a coordinating conjunction?

_____

Should you use a comma before a coordinating conjunction when a single subject has two verbs?

_____

◆ *P r a c t i c e   7*   **Identifying** In the following sentences, underline the subjects once and the coordinating conjunctions twice. Then circle any commas that are used incorrectly, and add any commas that are missing.

1. My computer crashed, so I lost my whole research paper.

2. The car looks great, and drives even better.

3. Going to the mountains was a good idea and we had a very nice time.

4. The cat will curl up on the chair, or the rug by the fireplace.

5. My cousin wants to get married but I think she's too young.

◆ *P r a c t i c e   8*   **Completing** Add the missing commas to the following paragraph.

> For my last birthday, my grandmother gave me $100 so I wanted to spend it on clothes. I went to the mall and I found three outfits that were perfect. I couldn't decide on just one but I didn't have enough money for them all. I needed the dressy outfit more yet the casual outfit was a great bargain. Finally, I settled on one pantsuit but I'm saving money to go back and get the others. I'll go back within a month or maybe I'll just wait until after my next holiday gift.

◆ *P r a c t i c e   9*   **Writing Your Own** Write a sentence of your own using each of the following coordinating conjunctions to separate two independent clauses.

1. or _____

2. and _____

3. so _____

4. but _____

5. yet _____

COMMAS WITH INTERRUPTERS

Use a comma before and after a word or phrase that interrupts the flow of a sentence.

Most words that interrupt a sentence are not necessary for understanding the main point of a sentence. Setting them off makes it easier to recognize the main point.

Word: My next-door neighbour, **Julio,** is from Portugal.

Word: I didn't hear the phone ring, **however,** because I was in the shower.

Phrase: My textbook, *Ancient Rome,* is on the desk.

Phrase: One of the most popular vacation spots, **according to recent surveys,** is Cuba.

Phrase: Mr. Colby, **chair of the school board,** has been elected mayor.

A very common type of interrupter is a clause that begins with *who, whose, which, when,* or *where* and is not necessary for understanding the main point of the sentence:

Clause: The new mall, **which is downtown,** has three large restaurants.

Because the information "which is downtown" is not necessary for understanding the main idea of the sentence, it is set off with commas.

Clause: Carol Roth, **who has a Ph.D. in history,** is my new tutor.

The main point here is that Carol Roth is my new tutor. Since the other information isn't necessary for understanding the sentence, it can be set off with commas.

Hint: Do not use commas with *who, whose, which, when,* or *where* if the information is necessary for understanding the main point of the sentence.

My friend **who is a circus clown** just arrived in town.

Because the information in the *who* clause is necessary to understand which friend just arrived in town, you should not set it off with commas.

Hint: Do not use commas to set off clauses beginning with *that:*

The mall **that is downtown** has three large restaurants.

REVIEWING COMMAS WITH INTERRUPTERS

Why should you use commas to set off words and phrases in the middle of a sentence?

_____

When should you use commas with who, whose, which, when, or where?

_____

_____

When should you not use commas before these words?

_____

◆ **P r a c t i c e   1 0   Identifying** Label each sentence C if commas are used correctly with the underlined words and phrases or X if they are not.

1. _____ Jaclyn Smith, <u>who used to be a model</u>, has a line of clothing at Kmart.

2. _____ My girlfriend <u>Cheri</u>, is almost 23 years old.

3. _____ The Famous Players theatre, <u>my hangout</u>, is located on Queen Street.

4. _____ Joe's leather jacket, <u>which he's had only four months</u> has a broken zipper.

5. _____ Rideau Hall, <u>the residence</u>, used by the Governor General, was built in 1838.

◆ **P r a c t i c e   1 1   Completing** Insert commas around the interrupting words and phrases in the following paragraph.

My favourite grandmother Gram turned 80 this year. My grandfather died last August, and we didn't want Gram living alone. She was able to take care of herself however and didn't want to go to a retirement home. Recently, we visited Rosewood which is a very popular retirement community and she was impressed with the facilities. There are group homes of course with "around the clock" care, but there are also condominiums where residents can live alone or with roommates. The entire neighbourhood is monitored by security guards which is reassuring and the medical staff is always available. Gram's been there for three weeks now and said when we asked that she's never been happier.

♦ *P r a c t i c e 1 2*   **Writing Your Own** Write a sentence of your own for each of the following phrases.

1. who is very brave _____

2. which costs over $100 _____

3. however _____

4. the mayor's wife _____

5. taking the keys _____

COMMAS WITH DIRECT QUOTATIONS

Use commas to mark direct quotations.

A direct quotation records a person's exact words. Commas set off the exact words from the rest of the sentence, making it easier to understand who said what.

Direct Quotation:	My friends often say, **"You are so lucky."**
Direct Quotation:	**"You are so lucky,"** my friends often say.
Direct Quotation:	**"You are so lucky,"** says my grandmother, **"to have good friends."**

Hint: If a quotation ends with a question mark or an exclamation point, do not use a comma. Only one punctuation mark is needed.

NOT	**"What did he want?,"** she asked.
Correct:	**"What did he want?"** she asked.

REVIEWING COMMAS WITH DIRECT QUOTATIONS

Why should you use commas with a direct quotation?

_____

Should you use a comma if the quotation ends with a question mark or an exclamation point? Why or why not?

_____

◆ *P r a c t i c e   1 3*   **Identifying** In the following sentences, circle the commas that are used incorrectly, and add any commas that are missing.

1. Tonya noted "I want the Canucks to win tonight."
2. "If you go now" he said "don't come back."
3. "Are you absolutely sure?," David asked.
4. "That cat," Christine said "sets off my allergies."
5. Mr. Avery remarked "The paper will not be accepted late."

◆ *P r a c t i c e   1 4*   **Completing** Add the missing commas to the following passage.

"Are you going to the game tonight?" Vijay asked Lonnie.
"Of course" she replied "I wouldn't miss it."
"But the Raptors will probably be slaughtered" Vijay said.
"What difference does that make?" she questioned.
Vijay answered "I just don't want to pay money to watch them lose."
"Well, I'm a real loyal fan!" Lonnie emphasized as she walked away.

◆ *P r a c t i c e   1 5*   **Writing Your Own** Write five sentences of your own using commas to set off direct quotations.

OTHER USES OF COMMAS

Use commas in the following ways.

Numbers:	What is **2,502,500** divided by **10,522?**
Dates:	My great-grandfather was born in December 1888 in London and died on **July 23, 1972,** in Kingston.

Notice that there is a comma both before and after the year.

Addresses:	Ashley moved from **Victoria, British Columbia,** to **1939 Queen St., Stratford, ON N6B 2C9.**

Notice that there is no comma between the province and postal code.

Letters:	**Dear Alicia,**
	Yours truly,

REVIEWING OTHER USES OF COMMAS

Give one example of commas in each of the following situations:

Numbers _____

Dates _____

Addresses _____

Letters _____

Why are these commas important?

_____

◆ *P r a c t i c e   1 6*   **Identifying** In the following sentences, circle the commas that are used incorrectly, and add any commas that are missing.

1. The new Honda Accord costs more than $23000.
2. Chris Bosh plays basketball with the Raptors and lives in Toronto Ontario.
3. My five-year anniversary is June 16 2005.
4. Jamie lives in Dryden, Ontario with her two kids.
5. Yours truly Deena

◆ *P r a c t i c e   1 7*   **Completing** Add the missing commas to the following paragraph.

Norma graduated from Fanshawe College in London Ontario on June 5 1999. There were more than 3000 people in the audience, including Norma's friends and family. Her parents drove all the way from Montreal Quebec and they stayed in London all weekend. After the graduation ceremonies, Norma and her loved ones spent the weekend visiting the Toronto area and other parts of Ontario that Norma didn't get to see while attending school.

◆ *P r a c t i c e   1 8*   **Writing Your Own** Write a sentence of your own for each of the following items.

1. your date of birth

_____

2. the city and province where you were born

_____

3. your full address, including the postal code

_____

4. the estimated number of people who attend your school

_____

5. the amount of money you would like to make per year after graduation

_____

CHAPTER REVIEW

Comma: separates items in a series; sets off an introductory word, phrase, or clause; joins independent clauses if used with a conjunction; sets off extra or non-essential information that interrupts a sentence; and differentiates a quote from the rest of the sentence

◆ *Review P r a c t i c e 1* **Writing Your Own** Write a paragraph about the importance of computer knowledge. What are the benefits of computer technology? Why should we be familiar with it?

◆ *Review P r a c t i c e 2* **Editing Through Collaboration** Exchange paragraphs from Review Practice 1 with another student, and then do the following:

1. Circle any misplaced commas.
2. Suggest corrections for the incorrect commas.

Then return the paper to its writer, and use the information in this chapter to correct any comma errors in your own paragraph. Record your errors on the Error Log in Appendix 3.

CHAPTER **44**

APOSTROPHES

☑ CHECKLIST for Using Apostrophes

✔ Are apostrophes used correctly in contractions?
✔ Are apostrophes used correctly to show possession?

Test Yourself

Add an apostrophe or an apostrophe and *-s* to the following sentences.

- The flight crew was surprised by the pilots rudeness when he boarded the plane.
- Its important that the car have its engine checked every 5,000 kilometres.
- Whats going to happen after Dominic is gone?
- The mens washroom is located on the third floor.
- James house is the third one on the left.

(Answers are in Appendix 8 on the Web site.)

The **apostrophe** looks like a single quotation mark. Its two main purposes are to indicate where letters have been left out and to show ownership.

MARKING CONTRACTIONS

Use an apostrophe to show that letters have been omitted to form a contraction.

A **contraction** is the shortening of one or more words. Our everyday speech is filled with contractions.

I have	=	I've (*h* and *a* have been omitted)
you are	=	you're (*a* has been omitted)
let us	=	let's (*u* has been omitted)

Here is a list of commonly used contractions.

Some Common Contractions

I am	=	*I'm*	*we have*	=	*we've*
I would	=	*I'd*	*we will*	=	*we'll*
I will	=	*I'll*	*they are*	=	*they're*
you have	=	*you've*	*they have*	=	*they've*
you will	=	*you'll*	*do not*	=	*don't*
he is	=	*he's*	*did not*	=	*didn't*
she will	=	*she'll*	*have not*	=	*haven't*
it is	=	*it's*	*could not*	=	*couldn't*

Hint: Two words that are frequently misused are *it's* and *its*.

> *it's* = contraction: it is (*or* it has)   **It's** too late to go to the movie.
>
> *its* = pronoun: belonging to it   **Its** eyes are really large.

To see if you are using the correct word, say the sentence with the words *it is*. If that is what you want to say, add an apostrophe to the word.

> **?**   I think **its** burning.
>
> **Test:**   I think it is burning.   **YES, add an apostrophe**

This sentence makes sense with *it is*, so you should write *it's*.

> **Correct:**   I think **it's** burning.

> **?**   The dog wagged **its** tail.
>
> **Test:**   The dog wagged it is tail.   **NO, so no apostrophe**

This sentence does not make sense with *it is*, so you should not use the apostrophe in *its*.

> **Correct:**   The dog wagged **its** tail.

REVIEWING CONTRACTIONS

What is the purpose of an apostrophe in a contraction?

_____

Write five contractions, and tell which letters have been omitted.

_____ _____

_____ _____

_____ _____

_____ _____

_____ _____

What is the difference between it's and its?

_____

◆ *P r a c t i c e   1*   **Identifying** In the following sentences, circle the apostrophes that are used incorrectly, and add any apostrophes that are missing.

1. Ive got to find a better job.
2. The attorney said shes working overtime on this case.
3. Theyll be glad to see you at the party.
4. It's a good thing they did'nt take their baby to the wedding.
5. Cameron doesnt get paid until Friday.

◆ *P r a c t i c e   2*   **Completing** Write contractions for the following words.

1. she + would = _____

2. did + not = _____

3. will + not = _____

4. they + will = _____

5. should + have = _____

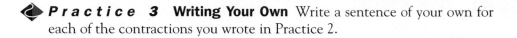 *P r a c t i c e 3* **Writing Your Own** Write a sentence of your own for each of the contractions you wrote in Practice 2.

SHOWING POSSESSION

Use an apostrophe to show possession.

1. For a singular word, use *'s* to indicate possession or ownership. You can always replace a possessive with *of* plus the noun or pronoun.

the soldier**'s** rifle	=	the rifle **of the soldier**
someone**'s** house	=	the house **of someone**
doctor**'s** office	=	the office **of the doctor**
yesterday**'s** paper	=	the paper **of yesterday**

2. For plural nouns ending in *-s*, use only an apostrophe.

the soldiers**'** rifles	=	the rifles **of the soldiers**
the doctors**'** office	=	the office **of the doctors**
the painters**'** studio	=	the studio **of the painters**
the students**'** grades	=	the grades **of the students**
the brothers**'** boat	=	the boat **of the brothers**

3. For plural nouns that do not end in *-s*, add *'s*.

the men**'s** pants	=	the pants **of the men**
the deer**'s** antlers	=	the antlers **of the deer**
the criteria**'s** importance	=	the importance **of the criteria**

REVIEWING POSSESSIVES

How do you mark possession or ownership for a singular word?

_____

How do you mark possession or ownership for a plural word that ends in -s?

_____

How do you mark possession or ownership for a plural word that doesn't end in -s?

_____

◆ *P r a c t i c e   4*   **Identifying** In the following sentences, circle the apostrophes that are used incorrectly, and add any apostrophes that are missing.

1. The boys bicycle had a flat tire.
2. The disaster was Jennifers' fault.
3. Our two cat's water bowl was empty.
4. We thought the airlines food would be tasty.
5. Todays' temperature reached 32 degrees.

◆ *P r a c t i c e   5*   **Completing** Write a possessive for each of the following phrases.

1. the feet of Charles _____

2. the guests of Dr. Blakeney _____

3. the tide of the ocean _____

4. the shirts of the men _____

5. the assignment of the students _____

◆ *P r a c t i c e   6*   **Writing Your Own** Write a sentence of your own for each of the possessives you wrote in Practice 5.

COMMON APOSTROPHE ERRORS

Two common errors occur with apostrophes. The following guidelines will help you avoid these errors.

No Apostrophe with Possessive Pronouns

Do not use an apostrophe with a possessive pronoun.

Possessive pronouns already show ownership, so they do not need an apostrophe.

Error	Correct
his'	his
her's or hers'	hers
it's or its'	its
your's or yours'	yours
our's or ours'	ours
their's or theirs'	theirs

No Apostrophe to Form the Plural

Do not use an apostrophe to form a plural word.

This error occurs most often with plural words ending in *-s*. An apostrophe indicates possession or contraction; it does *not* indicate the plural. Therefore, a plural word never takes an apostrophe unless it is possessive.

NOT	The **clothes'** are in the dryer.
Correct:	The **clothes** are in the dryer.

NOT	She bought three **DVD's** last week.
Correct:	She bought three **DVDs** last week.

NOT	Get your coffee and **doughnut's** here.
Correct:	Get your coffee and **doughnuts** here.

REVIEWING APOSTROPHE ERRORS

List three possessive pronouns.

_____

Why don't possessive pronouns take apostrophes?

_____

What is wrong with the apostrophe in each of the following sentences?

The last float in the parade is ours'.

_____

There must be 100 floats' in the parade.

_____

◆ **P r a c t i c e   7   Identifying** In the following sentences, circle the apostrophes that are used incorrectly, and add any apostrophes that are missing.

1. I've been to that store five time's, and I've never seen shoes like yours'.

2. My brother's are working for my father's company.

3. Sam left his' cars window's down, and it is starting to rain.

4. The soccer player's are meeting at noon.

5. The big story in the newspaper's is yesterday's flood.

◆ *P r a c t i c e 8*   **Completing** Write a possessive for each of the following phrases.

1. the house belonging to them _____

2. the pants she owns _____

3. the pop you are holding _____

4. the price of it _____

5. the feet of him _____

◆ *P r a c t i c e 9*   **Writing Your Own** Write a sentence of your own for each of the possessives you wrote in Practice 8.

CHAPTER REVIEW

Apostrophe: indicates ownership or where letters were left out in a contraction. Apostrophes should not be used with possessive pronouns. Apostrophes do not show that a word is plural.

◆ *Review P r a c t i c e 1*   **Writing Your Own** Write a paragraph about your favourite teacher. What was his or her name? What was special about this person?

◆ *Review P r a c t i c e 2*   **Editing Through Collaboration** Exchange paragraphs from Review Practice 1 with another student, and then do the following:

1. Circle any misplaced or missing apostrophes.

2. Indicate whether they mark possession (P) or contraction (C).

Then return the paper to its writer, and use the information in this chapter to correct any apostrophe errors in your own paragraph. Record your errors on the Error Log in Appendix 3.

QUOTATION MARKS

CHAPTER 45

✔ CHECKLIST for Using Quotation Marks

> ✔ Are quotation marks used to indicate someone's exact words?
>
> ✔ Are all periods and commas inside quotation marks?
>
> ✔ Are words capitalized correctly in quotations?
>
> ✔ Are quotation marks used to indicate the title of a short work, such as a short story or a poem?

Test Yourself

Add quotation marks where needed in the following sentences.

- Can we go out to dinner tonight? she asked.
- Jeri screamed, Don't go in there!
- If you can't find my house, Tom said, call me on your cell phone.
- My favourite poem is This Is a Photograph of Me by Margaret Atwood.
- David said, I'll fix your car this weekend.

(Answers are in Appendix 8 on the Web site.)

Quotation marks are punctuation marks that work together in pairs. Their most common use is to indicate someone's exact words. They are also used to mark the title of a short piece of writing, such as a short story or a poem.

DIRECT QUOTATIONS

Use quotation marks to indicate a **direct quotation**—someone's exact words.

Here are some examples that show the three basic forms of a direct quotation.

Direct Quotation: "I will not lend you the money," said the banker.

Here the quoted words come first.

Direct Quotation: The banker said, "I will not lend you the money."

Here the quoted words come after the speaker is named.

Direct Quotation: "I will not," the banker said, "lend you the money."

In this example, the quoted words are interrupted, and the speaker is named in the middle. This form emphasizes the first few words.

INDIRECT QUOTATIONS

If you just talk about someone's words, you do not need quotation marks. **Indirect quotations** usually include the word *that*, as in *said that*. In questions, the wording is often *asked if*. Look at these examples of indirect quotations.

Direct Quotation: "I lost my job at the supermarket," said Bob.

These are Bob's exact words, so you must use quotation marks.

Indirect Quotation: Bob **said that** he had lost his job at the supermarket.

This sentence explains what Bob said but does not use Bob's exact words. So quotation marks should not be used.

Direct Quotation: "The train trip took eight hours," said Kira.
Indirect Quotation: Kira **said that** the train trip took eight hours.

Direct Quotation: "Did you get the car fixed?" Mom asked.
Indirect Quotation: Mom **asked if** I had gotten the car fixed.

REVIEWING QUOTATION MARKS WITH QUOTATIONS

How do you show that you are repeating someone's exact words?

_____

What is an indirect quotation?

_____

◆ *P r a c t i c e 1* **Identifying** In the following sentences, circle the quotation marks used incorrectly, and add any quotation marks that are missing.

1. "Help me! yelled the drowning woman.
2. "If you can't take the heat," my mom used to say, stay out of the kitchen."
3. Martina asked, "Have you found my jacket?"
4. Steffan said, My goal is to "get into the Olympics."
5. Chonda said that "she enjoyed the movie last night."

◆ *P r a c t i c e 2* **Completing** Add the missing quotation marks to the following paragraph.

When I went into the salon, my hairdresser asked, How do you want your hair cut today? I don't really know, I replied, but I brought in a couple of pictures of haircuts I like. Those are cute she said. Do you think my hair would look good like that? I asked. Absolutely! she exclaimed. Then she set to work with the scissors. When she was finished, I looked in the mirror in horror. That's not what I had in mind, I told her. But it looks just like the pictures, she said. How can you say that? I exclaimed. The haircuts I showed you are shoulder-length, and mine is now above my ears. Well, she said, it will always grow back.

◆ *P r a c t i c e 3* **Writing Your Own** Write a sentence of your own for each of the following expressions.

1. a question asked by Claudia _____
2. a statement spoken by the manager _____
3. an exclamation spoken by Becky _____
4. an indirect question that Jared asked _____
5. a statement spoken by the electrician _____

CAPITALIZING AND USING OTHER PUNCTUATION MARKS WITH QUOTATION MARKS

When you are quoting someone's complete sentences, begin with a capital letter and use appropriate end punctuation—a comma, a period, a question mark, or an exclamation point. You do not need to capitalize the first word of a quotation if it is only part of a sentence. Here are some examples.

Capitalize the first letter of the words being quoted, and put a comma or a period at the end of the quotation if it is a statement. Separate the spoken words from the rest of the sentence with a comma.

> "He doesn't seem very nice," she said.
> He said, "Turn off the music."

If the quotation ends with a question mark or an exclamation point, use that punctuation instead of a comma or a period.

> "Why do you want to know?" she asked.
> He yelled, "Turn off that music!"

In a quotation that is interrupted, capitalize the first word being quoted, but do not capitalize words in the middle of the sentence. Use a comma both before and after the interruption. End with a period if it is a statement.

> "Yes," said the bus driver, "this bus goes downtown."

You do not need to capitalize the first word of a quotation that is only part of a sentence.

> I don't think that he will ever "find himself."

Hint: Look at the examples again. Notice when periods and commas go inside the quotation marks.

> **NOT**   "Yes", he said, "we're ready to leave".
> **Correct:** "Yes," he said, "we're ready to leave."

REVIEWING CAPITALIZATION AND PUNCTUATION WITH QUOTATION MARKS

When you quote someone's exact words, why should you begin with a capital letter?

_____

Where do commas go in relation to quotation marks? Where do periods go?

_____

◆ *P r a c t i c e   4*   **Identifying** In the following sentences, circle the quotation marks, capital letters, and other punctuation marks that are used incorrectly, and add any missing quotation marks and punctuation.

1. "Is there a doctor in the house"? the man screamed.

2. "I can't believe", she said, "That you've never seen the ocean."

3. Margarita asked, "Are you ever going to meet me for coffee."?

4. "This is the last time", he promised, "that I come home late".

5. Garrett said, "I want to take the bus to the restaurant on the corner".

◆ *P r a c t i c e   5*   **Completing** Add the missing quotation marks and punctuation to the following paragraph.

I was having car problems, so I drove to the garage on the corner. What do you think is wrong with my car? I asked the mechanic. I can't tell you he said, until I take a look at it myself. I replied, I'll leave it with you this afternoon, and you can tell me later today what you find out. That would be great, he said. Finally, around 4:00 p.m., he called me on the phone. Your car needs a new clutch, he said. No way! I exclaimed. Sorry, mister he calmly replied, but that's all I found to be wrong with it. I explained, But I just replaced the clutch four months ago. Well, he said I hope you saved your receipt and warranty paperwork.

◆ *P r a c t i c e   6*   **Writing Your Own** Write a sentence of your own for each of the following direct quotations, punctuated correctly.

1. "No, I won't" _____

2. "How are we going to do that" _____

3. "This is the most important priority" _____

4. "Yes" "you can come to the party" _____

5. "Don't worry" "you didn't miss anything" _____

QUOTATION MARKS AROUND TITLES

Put quotation marks around the titles of short works that are parts of larger works. The titles of longer works are put in italics (or underlined).

Quotation Marks	Italics/Underlining
"Last Snowstorm" (short story)	*Canadian Short Stories* (book)

"Song of Myself" (poem)   *Leaves of Grass* (book)

"My Girl" (song)   *The Temptations'*
Greatest Hits (CD)

"Explore Canada's Territories"   *Canadian*
(magazine article)   *Geographic*
(magazine)

"Convicts Escape" (newspaper article)   *The Globe and Mail*
(newspaper)

"The Wedding" (episode on TV series)   *Friends* (TV series)

REVIEWING QUOTATION MARKS WITH TITLES

When do you put quotation marks around a title?

_____

When do you italicize (or underline) a title?

_____

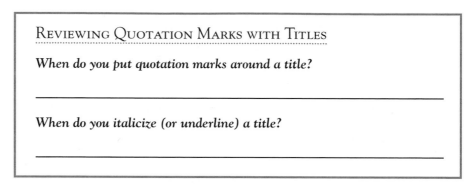 **P r a c t i c e 7**   **Identifying** Put an X in front of each sentence with errors in quotation marks or italics/underlining. Add any missing quotation marks and italics or underlining.

1. _____ My favourite song by the Beatles is *Yellow Submarine*.

2. _____ When Juliet was in high school, she read Shirley Jackson's famous short story The Lottery.

3. _____ Getting through *Moby Dick* by Herman Melville took me three weeks.

4. _____ My first boyfriend recited William Blake's poem *The Garden of Love* to me on my front porch.

5. _____ The "Globe and Mail" ran a long article called *Japan's Princess Gives Birth* about Crown Princess Masako.

P r a c t i c e 8   **Completing** Place quotation marks around the titles of short works, and underline the titles of long works in the following paragraph.

     Mark got a great job with the Toronto Star last summer. He is now working as the editor of the entertainment section, and he writes a column called Making a Mark. In his column, he reviews celebrity events and activities, such as concerts, hit movies, and best-selling books. For one article, he interviewed several people from Survivor, the popular reality TV show. He also attended a Tragically Hip concert and quoted lines from the song Scared on their album Day For Night. Another article featured Nikki Giovanni, who read her poem Dream during their interview. Mark has become friends with some very interesting and well-known people, and he is now looking forward to speaking with Atom Egoyan on the set of the latest sequel to Ararat.

◆ *P r a c t i c e 9*   **Writing Your Own** Write a sentence of your own for each of the following items. Make up a title if you can't think of one.

1. a short story _____

2. a song _____

3. a TV show _____

4. a CD _____

5. a magazine article _____

CHAPTER REVIEW

Quotation Marks: indicate someone's exact words or mark the title of a short piece of writing

◆ *Review P r a c t i c e   1*   **Writing Your Own** In paragraph form, record a conversation you had this week. Who were you talking to? What did you talk about? What were your exact words?

◆ *Review P r a c t i c e   2*   **Editing Through Collaboration** Exchange paragraphs from Review Practice 1 with another student, and do the following:

1. Circle any incorrect or missing quotation marks.

2. Underline any faulty punctuation.

3. Put an X over any incorrect use of italics/underlining.

Then return the paper to its writer, and use the information in this chapter to correct any errors with quotation marks and italics/underlining in your own paragraph. Record your errors on the Error Log in Appendix 3.

CHAPTER 46

OTHER PUNCTUATION MARKS

☑ CHECKLIST for Using Semicolons, Colons, Dashes, and Parentheses

> ✔ Are semicolons used to join two closely related complete sentences?
>
> ✔ Are long items in a series that already contain commas separated by semicolons?
>
> ✔ Are colons used correctly to introduce a list?
>
> ✔ Are dashes used to emphasize or further explain a point?
>
> ✔ Are parentheses used to include additional, but not necessary, information?

Test Yourself

Add semicolons, colons, dashes, or parentheses to the following sentences.

- Kris left for the dance Jean decided to stay home.
- We wanted to win therefore we practised every day.
- The computer's advertised price didn't include several important things a monitor, a printer, and speakers.
- Ray asked the best question during the interview "Why should we vote for you?"
- Bring the jelly to a "rolling boil" a boil that cannot be stirred down.

(Answers are in Appendix 8 on the Web site.)

This chapter explains the uses of the **semicolon, colon, dash,** and **parentheses.** We'll look at these punctuation marks one by one.

SEMICOLONS

Semicolons are used to join two closely related sentences. They are also used to avoid confusion when listing items in a series.

1. Use a semicolon to separate two closely related independent clauses.

   An independent clause is a group of words with a subject and a verb that can stand alone as a sentence. You might use a semicolon instead of a coordinating conjunction (*and, but, for, nor, or, so, yet*) or a period. Any one of the three options would be correct.

	independent	independent
Semicolon:	Sam never drove to school; **he** always rode his bike.	
Conjunction:	Sam never drove to school, **for** he always rode his bike.	
Period:	Sam never drove to school. **He** always rode his bike.	

2. Use a semicolon to join two independent clauses that are connected by such words as *however, therefore, furthermore, moreover, for example*, or *consequently*. Put a comma after the connecting word.

	independent	independent
Semicolon:	Travelling can be expensive; **nevertheless,** it's always enjoyable.	
Semicolon:	Brad is very smart; **furthermore,** he was offered seven scholarships.	
Semicolon:	He has trouble in math; **therefore,** he hired a tutor.	

3. Use a semicolon to separate items in a series when any of the items contain commas.

NOT	On the flight to Vancouver, Mei Lin read a popular new thriller with a surprise ending, took a long, relaxing nap, and watched an incredibly dull movie about a rock star.
Correct:	On the flight to Vancouver, Mei Lin read a popular new thriller with a surprise ending; took a long, relaxing nap; and watched an incredibly dull movie about a rock star.

REVIEWING SEMICOLONS
....

How are semicolons used between two independent clauses?

_____

How are semicolons used with items in a series?

_____

◆ *P r a c t i c e   **1***   **Identifying** In the following sentences, circle the semicolons that are used incorrectly, and add any commas and semicolons that are missing.

1. The car needed new front tires the old ones were quite bald.
2. Lisa's 10-month-old son didn't take a nap today however; he was very pleasant.
3. I must have lost my keys I can't; find them anywhere.
4. Our team is the strongest; and we are prepared to win.
5. Mr. Banderas teaches Spanish; writes novels; books; and short stories; and reviews movies in his spare time.

◆ *P r a c t i c e   **2***   **Completing** Add semicolons, where needed, to the following paragraph.

When I was in grade 9, my school had a big dance I dreaded it from the day it was announced. I didn't have a boyfriend I didn't have the right clothes, shoes, or hairstyle and I didn't have any money saved up for things like that. Even worse, I knew my parents felt I was too young to go nonetheless, I knew my friends would keep asking me if I was going. Finally, I thought of a good excuse: I told my friends my grandmother was having major surgery. My friends probably knew I was lying however, nobody said anything more to me about it.

◆ *P r a c t i c e   **3***   **Writing Your Own** Write five sentences of your own using semicolons correctly.

COLONS

1. The main use of the colon is to introduce a list or thought. Here are some examples:

   Colon: Buy the following items for the trip: toothpaste, tooth-brush, razor, soap, and makeup.

   Colon: The fair had some new attractions: a double ferris wheel, a roller coaster, and an antique merry-go-round.

   Colon: The choice was simple: return the merchandise.

   The most common error with colons is using one where it isn't needed.

2. Do not use a colon after the words *such as* or *including*. A complete sentence must come before a colon.

NOT   Cook only fresh vegetables, **such as:** green beans, broccoli, and spinach.

Correct: Cook only fresh vegetables, **such as** green beans, broccoli, and spinach.

NOT   We went to many countries in Europe, **including:** Spain and Portugal.

Correct: We went to many countries in Europe, **including** Spain and Portugal.

3. In addition, you should not use a colon after a verb or after a preposition. Remember that a complete sentence must come before a colon.

NOT   The movies to be reviewed **are:** *American Beauty* and *Wonder Boys*.

Correct: The movies to be reviewed **are** *American Beauty* and *Wonder Boys*.

NOT   The box was full **of:** books, old dolls, and scrapbooks.

Correct: The box was full **of** books, old dolls, and scrapbooks.

REVIEWING COLONS

What is the main use of a colon?

_____

Why should you not use a colon after such words as is *or* of*?*

_____

◆ *P r a c t i c e   4* **Identifying** In the following sentences, circle the colons that are used incorrectly, and add any colons that are missing.

1. The best things about summer are: swimming, biking, and picnics.

2. The man asked me for the following items my driver's licence, my Social Insurance number, and my credit cards.

3. We accidentally left many things at home, such as: my toothbrush, our hair dryer, and the baby's bottle.

4. I was most impressed by: the atmosphere, the prices, and the service.

5. The most expensive parts to repair were: the carburetor, the ignition system, and the fuel injector.

◆ *P r a c t i c e 5* **Completing** Add colons to the following paragraph.

Reading is an excellent way to spend free time. A good book can do many things take you to a faraway place, introduce you to different people, and expose you to extraordinary experiences. I especially like two kinds of books science fiction and romance novels. These genres are totally opposite, I know, but they have just what I like action, strange characters, and suspension of disbelief. When I am reading, I am in a world of my own. I escape all of my everyday problems my difficult job, my nagging mother, and sometimes even my homework.

◆ *P r a c t i c e 6* **Writing Your Own** Write five sentences of your own using colons correctly.

DASHES AND PARENTHESES

Dashes

1. Use dashes to emphasize or draw attention to a point.

   Dash: I know what I want to be—a doctor.

   In this example, the beginning of the sentence introduces an idea, and the dash then sets off the answer.

   Dash: Money and time—these are what I need.

   In this example, the key words are set off at the beginning, and the explanation follows. Beginning this way adds some suspense to the sentence.

   Dashes: I know what I want in a husband—a sense of humour— and I plan to get it.

   The dashes divide this sentence into three distinct parts, which makes the reader pause and think about each part.

Parentheses

Whereas dashes set off material that the writer wants to emphasize, parentheses do just the opposite. They are always used in pairs.

2. Use parentheses to set off information that is interesting or helpful but not necessary for understanding the sentence.

   Parentheses: When in Rome **(as the saying goes)**, do as the Romans do.

   Parentheses: The M.P.P.'s position on the proposal **(Bill 193)** has changed several times.

3. Parentheses are also used to mark a person's life span and to number items in a sentence.

Parentheses: Herman Melville **(1819–1891)** wrote the classic *Moby Dick*.

Parentheses: My boss gave me three things to do today: **(1)** answer the mail, **(2)** file receipts, and **(3)** send out bills.

REVIEWING DASHES AND PARENTHESES

What is the difference between dashes and parentheses?

_____

_____

When do you use dashes?

_____

When do you use parentheses?

_____

◆ *P r a c t i c e* **7** **Identifying** Use dashes or parentheses with the underlined words in the following sentences.

1. One powerful tool for student research is becoming more popular than the library <u>the Internet</u>.

2. My brother <u>the police chief</u> keeps his phone number unlisted.

3. Nick <u>head of the math department</u> hires the new teachers.

4. I signalled the oncoming car <u>by flashing my lights</u>, but it still didn't turn its headlights on.

5. Cheryl got her passport so she can <u>1</u> visit other countries <u>2</u> go diving in all of the seven seas, and <u>3</u> photograph royalty.

◆ *P r a c t i c e* **8** **Completing** Add dashes and parentheses to the following paragraph.

In high school, I volunteered to work on the yearbook. Mrs. Brady was our instructor a round lady with bright red cheeks and a strange laugh. She immediately set us to work on several things mostly after school, as we accumulated photos and news about the school's major events. I remember one lesson I learned in that class never procrastinate. If I failed to finish an assignment something that rarely happened, someone else would do it instead, and that person's work would be published instead of mine. I'll never forget my year with Mrs. Brady.

◆ *P r a c t i c e   9*   **Writing Your Own** Write three sentences of your own using dashes and two using parentheses.

CHAPTER REVIEW

Semicolon: used to join two closely related sentences or to separate items in a complex list

Colon: used to introduce a list or a thought. A complete sentence must come before a colon.

Dash: used to emphasize or draw attention to a point

Parentheses: set off interesting or helpful information. They are always used in pairs.

◆ *Review   P r a c t i c e   1*   **Writing Your Own** Write a paragraph explaining some of your five-year goals. What do you plan to be doing in five years? What do you want to have accomplished?

◆ *Review   P r a c t i c e   2*   **Editing Through Collaboration** Exchange paragraphs from Review Practice 1 with another student, and then do the following:

1. Circle any incorrect or missing semicolons.

2. Circle any incorrect or missing colons.

3. Circle any incorrect or missing dashes.

4. Circle any incorrect or missing parentheses.

Then return the paper to its writer, and use the information in this chapter to correct any punctuation errors in your own paragraph. Record your errors on the Error Log in Appendix 3.

CAPITALIZATION

☑ CHECKLIST for Editing Capitalization

> ✔ Are all proper nouns capitalized?
> ✔ Are all words in titles capitalized correctly?
> ✔ Have you followed the other rules for capitalizing correctly?

Test Yourself

Correct the capitalization errors in the following sentences.

- According to uncle Bob, mother makes the best nanaimo bars.
- Antonio is a new canadian.
- "the shortest path," he said, "Is down baker street."
- Issa loves to go to walt disney world.
- Last year, I saw the red hot chili peppers in concert.

(Answers are in Appendix 8 on the Web site.)

Because every sentence begins with a capital letter, **capitalization** is the best place to start discussing the mechanics of good writing. Capital letters signal where sentences begin. They also call attention to certain kinds of words, making sentences easier to read and understand.

Correct capitalization coupled with correct punctuation adds up to good, clear writing. Here are some guidelines to help you capitalize correctly.

1. Capitalize the first word of every sentence, including the first word of a quotation that forms a sentence.

> **M**y favourite city is Rome.
> "**R**ome is my favourite city," he said.
> **H**e said, "**M**y favourite city is Rome."

Do not capitalize the second part of a quotation that is split.

"My favourite city," he said, "is Rome."

2. Capitalize all proper nouns. Do not capitalize common nouns.

Common Nouns	Proper Nouns
person	Adrienne Clarkson
province	Newfoundland
building	CN Tower
river	St. Lawrence River

Here are some examples of proper nouns.

People:	Sarah, Shania Twain, Mike Weir
Groups:	Australians, Mohawk, Europeans, British, Latino
Languages:	Russian, Italian, French
Religions, Religious Books, Holy Days:	Catholicism, Buddhism, Koran, Bible, Yom Kippur, Kwanzaa, Easter
Organizations:	Toronto Blue Jays, New Democratic Party, Canadian Labour Congress, Kiwanis Club, Alpha Gamma Delta
Places:	Banff National Park, Antarctica, Kingston, Middlesex County, Bay Street, Highway 401, Bluewater Bridge, Lester B. Pearson Airport
Institutions, Agencies, Businesses:	Oakridge Secondary School, D. B. Weldon Library, United Way, Toronto Sick Children's Hospital, Petro-Canada
Brand Names, Ships, Aircraft:	Mustang, Tide, Pepsi, H.M.S. *Toronto*, *Avro Arrow*

3. Capitalize titles used with people's names or in place of their names.

Mr. Ralph W. Gerber, Ms. Rachel Lorca, Dr. Letitia Johnson, Aunt Jane, Grandpa Bob, Cousin Maria, Sis, Nana

Do not capitalize words that identify family relationships.

NOT	I saw my Grandfather yesterday.
Correct:	I saw my grandfather yesterday.
Correct:	I saw Grandfather yesterday.

4. Capitalize the titles of creative works.

Books:	*The Stone Angel*
Short Stories:	"The Sinking of the Mariposa Belle"
Plays:	*Goodnight Desdemona (Good Morning Juliet)*
Poems:	"In Flanders Fields"
Articles:	"Two New Inns Now Open for Business"
Magazines:	*Maclean's*
Songs:	"If I Had a Million Dollars"
Albums or CDs:	*Jagged Little Pill*
Films:	*The Sweet Hereafter*
TV Series:	*This Hour Has 22 Minutes*
Works of Art:	*Starry Night*
Computer Programs:	Create CD

Do not capitalize *a, an, the,* or short prepositions unless they are the first or last word in a title.

5. Capitalize days of the week, months, holidays, and special events.

Monday, July, Canada Day, Thanksgiving, St. Jean-Baptiste Day

Do not capitalize the names of seasons: *summer, fall, winter, spring.*

6. Capitalize the names of historical events, periods, and documents.

the French Revolution, the Jurassic Period, World War II, the Sixties, the Battle of Vimy Ridge, the Magna Carta

7. Capitalize specific course titles and the names of language courses.

Economics 201, Philosophy 101, Spanish 200, Civilizations of the Ancient World

Do not capitalize a course or subject you are referring to in a general way unless the course is a language.

my economics course, my philosophy course, my Spanish course, my history course

8. Capitalize references to regions of the country but not words that merely indicate direction.

If you travel north from Toronto, you will end up in Northern Ontario, probably in Sudbury or Timmins.

9. Capitalize the opening of a letter and the first word of the closing.

Dear Dr. Hamlin, Dear Sir,

Best wishes, Sincerely,

Notice that a comma comes after the opening and closing.

REVIEWING CAPITALIZATION

Why is capitalization important in your writing?

_____

_____

What is the difference between a proper noun and a common noun?

_____

_____

◆ **P r a c t i c e   1   Identifying** Correct the capitalization errors in the following sentences.

1. Revenue canada is auditing aunt Joan.

2. Debbie and Sue bought their mother a bottle of chanel's coco perfume for mother's Day.

3. In our History class, we are studying the great wall of china.

4. This Winter, emilio will visit uncle Luis, who lives somewhere in the south.

5. David Bowie's song "changes" is a classic from the seventies.

◆ **P r a c t i c e   2   Completing** Fill in each blank with words that complete the sentence. Be sure to capitalize words correctly. (You can make up titles if necessary.)

1. In my _____ class, we had to read _____.

2. Blanca bought a new truck, a _____.

3. _____ should be in charge of the charity drive.

4. I wish I could get tickets to see _____ in concert.

5. We are going to _____ for our vacation.

◆ **P r a c t i c e   3   Writing Your Own** Write five sentences of your own that cover at least five of the capitalization rules.

CHAPTER REVIEW

Capitalize the first word of every sentence.

Capitalize all proper nouns.

Capitalize titles used with people's names.

Capitalize the titles of creative works.

Capitalize days of the week, months, holidays, and special events.

Capitalize historical events, periods, and documents.

Capitalize specific course titles and the names of language courses.

Capitalize references to regions of the country, but not mere directions.

Capitalize the opening of a letter and the first word of the closing.

♦ *Review   P r a c t i c e   **1**   **Writing Your Own** Write a paragraph about the most unusual person you've met or the most unusual place you've visited. What made this person or place unique?

♦ *Review   P r a c t i c e   **2**   **Editing Through Collaboration** Exchange paragraphs from Review Practice 1 with another student, and then do the following tasks:

1. Circle any letters that don't follow the capitalization rules.
2. Write the rule number next to the error for the writer to refer to.

Then return the paper to its writer, and use the information in this chapter to correct any capitalization errors in your own paragraph. Record your errors on the Error Log in Appendix 3.

48

ABBREVIATIONS AND NUMBERS

☑ CHECKLIST for Using Abbreviations and Numbers

> ✔ Are titles before and after proper names abbreviated correctly?
> ✔ Are government agencies and other organizations abbreviated correctly?
> ✔ Are numbers *zero* through *nine* spelled out?
> ✔ Are numbers 10 and over written as figures (10, 25, 1–20, 324)?

Test Yourself

Correct the abbreviation and number errors in these sentences.

- He earned two million three hundred thousand dollars last year.
- My cat had 5 kittens.
- Mandy moved from England to the U.S.
- Mister Johnson always drinks hot chocolate in the mornings.
- I work for the Royal Canadian Mounted Police.

(Answers are in Appendix 8 on the Web site.)

Like capitalization, **abbreviations** and **numbers** are also mechanical features of writing that help us communicate what we want to say. Following the rules that govern their use will make your writing as precise as possible.

ABBREVIATIONS

1. Abbreviate titles before proper names.

Mr. Michael Charles, **Mrs.** Marschel, **Ms.** Susan Deffaa, **Dr.** Frank Hilbig, **Rev.** Billy Graham, **Sgt.** Arturo Lopez

Abbreviate religious, governmental, and military titles when used with an entire name. Do not abbreviate them when used only with a last name.

NOT   We thought that **Gov.** Peterson would be reelected.

Correct: We thought that **Governor** Peterson would be reelected.

Correct: We thought **Gov.** Richard Peterson would be reelected.

Professor is not usually abbreviated: **Professor** Mya Belle is teaching this class.

2. Abbreviate academic degrees.

B.S. (Bachelor of Science)

R.N. (Registered Nurse)

3. Use the following abbreviations with numbers.

a.m. or **A.M.**   **p.m.** or **P.M.**   **B.C.**   **B.C.E.**   **A.D.**

4. Abbreviate *United States* only when it is used as an adjective.

NOT   The **U.S.** is in North America.

Correct: The **United States** is in North America.

Correct: The **U.S.** Senate will consider this bill today.

5. Abbreviate only the names of well-known government agencies, businesses, and educational institutions by using their initials without periods.

RCMP (Royal Canadian Mounted Police)

C (Canadian)

UWO (University of Western Ontario)

6. Abbreviate province names when addressing mail or writing out the postal address. Otherwise, spell out the names of provinces.

Maria's new address is 7124 Funston Street, Winnipeg, **MB** R3G 2W4.

Maria has moved to Winnipeg, **Manitoba.**

REVIEWING ABBREVIATIONS

When you write, are you free to abbreviate any words you want?

_____

◆ *P r a c t i c e* **1**   **Identifying** Correct the underlined words in each of the following sentences.

1. <u>Prof.</u> Smith said that I was a wonderful writer.
2. The <u>United States</u> economy has many markets.
3. When I can't sleep, I watch <u>Music Television</u>.
4. Last night, <u>Sergeant</u> David Montgomery devised the winning strategy.
5. Candice moved to 237 Bella Avenue, Mississauga, <u>Ontario</u> L5N 1A5.

◆ *P r a c t i c e* **2**   **Completing** In each sentence, write either an abbreviation or the complete word, whichever is correct.

1. We were caught speeding at 10 _____ (p.m., post meridian).
2. Alisha will be attending _____ (UBC, University of British Columbia) and will get her _____ (B.A., bachelor of arts) degree in English.
3. Darryl and Pat are visiting relatives in Stratford, _____ (ON, Ontario).
4. We moved to _____ (P.E.I., Prince Edward Island) when I was four years old.
5. (Rev., Reverend) _____ Matthews always has a kind word.

◆ *P r a c t i c e* **3**   **Writing Your Own** Write a sentence of your own for each of the following abbreviations.

1. Mr. _____

2. a.m. _____

3. CBC _____

4. A.A. _____

5. N.W.T. _____

NUMBERS

Most writers ask the same question about using numbers: When should a number be spelled out, and when is it all right to use numerals? The following simple rules will help you make this decision.

1. Spell out numbers from *zero* to *nine*. Use figures for numbers 10 and higher.

   > I have **three** dogs.
   >
   > My mother-in-law has **19** grandchildren and **11** great-grandchildren.

   Do not mix spelled-out numbers and figures in a sentence if they refer to the same types of items. Use numerals for all numbers in that case.

   NOT   I have **three** dogs, **18** goldfish, and **two** canaries.

   Correct: I have **3** dogs, **18** goldfish, and **2** canaries.

2. For very large numbers, use a combination of figures and words.

   > The province's new budget is approximately **$32 million.**
   >
   > Computer sales for the company reached **2.1 million** units.

3. Always spell out a number that begins a sentence. If this becomes awkward, reword the sentence.

   > **Thirty-five** people died in the crash.
   >
   > Approximately **260,000** people live in Kitchener, Ontario.

4. Use figures for dates, addresses, postal codes, telephone numbers, identification numbers, and time.

   > On August **1, 1965,** my parents moved to **215** Circle Drive, Saskatoon, SK **PR5 2L7.**
   >
   > My new telephone number is **(555) 877-1420.**
   >
   > My Social Insurance number is **123-456-789.**
   >
   > My alarm went off at **5:00** a.m.

5. Use figures for fractions, decimals, and percentages.

   > To make the dessert, you need **125** ml butter and **450** g of chocolate.
   >
   > His blood-alcohol level was **.09.**
   >
   > Over **35 percent** of Quebecers are of French background.

   Notice that *percent* is written out and is all one word.

6. Use figures for exact measurements, including amounts of money. Use a dollar sign for amounts over $1.

   > The room measures **3** metres by **4** metres.
   >
   > She bought a bag of candy for 99 cents, $1.20 less than it was yesterday.

7. Use figures for the parts of a book.

   Chapter **10**   page **120**   Exercise **8**   questions **1** and **7**

   Notice that *Chapter* and *Exercise* are capitalized, but *page* and *question* are not.

REVIEWING NUMBERS

What is the general rule for spelling out numbers as opposed to using numerals?

_____

◆ *P r a c t i c e 4* **Identifying** Correct any errors with numbers in each of the following sentences.

1. On August third, 2001, sixteen dogs escaped from the kennel.

2. The park, which measures approximately 170 square metres, will cost five thousand dollars to landscape.

3. Mr. Thompson's old telephone number was three, nine, nine, four, two, zero, nine.

4. Almost twenty-five percent of my income comes from sales.

5. The earthquake that hit at six forty-five last night measured 6.0 on the Richter scale.

◆ *P r a c t i c e 5* **Completing** Fill in each blank in the following sentences with numbers in the proper form.

1. Please read Chapter _____ and answer questions _____ through _____.

2. I have _____ pencils, _____ notebooks, and _____ note cards; I am ready for this test.

3. _____ percent of my time is spent doing homework.

4. Christmas is on _____ every year.

5. He made $ _____ million last year.

◆ *P r a c t i c e   6*   **Write Your Own** Write a sentence demonstrating each of the following rules for numbers.

1. Spell out numbers *zero* through *nine*. Use figures for numbers 10 and higher.

2. For very large numbers, use a combination of figures and words.

3. Always spell out a number that begins a sentence.

4. Use figures for dates, addresses, postal codes, telephone numbers, identification numbers, and time.

5. Use figures for fractions, decimals, and percentages.

CHAPTER REVIEW

Abbreviate titles before proper names.

Abbreviate academic degrees.

Abbreviate names of well-known government agencies, businesses, and educational institutions.

Abbreviate province names when addressing mail or writing out the postal address.

Spell out numbers from *zero* to *nine*. Use figures for numbers 10 and higher.

For very large numbers, use a combination of figures and words.

Use figures for dates and addresses.

Use figures for fractions, decimals, and percentages.

Use figures for exact measurements and amounts of money.

Use figures for parts of a book.

◆ *Review   Practice   1*   **Writing Your Own** Write a paragraph describing the quickest route from your home to your school. Use numbers and abbreviations in your paragraph.

◆ *Review   Practice   2*   **Editing Through Collaboration** Exchange paragraphs from Review Practice 1 with another student, and do the following:

1. Underline all abbreviations, numbers, and figures.

2. Circle any abbreviations, numbers, or figures that are not in the correct form.

Then return the paper to its writer, and use the information in this chapter to correct any abbreviation and number errors in your own paragraph. Record your errors on the Error Log in Appendix 3.

Varying Sentence Structure

CHAPTER 49

✔ CHECKLIST for Varying Sentence Patterns

> ✔ Do you add introductory material to vary your sentence patterns?
>
> ✔ Do you occasionally reverse the order of some subjects and verbs?
>
> ✔ Do you move sentence parts to add variety to your sentences?
>
> ✔ Do you sometimes use questions and exclamations to vary your sentence structure?

Test Yourself

Turn each of the following pairs of sentences into one sentence that is more interesting.

- I work too much. I am tired.
- My cat is very lazy. She sleeps more than 14 hours a day.
- He enjoys reading. He likes mysteries.
- I live in an old house. My family has lived here for generations.
- My brother loves to eat. He will eat anything.

(Answers are in Appendix 8 on the Web site.)

Reading the same sentence pattern, sentence after sentence, can become very monotonous for your readers. This chapter will help you solve this problem in your writing. Look at the following example.

I have always loved animals. I am about to get my own dog for the first time. I am ready to be responsible enough to take care of it. I am excited about this new phase in my life. I got a part-time job. I can't wait to get my own dog.

This paragraph has some terrific ideas, but they are expressed in such a monotonous way that the readers might doze off. What this paragraph needs is variety in its sentence structure. Here are some ideas for keeping your readers awake and ready to hear your good thoughts.

ADD INTRODUCTORY WORDS

Add some introductory words to your sentences so that they don't all start the same way.

> **For as long as I can remember,** I have always loved animals. **Now** I am about to get my own dog for the first time. I am ready to be responsible enough to take care of it. I am excited about this new phase in my life. **To pay for my new friend,** I got a part-time job. I can't wait to get my own dog.

◆ *P r a c t i c e   1*   **Identifying** Underline the sentence in each pair that could be turned into an introductory word, phrase, or clause.

1. Misty had a terrible stomachache. It was late last night.
2. We went to the river. We skipped over the rocks.
3. We went to McDonald's for breakfast. We saw our friends.
4. The sunsets are beautiful. It was spring.
5. He is afraid of dogs. He was bitten by a dog once.

◆ *P r a c t i c e   2*   **Completing** Rewrite the sentences in Practice 1 by turning each sentence you underlined into an introductory word, phrase, or clause.

◆ *P r a c t i c e   3*   **Writing Your Own** Write five sentences of your own with introductory elements.

REVERSE WORDS

Reverse the order of some subjects and verbs. For example, instead of *I am so excited,* try *Am I ever excited.* You can also add or drop words and change punctuation to make the sentence read smoothly.

> For as long as I can remember, I have always loved animals. Now I am about to get my own dog for the first time. I am ready to be responsible enough to take care of it. **Am I ever excited** about this new phase in my life. To pay for my new friend, I got a part-time job. I can't wait to get my own dog.

◈ *P r a c t i c e* **4** **Identifying** Underline the words or phrases you could reverse in each of the following sentences.

1. I am happy to know you.
2. All the ingredients went into the pot.
3. The cat jumped out of the hat.
4. The children were happy.
5. A strange creature appeared out of nowhere.

◈ *P r a c t i c e* **5** **Completing** Rewrite the sentences in Practice 4 by reversing the words you underlined.

◈ *P r a c t i c e* **6** **Writing Your Own** Write five sentences of your own with subjects and verbs reversed.

MOVE SENTENCE PARTS

Move some parts of the sentence around. Experiment to see which order works best.

For as long as I can remember, I have always loved animals. Now I am about to get my own dog for the first time. I am ready to be responsible enough to take care of it. Am I ever excited about this new phase in my life. **My part-time job can help me pay for my new friend.** I can't wait to get my own dog.

◈ *P r a c t i c e* **7** **Identifying** Underline any parts of the following sentences that can be moved around.

1. To bake these cookies, you will need 500 ml of flour.
2. Finally, I knew the truth.
3. I was very full after lunch.
4. You will find your shoes underneath your bed.
5. If you enjoyed the film, you will probably like the book.

◈ *P r a c t i c e* **8** **Completing** Rewrite the sentences in Practice 7, moving the words you underlined.

◈ *P r a c t i c e* **9** **Writing Your Own** Write two sentences of your own. Then rewrite each sentence two different ways.

VARY SENTENCE TYPE

Use a question, a command, or an exclamation occasionally.

For as long as I can remember, I have always loved animals. **Have you?** Now I am about to get my own dog for the first time. I am ready to be responsible enough to take care of it. **Am I ever excited about this new phase in my life!** My part-time job can help me pay for my new friend. I can't wait to get my own dog.

Practice 10 Identifying Identify each of the following sentences as a statement (S), a question (Q), a command (C), or an exclamation (E).

1. _____ When is the meal being served
2. _____ Did you see that object flying in the sky
3. _____ Bring me a glass of iced tea and a bowl of grapes
4. _____ First do the prewriting exercises
5. _____ I just hate it when that happens

Practice 11 Completing Complete the following sentences, making them into questions, commands, or exclamations. Then supply the correct punctuation.

1. Wow, I can't believe _____

2. At the first intersection _____

3. Why is _____

4. Hand me _____

5. Did you hear _____

Practice 12 Writing Your Own Write two statements, two questions, two commands, and two exclamations of your own.

> REVIEWING WAYS TO VARY SENTENCE PATTERNS
>
> *Why is varying sentence patterns important in your writing?*
>
> _____

Name four ways to vary your sentence patterns.

_____

_____

_____

_____

What other kinds of sentences besides statements can you use for variety?

_____   _____   _____

USING THE ACTIVE VOICE

In the **active voice,** the subject performs the action. In the **passive voice,** the subject receives the action. Compare the following two examples:

Passive Voice: The mayor **was accused** of stealing **by the police.**

Active Voice: **The police accused** the mayor of stealing.

The active voice adds energy to your writing. Here is another example. Notice the difference between active and passive.

Passive Voice: **The cake was baked** for Tim's birthday **by my grandmother.**

Active Voice: **My grandmother baked the cake** for Tim's birthday.

REVIEWING ACTIVE AND PASSIVE VOICE

What is the difference between the active and passive voice?

_____

_____

Why is the active voice usually better than the passive?

_____

P r a c t i c e   1 3   **Identifying** Write A if the sentence is in the active voice and P if it is in the passive voice.

1. _____ The astronauts landed on the moon and planted a flag.
2. _____ Flowers are being sent to the funeral home.
3. _____ Jordan hit the ball over the fence into the neighbour's yard.
4. _____ The experimental medicines were shipped to the laboratory for further testing.
5. _____ People who heckle the politicians will be escorted from the building.

P r a c t i c e   1 4   **Correcting** Rewrite the passive sentences in Practice 13 in the active voice.

CHAPTER REVIEW

Add some introductory words to sentences so they don't all start the same way.

Reverse the order of some nouns and verbs.

Move parts of the sentences around.

Use a question, a command, or an exclamation occasionally.

Use the active voice to add energy to your writing.

Review   P r a c t i c e   1   **Writing Your Own** Write a paragraph about a good deed you have performed. What made you decide to do what you did? Try to use each of the four ways you have learned to make sentences interesting.

Review   P r a c t i c e   2   **Editing Through Collaboration** Exchange paragraphs from Review Practice 1 with another student, and then do the following:

1. Put brackets around any sentences that sound monotonous.
2. Suggest a way to vary each of these sentences.

Then return the paper to its writer, and use the information in this chapter to vary the sentence structure in your own paragraph. Record your errors on the Error Log in Appendix 3.

PARALLELISM

✔ CHECKLIST for Using Parallelism

> ✔ Can you use parallelism to add coherence to your sentences and paragraphs?
> ✔ Are all items in a series grammatically balanced?

Test Yourself

Underline the parts in each of the following sentences that seem awkward or unbalanced.

- Tony enjoys hockey, football, and runs.
- My mom and dad give money to help the homeless and for building new homes.
- I finished high school, started college, and I am beginning a new job.
- I love the mountains because they're cool, clean, and feel refreshing.
- Listening to music, watching television, or to read a book are good ways to relax.

(Answers are in Appendix 8 on the Web site.)

When sentences are **parallel,** they are balanced. That is, words, phrases, or clauses in a series start with the same grammatical form. Parallel structures make your sentences interesting and clear.

Following is a paragraph that could be greatly improved with parallel structures.

My brother Ricardo was not excited when he was called in to work at the hospital today. He had been looking forward to this day off—his first in three weeks. He was planning to work out in the morning, swimming in the afternoon, and going to a movie in the evening. Instead he will be helping the patients, assisting the nurses, and will aid the doctors.

Words and phrases in a series should be parallel, which means they should start with the same type of word. Parallelism makes your sentence structure smoother and more interesting. Look at this sentence, for example.

NOT   He had planned to **work out** in the morning,

          swimming in the afternoon, and

          going to a movie in the evening.

Parallel: He had planned to **work out** in the morning,

          swim in the afternoon, and

          go to a movie in the evening.

Parallel: He had planned on **working out** in the morning,

          swimming in the afternoon, and

          going to a movie in the evening.

Here is another sentence that would read better if the parts were parallel:

NOT   Instead he will be **helping** the patients,

          assisting the nurses, and

          will aid the doctors.

Parallel: Instead he will be **helping** the patients,

          assisting the nurses, and

          aiding the doctors.

Parallel: Instead he will be helping **the patients,**

          the nurses, and

          the doctors.

Now read the paragraph with these two sentences made parallel or balanced.

My brother Ricardo was not excited when he was called in to work at the hospital today. He had been looking forward to this day off—his first in three weeks. He had planned to work out in the morning, swim in the afternoon, and go to a movie in the evening. Instead he will be helping the patients, the nurses, and the doctors.

REVIEWING PARALLELISM

What is parallelism?

_____

_____

Why should you use parallelism in your writing?

_____

◆ *P r a c t i c e **1** **Identifying** Underline the parallel structures in each of the following sentences.

1. Scott plans to hide in his cottage, do some fishing, and work on his novel.
2. The car needs new windows, tires, and paint.
3. Georgia believes that she is the most wonderful person in the world and that she deserves everyone's love and attention.
4. They camped under the stars, swam in the cool lakes, and enjoyed the fresh air.
5. Because of the pouring rain, extreme cold, and bitter wind, we decided to stay inside.

◆ *P r a c t i c e **2** **Completing** Make the underlined elements parallel in each of the following sentences.

1. He will wear only clothes <u>that have designer labels</u> and <u>they are expensive</u>.

_____

2. <u>Regular exercise</u>, <u>drinking plenty of water</u>, and <u>eating lots of good food</u> will help keep you healthy.

_____

3. Deirdre went to the mall <u>to get a bite to eat</u>, <u>to do some shopping</u>, and <u>will visit friends</u>.

_____

4. Please do not <u>tap pens</u>, <u>talk to others</u>, or <u>eating food</u> during the exam.

_____

5. On his trip, he <u>took pictures of mountains</u>, <u>fed animals</u>, and <u>some enjoy-</u><u>able people</u>.

_____

◆ **P r a c t i c e   3**   **Writing Your Own** Write five sentences of your own using parallel structures in each.

CHAPTER REVIEW

Parallel Sentence: Words, phrases, or clauses in a series start with the same grammatical form.

◆ **Review P r a c t i c e   1**   **Writing Your Own** Write a paragraph about the best holiday you've ever had. What was the holiday? Why was it the best? Use two examples of parallelism in your paragraph.

◆ **Review P r a c t i c e   2**   **Editing Through Collaboration** Exchange paragraphs from Review Practice 1 with another student, and then do the following:

1. Underline any items in a series.
2. Put brackets around any of these items that are not grammatically parallel.

Then return the paper to its writer, and use the information in this chapter to correct any parallelism errors in your own paragraph. Record your errors on the Error Log in Appendix 3.

COMBINING SENTENCES

CHAPTER 51

✔️ CHECKLIST for Combining Sentences

> ✔ Do you combine sentences to avoid too many short, choppy sentences in a row?
>
> ✔ Do you use different types of sentences?

Test Yourself

Combine each set of sentences into one sentence.

- My brother is taking tennis lessons. He takes his lessons from a professional player.
- The baby is crying. She's hungry.
- It's too hot outside. Let's go for a swim.
- We moved overseas when I was 11 years old. I learned a lot about different cultures.
- I like to travel. Africa has many interesting animals and plants. I want to go to Africa.

(Answers are in Appendix 8 on the Web site.)

Still another way to add variety to your writing is to combine short, choppy sentences into longer sentences. You can combine simple sentences to make compound or complex sentences. You can also combine compound and complex sentences.

SIMPLE SENTENCES

A **simple sentence** consists of one independent clause. Remember that a clause has a subject and a main verb.

In the following examples, notice that a simple sentence can have more than one subject and more than one verb. (For more on compound subjects and compound verbs, see Chapter 32.)

s   v

I have several very good friends.

s   v   v

I have good friends and enjoy being with them.

s   s   v

Martin and Louis are good friends.

s   s   v   v

Martin and I go to interesting places and do interesting things.

REVIEWING SIMPLE SENTENCES

What does a simple sentence consist of?

_____

Write a simple sentence.

_____

◆ **P r a c t i c e   1   Identifying** Underline the subjects once and the verbs twice in each of the following sentences. Then label the simple sentences SS.

1. _____ Most cats don't like the water, but most dogs do.

2. _____ Tommy and I like listening to the same types of music and watching the same types of shows.

3. _____ I feel that our luck is about to change.

4. _____ We left quickly because of the smell.

5. _____ We have pictures of the family throughout the house.

◆ **P r a c t i c e   2   Completing** Make simple sentences out of the sentences in Practice 1 that are not simple.

◆ **P r a c t i c e   3   Writing Your Own** Write a simple sentence of your own for each of the following subjects and verbs.

1. Jessy and Leo _____

2. we're eating and drinking _____

3. the playful kittens _____

4. looking and listening _____

5. the hot pan _____

COMPOUND SENTENCES

A **compound sentence** consists of two or more independent clauses joined by a coordinating conjunction (*and, but, for, nor, or, so,* or *yet*). In other words, you can create a compound sentence from two (or more) simple sentences.

Simple:	I can swim fast.
Simple:	I am a good long-distance swimmer.
Compound:	I can swim fast, **and** I am a good long-distance swimmer.

Simple:	She has a very stressful job.
Simple:	She works out at the gym three times a week.
Compound:	She has a very stressful job, **so** she works out at the gym three times a week.

Simple:	My parents are leaving for Hawaii on Tuesday.
Simple:	They won't be here for my birthday party.
Compound:	My parents are leaving for Hawaii on Tuesday, **so** they won't be here for my birthday party.

Hint: As the examples show, a comma comes before the coordinating conjunction in a compound sentence.

REVIEWING COMPOUND SENTENCES

What does a compound sentence consist of?

_____

Write a compound sentence.

_____

◆ *P r a c t i c e 4* **Identifying** Underline the independent clauses in the following sentences, and circle the coordinating conjunctions.

1. I am not sick, and I feel fine.
2. You cannot bring food or drink into this building, but you can eat in the cafeteria.
3. We try not to gossip, for we know the damage rumours can cause.
4. I do not like raspberries, yet I do like raspberry pie.
5. Christy likes fast cars, so she is going to buy a sports car.

◆ *P r a c t i c e 5* **Completing** Combine each pair of simple sentences into a compound sentence.

1. I am leaving. I am late for an appointment.
2. Quickly, move out of the way. The angry elephant is going to charge us.
3. We usually take a month-long vacation. We are always happy to return home.
4. This food has been sitting out all day in the hot sun. It smells awful.
5. I have a lot of cousins. I haven't met them all.

◆ *P r a c t i c e 6* **Writing Your Own** Write five compound sentences of your own.

COMPLEX SENTENCES

A **complex sentence** is composed of one independent clause and at least one dependent clause. A **dependent clause** begins with either a subordinating conjunction or a relative pronoun.

Subordinating Conjunctions

after	because	since	until
although	before	so	when
as	even if	so that	whenever
as if	even though	than	where
as long as	how	that	wherever
as soon as	if	though	whether
as though	in order that	unless	while

Relative Pronouns

who	whom	whose	which	that

You can use subordinating conjunctions and relative pronouns to make a simple sentence (an independent clause) into a dependent clause. Then you can add the new dependent clause to an independent clause to produce a complex sentence that adds interest and variety to your writing.

How do you know which simple sentence should be independent and which should be dependent? The idea that you think is more important should be the independent clause. The less important idea will then be the dependent clause.

Following are some examples of how to combine simple sentences to make a complex sentence.

Simple: Myra has a large collection of movie videos.

Simple: Myra watches the same few films over and over.

                              dep
Complex: **Even though** Myra has a large collection of movie

                    ind
videos, she watches the same few films over and over.

This complex sentence stresses that Myra watches the same films over and over. The size of her collection is of secondary importance.

                    ind
Complex: Myra has a big collection of movie videos, **though** she

              dep
watches the same few films over and over.

In the previous complex sentence, the size of the collection is most important, so it is the independent clause.

Simple: The winner of the lottery was Laura.

Simple: Laura is my cousin.

                      ind   dep
Complex: The winner of the lottery was Laura, **who** is my cousin.

This complex sentence answers the question "Who won the lottery?" The information about Laura being the cousin is of secondary importance.

                  ind   dep
Complex: My cousin is Laura, **who** won the lottery.

This complex sentence answers the question "Who is your cousin?" The information that she won the lottery is secondary.

REVIEWING COMPLEX SENTENCES

What does a complex sentence consist of?

_____

Write a complex sentence.

_____

◆ *P r a c t i c e* **7** **Identifying** Label the underlined part of each sentence as either an independent (Ind) or a dependent (Dep) clause.

1. _____ <u>Although I was tired</u>, I still went to school.
2. _____ Here is the furniture <u>that you ordered</u>.
3. _____ <u>Trish moved to the coast</u> because she likes the beach.
4. _____ My doctor is Janet Wu, <u>who is also my mom</u>.
5. _____ If we cannot study at your house, <u>then let's study at the library</u>.

◆ *P r a c t i c e* **8** **Completing** Finish each sentence, and label the new clause either dependent (Dep) or independent (Ind).

1. _____ Whenever John's face turns red, _____.
2. _____ _____ because he forgot to call home.
3. _____ Maya's mother, who _____, is a great cook.
4. _____ I like the blue one, _____.
5. _____ He climbed the mountain _____.

◆ *P r a c t i c e* **9** **Writing Your Own** Write five complex sentences, making sure you have one independent clause and at least one dependent clause in each.

COMPOUND–COMPLEX SENTENCES

If you combine a compound sentence with a complex sentence, you produce a **compound–complex sentence.** That means your sentence has at least two independent clauses (to make it compound) and at least one dependent clause (to make it complex). Here are some examples.

Simple: My cousin likes scuba diving.
Simple: He is planning a trip to Hawaii.

Simple: He is excited about diving in Hawaii.

                                          ind   ind

Compound–Complex: My cousin likes scuba diving, **so** he is

                                                              dep

planning a trip to Hawaii, **which** he is
very excited about.

Simple: She bought a new house.

Simple: It has a pool and a spa.

Simple: The house was very expensive.

                                    ind   dep

Compound–Complex: She bought a new house, **which** has a

                                                        ind

pool and a spa, **but** it was very expensive.

Simple: Today's weather is very bad.

Simple: The rain could make it difficult to drive.

Simple: This could delay your departure for home.

                                    ind   ind

Compound–Complex: Today's weather is very bad, **and** the rain

                                                              dep

could make it difficult to drive, **which** could
delay your arrival home.

Hint: Notice that we occasionally have to change words in combined
sentences so that the sentences make sense.

Reviewing Compound–Complex Sentences

What does a compound–complex sentence consist of?

_____

Write a compound–complex sentence.

_____

♦ **Practice 10** **Identifying** Underline the clauses in each of the following compound–complex sentences. Then identify each clause as either independent (Ind) or dependent (Dep).

1. Whenever I travel, I set an alarm clock, and I arrange for a wake-up call.

2. Sandy likes Anthony because he is nice, but she also likes Mark.

3. After they fought, they decided to make up, and now they are inseparable.

4. The traffic, which is usually bad around noon, is very heavy today, so you'd better leave soon.

5. We went to the Virgin Islands because we love the sun, yet it rained the whole time.

♦ **Practice 11** **Completing** Expand each sentence into a compound–complex sentence.

1. The boy likes oranges and pears.

   _____

2. The box was very heavy, but he lifted it anyway.

   _____

3. Jill says that she will never fly in a plane.

   _____

4. John will be 21 soon.

   _____

5. I am watching MuchMusic and getting some rest.

   _____

◆ *P r a c t i c e 1 2* **Writing Your Own** Write five compound–complex sentences of your own.

CHAPTER REVIEW

Simple Sentence: consists of one independent clause

Compound Sentence: consists of two or more independent clauses joined by a coordinating conjunction

Complex Sentence: consists of one independent clause and at least one dependent clause

Subordinating Conjunctions: make an independent clause a dependent clause. Add this dependent clause to an independent clause to create a complex sentence.

Compound–Complex Sentence: has at least two independent clauses and one dependent clause

◆ *Review P r a c t i c e 1* **Writing Your Own** Write a paragraph about your fondest wish. What is it, and why do you wish for it?

◆ *Review P r a c t i c e 2* **Editing Through Collaboration** Exchange paragraphs from Review Practice 1 with another student, and then do the following:

1. Put brackets around any sentences that you think should be combined.
2. Underline sentences that are incorrectly combined (for example, ones that have a weak connecting word or no connecting word).

Then return the paper to its writer, and use the information in this chapter to combine sentences in your own paragraph. Record your errors on the Error Log in Appendix 3.

Standard and Nonstandard English

CHAPTER **52**

✔ CHECKLIST for Choosing the Right Word

> ✔ Do you consistently use standard English in your paper?
>
> ✔ Is your paper free of nonstandard, ungrammatical words?
>
> ✔ Have you changed any slang to standard English?

Test Yourself

Label the following sentences as correct, incorrect, or slang.

- You shoulda seen Claudia's new hairstyle. _____
- Where are my friends at? _____
- Your new bike is really hot. _____
- Randy was enthused about his date. _____
- Fatboy Slim's new video rocks. _____

(Answers are in Appendix 8 on the Web site.)

Choosing the right words for what you want to say is an important part of effective communication. This chapter will help you find the right words and phrases for the audience you are trying to reach.

Look, for example, at the following sentences. They all have a similar message, expressed in different words.

I want to do good in college, being as I can get a good job.

I be studying hard in college, so I can get a good job.

I'm going to hit the books so I can rake in the bucks.

I want to do well in college so I can get a good job.

Which of these sentences would you probably say to a friend or to someone in your family? Which would you most likely say in a job interview? Which would be good for a college paper?

548

The first three sentences are nonstandard English. They might be said or written to a friend or family member, but they would not be appropriate in an academic setting or in a job situation. Only the fourth sentence would be appropriate in an academic paper or in a job interview.

STANDARD AND NONSTANDARD ENGLISH

Most of the English language falls into one of two categories—either *standard* or *nonstandard*. **Standard English** is the language of college, business, and the media. It is used by reporters on television, by newspapers, in most magazines, and on Web sites created by schools, government, business, and organizations. Standard English is always grammatically correct and free of slang.

Nonstandard English does not follow all the rules of grammar and often includes slang. Nonstandard English is not necessarily wrong, but it is more appropriate in some settings (with friends and family) than others. It is not appropriate in college or business writing. To understand the difference between standard and nonstandard English, compare the following paragraphs.

Nonstandard English

I was stoked to find out I would be getting a $300 refund on my taxes. My first thought was to blow it on a trip, maybe somewheres like Montreal. But none of my friends was enthused by that. Then I thought being as I watch television alot, I would buy a new TV with a built-in DVD player. My brother got hisself one last year. Then it hit me, hey, I'm gonna need some money to buy new duds for my job. Alright, I decided, I gotta buy clothes with the dough, irregardless of what I'd like to do with it.

Standard English

I was thrilled when I found out I would be getting a $300 refund on my taxes. My first thought was to spend it on a trip, maybe somewhere like Montreal. But none of my friends were enthusiastic about that. Then I thought that since I watch television a lot, I would buy a new TV with a built-in DVD player. My brother got himself one last year. Then I realized that I am going to need some money to buy new clothes for my job. All right, I decided, I have to buy clothes with the money, regardless of what I'd like to do with it.

In the rest of this chapter, you will learn how to recognize and correct ungrammatical English and how to avoid slang in your writing.

> REVIEWING STANDARD AND NONSTANDARD ENGLISH
>
> *Where do you hear standard English in your daily life?*
>
> _____
>
> *What is nonstandard English?*
>
> _____
>
> *Give two examples of nonstandard English.*
>
> _____

NONSTANDARD ENGLISH

Nonstandard English is ungrammatical. It does not follow the rules of standard English that are required in college writing. The academic and business worlds expect you to be able to recognize and avoid nonstandard English. This is not always easy because some nonstandard terms are used so often in speech that many people think they are acceptable in writing. The following list might help you choose the correct words in your own writing

ain't

NOT	My economics professor **ain't** giving us the test today.
CORRECT	My economics professor **isn't** giving us the test today.

anywheres

NOT	Leah buys her clothes **anywheres** she can find them.
CORRECT	Leah buys her clothes **anywhere** she can find them.

be

NOT	I **be** so happy.
CORRECT	I **am** so happy.

being as, being that, seeing as how

NOT	Emilio will not get to go home over the weekend, **being as** he has to work.
CORRECT	Emilio will not get to go home over the weekend **because** he has to work.

coulda/could of, shoulda/should of

NOT   He **could of** earned a better grade on the test if he'd studied.

CORRECT He **could have** (or **could've**) earned a better grade on the test if he'd studied.

different than

NOT   She is **different than** us.

CORRECT She is **different from** us.

drug

NOT   She **drug** the mattress across the room.

CORRECT She **dragged** the mattress across the room.

enthused

NOT   Mary was **enthused** about the wedding.

CORRECT Mary was **enthusiastic** about the wedding.

everywheres

NOT   My dog follows me **everywheres** I go.

CORRECT My dog follows me **everywhere** I go.

goes

NOT   Then Lori **goes,** "I'm leaving without you."

CORRECT Then Lori **said,** "I'm leaving without you."

CORRECT Then Lori **said** that she was leaving without me.

hisself

NOT   Jerry made **hisself** a cheeseburger.

CORRECT Jerry made **himself** a cheeseburger.

in regards to

NOT   We received a letter **in regards to** your complaint.

CORRECT We received a letter **in regard to** your complaint.

irregardless

NOT   **Irregardless** of how long you study French, you'll never speak it like a native.

CORRECT **Regardless** of how long you study French, you'll never speak it like a native.

kinda/kind of, sorta/sort of

NOT   The rooms smells **kinda** sweet, **sorta** like vanilla.

CORRECT The room smells **rather** sweet, **much like** vanilla.

most

NOT	**Most** everyone accepted the invitation.
CORRECT	**Almost** everyone accepted the invitation.

must of

NOT	I **must of** lost my purse at the party.
CORRECT	I **must have** lost my purse at the party.

off of

NOT	Billy jumped **off of** the back of the truck.
CORRECT	Billy jumped **off** the back of the truck.

oughta

NOT	Sometimes I think I **oughta** watch less television.
CORRECT	Sometimes I think I **ought to** watch less television.

real

NOT	My boyfriend was **real** mad when I went out with another boy.
CORRECT	My boyfriend was **really** mad when I went out with another boy.

somewheres

NOT	Your jeans are **somewheres** in that pile of clothes.
CORRECT	Your jeans are **somewhere** in that pile of clothes.

suppose to

NOT	You were **suppose to** turn that paper in yesterday.
CORRECT	You were **supposed to** turn that paper in yesterday.

theirselves

NOT	They helped **theirselves** to the food in the buffet line.
CORRECT	They helped **themselves** to the food in the buffet line.

use to

NOT	I **use to** have a truck.
CORRECT	I **used to** have a truck.

ways

NOT	Curt's car broke down a long **ways** from home.
CORRECT	Curt's car broke down a long **way** from home.

where . . . at

NOT	**Where** is the nearest bakery **at?**
CORRECT	**Where** is the nearest bakery?

youse

> **NOT**   Can I get **youse** some coffee?
> **CORRECT** Can I get **you** some coffee?

REVIEWING NONSTANDARD ENGLISH

What is one reason using nonstandard English in written work is easy to do?

_____

Give four examples of nonstandard English; then correct them.

_____   _____

_____   _____

_____   _____

_____   _____

◆ **Practice 1A**   **Identifying** Underline the ungrammatical words or phrases in each of the following sentences.

1. Do you know where the children are at?
2. Then John goes, "There is no way I'm going to touch that."
3. Our production of *Romeo and Juliet* is kinda like the original, but sorta modern.
4. I coulda stayed at home instead of sitting here listening to this boring lecture.
5. Justin was suppose to mail the invitations.

◆ **Practice 1B**   **Correcting** Correct the ungrammatical words and expressions in Practice 1A by rewriting the incorrect sentences.

◆ **Practice 2**   **Completing** Underline the ungrammatical word or words in each phrase, and change them to standard English.

1. Anywheres I go   _____
2. She drug it   _____
3. We are a long ways   _____
4. He made hisself   _____
5. Being that Susan   _____

◆ *P r a c t i c e   3*   **Writing Your Own** Write five sentences of your own using the grammatical words and phrases you chose in Practice 2.

SLANG

Another example of nonstandard English is **slang,** popular words and ex-pressions that come and go, much like the latest fashions. For example, in the 1950s, someone might call his or her special someone *dreamy.* In the 1960s, you might hear a boyfriend or girlfriend described as *groovy,* and in the 1990s, *sweet* was the popular slang term. Today your significant other might be *hot* or *dope.*

These expressions are slang because they are part of the spoken lan-guage that changes from generation to generation and from place to place. As you might suspect, slang communicates to a limited audience who share common interests and experiences. Some slang words, such as *cool* and *neat,* have become part of our language, but most slang is temporary. What's in today may be out tomorrow, so the best advice is to avoid slang in your writing.

REVIEWING SLANG

What is slang?

_____

Give two examples of slang terms that were popular but aren't any longer.

_____

Give two examples of slang terms that you and your friends use today.

_____

◆ *P r a c t i c e   4*   **Identifying** Underline the slang words and expres-sions in each of the following sentences.

1. *Return of the Mummy* rocks!
2. "Wassup?" I yelled to my homies.
3. This party is da bomb.
4. My mom tripped out when I got my tattoo.
5. Stewart is zoning on the video game.

◆ *P r a c t i c e* **5** **Completing** Translate the following slang expressions into standard English.

1. Talk to the hand _____

2. hella good _____

3. flyboy _____

4. right back atcha _____

5. a wanna-be _____

◆ *P r a c t i c e* **6** **Writing Your Own** List five slang words or expressions, and use them in sentences of your own. Then rewrite each sentence using standard English to replace the slang expressions.

CHAPTER REVIEW

Standard English: the language of school, business, and the media

Non-standard English: does not follow the rules of grammar and often includes slang

Slang: popular words and expressions that come and go in the English language

◆ *R e v i e w   P r a c t i c e* **1** **Writing Your Own** Write a paragraph on how you spend your free time. Do you spend it with your friends or alone? What do you do and why?

◆ *R e v i e w   P r a c t i c e* **2** **Editing Through Collaboration** Exchange paragraphs from Review Practice 1 with another student, and then do the following:

1. Underline any ungrammatical language.
2. Circle any slang.

Then return the paper to its writer, and use the information in this chapter to correct any nonstandard or slang expressions in your own paragraph. Record your errors on the Error Log in Appendix 3.

53 EASILY CONFUSED WORDS

☑ CHECKLIST for Easily Confused Words

> ✔ Is the correct word chosen from the easily confused words?
>
> ✔ Are the following words used correctly: *its/it's, their/there/they're, to/too/two, who's/whose, your/you're?*

Test Yourself

Choose the correct word in parentheses.

- Miranda couldn't (choose, chose) a college.
- (It's, Its) time to leave for the show.
- I can't (hear, here) with all this noise.
- (Weather, Whether) you go or not, I'm still going to attend.
- (Who's, Whose) responsible for this mess?

(Answers are in Appendix 8 on the Web site.)

Some words are easily confused. They may look alike, sound alike, or have similar meanings, but they all play different roles in the English language. This chapter will help you choose the right words for your sentences.

EASILY CONFUSED WORDS, PART I

a/an: Use *a* before words that begin with a consonant. Use *an* before words that begin with a vowel (*a, e, i, o, u*).

> **a** bill, **a** cat, **a** zebra
> **an** artichoke, **an** island, **an** occasion

accept/except: *Accept* means "receive." *Except* means "other than."

> Mary will not **accept** the gift.
> Everyone went **except** Harry.

advice/advise: *Advice* means "helpful information." *Advise* means "give advice or help."

> My mother usually gives me very good **advice.**
>
> My parents **advise** me when I'm trying to make an important decision.

affect/effect: *Affect* (verb) means "influence." *Effect* means "bring about" (verb) or "a result" (noun).

> She hopes having children won't **affect** her chance at promotion.
>
> I believe that changes in the law will **effect** positive changes in society.
>
> The weather had a bad **effect** on his health.

already/all ready: *Already* means "in the past." *All ready* means "completely prepared."

> I have **already** taken that class.
>
> We had packed the car and were **all ready** to go when the accident happened.

among/between: Use *among* when referring to three or more people or things. Use *between* when referring to only two people or things.

> The students discussed the issues **among** themselves.
>
> I can't decide **between** the two dresses.

bad/badly: *Bad* means "not good." *Badly* means "not well."

> That meat is **bad,** so don't eat it.
>
> He felt **bad** about the accident.
>
> He was hurt **badly** in the accident.

beside/besides: *Beside* means "next to." *Besides* means "in addition (to)."

> She sat **beside** him at lunch.
>
> **Besides** sleeping, I can think of nothing else I want to do.

brake/break: *Brake* means "stop" or "the parts that stop a moving vehicle." *Break* means "shatter, come apart" or "a rest between work periods."

> She didn't **brake** soon enough to avoid the other car.
>
> I watched the limb **break** off the tree.
>
> Can we take a **break?**

breath/breathe: *Breath* means "air." *Breathe* means "taking in air."

Take a long, slow **breath.**

The air we have to **breathe** is unhealthy.

choose/chose: *Choose* means "select." *Chose* is the past tense of choose.

Please **choose** an answer.

He **chose** the wrong answer.

REVIEWING WORDS THAT ARE EASILY CONFUSED, PART I

Do you understand the differences in the sets of words in Part I of the list?

_____

Have you ever confused any of these words? If so, which ones?

_____

◆ **P r a c t i c e 1** **Identifying** Underline the correct word in each of the following sentences.

1. I can (advice, advise) you on what courses to take.
2. The little boy behaved (bad, badly) when his father left.
3. We were (already, all ready) to leave the house when she realized she didn't have her purse.
4. (Among, Between) the three of us, we should have enough money to buy lunch.
5. The cold water took my (breath, breathe) away.

◆ **P r a c t i c e 2** **Completing** Complete the following sentences with a correct word from Part I of the list of easily confused words.

1. I _____ you to be on my team last year.
2. _____ for the humidity, we had a wonderful trip.
3. We have to keep the secret _____ you and me.
4. Corkey was a _____ dog; he chewed up my shoes.
5. Take my _____ and bring a jacket.

♦ *P r a c t i c e 3* **Writing Your Own** Use each pair of words correctly in a sentence of your own.

1. a/an _____

2. breath/breathe _____

3. affect/effect _____

4. already/all ready _____

5. beside/besides _____

EASILY CONFUSED WORDS, PART II

coarse/course: *Coarse* refers to something that is rough. *Course* refers to a class, a process, or a part of a meal.

> This pavement is **coarse.**
> My **course** in math is very interesting.
> I will prepare a four-**course** meal.

desert/dessert: *Desert* refers to dry, sandy land or means "abandon." *Dessert* refers to the last course of a meal.

> It is difficult to live in the **desert.**
> He **deserted** his family.
> We had strawberry shortcake for **dessert.**

Hint: You can remember that **dessert** has two *s*'s if you think of *strawberry shortcake*.

does/dose: *Does* means "performs." *Dose* refers to a specific portion of medicine.

> My sister **does** whatever she wants.
> Children should have only a small **dose** of the medicine.

fewer/less: *Fewer* refers to things that can be counted. *Less* refers to things that cannot be counted.

> There are **fewer** cotton fields than there used to be.
> She has much **less** time now that she has a new job.

good/well: *Good* modifies nouns. *Well* modifies verbs, adjectives, and adverbs. *Well* also refers to a state of health.

> Bill looks **good** in his new suit.
> I'm afraid I didn't do **well** on the test.
> Kate isn't feeling **well** today.

hear/here: *Hear* refers to the act of listening. *Here* means "in this place."

> My father can't **hear** as well as he used to.
> **Here** is the book you asked for.

it's/its: *It's* is the contraction for *it is* or *it has*. *Its* is a possessive pronoun.

> The teacher said **it's** important to answer all the questions.
> The dog chased **its** tail.

knew/new: *Knew* is the past tense of *know*. *New* means "recent."

> I thought everyone **knew** I had a **new** boyfriend.

know/no: *Know* means "understand." *No* means "not any" or is the opposite of *yes*.

> We all **know** that we have **no** hope of defeating the other team.

lay/lie: *Lay* means "set down." (Its principal parts are *lay, laid, laid*.) *Lie* means "recline." (Its principal parts are *lie, lay, lain*.)

> He **lays** brick for a living.
> He **laid** down the heavy sack.
> She **lies** down at 2 p.m. every day for a nap.
> I **lay** in the grass.

(For additional help with *lie* and *lay*, see Chapter 35, "Regular and Irregular Verbs.")

loose/lose: *Loose* means "free" or "unattached." *Lose* means "misplace" or "not win."

> Hal's pants are too **loose.**
> If I **lose** another $10, I'm going to quit gambling.

passed/past: *Passed* is the past tense of pass. *Past* refers to an earlier time or means "beyond."

> John **passed** by his old house on the way to school.
> It is interesting to study the **past.**
> The dog ran **past** me and into the street.

> REVIEWING WORDS THAT ARE EASILY CONFUSED, PART II
>
> *Do you understand the differences in the sets of words in Part II of the list?*
>
> _____
>
> *Have you ever confused any of these words? If so, which ones?*
>
> _____

◆ **P r a c t i c e 4 Identifying** Underline the correct word in each of the following sentences.

1. We (passed, past) Edward on the highway.
2. I think you have made a (good, well) choice.
3. With her second job, Marsha has (fewer, less) time to spend with her friends.
4. (It's, Its) going to be a beautiful day.
5. I cannot (loose, lose) this ring; it was given to me by my grandmother.

◆ **P r a c t i c e 5 Completing** Complete the following sentences with a correct word from Part II of the list.

1. The restaurant served peach cobbler for _____.
2. How do you like my _____ car?
3. Mike _____ not want to go to the concert with us.
4. This business _____ will benefit me on the job.
5. I am not feeling _____ today.

◆ **P r a c t i c e 6 Writing Your Own** Use each pair of words correctly in a sentence of your own.

1. fewer/less _____

2. knew/new _____

3. hear/here _____

4. it's/its _____

5. lay/lie _____

EASILY CONFUSED WORDS, PART III

principal/principle: *Principal* means "main, most important," "a school official," or "a sum of money." A *principle* is a rule. (Think of *principle* and *rule*—both end in *-le*.)

> My **principal** reason for moving is to be closer to my family.
> Mr. Kobler is the **principal** at Westside Elementary School.
> He lives by one main **principle**—honesty.

quiet/quite: *Quiet* means "without noise." *Quite* means "very."

> The house was **quiet.**
> I am **quite** happy with my new car.

raise/rise: *Raise* means "increase" or "lift up." *Rise* means "get up from a sitting or reclining position."

> The state is going to **raise** the tax on cigarettes.
> Jane can **rise** slowly from her wheelchair.

set/sit: *Set* means "put down." *Sit* means "take a seated position."

> **Set** the vase on the table.
> I don't like to **sit** at a desk for long periods of time.

than/then: *Than* is used in making comparisons. *Then* means "next."

> My mother is younger **than** my father.
> I took piano lessons; **then** I took guitar lessons.

their/there/they're: *Their* is possessive. *There* indicates location. *They're* is the contraction of *they are.*

> **Their** house burned down last year.
> Too many people are living **there.**
> **They're** all going to London.

threw/through: *Threw,* the past tense of throw, means "tossed." *Through* means "finished" or "passing from one point to another."

> The pitcher **threw** the ball.
> I am **through** with dinner.
> My brother and I rode **through** the forest on our bikes.

to/too/two: *To* means "toward" or is used with a verb. *Too* means "also" or "very." *Two* is a number.

> I went to the store **to** buy some bread.
> I bought some artichokes **too,** even though they were **too** expensive for my budget.
> My mother has **two** sisters.

wear/were/where: *Wear* means "have on one's body." *Were* is the past tense of *be*. *Where* refers to a place.

> Can you **wear** shorts to school?
> **Where were** you yesterday?

weather/whether: *Weather* refers to outdoor conditions. *Whether* expresses possibility.

> No one knows **whether** the **weather** will get better or worse.

who's/whose: *Who's* is a contraction of *who is* or *who has*. *Whose* is a possessive pronoun.

> **Who's** going to decide **whose** car to take?

your/you're: *Your* means "belonging to you." *You're* is the contraction of *you are*.

> **Your** attention to details proves that **you're** a good worker.

REVIEWING WORDS THAT ARE EASILY CONFUSED, PART III

Do you understand the differences in the sets of words in Part III of this list?

_____

Have you ever confused any of these words? If so, which ones?

_____

◆ *P r a c t i c e 7*   **Identifying** Underline the correct word in each of the following sentences.

1. Janice was (quiet, quite) pleased with your work.
2. (Your, You're) the best choice for this task.
3. Please (set, sit) here and wait for the doctor.
4. (Who's, Whose) planning on going to tonight's game?
5. Our (principal, principle) is retiring at the end of the year.

◆ *P r a c t i c e 8*   **Completing** Complete the following sentences with a correct word from Part III of this list.

1. After the performance, the audience _____ flowers at the performer's feet.
2. Beatrice's _____ reason for quitting her job was the pay.
3. Finish your homework, and _____ you can watch television.
4. _____ are you going dressed like that?
5. Why did you _____ shorts in the winter?

◆ *P r a c t i c e 9*   **Writing Your Own** Use each set of words correctly in a sentence of your own.

1. raise/rise _____

2. their/there/they're _____

3. your/you're _____

4. set/sit _____

5. who's/whose _____

CHAPTER REVIEW

◆ *Review P r a c t i c e 1*   **Writing Your Own** Write a paragraph explaining the qualities of a good friend. What are the qualities, and why do you think they are important? Try to use some of the easily confused words from this chapter.

◆ *Review P r a c t i c e 2*   **Editing Through Collaboration** Exchange paragraphs from Review Practice 1 with another student, and then do the following:

1. Circle any words used incorrectly.
2. Write the correct form of the word above the error.

Then return the paper to its writer, and use the information in this chapter to correct any confused words in your own paragraph. Record your errors on the Error Log in Appendix 3.

CHAPTER 54

SPELLING

✔ CHECKLIST for Identifying Misspelled Words

> ✔ Do you follow the basic spelling rules?
> ✔ Are all words spelled correctly?

Test Yourself

Correct the misspelled words in the following sentences.

- What is your new addres?
- Turn left on the third avenu.
- I was using the wrong calender when I made out the schedule.
- The dealer delt me a good hand.
- Please get all the items on the grocry list.

(Answers are in Appendix 8 on the Web site.)

If you think back over your education, you will realize that teachers believe spelling is important. There is a good reason they feel this way: Spelling errors send negative messages. Misspellings seem to leap out at readers, creating serious doubts about the writer's abilities in general. Because you will not always have access to spell-checkers—and because spell-checkers do not catch all spelling errors—improving your spelling skills is important.

SPELLING HINTS

The spelling rules in this chapter will help you become a better speller. But first, here are some practical hints that will also help you improve your spelling.

1. Start a personal spelling list of your own. Use the list of commonly misspelled words on pages 570–574 as your starting point.

2. Study the lists of easily confused words in Chapter 53.

3. Avoid all nonstandard expressions (see Chapter 52).

4. Use a dictionary when you run across words you don't know.

5. Run the spell-check program if you are writing on a computer. Keep in mind, however, that spell-check cannot tell if you have incorrectly used one word in place of another (such as *to, too,* or *two*).

REVIEWING HINTS FOR BECOMING A BETTER SPELLER

Name two things you can do immediately to become a better speller.

_____

Why can't you depend on a spell-check program to find every misspelled word?

_____

◆ *P r a c t i c e   1 A*   **Identifying**   Underline the misspelled words in each of the following sentences. Refer to the list of easily confused words in Chapter 53 and to the spelling list in this chapter as necessary.

1. "We want to go to," cried the children.

2. The baloon floated away in the breeze.

3. With John's promotion came a better salry.

4. This vacation has had a relaxing affect on my attitude.

5. It was an akward situation when the bride wouldn't say, "I do."

◆ *P r a c t i c e   1 B*   **Correcting**   Correct the spelling errors in Practice 1A by rewriting the incorrect sentences.

◆ *P r a c t i c e   2*   **Completing**   Fill in each blank in the following sentences with hints that help with spelling.

1. Use a _____ to look up words you don't know.

2. You can always use the _____ on your computer, but you should remember that it cannot catch confused words, only misspelled words.

3. Start a _____ to help you remember words you commonly misspell.

4. Study the list of _____ in Chapter _____.

5. Try to avoid all _____ English.

◄► *P r a c t i c e 3* **Writing Your Own** Choose the correctly spelled word in each pair, and write a sentence using it. Refer to the spelling list on pages 570–574 if necessary.

1. concieve/conceive _____

2. absence/absense _____

3. vaccum/vacuum _____

4. library/libary _____

5. delt/dealt _____

SPELLING RULES

Four basic spelling rules can help you avoid many misspellings. It pays to spend a little time learning them now.

1. **Words that end in -e:** When adding a suffix beginning with a vowel (*a, e, i, o, u*), drop the final -e.

achieve + -ing	=	achieving
include + -ed	=	included
value + -able	=	valuable

   When adding a suffix beginning with a consonant, keep the final -e.

aware + -ness	=	awareness
improve + -ment	=	improvement
leisure + -ly	=	leisurely

2. **Words with *ie* and *ei*:** Put *i* before *e* except after *c* or when sounded like *ay* as in *neighbour* and *weigh*.

c + ei	(no c) + ie
receive	grieve
conceive	niece
deceive	friend
	relief

3. **Words that end in -y:** When adding a suffix to a word that ends in a consonant plus -y, change the y to i.

happy + -er	=	happier
dry + -ed	=	dried
easy + -est	=	easiest

4. **Words that double the final consonant:** When adding a suffix starting with a vowel to a one-syllable word, double the final consonant.

big + -est = biggest
quit + -er = quitter
bet + -ing = betting

With words of more than one syllable, double the final consonant if the word ends in a single vowel plus a single consonant.

begin + -ing   = beginning
transmit + -ing = transmitting
excel + -ed   = excelled

REVIEWING FOUR BASIC SPELLING RULES

What is the rule for adding a suffix to words ending in -e (such as date + -ing)?

_____

_____

What is the rule for spelling ie *and* ei *words (such as* receive, neighbour, *and* friend)?

_____

_____

When do you change y *to* i *before a suffix (such as* sunny + -est)?

_____

When do you double the final consonant of a word before adding a suffix (such as cut, begin, *or* travel + -ing)?

_____

_____

◆ *P r a c t i c e 4 A* **Identifying** Underline the spelling errors in each of the following sentences.

1. It's not like we're commiting a crime.
2. The boundarys have been clearly marked.

3. My suitcase wieghs too much.

4. Our bagage was lost somewhere in Calgary.

5. The facilitys are near one another.

◆ *P r a c t i c e*   **4 B**   **Correcting** Correct the spelling errors in Practice 4A by rewriting the incorrect sentences.

◆ *P r a c t i c e*   **5**   **Completing** Complete the following spelling rules.

1. When adding a suffix beginning with a vowel to a word that ends in *-e*, _____.

2. With words of more than one syllable, _____ the final consonant if the word ends in a single _____ plus a single _____.

3. Put *i* before *e* except after _____ or when sounded like _____ as in _____.

4. When adding a suffix starting with a _____ to a one-syllable word, _____ the final consonant.

5. When adding a suffix to a word the ends in a consonant plus *-y*, change the _____ to _____.

◆ *P r a c t i c e*   **6**   **Writing Your Own** Make a list of words you commonly misspell. Then choose five of the words, and use each correctly in a sentence.

MOST COMMONLY MISSPELLED WORDS

Use the following list of commonly misspelled words to check your spelling when you write.

abbreviate	accumulate	advertisement
absence	accurate	afraid
accelerate	ache	aggravate
accessible	achievement	aisle
accidentally	acre	although
accommodate	actual	aluminum
accompany	address	amateur
accomplish	adequate	ambulance

ancient	burglar	conceive
anonymous	business	concession
anxiety	cabbage	concrete
anxious	cafeteria	condemn
appreciate	calendar	conference
appropriate	campaign	congratulate
approximate	canoe	conscience
architect	canyon	consensus
arithmetic	captain	continuous
artificial	career	convenience
assassin	carriage	cooperate
athletic	cashier	corporation
attach	catastrophe	correspond
audience	caterpillar	cough
authority	ceiling	counterfeit
autumn	cemetery	courageous
auxiliary	census	courteous
avenue	certain	cozy
awkward	certificate	criticize
baggage	challenge	curiosity
balloon	champion	curious
banana	character	curriculum
bankrupt	chief	cylinder
banquet	children	dairy
beautiful	chimney	dangerous
beggar	coffee	dealt
beginning	collar	deceive
behaviour	college	decision
benefited	column	definition
bicycle	commit	delicious
biscuit	committee	descend
bought	communicate	describe
boundary	community	description
brilliant	comparison	deteriorate
brought	competent	determine
buoyant	competition	development
bureau	complexion	dictionary

difficulty	extinct	height
diploma	extraordinary	hesitate
disappear	familiar	hoping
disastrous	famous	humorous
discipline	fascinate	hygiene
disease	fashion	hymn
dissatisfied	fatigue	icicle
divisional	faucet	illustrate
dormitory	February	imaginary
economy	fiery	immediately
efficiency	financial	immortal
eighth	foreign	impossible
elaborate	forfeit	incidentally
electricity	fortunate	incredible
eligible	forty	independence
embarrass	freight	indispensable
emphasize	friend	individual
employee	fundamental	inferior
encourage	gauge	infinite
enormous	genius	influential
enough	genuine	initial
enthusiastic	geography	initiation
envelope	gnaw	innocence
environment	government	installation
equipment	graduation	intelligence
equivalent	grammar	interfere
especially	grief	interrupt
essential	grocery	invitation
establish	gruesome	irrelevant
exaggerate	guarantee	irrigate
excellent	guess	issue
exceptionally	guidance	jealous
excessive	handkerchief	jewellery
exhaust	handsome	journalism
exhilarating	haphazard	kindergarten
existence	happiness	knife
explanation	harass	knowledge

knuckles	miscellaneous	personnel
laboratory	mischievous	persuade
laborious	miserable	physician
language	misspell	pitcher
laugh	monotonous	pneumonia
laundry	mortgage	politician
league	mysterious	possess
legible	necessary	prairie
legislature	neighbourhood	precede
leisure	niece	precious
length	nineteen	preferred
library	ninety	prejudice
licence (n.)/license (v.)	noticeable	previous
lieutenant	nuisance	privilege
lightning	obedience	procedure
likeable	obstacle	proceed
liquid	occasion	pronounce
listen	occurred	psychology
literature	official	publicly
machinery	omission	questionnaire
magazine	omitted	quotient
magnificent	opponent	realize
majority	opportunity	receipt
manufacture	opposite	recipe
marriage	original	recommend
material	outrageous	reign
mathematics	pamphlet	religious
maximum	paragraph	representative
mayor	parallel	reservoir
meant	parentheses	responsibility
medicine	partial	restaurant
message	particular	rhyme
mileage	pastime	rhythm
miniature	patience	salary
minimum	peculiar	satisfactory
minute	permanent	scarcity
mirror	persistent	scenery

schedule	syllable	valuable
science	symptom	various
scissors	technique	vegetable
secretary	temperature	vehicle
seize	temporary	vicinity
separate	terrible	villain
significant	theatre	visible
similar	thief	volunteer
skiing	thorough	weather
soldier	tobacco	Wednesday
souvenir	tomorrow	weigh
sovereign	tongue	weird
spaghetti	tournament	whose
squirrel	tragedy	width
statue	truly	worst
stomach	unanimous	wreckage
strength	undoubtedly	writing
subtle	unique	yacht
succeed	university	yearn
success	usable	yield
sufficient	usually	zealous
surprise	vacuum	zoology

REVIEWING COMMONLY MISSPELLED WORDS

Why is spelling important in your writing?

_____

Start a personal spelling log of your most commonly misspelled words.

_____ _____ _____ _____

_____ _____ _____ _____

_____ _____ _____ _____

♦ *P r a c t i c e*   **7 A**   **Identifying** Underline any words that are misspelled in the following sentences.

1. This steak and lobster dinner is incredable.
2. You shouldn't condem others for doing what you do.
3. Valentine's Day is in Febuary.
4. How long have you been writting that novel?
5. I know you will suceed in college.

♦ *P r a c t i c e*   **7 B**   **Correcting** Correct any spelling errors that you identified in Practice 7A by rewriting the incorrect sentences.

♦ *P r a c t i c e*   **8**   **Completing** Correct the spelling errors in the following paragraph.

I was eating a plate of spagetti when the phone rang. It was my nieghbour. He said, "The big game is begining in 15 minutes, and my television screen just went out." He then beged me to let him come over and watch it at my house. So I told him that was fine. He neglected to tell me, however, that he wouldn't be alone. He and seven of his rowdy freinds invaded my house, ate my spagetti and drank my pop, and left a catastrophy behind. I think the next time I have a party, I'll have it at his house.

♦ *P r a c t i c e*   **9**   **Writing Your Own** Write a complete sentence for each word listed here.

1. appreciate ⎯⎯⎯⎯⎯⎯⎯⎯⎯⎯⎯⎯⎯⎯⎯⎯⎯⎯⎯⎯⎯⎯

2. laundry ⎯⎯⎯⎯⎯⎯⎯⎯⎯⎯⎯⎯⎯⎯⎯⎯⎯⎯⎯⎯⎯⎯⎯

3. marriage ⎯⎯⎯⎯⎯⎯⎯⎯⎯⎯⎯⎯⎯⎯⎯⎯⎯⎯⎯⎯⎯⎯

4. excellent ⎯⎯⎯⎯⎯⎯⎯⎯⎯⎯⎯⎯⎯⎯⎯⎯⎯⎯⎯⎯⎯⎯

5. opposite ⎯⎯⎯⎯⎯⎯⎯⎯⎯⎯⎯⎯⎯⎯⎯⎯⎯⎯⎯⎯⎯⎯

CHAPTER REVIEW

◆ *Review Practice 1* **Writing Your Own** Write a paragraph explaining how to become a better speller. Are there any hints that may help?

◆ *Review Practice 2* **Editing Through Collaboration** Exchange paragraphs from Review Practice 1 with another student, and then do the following:

1. Underline any words that are used incorrectly.
2. Circle any misspelled words.

Then return the paper to its writer, and use the information in this chapter to correct any spelling errors in your own paragraph. Record your errors on the Spelling Log in Appendix 4.

APPENDIX 1A

Revising
Peer Evaluation Form

Use the following questions to evaluate your partner's essay. Direct your comments to your partner.

Writer: _____ **Peer:** _____

Describing

1. Is the dominant impression clearly communicated? Explain your answer.

Thesis Statement

2. Does the thesis statement contain the essay's controlling idea and an opinion about that idea?

3. Does the thesis appear as the last sentence of the introduction? Explain your answer.

Basic Elements

4. Does the essay have all the basic elements? Is each one effective? Explain your answer.

Development

5. Does each paragraph support the thesis statement? Does each paragraph contain enough specific details to develop its topic sentence? Explain your answer.

Unity

6. Do all the essay's topic sentences relate directly to the thesis statement? Do the details in each paragraph support its topic sentence? Explain your answer.

Organization

7. Is the essay organized logically? Is each body paragraph organized logically? Explain your answer.

Coherence

8. Are transitions used effectively so that paragraphs move smoothly and logically from one to the next? Do the sentences move smoothly and logically from one to the next? Explain your answer.

Forms for evaluating specific types of essays are available on the Web site.

APPENDIX 1B Editing Peer Evaluation Form

Use the following questions to help you find editing errors in your partner's essay. Mark the errors directly on your partner's paper using the editing symbols on the inside back cover.

Writer: _____ **Peer:** _____

Sentences

1. Does each sentence have a subject and verb?

   Mark any fragments you find with **frag.**

   Put a slash (/) between any fused sentences and comma splices.

2. Do all subjects and verbs agree?

   Mark any subject–verb agreement errors you find with **sv.**

3. Do all pronouns agree with their nouns?

   Mark any pronoun errors you find with **pro agr.**

4. Are all modifiers as close as possible to the words they modify?

   Mark any modifier errors you find with **ad** (adjective or adverb problem), **mm** (misplaced modifier), or **dm** (dangling modifier).

Punctuation and Mechanics

5. Are sentences punctuated correctly?

   Mark any punctuation errors you find with the appropriate symbol under Unit 5 of the editing symbols (inside back cover).

6. Are words capitalized properly?

   Mark any capitalization errors you find with **lc** (lowercase) or **cap** (capital).

Word Choice and Spelling

7. Are words used correctly?

   Mark any words that are used incorrectly with **wc** (word choice) or **ww** (wrong word).

8. Are words spelled correctly?

   Mark any misspelled words you find with **sp.**

APPENDIX 2 Editing Quotient Error Chart

Put an X in the square that corresponds to each question that you missed. Then record your errors in the categories below to find out where you might need help.

	a	b	c	d	e	f	g
1							
2							
3							
4							
5							
6							
7							

Fragments   1b _____ 1c _____ 2b _____ 2e _____ 7c _____

Fused sentences   1a _____ 1d _____ 2d _____ 3d _____ 5b _____
and comma splices
                       7b _____ 7f _____

Subject–verb agreement   3a _____ 3c _____

Verb forms   6e _____

Pronoun errors   4b _____

Pronoun agreement 3b _____ 7a _____

Modifiers   7e _____

End punctuation   1d _____ 2d _____ 3d _____ 5b _____ 7b _____

                       7f _____

Commas   4e _____ 4f _____ 5e _____ 6a _____ 6b _____ 6c _____

Apostrophes   4g _____ 7d _____

Capitalization   2a _____ 2c _____ 4c _____ 4d _____

Confused words   4g _____ 5a _____ 5d _____

Spelling   4a _____ 5c _____ 5d _____ 6f _____

APPENDIX 3 Error Log

List any grammar, punctuation, and mechanics errors you make in your writing on the following chart. Then, to the right of this label, record (1) the actual error from your writing, (2) the rule for correcting this error, and (3) your correction.

Error	
	Example I went to the new seafood restaurant and I ordered the lobster.
Comma	**Rule** Use a comma before *and, but, for, nor, or, so,* and *yet* when they join two independent clauses.
	Correction I went to the new seafood restaurant, and I ordered the lobster.
Error	**Example**
	Rule
	Correction
Error	**Example**
	Rule
	Correction
Error	**Example**
	Rule
	Correction
Error	**Example**
	Rule
	Correction
Error	**Example**
	Rule
	Correction
Error	**Example**
	Rule
	Correction
Error	**Example**
	Rule
	Correction
Error	**Example**
	Rule
	Correction

Error	Example
	Rule
	Correction
Error	Example
	Rule
	Correction
Error	Example
	Rule
	Correction
Error	Example
	Rule
	Correction
Error	Example
	Rule
	Correction
Error	Example
	Rule
	Correction
Error	Example
	Rule
	Correction
Error	Example
	Rule
	Correction
Error	Example
	Rule
	Correction
Error	Example
	Rule
	Correction
Error	Example
	Rule
	Correction

Appendix 4 Spelling Log

On this chart, record any words you misspell, and write the correct spelling in the space next to the misspelled word. In the right column, write a note to yourself to help you remember the correct spelling. (See the first line for an example.) Refer to this chart as often as necessary to avoid misspelling the same words again.

Misspelled Word	Correct Spelling	Definition/Notes
there	their	there = place; their = pronoun; they're = "they are"

APPENDIX 5 Presentation Techniques

The following Guidelines will help you to prepare your oral presentation. They will help make your presentation a more enjoyable and less stressful experience. Good luck!

Guidelines for Using PowerPoint

1. **Avoid having too much information on a slide.** If you type your whole speech onto the slide, your audience's attention will be divided. They won't know if they should listen to you, read the information on the slide, or write everything down. Use the main points of your topic on your PowerPoint slides. If you put the main points on the slide, the audience can see them and then listen to you discuss them. A good rule to follow is the 6×6 rule: Try to use no more than 6 words across and 6 words down on each side.

2. **Avoid using too many bells and whistles.** The swirling letters and dancing graphics are fun; however, can you imagine sitting through an hour-long presentation where each letter falls individually from the top of the screen and makes a typewriter sound as it reaches its place? Use these functions sparingly. You don't want to annoy your audience or have their attention pulled away from what you are saying.

3. **Always have a consistent background.** Your presentation will look more professional and will be seen as a united whole if you use the same background on every slide. This is important to remember if you are presenting with a group. Each presenter should have the same background slides. This consistency will help the audience to link the group's topic together as a unified whole presentation.

4. **Always have a backup plan.** Sometimes the technology will fail on the day of your presentation. The computer may crash, the disk may be flawed, or the bulb on the projector may burn out. It's always a good idea to have a backup plan in case anything unforeseen happens. Perhaps have a handout with your main points on it. You may want to put some of your slides on overhead to use in case there's an unfixable problem. It's a good idea to do a trial run with the equipment to make sure everything is in order. It's also a good idea to show up early enough to get things set up and to make sure everything is working.

Guidelines for Presenting

1. **Maintain eye contact with your audience.** By keeping eye contact, you will engage and interact with your audience. This interaction will help keep your audience's attention. It's difficult to daydream when the presenter is looking at you!

2. **Don't be afraid to move around.** Movement will engage your audience. If you are standing motionless behind a lectern, the audience's attention will wander. If you move around, you will look more comfortable and your audience will be more engaged with your presentation. If you are in a group, have another member click the mouse to change the PowerPoint slide. If you are presenting alone, and you don't have a portable mouse, put the mouse in a position where you can move around in front of the audience and still get back to reach the mouse.

3. **Be aware of your voice level.** Be sure to speak to the people in the back of the room. You want to make sure everyone can hear you. It's frustrating for the audience if they can't hear you, so they will stop listening. Sometimes you may mumble because you are nervous. Perhaps have someone sit in the back who can give you a visual clue to show that he or she can/cannot hear you. Another option may be to have a group member cue you. You are all members of a team, so don't be afraid to help each other out.

4. **Keep your notes organized.** Number your cue cards to keep them in order. This will help if you accidentally drop them and they get out of order. Have the main points in large type so they stand out, even if you're nervous. Highlight information so that you can glance down and see it quickly. Write notes to yourself on your cue cards. Remind yourself to speak slowly, loudly, and clearly. Remind yourself to move around and look comfortable. Remind yourself to look up and keep eye contact with your audience.

How to Keep from Reading Your Material

1. **Trust yourself and your knowledge of your topic.** You've spent a lot of time research-ing and preparing for your presentation. Do not wait until the day before to prepare your material! You know your topic. Trust that knowledge.

2. **Write only the main points on your cue cards.** If you have notes, don't write out your whole speech. This will only tempt you to read word for word what is on your page. It's hard for an audience to pay attention to someone who is reading the presentation. If you have only the main points, then you are forced to discuss your topic rather than read your topic to the audience. Again, trust your knowledge of the topic.

3. **Practise your presentation.** Rehearse what you want to say. If you can avoid reading, your presentation will be more interesting to listen to. Practising your presentation out loud will help you learn your material and get used to discussing it aloud at the same time. Say difficult words aloud a few times in order to get used to wrapping your mouth around them. The more you practise, the more comfortable you will become and the less you will need to rely on your notes.

Guidelines for Fighting Nervousness

1. **Be prepared.** If you are comfortable with your information, you will be less nervous. Try not to procrastinate and leave your presentation preparation until the day before. The longer in advance you are prepared, the more time you have to practise and rehearse your presentation. If you can step in front of the audience confident that you know your material, you will be far less nervous.

2. **Take a drink of water.** If you are nervous and forget what you want to say, then take a drink of water. It's perfectly acceptable for a presenter to have water with him or her. If you get lost for a moment, take a drink of water. This will give you a moment to regain your thoughts or composure.

3. **Move around the room.** It's very difficult to be stiff and terrified if you walk or move around. The action of walking forces you to relax stiff leg and arm muscles. Once you are moving, your relaxed state will spread and you will find that your nervousness will dissipate.

4. **Remember that everyone gets nervous.** Even professional presenters get nervous. It's natural to be nervous when you are speaking in front of a group of people. Try to channel the nervous energy into your presentation. Use it to your advantage. Your mind can focus on the information. Focus the energy into your presentation. Move around. Make eye contact. Don't give in to the nervousness!

CREDITS ❖

CHAPTER **31**

"We Are Training Our Kids to Kill," by Dave Grossman, *Saturday Evening Post,* July, 1999. Reprinted by permission of the author.

"Ban Spam? What, and Banish All the World?" by Doug Saunders is reprinted with permission from *The Globe and Mail.*

"Ban Spam: E-nough Is E-nough" by Rick Broadhead: Rick Broadhead is a best-selling author, technology analyst, public speaker, and literary agent. His most recent book is *Dear Valued Customer: You Are a Loser!—And Over 100 Other Embarrassing and Funny Stories of Technology Gone Mad* (Andrews McMeel Publishing, 2004). He can be reached by email at **rickb@rickbroadhead.com** © 2004 by Rick Broadhead. All rights reserved. No reproduction in any form without permission.

Index ❖